"In *Against the Darkness*, Graham Cole demonstrates once again why he is considered a trusted theological voice for our time. Bringing his careful research and wide-ranging interaction with major theological voices throughout the centuries alongside his own fresh theological engagement, Cole applies his superb theological skills to the oft-neglected themes of angels, Satan, and demons. Moreover, this thoughtfully designed and accessible volume offers several fuller treatments of controversial subjects and challenging biblical texts, providing readers an opportunity to learn from Cole's insightful wisdom. It is a genuine joy to recommend this thoroughly biblical, theologically faithful, and purposefully pastoral contribution to the highly regarded Foundations of Evangelical Theology series."

David S. Dockery, Chancellor, Trinity Evangelical Divinity School

"While the doctrine of angels and demons may be less central than doctrines such as the Trinity, the hypostatic union, and substitutionary atonement, nevertheless angels and demons play a role in nearly every other doctrine of the Christian faith. In fact, what Graham Cole successfully does in this volume is demonstrate just how important their role is to the outworking of God's plans and purposes in creation, in providence, and in all of redemptive history. I am deeply grateful for the careful attention he has shown to biblical teaching, along with his fair and winsome interaction with scholarship throughout this volume. The Christian faith as well as the Christian life is affected by the role and activity of angels and demons in significant ways, and this volume goes a long way in informing us of just how much we may have been missing."

Bruce A. Ware, T. Rupert and Lucille Coleman Professor of Christian Theology,
The Southern Baptist Theological Seminary

"The structure of this book contributes to its appeal. The nine chapters cover the theological meat of the theme, the five excursuses address such sidebars as the meaning of Genesis 6:1–4 and how to test the spirits, and the three appendices survey adjacent but highly relevant themes (how these themes are treated in Islam on the one hand, and in various Christian creeds on the other). The book is comprehensive and edifying—and more important than one might initially think, in a culture that wants to be touched by an angel."

D. A. Carson, Emeritus Professor of New Testament, Trinity Evangelical Divinity
School; Cofounder, The Gospel Coalition

"In a modern secular age, it is all too easy for Christians to overlook the major source of conflict in the drama of redemption: the devilish powers of darkness that seek to seduce hearts away from the truth of the gospel with glittering images and empty promises. Graham Cole rightly reminds us that, while angels and demons are not at the heart of biblical revelation, to ignore them is to risk being blindsided. *Against the Darkness* is a model of how to judiciously read Scripture and formulate Christian doctrine on matters that are both peripheral and essential to the Bible's main storyline. This is theology for the twenty-first-century church, and Cole helpfully draws out the pastoral implications of angelology and demonology—all the while never losing sight of the centrality of Jesus Christ and his lordship over the angelic and earthly realms."

Kevin J. Vanhoozer, Research Professor of Systematic Theology, Trinity
Evangelical Divinity School; author, *The Drama of Doctrine*; *Hearers and Doers*;
Biblical Authority after Babel; and *Faith Speaking Understanding*

"We live in a culture that pretends the spiritual realm does not exist. Reducing that which is real to that which can be seen and touched, our culture catechizes its pupils in a worldview that dismisses angels and demons. It laughs at those who believe in the devil and his hell. So when we act disinterested in angels, Satan, and demons, we invite this secular outlook to control the biblical narrative. Although we profess faith in a God who has overcome the evil one, in reality our indifference reveals us to be practical atheists. Graham Cole exposes this blind spot, demonstrating that our theology of angels, Satan, and demons is not irrelevant but takes us to the center of the gospel itself. For if Christ has suffered for our sins and risen for our justification, then Satan no longer has power and victory over us. Read *Against the Darkness* and discover how God has delivered us from the domain of darkness and transferred us to the kingdom of his beloved Son."

Matthew Barrett, Associate Professor of Christian Theology, Midwestern Baptist Theological Seminary; Executive Editor, *Credo* magazine; author, *None Greater*

"This is theology at its best. Written by one of evangelicalism's finest theologians, *Against the Darkness* is biblical, systematic, pastoral, fresh, and faithful. It is exegetically driven, historically rooted, philosophically astute, globally aware, systematically related, and crisply written. And it is downright interesting, addressing pressing questions with carefulness and candor."

Christopher W. Morgan, Dean and Professor of Theology, California Baptist University; editor, Theology in Community series; coeditor, *ESV Systematic Theology Study Bible*

"We commit heresy by contradicting or distorting Biblical revelation. We also commit heresy by politely ignoring the bits we find difficult or unacceptable! So even in orthodox circles, we commit heresy by ignoring what the Bible reveals about angels, Satan, and demons. We are syncretists, captive to the rationalistic Enlightenment. What we ignore in the Biblical revelation distorts our gospel preaching and teaching. Graham Cole's excellent book is a timely and judicious study of what the Bible teaches on these topics, in the context of historical theology, contemporary thinking, and the practice of Christian life and ministry. He shows us that we must not misunderstand these topics, but that we also cannot ignore them. We need this book!"

Peter Adam, Vicar Emeritus, St. Jude's Carlton; Former Principal, Ridley College, Melbourne

AGAINST THE DARKNESS

AGAINST THE DARKNESS

THE DOCTRINE OF ANGELS, SATAN, AND DEMONS

GRAHAM A. COLE

WHEATON, ILLINOIS

Library of Congress Cataloging-in-Publication Data

Names: Cole, Graham A. (Graham Arthur), 1949- author.
Title: Against the darkness: the doctrine of angels, satan, and demons / Graham A. Cole.
Description: Wheaton, Illinois : Crossway, [2019] | Series: Foundations of evangelical theology series | Includes bibliographical references and index.
Identifiers: LCCN 2018048953 (print) | LCCN 2018053994 (ebook) | ISBN 9781433533167 (pdf) | ISBN 9781433533174 (mobi) | ISBN 9781433533181 (epub) | ISBN 9781433533150 (hc : alk. paper) | ISBN 9781433533181 (ePub) | ISBN 9781433533174 (Mobipocket)
Subjects: LCSH: Angels—Biblical teaching. | Devil—Biblical teaching. | Demonology—Biblical teaching. | Spiritual warfare—Biblical teaching. | Theology, Doctrinal.
Classification: LCC BT963 (ebook) | LCC BT963 .C65 2019 (print) | DDC 235—dc23
LC record available at https://lccn.loc.gov/2018048953

CONTENTS

Why another series of works on evangelical systematic theology? This is an especially appropriate question in light of the fact that evangelicals are fully committed to an inspired and inerrant Bible as their final authority for faith and practice. But since neither God nor the Bible change, why is there a need to redo evangelical systematic theology?

Systematic theology is not divine revelation. Theologizing of any sort is a human conceptual enterprise. Thinking that it is equal to biblical revelation misunderstands the nature of both Scripture and theology! Insofar as our theology contains propositions that accurately reflect Scripture or match the world and are consistent with the Bible (in cases where the propositions do not come per se from Scripture), our theology is biblically based and correct. But even if all the propositions of a systematic theology are true, that theology would still not be equivalent to biblical revelation! It is still a human conceptualization of God and his relation to the world.

Although this may disturb some who see theology as nothing more than doing careful exegesis over a series of passages, and others who see it as nothing more than biblical theology, those methods of doing theology do not somehow produce a theology that is equivalent to biblical revelation either. Exegesis is a human conceptual enterprise, and so is biblical theology. All the theological disciplines involve human intellectual participation. But human intellect is finite, and hence there is always room for revision of systematic theology as knowledge increases. Though God and his word do not change, human understanding of his revelation can grow, and our theologies should be reworked to reflect those advances in understanding.

Another reason for evangelicals to rework their theology is the nature of systematic theology as opposed to other theological disciplines. For example, whereas the task of biblical theology is more to describe biblical teaching on whatever topics Scripture addresses, systematics should make a special point to relate its conclusions to the issues of one's day. This does not mean that the systematician ignores the topics biblical writers address. Nor does it mean that theologians should warp Scripture to address issues it never intended to address. Rather it suggests that in addition to expounding what biblical writers teach, the theologian should attempt to take those biblical teachings (along with the biblical mind-set) and apply them to issues that are especially confronting the church in the theologian's own day. For example, 150 years ago, an evangelical theologian doing work on the doctrine of man would likely have discussed issues such as the creation of man and the constituent parts of man's being. Such a theology might even have included a discussion about human institutions such as marriage, noting in general the respective roles of husbands and wives in marriage. However, it is dubious that there would have been any lengthy discussion with various viewpoints about the respective roles of men and women in marriage, in society, and in the church. But at our point in history and in light of the feminist movement and the issues it has raised even among many conservative Christians, it would be foolish to write a theology of man (or, should we say, a "theology of humanity") without a thorough discussion of the issue of the roles of men and women in society, the home, and the church.

Because systematic theology attempts to address itself not only to the timeless issues presented in Scripture but also to the current issues of one's day and culture, each theology will to some extent need to be redone in each generation. Biblical truth does not change from generation to generation, but the issues that confront the church do. A theology that was adequate for a different era and different culture may simply not speak to key issues in a given culture at a given time. Hence, in this series we are reworking evangelical systematic theology, though we do so with the understanding that in future generations there will be room for a revision of theology again.

How, then, do the contributors to this series understand the nature of systematic theology? Systematic theology as done from an evangelical Christian perspective involves study of the person, works, and relationships of God. As evangelicals committed to the full inspiration, inerrancy, and final authority of Scripture, we demand that whatever appears in a systematic theology correspond to the way things are and must not contradict any claim taught in Scripture. Holy Writ is the touchstone of our theology, but we do not limit the source material for systematics to Scripture alone. Hence, whatever information from history, science, philosophy, and the like is relevant to our understanding of God and his relation to our world is fair game for systematics. Depending on the specific interests and expertise of the contributors to this series, their respective volumes will reflect interaction with one or more of these disciplines.

What is the rationale for appealing to other sources than Scripture and other disciplines than the biblical ones? Since God created the universe, there is revelation of God not only in Scripture but in the created order as well. There are many disciplines that study our world, just as does theology. But since the world studied by the nontheological disciplines is the world created by God, any data and conclusions in the so-called secular disciplines that accurately reflect the real world are also relevant to our understanding of the God who made that world. Hence, in a general sense, since all of creation is God's work, nothing is outside the realm of theology. The so-called secular disciplines need to be thought of in a theological context, because they are reflecting on the universe God created, just as is the theologian. And, of course, there are many claims in the nontheological disciplines that are generally accepted as true (although this does not mean that every claim in nontheological disciplines is true, or that we are in a position with respect to every proposition to know whether it is true or false). Since this is so, and since all disciplines are in one way or another reflecting on our universe, a universe made by God, any true statement in any discipline should in some way be informative for our understanding of God and his relation to our world. Hence, we have felt it appropriate to incorporate data from outside the Bible in our theological formulations.

As to the specific design of this series, our intention is to address all areas of evangelical theology with a special emphasis on key issues in each area. While other series may be more like a history of doctrine, this series purposes to incorporate insights from Scripture, historical theology, philosophy, etc., in order to produce an up-to-date work in systematic theology. Though all contributors to the series are thoroughly evangelical in their theology, embracing the historical orthodox doctrines of the church, the series as a whole is not meant to be slanted in the direction of one form of evangelical theology. Nonetheless, most of the writers come from a Reformed perspective. Alternate evangelical and nonevangelical options, however, are discussed.

As to style and intended audience, this series is meant to rest on the very best of scholarship while at the same time being understandable to the beginner in theology as well as to the academic theologian. With that in mind, contributors are writing in a clear style, taking care to define whatever technical terms they use.

Finally, we believe that systematic theology is not just for the understanding. It must apply to life, and it must be lived. As Paul wrote to Timothy, God has given divine revelation for many purposes, including ones that necessitate doing theology, but the ultimate reason for giving revelation and for theologians doing theology is that the people of God may be fitted for every good work (2 Tim. 3:16–17). In light of the need for theology to connect to life, each of the contributors not only formulates doctrines but also explains how those doctrines practically apply to everyday living.

It is our sincerest hope that the work we have done in this series will first glorify and please God, and, secondly, instruct and edify the people of God. May God be pleased to use this series to those ends, and may he richly bless you as you read the fruits of our labors.

John S. Feinberg
General Editor

This study has surprised me in how fascinating it turned out to be. Angelology is not the heart of the biblical revelation. Even so, angels play their part in salvation history and are worth their due. Systematic theology by definition is comprehensive and so angels, Satan, and demons need our attention. I have written this study as a church scholar and not as a guild scholar. Both kinds of scholars have their place in the sun. On the one hand, the guild scholar writes in the first instance to address the academy of fellow scholars, providing research that pushes the boundaries of knowledge. On the other hand, the church scholar writes in the first instance to address the church. Hopefully, what the church scholar writes has value for guild scholars and likewise guild scholars write what proves valuable to the church. Since this is a work addressed to the church, each substantive chapter attempts to tease out implications for Christian belief and behavior. My aim is not simply to address the church but to serve the church. In researching and writing I owe many. I owe a great debt to John Feinberg for his judicious editing and advice. This is a better book because of his insights. I would also like to thank my master's class at Beeson Divinity School and my doctoral class at Trinity Evangelical Divinity School. This book is written especially with such students, as well as pastors, in mind. Two of my students in particular come to mind. Both of them were my teaching assistants. Dwight Davis at Beeson and David Moser at Trinity have been so very helpful and I am grateful. I have also valued the input of Jonathan King, now teaching in Indonesia. I am very grateful to Bill Deckard of Crossway, who has proved to be an invaluable editor. My special thanks to Jules, my beloved wife, for her never failing encouragement and delightful companionship.

ABC	*Africa Bible Commentary*
CCC	*Catechism of the Catholic Church*
CD	Karl Barth, *Church Dogmatics*. Edited by G. W. Bromiley and T. F. Torrance. 13 vols. Edinburgh: T&T Clark, 1936–1977.
CJCC	*The Comprehensive John Calvin Collection* (Rio, WI: Ages Software, 2002), CD-Rom version.
CNTUOT	*Commentary on the New Testament Use of the Old Testament*
DECB	*A Dictionary of Early Christian Beliefs*
DJG	*Dictionary of Jesus and the Gospels*
DPL	*Dictionary of Paul and His Letters*
EBC	*The Expositor's Bible Commentary*. Edited by Frank E. Gaebelein. Grand Rapids, MI: Zondervan, 1976–. CD-Rom version.
ECB	*Eerdmans Commentary on the Bible*
JSB	*The Jewish Study Bible*
NBC	*New Bible Commentary, Twenty-first Century Edition*, 4th ed., ed. D. A. Carson (Leicester, UK, and Downers Grove, IL: InterVarsity Press, 1994)
NIB	*The New Interpreter's Bible*
NIDB	*The New Interpreter's Dictionary of the Bible*
NIVAC	NIV Application Commentary
OBC	*Oxford Bible Commentary*. Edited by John Barton and John Muddiman. Oxford: Oxford University Press, 2001.
SBJT	*Southern Baptist Journal of Theology*
ST	*Summa Theologica* (Thomas Aquinas)
TBST	The Bible Speaks Today
TNTC	Tyndale New Testament Commentaries
TOTC	Tyndale Old Testament Commentaries
WBC	Word Biblical Commentary
WTJ	*Westminster Theological Journal*

INTRODUCTION

One of the questions that animates so many today is whether we are alone in the universe. The thought that humanity is the lonely product of blind evolutionary processes chills. Peter Kreeft expresses the point well: "We can't stand being alone in the universe."[1] Surely there is other intelligent life in such a vast expanse as space. Some clearly think so. Indeed, this is the question informing many a film (e.g., *First Contact* and *Close Encounters of the Third Kind*) and many a TV show (e.g., "The X-Files"). Indeed the human imagination is not content with such solitariness, and so we find all sorts of alien beings frequenting popular entertainment. The many versions of *Star Trek* provide a case in point.

Christians should not be surprised by any of this. We affirm that humanity is not a cosmic orphan, thrown up by blind evolutionary processes. As theists we believe that there is the Creator and ourselves, but is that the whole story? Not according to Scripture. There is another order of intelligent life that must be factored into the discussion: the angels, both fallen and unfallen. Yet although Christians espouse belief in such an order of intelligent life, I wonder whether, operationally speaking, many of us—at least in the secularized West—live as though we are effectively alone.

A CRITICAL ASSUMPTION

Despite the popular entertainments that deal in the supernatural, more and more folk in the West seem to be embracing a naturalistic worldview. This trend began a few centuries ago in the West. Darren Oldridge describes it well: "The withdrawal of the Devil [his case in point] from public affairs was associated with more general trends in the history of Christianity. The process began with the emergence in the late 17th century of a naturalistic view of the world that excluded the immediate influence of supernatural powers."[2] As for today's

---

[1] Peter Kreeft, *Angels and Demons: What Do We Really Know about Them?* (San Francisco: Ignatius, 1995), 3.
[2] Darren Oldridge, *The Devil: A Very Short Introduction* (Oxford: Oxford University Press, 2012), 40.

context, Oldridge observes, "As medicine became more effective, so the range of Satan's operations shrank. More broadly, the expansion of literacy and mass media exposed a growing section of the population to secular opinions and entertainments, while mass education circulated a naturalistic view of the world."[3] Stephen F. Noll adds to this account with reference to two important philosophers:

> The reserve about angels that was characteristic of the Reformation [e.g., Calvin] developed into a complete rejection of them during the Enlightenment. Taking the principle of parsimony to its limit, René Descartes argued that only God and human consciousness could be rationally proved and, therefore, the existence of other intelligences in the universe was purely conjectural and unnecessary to the conduct of everyday life. Descartes' method, extended by John Locke in his *Essay on Human Understanding*, has formed the fundamental mindset of modern scepticism towards angels.[4]

The "social imaginary" has changed, as Charles Taylor contends.[5]

The Western church has not been immune from this trend. Rudolf Bultmann (1884–1976) famously or infamously launched his demythologizing program in the 1940s. This German NT scholar argued that modern man was not bound by ancient superstitions. The mythical NT world picture needs to be denuded of its mythic garb and reclothed in existentialist philosophical dress. Bultmann maintained, "We cannot use electric lights and radios and, in the event of illness, avail ourselves of modern medical and clinical means and at the same time believe in the spirit and wonder world of the New Testament."[6] Scot McKnight terms Bultmann-like dismissals of angels in the biblical testimony as the "de-angelification of the Bible, the church, and the faith."[7]

The rise of the new atheists serves as a case in point. Richard Dawkins, Christopher Hitchens, and Daniel Dennett have their following.[8] In such a

---

[3] Oldridge, *Devil: A Very Short Introduction*, 43–44.

[4] Stephen F. Noll, "Angels," in *New Dictionary of Christian Apologetics*, ed. W. C. Campbell-Jack and Gavin J. McGrath (Leicester, UK, and Downers Grove, IL: InterVarsity Press, 2006), 73–74.

[5] The magisterial study of the move in the West from an enchanted to an unenchanted worldview is found in Charles Taylor, *A Secular Age* (Cambridge, MA: Belknap Press of Harvard University Press, 2007). Taylor himself is a professing Christian. (He is one of those featured in James L. Heft, ed., *Believing Scholars: Ten Catholic Intellectuals* [New York: Fordham University Press, 2005], 10–35). For Taylor, the social imaginary is the way a particular social group imagines its life, its beliefs, symbols, and values.

[6] Rudolf Bultmann, "The New Testament and Mythology: The Problem of Demythologizing the New Testament Proclamation" (1941), quoted in *The New Testament and Mythology and Other Basic Writings*, ed. Schubert Ogden (Philadelphia: Fortress, 1984), 4. For a counter to Bultmann's anti-supernaturalism, see Craig S. Keener's magisterial *Miracles: The Credibility of New Testament Accounts*, 2 vols. (Grand Rapids, MI: Baker, 2011).

[7] Scot McKnight, *The Hum of Angels: Listening for the Messengers of God around Us* (New York: Waterbrook, 2017), 8.

[8] See Richard Dawkins, *The God Delusion* (New York: Mariner, 2008); Christopher Hitchens, *God Is Not Great: How Religion Poisons Everything* (New York: Twelve, 2007); and Daniel C. Dennett, *Breaking the Spell: Religion as a Natural Phenomenon* (London: Penguin, 2007). For a spirited riposte, see David Bentley Hart, *Atheist Delusions: The Christian Revolution and Its Fashionable Enemies* (New Haven, CT, and London: Yale University Press, 2009).

worldview there is no room for the supernatural. One philosopher, William H. Halverson, expresses the importance of this matter well. He argues,

> It may be helpful to bear in mind from the beginning, however, that one theme that underlies nearly all philosophical discussion is the perpetual conflict be-tween *naturalistic* and *nonnaturalistic* world views. A *naturalistic* world view is one in which it is affirmed that (a) there is only one order of reality, (b) this one order of reality consists entirely of objects and events occurring in space and time, and (c) this one order of reality is completely self-dependent and self-operating. . . . Any world view that denies any of the above-stated tenets of naturalism, then, may be termed *nonnaturalistic*.[9]

Our present study is nonnaturalistic.[10] Daniel J. Treier rightly contends, "[E]vangelicals are confessedly orthodox, rejecting 'liberal theologies' and anti-supernaturalistic approaches to the Bible."[11] Indeed it is hard to imagine a naturalistic expression of an evangelical faith, although with tongue in cheek the new atheists have been described as evangelical atheists, given their mis-sionary zeal.[12]

THE THEME OF THE STUDY

This study explores an evangelical doctrine of angels both fallen and unfallen.[13] But what does an evangelical doctrine of angelic order and disorder assume? For a start, the Scriptures are construed as the *norma normans* (the norming norm).[14] Thus understood, Scripture is the final court of appeal in any contest

---

[9] William H. Halverson. *A Concise Introduction to Philosophy*, 4th ed. (Boston: McGraw Hill, 1981). 9–10 (em-phases original).

[10] For an excellent discussion of the defense of the truth of the faith, see John S. Feinberg, *Can You Believe It's True?: Christian Apologetics in a Modern and Postmodern Era* (Wheaton, IL: Crossway, 2013).

[11] Daniel J. Treier, "Scripture and Hermeneutics," in *The Cambridge Companion to Evangelical Theology*, ed. Timothy Larsen and Daniel J. Treier (Cambridge: Cambridge University Press, 2007), 36. The father of liberal theology, Friedrich Schleiermacher (*The Christian Faith*, ed. H. R. Macintosh and J. S. Stewart, various trans. [Edinburgh: T&T Clark, 1948], 160) argued that angelology ought not to be a dogmatic topic but a matter for private and liturgical use.

[12] For example, Chris Stedman, "Evangelical Atheists: Pushing for What?," in the *Huffington Post*, posted 10/18/2010, http://www.huffingtonpost.com/chris-stedman/evangelical-atheists-what_b_765379.html, accessed 8/2/2013. Stedman writes, "There is, as has often been noted, something peculiarly evangelistic about what has been termed the new atheist movement. . . . It is no exaggeration to describe the movement popularized by the likes of Richard Dawkins, Daniel Dennett, Sam Harris, and Christopher Hitchens as a new and particularly zealous form of fundamentalism—an atheist fundamentalism."

[13] For an excellent brief history of angelology from Philo of Alexandria to Walter Wink, see Stephen F. Noll, "Thinking about Angels," in *The Unseen World: Christian Reflections on Angels, Demons, and the Heavenly Realm*, ed. Anthony N. S. Lane (Grand Rapids, MI: Paternoster/Baker, 1996), 1–27. This is a very valuable volume. A generally first-rate bibliography on angels is found in David Albert Jones, *Angels: A Very Short Introduction* (Oxford: Oxford University Press, 2011), 124–128. The omission of Karl Barth's discussion is a weakness, however. In fact, Barth offers a most useful brief history himself in *CD*, III/3 (380–401).

[14] An evangelical systematic theology presupposes a closed canon of inspired Scripture and works within its param-eters. Angelology more broadly conceived would take into account ancient Near Eastern comparisons and inter-testamental developments including Qumran. There is much that is interesting in such studies, but they lie outside the purview of this work. For the broader canvas, see Maxwell John Davidson, "Angel," in *NIDB*, ed. Katharine Doob Sakenfeld, 5 vols. (Nashville: Abingdon, 2006), 1:148–155. In terms of the delimitations of this kind of study, what Charles H. H. Scobie argues in relation to his own discipline of biblical theology applies *mutatis mutandis* to a systematic theology informed by a biblical theology approach like this one. Speaking of the cosmic forces of evil, Scobie states, "No doubt it [the New Testament] reflects developments that had taken place within Judaism.

between authorities, including reason or tradition or experience. The latter three operate in all of our lives as *norma normata* (ruled norms) but not as having the final say. So an evangelical doctrine of X or Y or Z needs sound scriptural grounding if it is to bind the Christian's conscience. The distinction is an important one, as there has been much speculation about angels at various times in church history, as we shall see when we discuss Dionysius the Areopagite's *Celestial Hierarchy* in a later chapter. John Wesley (1703–1791) wisely said, "Revelation only is able to . . . [give] a clear, rational, consistent account of those whom our eyes have not seen, nor our ears heard; of both good and evil angels."[15]

The question now becomes, what does sound scriptural grounding look like?[16] For a start, scriptural grounding means exegesis (i.e., legitimately read out of Scripture) not eisegesis (illegitimately read *into* Scripture). Such grounding can be hard to see in the classic method of *dicta probantia* (proving statements), when some doctrinal claim is made and texts from Scripture are cited, usually in parentheses at the end of a sentence. Here is an example from Millard J. Erickson's discussion of angels: "When angels are seen, they ordinarily have a humanlike appearance, so that they may well be mistaken for humans (Gen. 18:2, 16, 22; 19:1, 5, 12, 15, 16; Judg. 13:6; Mark 16:5; Luke 24:4)."[17] This time-honored method has its place. It saves time. However, it may also beg the question of selection.[18] A complementary method is that of contextualized affirmations. A key text which mentions angels is not simply cited but is quoted, placed in its context in its literary unit in its book in the canon in the light of the flow of redemptive history before doctrinal implications are considered. An advantage of this method is that it can show why the chosen text is described as a key one. Paying attention to the flow of redemptive history is important to both methods. A comparison between OT and NT references to Satan provides a case in point. J. I. Packer wisely observes, "The level and intensity of demonic manifestations in people during Christ's ministry was unique, having no parallel in Old Testament times or since; it was doubtless part of Satan's desperate battle for his kingdom against Christ's attack on it (Matt. 12:29)."[19]

. . . though BT [Biblical Theology] is concerned only with the material that appears in the biblical text" (*The Ways of Our God: An Approach to Biblical Theology* [Grand Rapids, MI, and Cambridge: Eerdmans, 2003], 251).

[15] John Wesley, "Of Good Angels, Sermon 71," www.umcmission.org/Find-Resources/John-Wesley-Sermons /Sermon-71-Of-Good-Angels, accessed 2/2/2019. I owe this reference to Lyle Dorsett, my former colleague at Beeson Divinity School.

[16] The search for scriptural grounding is of a piece with an evidence-based approach, which is an epistemological protocol that appeals to biblical evidence to support truth claims. As for evidence, it is best understood as information which counts toward establishing the truth or falsity of a proposition.

[17] Millard J. Erickson, *Christian Theology*, 3rd ed. (Grand Rapids, MI: Baker, 2013), 410.

[18] In Erickson's case, he has chosen texts well.

[19] J. I. Packer, *Concise Theology: A Guide to Historic Christian Beliefs* (Wheaton, IL: Tyndale), 67–68.

THE APPROACH OF THIS STUDY

This study is both descriptive and prescriptive in approach. Not only will careful attention be given to describing what is in the biblical testimony to angels, Satan, and demons. In the end, normative questions need to be asked: what ought we to believe about angels fallen and unfallen and their roles in our lives? Biblical theology as a discipline plays an important role in constructing doctrine as it pays careful attention to the task of description. It is a phenomenological exercise. The eminent Jewish thinker Abraham Joshua Heschel (1907–1972) explains the phenomenological approach aptly when he writes, "The principle to be kept in mind is to know what we see rather than to see what we know."[20] Exegesis enables the former; eisegesis leads to the latter. Evangelical systematic theology addresses the prescriptive questions in ways that are informed by biblical theology, and with an awareness also of the history of the discussion of the topic in the church, and a concern for application to today's world.[21]

AVOIDING A BLIND SPOT

Noted Christian anthropologist and missiologist Paul Hiebert (1932–2007) identified a blind spot in much of Western Christianity, which he called the "flaw of the excluded middle." So many Christians in the West live as though the story of creation involved in the main just two important characters, God and ourselves. The majority world, however, in contrast, has never forgotten that there is another order of intelligent created life playing its role in the story: namely, the angelic order.[22] Hiebert himself, as a Western-trained theologian and as a social scientist—albeit a Christian one—had forgotten this creaturely order. He confesses,

> The reasons for my uneasiness with the biblical and Indian worldviews should be clear. I had excluded the middle level of supernatural this-worldly beings and forces from my own worldview. As a scientist I had been trained to deal with the empirical world in naturalistic terms. As a theologian I was taught to answer ultimate questions in theistic terms. For me the middle zone did not

---

[20] Abraham Joshua Heschel, *The Prophets*, vol. 1 (New York: Harper & Row, 1962), xi.

[21] For my understanding of how biblical theology and systematic theology relate as disciplines to enable the theological interpretation of Scripture, see my *The God Who Became Human: A Biblical Theology of Incarnation* (Downers Grove, IL: InterVarsity Press, 2013), 171–174.

[22] See Matthew Michael, *Christian Theology and African Traditions* (Eugene, OR: Wipf & Stock, 2013), 92–100. Michael usefully points out the similarities and differences between the biblical view of spirits and the traditional African one. See also the discussion of the spirit world in Emiola Nihinlola, *Theology under the Mango Tree: A Handbook of African Christian Theology* (Lagos, Nigeria: Fine Print, 2013), 66–71. Nihinlola posits five major themes in this order in his work on African theology: the nature of God, the nature of creation, the spirit world, the nature of human beings, and the doctrine of atonement (66–71). The need to hear majority world voices is shown by a question asked by Richard Beck in his *Reviving Old Scratch: Demons and the Devil for Doubters and the Disenchanted* (Minneapolis: Fortress, 2016), 15: "Why do the majority of Christians doubt the literal existence of the Devil?" By his apparent misunderstanding of what constitutes a "majority" of Christians, Beck shows his Western ethnocentricity.

really exist. Unlike Indian villagers, I had given little thought to spirits of this world, to local ancestors and ghosts, or to the souls of animals. For me these belonged to the realm of fairies, trolls, and other mythical beings.[23]

In Hiebert's view, Western Christianity needs to learn from the global south, where, incidentally, the center of gravity now resides as far as the Christian faith is concerned.[24]

A brief survey of references to angels, Satan, and demons found in the indexes and chapter contents in current systematic theologies largely bears out his contention.[25] *The Cambridge Companion to Christian Theology*, edited by Colin E. Gunton, is devoid of references to angels, Satan, and demons.[26] Unsurprisingly, Gunton's *The Christian Faith: An Introduction to Christian Doctrine* is similarly bare of such references. *The Cambridge Companion to Evangelical Theology* fares no better.[27] William C. Placher has edited a volume with the title *Essentials of Christian Theology*.[28] Since it includes nothing about angelology, that subject clearly belongs to the nonessentials as far as this volume is concerned. Daniel L. Migliore's *Faith Seeking Understanding: An Introduction to Christian Theology* is bereft of references to the angelic order whether fallen or unfallen.[29] Alister E. McGrath's *Christian Theology: An Introduction* gives no focused attention to angels, Satan, and demons in their own rights, although there is one reference to Satan in the historical material and three pages in relation to the *Christus Victor* view of the atonement.[30] Kevin J. Vanhoozer's wonderfully creative *The Drama of Doctrine: A Canonical Linguistic Approach to Christian Theology* makes drama the organizing idea. Surprisingly, though, it is drama without conflict. There are no references to angels, or to Satan, or to

---

[23] Paul. G. Hiebert, *Anthropological Reflections on Missiological Issues* (Grand Rapids, MI: Baker, 1994), 196. The blind spot identified by Hiebert is spectacularly illustrated by the work by Miguel A. De La Torre and Albert Hernandez, *The Quest for the Historical Satan* (Minneapolis: Fortress, 2011). In this work the authors end their "quest" in this way: "We have ended the quest for the historical Satan by finding him in the mirror. We have seen Satan, and much too often over the past twenty centuries he has been us Christians. The real quest that now lies before us is finding a way to exorcize this Satan and the demonic legions lodged within the heart of and mind of an exclusivist and persecuting tradition" (220–221). This is ideology parading as historiography.

[24] Peter G. Bolt and Donald S. West, "Christ's Victory over the Powers and Pastoral Practice," in *Christ's Victory over Evil: Biblical Theology and Pastoral Ministry*, ed. Peter G. Bolt (Nottingham, UK: Inter-Varsity Press, 2009), 222, suggest that an implication could be drawn from Hiebert's thesis that Western secularists need to become animists. This is quite a stretch, to put it mildly. That said, however, the work of Bolt and West is full of insight, provocative argument, and a serious engagement with the biblical testimony in the light of controversial contemporary Christian practices.

[25] See also Andreas J. Köstenberger, L. Scott Kellum, and Charles L. Quarles, *The Cradle, the Cross, and the Crown: An Introduction to the New Testament*, 2nd ed. (Nashville: B&H, 2016), Even though this work is more than a thousand pages long, its index contains no references to angels, Satan or devil, or demons.

[26] Colin E. Gunton, ed., *The Cambridge Companion to Christian Theology* (Cambridge: Cambridge University Press, 1997).

[27] Timothy Larsen and Daniel J. Treier, eds., *The Cambridge Companion to Evangelical Theology* (Cambridge: Cambridge University Press, 2007). Interestingly this volume contains no chapter on creation. Perhaps that helps explain the absence of references to angels.

[28] William C. Placher, ed., *Essentials of Christian Theology* (Louisville: Westminster John Knox, 2003).

[29] Daniel L. Migliore, *Faith Seeking Understanding: An Introduction to Christian Theology*, 2nd ed. (Grand Rapids, MI: Eerdmans, 2004).

[30] Alister E. McGrath, *Christian Theology: An Introduction*, 5th ed. (Chichester, West Sussex, UK: Basil-Wiley, 2011).

demons, or to conflict in the work. The latter lacuna is significant since conflict is of the essence of drama.[31] Even Timothy C. Tennent's very important and groundbreaking *Theology in the Context of World Christianity: How the Global Church Is Influencing the Way We Think about and Discuss Theology* has little on angels, Satan, and demons per se. One would have expected much more on the subject in his chapter on Christology in Africa. He thematizes Christ as healer and as ancestor but not as *Christus Victor* per se. This is the case even though he writes,

> Fourth, despite the diverse Christological images developed by African writers, a common underlying theme is an emphasis on the power and victory of Christ. . . . Harold Turner, in his *Profile through Preaching*, has documented this emphasis in the popular preaching of African independent church leaders. He discovered that African preachers often focus on Jesus' victory over the devil, his works of healing and demonic deliverance, his announcement of deliverance for the captives, his triumphal entry into Jerusalem, and his resurrection.[32]

For some theologians, a reference to the devil is judged to be actually dangerous. For example, when Douglas John Hall writes of apocalyptic language he is strident: "When its resort to biblical and medieval imagery (the Devil, Antichrist, cosmic struggle, the Beast and the Dragon, etc.) is not just anachronistic and apologetically irresponsible, it too easily encourages a mood of paranoia and irrationality that is never far from the surface of human social consciousness."[33]

In contrast, Karl Barth (1886–1968) covered angelology and demonology in depth—over one hundred fifty passages—in his massive *Church Dogmatics* under the heading of "The Kingdom of Heaven, The Ambassadors of God and Their Opponents."[34] Both Millard Erickson and Wayne Grudem likewise avoid the blind spot mentioned earlier. Pleasingly, in both of their systematic

---

[31] Kevin J. Vanhoozer, *The Drama of Doctrine: A Canonical Linguistic Approach to Christian Theology* (Louisville: Westminster John Knox, 2005). In literary terms a drama is "[a] composition in prose or verse presenting, in pantomime and dialogue, a narrative involving conflict between a character or characters and some external or internal force (see conflict)." This definition is found in "Literary Terms and Definitions," http://web.cn.edu/kwheeler/lit_terms_D.html, accessed 7/18/2013. In more recent work, Vanhoozer does indeed thematize the devil and demons. See his *Faith Seeking Understanding* (Louisville: Westminster John Knox, 2014), 87–89. This section is entitled, "Satan and His Minions."

[32] Timothy C. Tennent, *Theology in the Context of World Christianity: How the Global Church Is Influencing the Way We Think about and Discuss Theology* (Grand Rapids, MI: Zondervan, 2007), 115–116.

[33] John Douglas Hall, *The Cross in Our Context: Jesus and the Suffering World* (Minneapolis: Fortress, 2003), 227.

[34] Barth, *CD*, III/3 (369–531). Stanley J. Grenz, *Theology for the Community of God* (Grand Rapids, MI: Eerdmans, 2000), 218, suggests, "Perhaps no theologian in the twentieth century has explored angelology in general and the concept of the demonic in particular in greater depth than has Paul Tillich." This is puzzling, given the sustained attention Barth gave to the topic. A close reading of Tillich shows that he gave an inordinate amount of attention to the demonic in the abstract rather than to angelology per se, especially in volume 3 of his *Systematic Theology: Life and the Spirit: History and the Kingdom of God* (Chicago: University of Chicago Press, 1976), passim.

theologies there are chapters on our theme.[35] Significantly, some multiauthored systematic theologies also give sustained attention to angelology. Peter R. Schemm Jr., in one such volume, maintains,

> The greatest of Christian thinkers have consistently recognized that angels and demons are far more than a divine embellishment designed to make the Bible interesting. Angels are actual beings whose existence affects human life. Augustine's classic *The City of God* explains the origin, history, and destiny of two cities and the angelic servants that attend to them—the earthly city under the power of the devil and his minions and the heavenly city ruled by God and his host. John Bunyan's work *The Pilgrim's Progress* features Apollyon as the most formidable foe that Christian encountered. By deception and force, Apollyon tries to turn Christian back to the City of Destruction from which he has come. Clive Staples Lewis's *The Screwtape Letters* details the correspondence between the affectionate Uncle Screwtape and another demon, his nephew Wormwood, whose strategy is marked by a consistent yet subtle undermining of the faith of the believer to whom he is assigned.[36]

Whether in apology (*The City of God*) or allegory (*The Pilgrim's Progress*) or fantasy (*The Screwtape Letters*), the significance of angels both good and evil is accented.

So then what is the balance that is needed? C. S. Lewis (1898–1963) wrote of two errors when it comes to the fallen angels: excessive interest and excessive disinterest.[37] His warning applies to unfallen angels as well. In a similar vein, J. I. Packer argues, "He [Satan] should be taken seriously, for malice and cunning make him fearsome; yet not so seriously as to provoke abject terror of him, for he is a beaten enemy."[38] In this study, then, I will endeavor carefully to make it clear when I am merely giving an opinion or speculating—when I have run out of revelatory data. The need to do so is simple: Scripture is not addressed to the angelic realm; Scripture addresses humankind. This constitutes a difficulty for constructive theology.[39] As Erickson points out, "Every [biblical] reference

[35] Erickson, *Christian Theology*, chapter 19, "God's Special Agents: Angels"; and Wayne Grudem, *Systematic Theology: An Introduction to Biblical Doctrine* (Grand Rapids, MI: Zondervan, 1995), chapter 19, "Angels," and chapter 20, "Satan and Demons."
[36] Peter R. Schemm Jr., "The Agents of God: Angels," in *A Theology for the Church*, rev. ed., ed. Daniel L. Akin (Nashville: B&H, 2014), 249. Another example is Robert P. Lightner, "Angels, Satan, and Demons: Invisible Beings That Inhabit the Spiritual World," in *Understanding Christian Theology*, ed. Charles R. Swindoll and Roy B. Zuck (Nashville: Thomas Nelson, 2003), 539–640.
[37] C. S. Lewis, *The Screwtape Letters: Letters from a Senior to a Junior Devil* (London and Glasgow: Fontana, 1966), 9. Heinz-Dieter Neef observes, concerning the neglect of theological attention to angels, "The angel boom in our secularized world stands in contrast to a significantly growing absence of angels in the proclamation of the church" ("The Angels of God in the Bible," in *Comfortable Words: Essays in Honor of Paul F. M. Zahl*, ed. John D. Koch Jr. and Todd H. W. Brewer [Eugene, OR: Pickwick, 2013], 72). Neef is speaking especially of the scene in Germany, and if he is right, one can see there the dangers of both excess and neglect.
[38] Packer, *Concise Theology*, 71. A strength of Packer's work is three brief chapters on angels, Satan, and demons.
[39] Barth, *CD*, III/3 (369), describes a theology of angels in these terms: "The dogmatic sphere which we have to enter and traverse . . . is the most remarkable and difficult of all."

to angels is incidental to some other topic. They are not treated in themselves. God's revelation never aims at informing us regarding the nature of angels."[40]

Questions to Be Considered

Questions are the life blood of academic discourse. By the quality of their questions you can know them, one might say. Here are some of the questions animating this study:

- Who are angels?
- What is their nature?
- Are there different kinds of angels?
- Does the category of "angel" cover every kind of spiritual beings?
- Where do angels fit in the scheme of God's creation?
- What roles do angels perform?
- Are angels active in our world today?
- Are there guardian angels?
- Is it wrong to pray to angels?
- Do angels have wings?
- Should we expect to encounter them in today's world?
- What is "angelism" and what danger does it pose?
- If some angels have never fallen, in what sense is it right to speak of a "fallen creation"?
- How did disorder in the angelic realm come about?
- Who and what is Satan?
- How did Satan fall?
- What was Satan's sin?
- What role does he play in disordering creation?
- Who and what are demons?
- What role do they play in disordering creation?
- Are there exorcisms today?
- Can the Christian believer be influenced by demons?
- Can the Christian believer be tempted by demons?
- Can the Christian believer be oppressed by demons?
- Can the Christian believer ever be demon-possessed?
- How do demons relate to Satan?
- Is Michael the archangel the restrainer of 2 Thessalonians 2:6–7?
- How does the Antichrist relate to Satan?
- How are Satan and demons related to the problem of evil?
- Is there a relation between some mental illness and the demonic?
- How are Satan and demons defeated?
- What is the future of the angelic order?
- How have angels, Satan, and demons been understood down through the ages?
- How are angels, Satan, and demons to be understood in relation to other religions?

---

[40] Erickson, *Christian Theology*, 404.

- How important doctrinally are angels, Satan, and demons?
- How important existentially are angels, Satan, and demons to the life of the Christian?
- What place do angels, Satan, and demons play in an understanding of spiritual warfare?
- What is an apocalyptic imagination and why is it important?

The Shape of This Study

The second chapter explores the doctrine of creation and angelology. The biblical account reveals a creation multiplex. Creatures are of different kinds and of differing capacities. Some creatures are persons who are self-aware and morally accountable for their actions. Humankind and angel-kind are members of the realm of the personal. Both can self-consciously say "I." Both humankind and angel-kind are judged.[41] Scripture gives no hint that other creatures—clever though some may be—are part of this realm of the personal (e.g., dolphins, higher primates). The nature of angels as spirits is considered and the role of angels in the heavenly realm is examined insofar as Scripture provides insight. The chapter concludes with a discussion of its implications for belief and practice.[42] John M. Frame rightly suggests that theology's definition is "the application of the Word of God to all areas of life."[43] An excursus treats the question of the nature of spirit.

Chapter 3 continues the treatment of angels. In this chapter, however, the accent falls on angelic activity on earth in relation not just to individuals but also to nations. An intriguing and influential discussion of angels emanating from the pen of Pseudo-Dionysius in the early church period will be examined. Thomas Aquinas's discussion of angelology also comes into view as the high point of medieval speculation on the subject. Some wisdom from Barth on the subject of speculation is considered. In the section on the implications for belief and action we will look at the question—among others—of our expectations with regard to encountering angels today. An excursus follows which deals with angelophanies (appearances of angels).

Satan is the subject of chapter 4. A dark note is introduced in this chapter as a rupture has taken place in the created order and it is Satan who stands revealed as the great spoiler. There is rebellion in the angelic order. As a consequence, the created order in which we now live is a dramatic one. That is to

---

[41] I. Howard Marshall argues, "*Alone* of created beings he [meaning a human being] is capable of moral behavior; he knows the difference between right and wrong, between love and hatred" (*Pocket Guide to Christian Beliefs* [Leicester, UK: Inter-Varsity Press, 1990], 57, emphasis mine). This is puzzlingly reductionist, since angels are held accountable for their actions (Jude 6).
[42] Each of the main chapters will have a section on implications for belief and action. For the purposes of this study I understand a sound application of the findings of a chapter to be the implications drawn from the biblical text relevantly connected to a contemporary context. In this way, application avoids being an imposition on the text.
[43] John M. Frame, *The Knowledge of God* (Phillipsburg, NJ: P&R, 1987), 81. I would nuance Frame's definition by covering more than application in a definition of theology.

say, there is a great conflict underway between good and evil. Satan's role in the great rupture is examined and the exact nature of his condemnation discussed. Hints in the OT as to Satan's sin are brought into view, as well as the much fuller NT revelation. The progressive nature of biblical revelation is to the fore in this chapter as we see how the NT picture is so much fuller than the OT one. What it means for the NT to describe Satan as the god of this world will be discussed.

Chapter 5 is concerned with the demonic disorder. Satan is not alone in his rebellion. There are other principalities and powers involved. Their nature is examined, and how they relate to Satan is discussed. In the section on the implications for belief and action we will investigate the question of demon-possession and whether a genuine believer, who is the temple of the Holy Spirit of God, can be so possessed. An excursus is added that explores the question of the identity of the "sons of God" referenced in Genesis 6 and the methodological questions that the exegesis of such a passage raises.

Christology is front and center in chapter 6. The controversial claim by some that the mysterious "angel of the Lord" found in the OT witness is none other than the preincarnate Son of God and anticipatory of the incarnation will be analyzed. Jesus's ministry as an exorcist will be examined, as well as the role of the Holy Spirit in Jesus's binding the strong man and spoiling his goods. Particular attention will be given to the story of Good Friday's cross and how Jesus defeats Satan there. Holy Saturday will also be discussed in relation to Jesus's death and the defeat of evil. The resurrection is a key part of that story too. *Christus Victor* features prominently in this part of the study, and how exactly Jesus overcomes the evil one shall be explored.

Chapter 7 deals with spiritual warfare as seen in Jesus's ministry, and as found articulated in the writings of Luke–Acts, Paul, Peter, and John. Seven contemporary views of spiritual warfare will be critically examined. I will offer my own approach as a biblically defensible model of spiritual warfare. An excursus examines the question of how to discern whether a spirit is from God.

The eighth chapter looks to the end of history: the destiny of the darkness and the victory of the light. The witness of Revelation is especially important here. "God wins" is its message, as we shall see. The world to come reveals order restored and evil defeated, with God's people at home with God, living in shalom. The judging of angels will be discussed, as will the salvation or otherwise of Satan (*apocatastasis*). An excursus deals with 2 Thessalonians 2:6–7 and the question of whether the archangel Michael is the restrainer.

Chapter 9 is a brief conclusion, followed by three appendices. The first deals with the stratified nature of creation, the second treats angelology in Islam, and the final one explores the witness of creeds, articles of faith, confessions, and catechisms to angels, Satan, and demons. A glossary of key terms and some suggestions for further reading complete the study.

Even though the present work addresses a topic in systematic theology, the shape of the study pays attention to the biblical plotline, moving as it does from the good creation in chapter 2 to the new heavens and new earth (chapter 8) with Christ at the heart of it (chapter 6). Thus the work moves through the key motifs of creation, fall, redemption, and consummation.

A WARNING ABOUT ANGELOLOGY AND "GOSPEL SPOILING"

J. C. Ryle (1816–1900) wrote a seminal essay on evangelicalism titled, "Evangelical Religion."[44] In it he discusses how the gospel may be "spoiled" in various ways. One of the ways he draws attention to is spoiling through disproportion. By this he means attaching *"an exaggerated importance to the secondary things of Christianity, and a diminished importance to the first things, and the mischief is done."*[45] Ryle's concern for a gospel spoiled by disproportion is especially relevant to this study. Recall C. S. Lewis's warning of two dangers concerning Satan and demons: excessive interest in them or excessive disinterest: "There are two equal and opposite errors into which our race can fall about the devils. One is to disbelieve in their existence. The other is to believe, and to feel an excessive and unhealthy interest in them."[46] With regard to the latter, Karl Barth rightly comments, "A good deal of hampering rubbish has accumulated in this field in both ancient and more modern times."[47] Even so, angelology ought not be allowed to fall into theological neglect. Again Barth puts it well: "At a pinch and in the forbearance of God, which sustains it in spite of its defects, the Church and its proclamation may well survive without this dimension of faith [angelology], although not without hurt, and not without an underlying awareness that something is missing."[48]

An aim of this particular study is to provide a balanced account of angels, Satan, and demons which does not give more weight to the subject than is due. And happily, being one of a series of studies in evangelical systematic theology helps because this work finds its place in that larger theological scheme.

---

[44] J. C. Ryle, "Evangelical Religion," in *Knots Untied* (London: James Clarke, 1959), 9–22.
[45] Ryle, "Evangelical Religion," emphasis original. Surprisingly, Ryle does not ground his categories in the NT. However, his categories can be illustrated from the NT. For example, spoiling the gospel through disproportion: secondary matters become primary matters. Was this one of the problems at Corinth, where the more sensational gifts of the Spirit were overemphasized and the importance of a loving use of them was lost sight of (1 Corinthians 12–13)?
[46] Lewis, *Screwtape Letters*, 9.
[47] Barth, *CD*, III/3 (xi).
[48] Barth, *CD*, III/3 (380).

ANGELS, THEIR KINDS, AND

HEAVENLY ACTIVITY

In Shakespeare's *Hamlet* there is a celebrated scene involving Hamlet, the ghost of Hamlet's father, and Hamlet's friend Horatio. Horatio, like Hamlet, is a student at the University of Wittenberg. He is skeptical about ghosts and finds the idea of Hamlet conversing with the ghost of his father "wondrous strange." To which Hamlet responds, "There are more things in heaven and earth, Horatio, Than are dreamt of in your philosophy."[1] How right Hamlet was. In this chapter we consider not ghosts but those wondrous strange creatures the Bible calls angels.[2] To do so we need to frame our study in the broadest of terms. So first we consider angels in the scheme of created things. Next, we consider the angelic realm and its inhabitants, ranging from angels to seraphim. Then we explore questions concerning the nature of angels as created beings. We also canvas the provocative thesis of Amos Yong on angelic nature. To be practical, we consider the implications of our findings for belief and practice, before drawing the threads together by way of a conclusion. An excursus on the nature of angels as spirits then follows.

ANGELS IN THE SCHEME OF CREATED THINGS

The basic metaphysical distinction in Scripture is that between the Creator and the creature (Gen. 1:1), not that between being and becoming, or between the

---

[1] *Hamlet*, act 1, scene 5. Not all Christian theologians would find Hamlet persuasive. For example, Nancey Murphy is dismissive of angels as presented in Scripture as "merely figurative or literary devices." See William A. Dembski's personal account of Murphy's speaking at a Baylor University conference, in Peter S. Williams, *The Case for Angels* (Carlisle, UK and Waynesboro, GA: Paternoster, 2000), ix–x. Williams offers an acute philosophical defense of the existence of angels in contradistinction to a naturalistic worldview. See also Mortimer J. Adler, *The Angels and Us*, reissue ed. (Lexington, KY: Touchstone, 2016). This work was first published in 1982 by Scribner. Writing as a philosopher, Adler argues that the idea of angels is one of the great ones in Western thought (xi). The philosophical treatment of angels, unlike the theological one, works with the Bible closed. It is an exercise in natural theology.

[2] The appeal to the opened Bible is fundamental to an evangelical systematic theology, and Scripture makes it clear that these creatures exist. For a rather speculative natural theology argument for the existence of angels, predicated on some theory of a great chain of being where angels fill the gap between God and ourselves just as other creatures fill the gap between us and the lowest form of organic life, see Peter Kreeft, *Angels and Demons: What Do We Really Know about Them?* (San Francisco: Ignatius, 1995), 33–36. Natural theology by definition leaves the Bible closed.

infinite and the finite. These latter two distinctions have their place in theological discourse, but not first place.[3] Angels stand on the creature side of the ledger, as we do. Their origin, like our own, lies in the creative action of God.[4] In Psalm 148:1–5, angels are commanded along with other creatures to praise the name of their God, who "commanded and they [the angels] were created."[5] Angels are of heaven and we are of the earth. The heavens and the earth encompass the creaturely domain in biblical perspective.

Creatures are of different kinds and values. The testimony of Genesis 1 provides evidence for a myriad of creaturely kinds (Gen. 1:11, 12, 21, 24, 25). Regarding creaturely value, Jesus argued, for example, that human beings are of more value than many sparrows or sheep (Matt. 10:31 and 12:12, respectively). In the hierarchy of creaturely value, humanity stands higher than other terrestrial life forms. But what of angels? Are they superior to human beings? Like human beings, angels bear personal names (e.g., Gabriel, as in Luke 1:19), they are speech agents (again Gabriel in Luke 1:19), intelligent, and are held morally accountable by the Creator (e.g., Satan, as in Rev. 20:1–4). Kevin J. Vanhoozer describes angels as "[a] third species of communicative agents."[6] Like us they belong in the realm of the person.[7] However, they are nowhere described as the images of God, and in fact they are to be judged by believers (1 Cor. 6:3). Interestingly, we are called upon to love God, the people of God, our neighbors, and even our enemies (cf. Matt. 22:34–40; Rom. 13:8; and Matt. 5:43–44), but nowhere in Scripture are we commanded to love angels. Moreover, the second person of the triune Godhead became human, not angelic (Heb. 2:14). In the light of this, Peter Kreeft's suggestion is baffling in places. He argues, "Humans are the lowest (least intelligent) of spirits and the highest (most intelligent) of animals. We are rational animals, incarnate minds,

---

[3] As I have argued in my "Towards a New Metaphysic of the Exodus," in *Reformed Theological Review* 42 (1983): 75–84.

[4] Interestingly, the medieval divines coined a term for the kind of time that angels enjoy. "*Aeviternity*" refers to the fact that angels have a beginning but no end of existence. They experience no duration. Hence they do not age. For a useful discussion of this speculation see Kreeft, *Angels and Demons*, 92–93. Kreeft mistakenly has "aeveternity."

[5] How one could place the angels' creation within the flow of God's creative acts I would not even begin to know, since they are spirits. Augustine believed that they were created on the first of the Genesis days. However, Basil the Great, Gregory the Theologian, John Chrysostom, Ambrose of Milan, John of Damascus, and Jerome posited that the angels were created *before* the first of the six days of Genesis. See Sergius Bulgakov, *Jacob's Ladder: On Angels*, trans. Thomas Allan Smith (Grand Rapid, MI and Cambridge: Eerdmans, 2010), 22–23. On the latter view, the reference to the heavens in Genesis 1:1 refers to the angelic realm.

[6] Kevin J. Vanhoozer, *Remythologizing Theology: Divine Action, Passion, and Authorship* (Cambridge: Cambridge University Press, 2010), 221. The other two, according to Vanhoozer, are God and human beings. I am not sure that I would use "species" of the incomparable God.

[7] Karl Barth, CD, III/3 (410). Barth argues, ". . . the biblical doctrine of angels gives us no information whatever. It tells us nothing, for example, about the much ventilated question of the 'nature' of angels, whether they are persons . . ." Barth is clearly wrong in this. A creature that is a speech agent, intelligent, and morally accountable seems robustly personal, whatever else they might be. Philosopher Elton Trueblood, in *The New Man for Our Time* (New York: Harper & Row, 1970), 122, offers wisdom on this matter: "An examination of the Biblical use of the language of direct intimacy offers a deeper understanding of what it means to be a person. A person is any being to whom the word 'thou' or even 'you' can be intelligibly addressed! No one ever says 'thou' to a physical object or to a principle or a law."

the smartest of animals and the stupidest of spirits."[8] How this fits with a Chalcedonian Christology, which posits that one person is perfectly God and perfectly human, is not clear.[9]

THE ANGELIC REALM

As Stephen F. Noll rightly points out, "The term 'angel' itself (Hebrew: mal'ak; Greek: angelos) is functional, denoting a messenger, whether human or divine."[10] He is right, but in relation to "divine" messengers, confusion may arise. Millard J. Erickson, for example, would not describe angels as "divine beings" but instead as "superhuman."[11] There is some merit in this proposal. However, it might be better to describe these celestial beings as "suprahuman" (i.e., "supra," beyond the human) to reflect something of their celestial origins or habitat.

Even more nuance is in order. Let me stipulate for the purposes of this study that "angels" broadly considered covers all sorts of spiritual beings, from seraphim to archangels to Satan and demons. Hence we have the theological topic of angelology, which covers both unfallen and fallen spiritual beings of heavenly origin. Narrowly considered, however, "angels" might refer to only some of the heavenly agents (archangels and angels).

N. T. Wright offers a helpful analogy when it comes to understanding a doctrine, which I will tweak in my own way.[12] A doctrine is like a suitcase. In it are packed all the relevant biblical testimonies, organized in a useful way. The suitcase labeled "Atonement" might contain not only relevant biblical passages such as Romans 3:21–26 but also some key theories generated through Christian history, such as penal substitution or Christus Victor, to name just two. "Angelology" labels a particular doctrinal suitcase, and a variety of articles of clothing, such as seraphim or archangel, are to be found in it, together with their relevant biblical testimonies and, in addition, theories promulgated in the course of theological discussion and debate over time.

We begin broadly and positively with the unfallen angels (broad definition). "Angel" as the label for the consideration of fallen angels will come in later chapters. But as we do, we need to recognize that, when it comes to the

---

[8] Kreeft, Angels and Demons, 19.

[9] More apposite is Adler's comment: "If neither an angel nor a brute, but occupies a middle ground between the real world of material things and the world, either real or possible, of purely spiritual beings, then a right understanding of human nature requires us to avoid lowering man's nature to the level of the brutes, while not trying to raise it to the level of angels" (Angels and Us, 21).

[10] Stephen F. Noll, "Angels, Doctrine of," in Dictionary for Theological Interpretation of the Bible, ed. Kevin J. Vanhoozer (Grand Rapids, MI: Baker Academic, 2005), 45. Most references to angels, however, refer to "a transcendent power who carries out various missions or tasks" as Bauer, Gingrich, and Danker point out, in W. Bauer, F. W. Gingrich, and F. W. Danker, A Greek-English Lexicon of the New Testament and Other Early Christian Literature, 2nd ed. (Chicago: University of Chicago Press, 1979), 8.

[11] Millard J. Erickson, Christian Theology, 3rd ed. (Grand Rapids, MI: Baker, 2013), 403.

[12] See N. T. Wright, "Reading Paul, Thinking Scripture," in http://ntwrightpage.com/Wright_Reading_Paul _Thinking_Scripture.htm, accessed 2/3/2015.

heavenly angels (the broad definition), the Scriptures offer a plethora of terms that are not easy to systematize, and it is to the main terms that we now turn.[13]

Archangels

There are only two references to an archangel per se in Scripture (1 Thess. 4:16 and Jude 9). Jude 9 is of particular interest: "But when the archangel [*archangelos*] Michael, contending with the devil, was disputing about the body of Moses, he did not presume to pronounce a blasphemous judgment, but said, 'The Lord rebuke you.'" It is a fascinating text for a number of reasons. For a start, there is Jude's use of a story referring to Michael that is probably drawn from a pseudepigraphal work known as the *Assumption of Moses*, which is also possibly behind Jude 6. Was he writing ad hominem in using such a source, or was this extracanonical tradition an authority for him?[14] For our purposes what is significant is that Michael is of such a stature that he can confront the devil himself. Indeed in Revelation 12:7 he is named as the leader of the good angels in the war in heaven against the dragon and its angelic forces. Moreover, he bears a personal name. Angels are therefore not impersonal heavenly forces or influences. Gabriel is another angel who is named in Scripture (Luke 1:19), and he is traditionally identified as an archangel, although Scripture does not go that far.[15]

Angels

Angels are God's messengers and appear to be the most numerous of the celestial spiritual beings.[16] A good biblical example of angels as messengers is found in the Lukan story of the shepherds, in Luke 2:8–15. We read in verses 10–11, "And the angel said to them, 'Fear not, for behold, I bring you good news of

---

[13] The terminology of Scripture is not systematic when it comes to angelology. In this there is a parallel with the biblical terminology for human psychology. In both areas there are considerable challenges to ordering the discussion. The various English translations show the difficulties. For example, in Colossians 1:16 the NIV translates *kyriotētes* as "powers" while the ESV renders it "dominions." For the purposes of this part of the discussion I will follow the ESV translation. For an excellent discussion of the terminology, see Maxwell John Davidson, "Angel," in *NIDB*, ed. Katharine Doob Sakenfeld, 5 vols. (Nashville: Abingdon, 2006), 1:148–155.

[14] For an extensive discussion of the issues, see Richard J. Bauckham, *Jude, 2 Peter*, WBC (Dallas: Word, 2002), 64. Michael Green favors the ad hominem explanation (*2 Peter and Jude*, TNTC [Downers Grove, IL: IVP Academic, 1987], 196). Christopher Green makes the helpful point that "*[T]here is nothing unusual in biblical writers referring to or quoting books that are not in our Bibles*. In the Old Testament we find references to 'the Book of the Wars of the LORD,' the records of Nathan the prophet and of Gad the seer, the annals of the kings of Israel and the annals of the kings of Judah" (Dick Lucas and Christopher Green, *The Message of 2 Peter and Jude* [Leicester, UK: Inter-Varsity Press, 1995], 191, emphasis original; Lucas wrote the introduction to the two books, and Green did the commentary and exposition). An alternative argument is that the story of Michael and the devil in *Assumption of Moses* is a true one, and when included in Holy Scripture such truth becomes biblical truth.

[15] In extracanonical tradition, two groups of archangels emerged. One group consisted of Michael, Gabriel, Raphael, and Sariel (e.g., *1 Enoch* 9:1). The other had seven members: the four already mentioned plus Uriel, Raguel, and Remiel (e.g., *1 Enoch* 20 and *Tobit* 12:15) (Davidson, "Angel," 152).

[16] There are synonyms for angels in Scripture, such as "gods" (*'elohim*), as in Psalm 138:1, or "sons of God" (*bene ha 'elohim*), as in Job 1:6. According to C. Fred Dickason (*Angels: Elect and Evil*, rev. and expanded ed. [Chicago: Moody, 1995], 14), there are 17 books of the OT that refer to angels and 17 of the NT. On his count, there are 273 references to angels in Scripture.

great joy that will be for all the people. For unto you is born this day in the city of David a Savior, who is Christ the Lord.'" The content of the message is both Christological and soteriological, set within the Davidic promises of old. As for the number of these angels, verses 13–14 are eloquent: "And suddenly there was with the angel a multitude of the heavenly host praising God and saying, 'Glory to God in the highest, and on earth peace among those with whom he is pleased!'" Angels do other tasks besides communicating the divine will, as we shall see anon.

Seraphim

Only one passage of Scripture refers to seraphim per se, but it is a magnificent one. In Isaiah 6:1–4 we find this description:

> In the year that King Uzziah died I saw the Lord sitting upon a throne, high and lifted up; and the train of his robe filled the temple. Above him stood the seraphim. Each had six wings: with two he covered his face, and with two he covered his feet, and with two he flew. And one called to another and said:
>
> > "Holy, holy, holy is the LORD of hosts;
> > the whole earth is full of his glory!"

These creatures along with the cherubim (more anon) are well described by Noll as "throne angels."[17] They seem to be associated with the glorious presence of God and with purifying fire.[18]

Cherubim

Cherubim come into view very early on in the canonical presentation and are more frequently mentioned in Scripture than are the seraphim (e.g., 1 Sam. 4:4; 2 Sam. 6:2; 2 Kings 19:15; Pss. 80:1; 99:1, inter alia).[19] The primal pair are expelled from the garden, and cherubim guard the entrance to prevent reentry (Gen. 3:24): "He drove out the man, and at the east of the garden of Eden he placed the cherubim [kᵉrûḇîm] and a flaming sword that turned every way to guard the way to the tree of life."[20] In Ezekiel 10:14–21, cherubim are presented as having four faces (cherub, man, lion, and eagle) as well as four wings, but in the later vision of Ezekiel 41:18–19 they are described as having only two

---

[17] Stephen F. Noll, "Angels and Heaven," in *Heaven*, ed. Christopher W. Morgan and Robert A. Peterson (Wheaton, IL: Crossway, 2014), 206.

[18] John H. Walton, Victor H. Matthews, and Mark W. Chavalas, *The IVP Bible Background Commentary: Old Testament*, electronic ed. (Downers Grove, IL: InterVarsity Press, 2000), 592 (comment on Isa. 6:2): "Since the Hebrew root *sarap* is usually associated with 'burning,' there is also good reason to associate these creatures with fire."

[19] The etymology of "cherubim" is uncertain.

[20] The relation between the flaming sword and the cherubim is not clear in this context. Is one of the cherubim holding it? The reference to cherubim and the flaming sword is unique in the OT, as Terence E. Fretheim points out ("Genesis," in *NIB*, 12 vols. [Nashville: Abingdon, 1993–2002], 1:365).

faces (of a human and a lion). There is plasticity when it comes to the prophet's description of these strange celestial beings.[21] These creatures are real but their description is symbol-laden. Ezekiel 10 is particularly interesting because these creatures form the visible pedestal for the invisible God (vv. 1–17).

Some suggest that seraphim and cherubim are the same creatures. A. A. Hodge wrote, "The word [seraphim] signifies *burning, bright, dazzling*. . . . It probably presents, under a different aspect, the ideal beings commonly designated cherubim and living creatures."[22] Others clearly distinguish them.[23] Erickson shows admirable modesty in mining the biblical testimony: "The most cautious position is simply to regard the seraphim and cherubim as being among spiritual creatures designated by the general term 'angel'."[24] He is also correct in my view to argue, "[W]e cannot assume that the characteristics of either seraphim or cherubim can be predicated of all angels. And whether they are of the higher or lower ranks, if indeed there are such ranks, we do not know."[25] The difference among the commentators highlights the need for caution in theologizing in angelology. Theological overreach is all too possible.

Thrones, Dominions, Rulers, and Authorities

Paul, in writing to the Colossians, magnificently describes Christ's role in creation and in doing so makes an intriguing reference to four created realities (Col. 1:16–20): "For by him [Christ] all things were created, in heaven and on earth, visible and invisible, whether thrones [*thronoi*] or dominions [*kyriotēs*] or rulers [*archai*] or authorities [*exousiai*]—all things were created through him and for him." Distinguishing among thrones, dominions, rulers, and authorities is extremely difficult. Wittgenstein has taught us, "For a *large* class of cases—though not for all—in which we employ the word 'meaning' it can be defined thus: the meaning of a word is its use in the language."[26] Our problem is that, unlike the term "angel," these terms are used far less frequently, and concrete examples are not given in the biblical testimony.[27] Since these spiritual

---

[21] The plasticity can be seen in comparing the creatures of Ezekiel 1 ("living creatures") and 10 (e.g., the face of an ox in Ezekiel 1 and that of a cherub in Ezekiel 10, unless the face of a cherub is in fact the face of an ox).
[22] For example, A. A. Hodge, *Outlines of Theology* (Edinburgh: Banner of Truth Trust, 1983), 250. Others see significant differences between the two, such as the number of faces and wings (e.g., Leon Morris). If seraphim, cherubim, and the living creatures are different celestial beings, perhaps they can be grouped as "throne angels," as a subset of angels viewed as a general category (the broad definition of "angel"). However, it may be another case of the plasticity of symbolic description, and Ezekiel 1, 10, and Revelation 4 are referring to the same species of celestial being. Richard Bauckham, *The Theology of the Book of Revelation* (Cambridge: Cambridge University Press, 2016), 33–34, provides an insightful discussion of the living creatures.
[23] For example, Dickason, *Angels: Elect and Evil*, 64–69.
[24] Erickson, *Christian Theology*, 412.
[25] Erickson, *Christian Theology*, 412.
[26] Ludwig Wittgenstein, *Philosophical Investigations*, trans. G. E. M. Anscombe (Oxford: Bail Blackwell, 1986), 43, emphasis original, http://gormendizer.co.za/wp-content/uploads/2010/06/Ludwig.Wittgenstein.-.Philosophical .Investigations.pdf, accessed 1/13/2015.
[27] For example, "angel" (*angelos*) used of spiritual beings occurs hundreds of times in the LXX and Greek New Testament combined. However, with regard to what appear to be spiritual beings, thrones (*thronos*) is found only in Colossians 1:16; rulers (*archai*) in Colossians 1:16 and 2:15; Ephesians 1:21 (possibly); 3:10 and 6:12; Romans

beings are mentioned in occasional letters addressed to particular congrega-
tions, we are very much listening in on one end of the conversation. Gregory A.
Boyd is right to say, "Thus while these terms may indeed be somewhat opaque
to us, in all likelihood they were not so to Paul's original audience."[28] The
original addressees presumably could pour content into these terms in ways
inaccessible to us unless we care to speculate.

Powers

In 1 Peter there is a description of the victory of Christ and his subsequent ascension which refers to angels, authorities, and powers (1 Pet. 3:22): ". . . who
has gone into heaven and is at the right hand of God, with angels, authorities,
and powers [dynameis] having been subjected to him." This Petrine text is
suggestive. The victorious Christ is now at the place of executive power at the
right hand of God. This would have been readily understood by first-century
readers familiar with court protocols. Spiritual beings are now subjected to his
authority. The fact that angels are listed gives support to the view that authorities and powers are spiritual beings as well in this context.[29]

THE NATURE OF ANGELS

In discussing the place of angels in the scheme of created things and the angelic realm per se, a question has been begged which it is now time to consider.
What is an angel's nature? (I am using "angel" in the broader sense of an
exclusively spiritual being.) To ask questions about the nature of X is to enter
deep metaphysical waters.[30] At this juncture in our discussion we will proceed
more simply with Peter R. Schemm Jr's excellent analysis of the nature of
angels in six propositions, only one of which I find problematic.[31] First, he
rightly argues that, in substance, angels are personal spirits who normally do
not appear in bodily form, but on occasion do.[32] He rightly cites Hebrews

---

8:38; authorities (exousiai) in Colossians 1:16 and 2:15; Ephesians 1:21 (possibly); 3:10 and 6:12; and dominions
(kuriotēs) is found only in Colossians 1:16 and Ephesians 1:21 (possibly).

[28] Gregory A. Boyd, God at War: The Bible and Spiritual Conflict (Downers Grove, IL: IVP Academic, 1997), 271.
His discussion of these terms is most careful and illuminating. He concludes, "In sum, Paul viewed the various
cosmic powers as transcendent personal beings, created by God and ordered in a hierarchical fashion. At least
some of these powers have now become evil and thus have to be fought against by the church and overthrown by
Christ" (276).

[29] The chart in Dickason, Angels: Elect and Evil, 93, omits 1 Peter 3:22.

[30] The excursus attached to this chapter goes deeper into those metaphysical waters.

[31] Peter R. Schemm Jr., "The Agents of God: Angels," in A Theology for the Church, rev. ed., ed. Daniel L. Akin
(Nashville: B&H, 2014), 251–252.

[32] Noll suggests that "the heavenly angels have a personal or bodily—though not a body of flesh—identity distinct
from a formless demonic spirit ever in search of a body (Mark 5:12)" ("Angels and Heaven," 204). This is an interesting speculation but its truth value is difficult to decide. For a contrary and more traditional view, which maintains
that angels are pure spirits, see Peter Kreeft, Angels and Demons, 47. On the question of whether, as spirits, angels
have gender, see Robert P. Lightner, "Angels, Satan, and Demons: Invisible Beings That Inhabit the Spiritual World,"
in Understanding Christian Theology, ed. Charles R. Swindoll and Roy B. Zuck (Nashville: Thomas Nelson, 2003),
631–632. I agree with Lightner that gender does not apply to angels.

1:14 among other texts to support this contention.[33] Second, he maintains that angels are often glorious in appearance, as Revelation 18:1 suggests.[34] Third, angels are wise but not omniscient. They interpret dreams, for example, as in Daniel 8:16. Moreover, they can learn. Their knowledge can be dependent on unfolding events involving salvation and the church (cf. Eph. 3:10–11 and 1 Pet. 1:10–12). Fourth, they are powerful but not omnipotent. Schemm adduces as evidence 1 Peter 2:11 here, but the text should be 2 Peter 2:11. Fifth, angels can be in many places but are not omnipresent. They move from place to place for instance, as in Job 1:7. His last claim is that, in status, angels are more glorious than man. There is certainly biblical evidence that angels are glorious beings. In Revelation 18:1–2 the seer sees an angel "coming down from heaven, having great authority, and the earth was made bright with his glory [*doxēs*; "glory," "splendor"]." Such texts don't, however, make a comparison between angel-kind and humankind.

Schemm finds evidence for his contention in Psalm 8. Psalm 8 reads like a commentary on Genesis 1. It begins and ends (vv. 1, 9) by declaring the majesty of the divine name in all the earth: "O LORD, our Lord, how majestic is your name in all the earth!" This *inclusio* shows that the majesty of God provides the frame of reference for the psalmist's reflection on creation, angels, and humankind. Humankind is depicted as the ruler of the earth (vv. 6–8): "You have given him dominion over the works of your hands; you have put all things under his feet, all sheep and oxen, and also the beasts of the field, the birds of the heavens, and the fish of the sea, whatever passes along the paths of the seas." For our purpose the key verse is verse 5: "Yet you have made him a little lower than the heavenly beings [Hb. *'elohim*, "God," "gods"; LXX *angeloi*, "angels"]." For Schemm this is evidence of the superiority of angels. The angels have heavenly glory while humankind has earthly glory. He rightly argues, "The passage is not clear as to exactly how man is 'lower' than the angels." He suggests tentatively that "the holy angels are more glorious than man in that they bear a more immediate and brilliant display of their Creator's glory."[35] On this view, is humankind lower than angels ontologically, or functionally, or in terms of moral status, or is it spatial in some sense (angels are of the heavens, humankind is of the earth)?

I favor a different reading. If Psalm 8 is in part a reflection on the truths of Genesis 1, then it needs to be noted that Genesis 1 does not refer to angels.[36] The majestic God of creation dominates the Genesis text. Humankind, male

---

[33] Hebrews 1:14 is clear that angels can be described as "spirits" (*pneumata*).
[34] The appearance of an angel is an angelophany, in contradistinction to a theophany, which is an appearance of God himself (cf. Matt. 1:20 and Ex. 34:5). See excursus.
[35] Schemm, "Agents of God: Angels," 252.
[36] Some adopt a different view and argue that the "Let us" of Genesis 1 refers to God and the angelic assembly. John Sailhamer, *Pentateuch as Narrative* (Grand Rapids, MI: Zondervan, 1992), 95, effectively critiques this view.

and female, are given a godlike task of exercising dominion. The NRSV renders the Hebrew of Psalm 8:5 as, "Yet you have made them a little lower than God, and crowned them with glory and honor." Peter C. Craigie favors this translation but in doing so mentions a plausible reason for the LXX's translation, which has "angels":

> Many of the earliest versions took the word אלהים (literally, "God, gods") to mean "angels" (so G, S, Tg. and Vg), and in some texts that would be an appropriate translation. But other versions (Aquila, Symmachus, and others) translated *God*. The translation *angels* may have been prompted by modesty, for it may have seemed rather extravagant to claim that mankind was only a little less than God. Nevertheless, the translation *God* is almost certainly correct, and the words probably contain an allusion to the image of God in mankind and the God-given role of dominion to be exercised by mankind within the created order.[37]

Whatever the answer is to the question of the right translation, what is clear is that humankind may begin in a lowly way but in this psalm they become exalted creatures "crowned . . . with glory and honor." This point is not lost on the writer to the Hebrews, who employs this psalm as a lens through which to view the humiliation and exaltation of Christ (Heb. 2:5–9).

Human beings are not only rational creatures but emotional ones as well. What about angels? Do angels have emotion? If so, this is an aspect of angelic nature overlooked in theological literature. One theologian who has not neglected the question is Sergius Bulgakov (1871–1944). In one of the major works on angelology in the twentieth century, this Russian Orthodox divine argued, "Thus the labor of love and the creative work of angelic love for humans naturally contains for angels themselves the source of particular joys with humans and for humans which they share with the human world."[38] Although Scripture has no references to angelic love for humankind, there is a striking statement in Luke's Gospel that may support Bulgakov's contention about angelic joy. In his parable of the lost coin, Jesus says (Luke 15:8–10),

> Or what woman, having ten silver coins, if she loses one coin, does not light a lamp and sweep the house and seek diligently until she finds it? And when she has found it, she calls together her friends and neighbors, saying, "Rejoice with me, for I have found the coin that I had lost." Just so, I tell you, there is joy before [*enōpion*, "before"] the angels of God over one sinner who repents.

---

[37] Peter C. Craigie, *Psalms 1–50*, WBC (Dallas: Word, 2004), 108.

[38] Bulgakov, *Jacob's Ladder*, 14. Much in Bulgakov is both lyrical and fanciful. On this question, though, he is worth taking seriously. However, there are elements in his angelology that are simply strange. For example, he argues that angels are changeable in that they grow. If he means they grow in knowledge of the purpose of God then he has scriptural warrant (see 1 Pet. 1:12, "things into which angels long to look"). If his claim is an ontological one and not simply an epistemological one, then it is highly problematic.

Some commentators argue that the reference to angels in verse 10 is a Jewish idiomatic way of indirectly referring to God.[39] These commentators take "before" (*enōpion*) in verse 10 to mean in the presence of God, who is the one who is rejoicing. And so angels are not on view at all. Others, like Calvin, maintain that angels experience joy at human repentance. Calvin wrote, "If *angels* mutually rejoice with each other in heaven, when they see that what had wandered is restored to the fold, we too, who have the same cause in common with them, ought to be partakers of the same *joy*."[40] I, for one, find it hard to imagine that the angelic singing of Revelation 5:11–12 was a passionless affair.

Regarding angels, both their nature and function, the great early church father Augustine (354–430) made a useful distinction. Augustine suggested, "'Angel' is the name of their office, not of their nature. If you seek the name of their nature, it is 'spirit'; if you seek the name of their office, it is 'angel': from what they are, 'spirit,' from what they do, 'angel.'"[41] Having considered the nature of these spiritual beings, we now turn to their function according to the biblical witness. And that witness shows great continuity between the Old Testament and the New, as Maxwell J. Davidson accurately claims:

> Compared with the OT, intertestamental Jewish literature such as *1 Enoch, Jubilees* and the writings of the Qumran community, evidence a wide proliferation of ideas about angels. Nevertheless, the essential elements of the beliefs we encounter in the Gospels are already present in the OT. It is unnecessary to seek elsewhere, such as in Greek mystery religions, for the origins of NT beliefs concerning angels.[42]

I would argue that Davidson's observations concerning the intertestamental Jewish literature and the Gospels are also true of the rest of the NT literature.

THE NATURE OF ANGELS ACCORDING TO AMOS YONG

The always interesting Pentecostal theologian Amos Yong offers a provocative set of proposals concerning the nature of creation in what he calls "a Pneuma-

[39] I. Howard Marshall, "Luke," in *NBC*, comment on Luke 15:10.

[40] John Calvin, *Commentaries on the Harmony of the Gospels*, vol. 2 (*CJCC*), comment on Luke 15:10 (emphasis original). For a more recent example, see Michael Wilcock, *The Savior of the World: The Message of Luke's Gospel* (Downers Grove, IL: InterVarsity Press, 1979), 155 (comment on Luke 15:10). The "before" (*enōpion*) in verse 10 can be translated in certain contexts as "among."

[41] Augustine, *Enarrationes in Psalmos* 103, 1, 15, quoted in CCC (Liguori, MO: Liguori, 1994), 329, 85; Barth, *CD*, III/3 (381), has problems with any attempt to explore the question of the nature of angels. He sees this exploration starting in the early church and argues that it received its classic formulation at the hands of Augustine in this quotation. In his view, to consider the nature of angels per se is to draw attention away from the biblical emphasis on the function of angels as messengers of God. However, given that Scripture does describe angels as spirits, I think Barth's anxiety on this point is overblown.

[42] Maxwell J. Davidson, "Angels," in *DJG*, ed. Joel B. Green, Jeannine K. Brown, and Nicholas Perrin, 2nd ed. (Downers Grove, IL: InterVarsity Press, 2013), 8.

tological Cosmology."[43] He draws on the work of Philip Clayton in particular in seeking "the cross-fertilization . . . between a metaphysic of emergence and a pneumatological theology."[44] In Yong's mind, the cosmos is pluralistic in nature. It is a world that is "Spirit-Filled," and by that he means not just by the Holy Spirit of God.[45] In the cosmos, human life emerges through an evolutionary process followed by the emergence of angelic spirits: "Just as the human spirit emerges from and supervenes upon embodied relations that constitute our existence, so also, I suggest, do benevolent spiritual realities emerge from the complex material and personal relationships through which God's redemption is at work."[46] He elaborates:

> On the one hand, as agents of God who assist in the salvation of personal beings, they also are personal realities; on the other hand, as emergent from the complex matrices that constitute human relationships and their multiple environments, what we call angels are higher-level transpersonal or suprapersonal realities, constituted by and supervening upon the human relations *from which they derive*. Yet once emergent, they are irreducible to their underlying parts, even to the point of being capable of exercising "top-down" influence and agency in relationship to their lower-level realities [e.g., humans?].[47]

This statement leaves one puzzled as to what angels are in nature. Are they personal realities or are they transpersonal realities or are they suprapersonal ones? If they are "trans" or "supra" then they go beyond the personal. As for the creation sequence, Yong argues that the creation account, for example, in Psalm 8, "does not require that angels were created prior to or emerged before humanity."[48] We shall return to Yong's work when we discuss demonology in a later chapter.

So what are the angels up to, both in heaven and on earth? In this chapter we will address the "in heaven" question, and in the next the "on earth" one.

ANGELIC ACTIVITY IN HEAVEN

In Scripture, God the King has his court.[49] Heaven is that created sphere where his throne is found and that constitutes his dwelling place. Heaven is the seat of his sovereignty in the created realm. Charles H. H. Scobie rightly describes

---

[43] Amos Yong, *The Spirit of Creation: Modern Science and Divine Action in the Pentecostal-Charismatic Imagination* (Grand Rapids, MI, and Cambridge: Eerdmans, 2011), chapter 6. "Imagination" is well chosen as part of his title. To his credit, Yong acknowledges how speculative his theses are (207).

[44] Yong, *Spirit of Creation*, 151.

[45] Yong, *Spirit of Creation*, 173.

[46] Yong, *Spirit of Creation*, 213. His view may be usefully described as a non-reductive angelology, perhaps.

[47] Yong, *Spirit of Creation*, 216, emphasis mine.

[48] Yong, *Spirit of Creation*, 213n104.

[49] For an illuminating discussion of the heavenly court, with its royal imagery and its relation to its ancient Near Eastern background, see Leland Ryken, James C. Wilhoit, Tremper Longman III, Colin Duriez, Douglas Penney, and Daniel G. Reid, eds., *Dictionary of Biblical Imagery*, electronic ed. (Downers Grove, IL: InterVarsity Press, 2000), 50 ("Assembly, Divine").

angels as "God's attendants in his glory in heaven."[50] Angels attend him there with praise (Ps. 148:1–2 and Rev. 7:11–12). The heavenly court is not only the sphere in which God is glorified and praised by angelic creatures. It is also the place of divine decrees and deliberation, i.e., a council (Jer. 23:18).[51] Micaiah the OT prophet has a vision of the heavenly assembly (1 Kings 22:19–23). In the vision, God is enthroned with angels ("the host of heaven") standing on both the left and the right of the seated deity. The NT picture is far more expansive. The seer of Revelation sees the throne room teeming with celestial figures (Revelation 4–5): God, the Lamb, twenty-four elders, the four living creatures, and myriads of angels. The imagery is highly pictorial but reality-depicting. The universe has only one sovereign. As for the throne room itself, Michael F. Bird puts it vividly: "When John the Seer receives a vision of heaven in Revelation 4–5, it is like he's summoned to a cross between a military headquarters and the throne room of a monarch."[52]

Importantly, the activity on view in Revelation 4–5 is worship in the classic sense of the protocol adopted in the presence of great majesty (Rev. 4:9–11; 5:11–14). The statement in Revelation 4 and the song in Revelation 5 begin with an acknowledgment of the worthiness of God the Creator and of the Lamb the Redeemer, respectively: "Worthy are you!" is the cry in both passages. And the expression of the worth of God and of his Christ are the traditional way in which worship has been understood in the churches.[53] So the space depicted in Revelation 4–5 is not only a military headquarters in the sense and a monarch's throne but is also cathedral-like in its purpose.

---

[50] Charles H. H. Scobie, *The Ways of Our God: An Approach to Biblical Theology* (Grand Rapids, MI, and Cambridge: Eerdmans, 2003), 114.

[51] Ryken et al., *Dictionary of Biblical Imagery*, 50 (Assembly, Divine). Psalm 82, which also depicts the heavenly assembly, in verse 1 may be describing angels as gods. However, exegetes divide over whether the reference to gods is to angelic beings or to human magistrates (Derek Kidner, *Psalms 73–150*, TOTC (Downers Grove, IL: InterVarsity Press, 1975), 328, argues for angelic beings. In contrast, Walter C. Kaiser Jr., *Hard Sayings of the Bible* (Downers Grove, IL: InterVarsity Press, 1997), 279, contends for human magistrates. The rabbis understood Psalm 82 as referring to human judges (W. Derek Suderman, "Psalms," in *The Old Testament and Apocrypha: Fortress Commentary on the Bible*, ed. Gale A. Yee, Hugh R. Page Jr., and Matthew J. M. Coomber, [Minneapolis: Fortress, 2014], 572, who cites *Midrash on the Psalms* [*Midrash Tehillim*]). In contrast to the rabbis, Michael S. Heiser is in no doubt that divine beings are on view (*The Unseen Realm: Recovering the Supernatural Worldview of the Bible* [Bellingham, WA: Lexham, 2015], cf. 82 and 28–29). In John 10:34, Jesus, in debate with Jews calling him a blasphemer for making himself equal to God though he was so obviously a man to them (v. 33), replied by quoting Psalm 82:6, "Is it not written in your Law, 'I said, you are gods'?" Heiser's work is both highly stimulating and provocative. However, he is overconfident, in my view, in his attempt to explain the quotation in terms of Jesus's claiming to be a superior being to the "gods" of Psalm 82 (Heiser, *Unseen Realm*, 268n3). There are other views that are consistent with the biblical text. For example, Jesus may have been simply using the OT Scripture to point out an irony in the Jews' charge against him. Or Jesus may have been using an implied a fortiori argument: If human beings to whom the word of God came can be called "gods," how much more can Jesus be called "God," since he brings the word of God to humankind. See Colin G. Kruse, *John*, TNTC (Downers Grove, IL: InterVarsity Press, 2003), 241. Scholarly debate continues over the exegesis of Psalm 82 and John 10:34. Likewise, Heiser is overconfident (by going beyond the biblical evidence) in arguing that God is "in the family business," wanting a family in heaven (the angels or gods) and its mirror image on earth (e.g., 97).

[52] Michael F. Bird, *Evangelical Theology: A Biblical and Systematic Introduction* (Grand Rapids, MI: Zondervan, 2013), 327.

[53] In the NT there is another dimension to worship, which is the whole of life lived in response to the gospel (Rom. 12:1–2). A full-orbed understanding of Christian worship needs to reckon with both the narrow and the broad concepts found in the NT.

IMPLICATIONS FOR BELIEF AND PRACTICE

We turn now to drawing out some of the implications for belief and practice of what we have seen thus far, beginning with an idea that sometimes is heard in popular Christian rhetoric: that creation is fallen or broken. There is truth in this claim, but it is not the whole of the truth, given the witness of Scripture.

Not All Creation Is Fallen, Broken, or in Need of Healing

It is clear from the Genesis 3 account that the fall ruptures relations not only between humankind and God but also between humankind and the natural order. The apostle Paul takes up the cosmic dimension of the problem when he personifies creation in a remarkable way. To the Romans he writes (Rom. 8:18–22),

> For I consider that the sufferings of this present time are not worth comparing with the glory that is to be revealed to us. For the creation waits with eager longing for the revealing of the sons of God. For the creation was subjected to futility, not willingly, but because of him who subjected it, in hope that the creation itself will be set free from its bondage to corruption and obtain the freedom of the glory of the children of God. For we know that the whole creation has been groaning together in the pains of childbirth until now.

In another letter he writes of a reconciliation that seems all-encompassing (Col. 1:19–20): "For in him all the fullness of God was pleased to dwell, and through him to reconcile to himself all things, whether on earth or in heaven, making peace by the blood of his cross."

The above is an example of where G. Campbell Morgan's important dictum about never saying "it is written but again it is written and again it is written" comes into play. In other words, Scripture X needs to be in conversation with Scripture Y and Scripture Z. A *tota scriptura* approach is necessary. According to biblical testimony, not all of God's creatures have fallen away from their Creator and need reconciliation or, as far as we know, are groaning while awaiting redemption.[54] These unfallen creatures are God's unfallen angels.[55] Hence, theologians need to be nuanced when speaking or writing about "fallen nature" or "fallen creation." Stephen H. Webb shows the need when he writes, "Darwinians are right, in my view, to emphasize the wanton cruelty and apparent senselessness of evolution, but they are not right to think that disproves

---

[54] C. S. Lewis posits a universe in which only a local part of it was "bent," in his *Out of the Silent Planet*. In this work of science fiction, the "silent" planet is Thulcandra, which clearly represents earth. For a useful discussion of the work, see Colin Duriez, *The C. S. Lewis Handbook: A Comprehensive Guide to His Life, Thought, and Writings* (Eastbourne, UK: Monarch, 1990), 150–153.

[55] Barth rejects the categories of unfallen and fallen angels, and argues that the distinction was "responsible for very serious confusion" (*CD*, III/3 [520]). I find his argument obscure. More concerning is Bulgakov, *Jacob's Ladder*, 66, who in relation to Revelation 5 writes that "*Angels together with humans speak of their redemption through the blood of the Lamb*" (emphasis original).

the idea of an intelligent and beneficent designer. Instead, it points to the need for a post-Darwinian retrieval of the Genesis teaching about *nature's fall.*"[56] Perhaps it would be better to speak in terms of "our broken world."

Angelology, Theological Anthropology, and the Imago Dei

In theological anthropology, the biblical phrase "image of God" (*imago dei*) plays a key role. The phrase is found famously in the opening chapter of Scripture (Gen. 1:26–28) and sets humankind apart from other creatures. One of the major ways the phrase is understood Erickson calls the "substantive view." On this view, the image of God, i.e., our likeness to God, lies in certain properties we have. Regarding the *imago dei* Erickson states, "It is located within humans as a resident quality or capacity."[57] He rightly contends that this is the view that predominates over church history. But what are these qualities? Rationality is a commonly adduced one. Volition is another. Erickson himself argues for the substantive view after a detailed evaluation of its two competitors (the relational and functional models).[58]

However, if rationality and volition constitute the image of God, then is not the serpent of Genesis 3 in God's image too? Aquinas contended that angels as pure minds were more perfectly the image of God than human beings, who have bodies. He argued, "[W]e must grant that, absolutely speaking, the angels are more the image of God than man is."[59] The substantive view may be part of the theological story of *imago dei*, but I doubt that it is the whole story. The accent in Genesis 1:26–28 seems to fall on imaging God by acting as royalty in God's world (the dominion motif). All this is to say the fact that angels have both rationality and will, whether fallen or not, should act as a caution against reducing the *imago dei* to substance alone.

The Danger of "Angelism"

Peter Kreeft usefully draws attention to two dangers confronting us. One is "animalism." Animalism is that view that reduces us to mere animals, higher primates. "Angelism" confuses the human and the suprahuman and sees hu-

---

[56] Stephen H. Webb, *The Dome of Eden: A New Solution to the Problem of Creation and Evolution* (Eugene, OR: Cascade, 2010), 8, and also 6 and 9, emphasis mine. This is a highly stimulating work.
[57] Erickson, *Christian Theology*, 463.
[58] Erickson, *Christian Theology*, 463. Erickson's careful treatment (457–474) repays close study. In theological reflection, one might argue that the exercise of the God-given task of exercising dominion requires rationality and will as necessary conditions. This would also apply to the relational view. In this way the three views might be theologically synthesized. It must be remembered that, in systematic theology, biblical phrases translated into English may take on depths that in individual passages in an English Bible they might not have. "Sanctification" and its cognates are cases in point. As a theological master concept it encompasses both positional and progressive concepts. Individual biblical passages, however, might only allow one of these ideas. For example, "sanctified" in 1 Corinthians 1:2 is clearly positional. In the light of the whole epistle it is clear that the Corinthians had made little progress in progressive sanctification or growth in holiness.
[59] Thomas Aquinas, *ST*, I, Q 93. Aquinas's discussion is more nuanced than this quotation suggests but his point is clear. Bulgakov, *Jacob's Ladder*, 66, also argues that angels are in the image of God: "The image of God is imprinted *in two ways*: in the world of angels and in the human world" (emphasis original).

manity in angel terms.[60] Kreeft muddies his own distinction by going on to argue that "Man is the only being that is both angel and animal, both spirit and body."[61] A popular view in some quarters is to claim that when we die we become angels—especially children who die. This is a text-less doctrine. Indeed, Jesus did say, in debate with the Sadducees reported in Matthew 22:23–33, that after death we become like the angels in heaven as far as marital status is concerned. But clearly likeness (*hos*) is not identity.

Is It Wrong to Worship Angels?

The biblical answer to this question is emphatic. Only the living God is to be worshiped. Any other object of worship is an idol. The seer of Revelation made a misstep in this regard. We read in Revelation 22:8, "I, John, am the one who heard and saw these things. And when I heard and saw them, I fell down to worship at the feet of the angel who showed them to me." The angel will have none of this, as the next verse shows: "But he said to me, 'You must not do that! I am a fellow servant with you and your brothers the prophets, and with those who keep the words of this book. Worship God'" (v. 9). The angel sees John as a fellow servant and knows where true worship is to be directed. Angels may be glorious beings that evoke wonder, but God they are not.

In fact, Hebrews 1:6 makes it clear that angels are commanded to worship another: the son of God.[62] Richard Bauckham rightly argues that Hebrews 1 makes it plain that Jesus is superior to angels: "This superiority is both imaged as spatial height (1:3–4) and expounded as qualitative difference. The angels, argues the passage, are no more than servants of God, whereas Christ, who occupies the divine throne itself, participates in God's own sovereignty and is, therefore, served by the angels (1:7–9, 13–14)."[63] He adduces Ephesians 1:22–23 as similar evidence of "Jesus' exaltation and sovereignty over all the angelic powers, sometimes with emphatic use of the potent Jewish imagery of height."[64]

Paul's letter to the Colossians is also relevant to the question. This church was troubled by false teachers.[65] One aspect of their false teaching appears to have been the exaltation of angels as intermediaries between God and ourselves. Paul warns the Colossians, in Colossians 2:18–19,

[60] Famously, the eminent Roman Catholic philosopher Jacques Maritain accused Descartes of the sin of angelism, given Descartes's accent on the mind, in *The Dream of Descartes*, trans. Mabelle L. Andison (New York: Philosophical Library, 1944), 28.

[61] Peter Kreeft, *Angels and Demons*, 104.

[62] For a rich discussion of Hebrews 1:6 and its use of Deuteronomy 32:43 in relation to the differing Hebrew and LXX texts, see George H. Guthrie, "Hebrews," in *CNTUOT*, ed. G. K. Beale and D. A. Carson (Grand Rapids, MI: Baker Academic, 2007), 930–933.

[63] See Richard Bauckham, *God Crucified: Monotheism and Christology in the New Testament* (Grand Rapids, MI, and Cambridge: Eerdmans, 1998), 33. This is an important book.

[64] Bauckham, *God Crucified*, 32.

[65] On the syncretistic nature of the false teaching, with its Hellenistic and Jewish elements, see the discussion in D. A. Carson and Douglas J. Moo, *An Introduction to the New Testament*, 2nd ed. (Grand Rapids, MI: Zondervan, 2005), 523–525.

Let no one disqualify you, insisting on asceticism and worship [*thrēskeia*, "veneration"] of angels, going on in detail about visions, puffed up without reason by his sensuous mind, and not holding fast to the Head, from whom the whole body, nourished and knit together through its joints and ligaments, grows with a growth that is from God.

Christology is not to be displaced by angelology. For the false teachers at Colossae, this displacement took the form either of worshiping angels per se or of attempting mystically to participate in the angels' worship of God, or of ironically so emphasizing angels that it seemed as though they were worshiping them.[66]

Joining the Angels Worshiping in Heaven

If, on the one hand, worshiping angels is deleterious, worshiping *with* angels, on the other hand, is an entirely different story. The NT describes the public assembling of Christians in various ways. For example, it can be seen as the forming of a living temple (1 Pet. 2:4–5) or as a gathering of the household (4:17) or the flock (e.g., 5:1–4), or a meeting of a brotherhood that is worldwide (e.g., 5:9).[67] Hebrews has a striking way of describing the transcendent dimension of the Christian assembly (Heb. 12:22–24):

But you have come to Mount Zion and to the city of the living God, the heavenly Jerusalem, and to innumerable angels in festal gathering, and to the assembly of the firstborn who are enrolled in heaven, and to God, the judge of all, and to the spirits of the righteous made perfect, and to Jesus, the mediator of a new covenant, and to the sprinkled blood that speaks a better word than the blood of Abel.

Believers are already citizens of the City of God and are, in a mysterious sense, there with the angels.[68] In Pauline terms, we are seated in the heavenlies: "And God raised us up with Christ and seated us with him in the heavenly realms in Christ Jesus" (Eph. 2:6 NIV).[69]

---

[66] N. T. Wright, *Colossians and Philemon*, TNTC (Downers Grove, IL, IVP Academic, 2008), 126, discusses these three possibilities before concluding, "This third view [the ironic one] fits the tone and context of Colossians 2 very well." Daniel J. Ebert IV, *Wisdom Christology: How Jesus Becomes God's Wisdom for Us* (Phillipsburg, NJ: P&R, 2011), 87, advocates Wright's second possibility.

[67] It is fascinating that 1 Peter has so many ways of describing the corporate dimension of the faith, and that "church" (*ekklēsia*) is not one of them. Perhaps the term "church" has been given too much work in theology and in describing Christian corporate life, to the neglect of a plethora of other biblical images.

[68] Perhaps the reference to angels in 1 Corinthians 11:10 ("because of the angels") in the context of the discussion of decorum in worship is further evidence of our joining the worship of heaven. For a contrary view see Bruce W. Winter, *After Paul Left Corinth: The Influence of Secular Ethics and Social Change* (Grand Rapids, MI: Eerdmans, 2001), 133–137. Winter argues that the angels are human messengers. On his view, they are imperial spies who are looking for those who disturb the social order in order to report them.

[69] The best explanation for the language of Hebrews and Ephesians lies in the relation of Christology and ecclesiology. As members of Christ, who is the head of his body, which is the church, there is a sense that where the head is, so are the members. Again Paul captures this in Colossians 3:1–3: "If then you have been raised with Christ, seek the things that are above, where Christ is, seated at the right hand of God. Set your minds on things that are above, not on things that are on earth. For you have died, and your life is hidden with Christ in God." This is obviously a matter of faith, not sight.

In liturgical churches like Anglican ones, a sense of the angelic order is built into the liturgy. For example, in Morning and Evening Prayer the congregation might praise God in these ancient words, which date from the fourth or fifth century:

> WE praise thee, O God: we acknowledge thee to be the Lord.
> All the earth doth worship thee: the Father everlasting.
> To thee all Angels cry aloud: the Heavens, and all the Powers therein.
> To thee Cherubin [sic] and Seraphin [sic]: continually do cry,
> Holy, Holy, Holy: Lord God of Sabaoth;
> Heaven and earth are full of the Majesty: of thy glory.[70]

The Holy Communion service likewise places the human worshiper in a bigger landscape as they are invited to pray, "**THEREFORE** with Angels and Archangels, and with all the company of heaven, we laud and magnify thy glorious Name; evermore praising thee, and saying, Holy, holy, holy, Lord God of hosts, heaven and earth are full of thy glory: Glory be to thee, O Lord most High. Amen."[71] It is not difficult to see the heavenly scene as set out in Revelation 4 informing this. It is in Revelation 4:8, on the lips of the four living creatures, that we find the *trisagion* ("Holy, holy, holy").[72] In worship we join the angels in adoration of the living God.[73] And the doxologies that angel-kind and humankind are jointly involved in show that angels as well as humans are capable of artistic expression. Song is a union of form, sound, and words. It is art, as Bulgakov helpfully points out.[74] Regarding song, John Anthony McGuckin, with the book of Revelation in mind, describes angels as "the preeminent singers of God's glory."[75]

In non-liturgical churches, unless the pastor is intentional about worship and the pastoral prayer, and if there is no systematic exposition of Scripture, then angelology might be neglected all together. One thinks of the ancient rule *lex orandi lex credendi* ("the law of praying is the law of believing"). What we really believe comes out in what we pray. This neglect could lead to an impoverished

---

[70] *Book of Common Prayer* (1662). In liturgics, this is known as the *Te Deum* (Latin for the opening words).

[71] *Book of Common Prayer* (1662).

[72] Barth will have none of this. He writes, "Imitation of angels is not what is demanded of man and the Church by the ministry of angels. Thus the earthly Church will never see its decisive task in copying the cultus of heaven. May it always be restrained from doing so!" (*CD*, III/3 [475]). I find it hard to follow his reasoning here, especially if the twenty-four elders represent not angelic beings (contra Barth) but representatives of old and new covenant believers, as Craig S. Keener contends (*Revelation*, NIVAC [Grand Rapids, MI: Zondervan, 1999], 168–199). In contrast to Keener, Richard Bauckham (*Theology of the Book of Revelation*, 34) draws on OT (Isa. 24:23 and Dan. 7:9–10) and extrabiblical literature (2 *Enoch* 4:1 and *T. Levi* 3:8) to argue that the twenty-four elders are angelic personages.

[73] Wayne Grudem, *Systematic Theology: An Introduction to Biblical Doctrine* (Grand Rapids, MI: Zondervan, 1995), 404, argues that angels are examples for us in both their worship and their obedience. However, this interesting idea is text-less and therefore can only remain suggestive.

[74] Bulgakov, *Jacob's Ladder*, 122–124. Also, as Noll ("Angels and Heaven," 195) observes, at least some angelic beings play harps, according to Revelation 5:8. This is the only such reference in Scripture.

[75] John Anthony McGuckin, *The Westminster Handbook to Patristic Theology* (Louisville and London: Westminster John Knox, 2004), 12.

Christian worldview and the blind spot of which Paul Hiebert wrote in his seminal article referred to in the "Introduction" to the present work (ch. 1).

In addition, and this may be a peculiarity of the writer, I find great comfort in the fact that the living God is the object of ceaseless worship and praise, when on earth the name of God and his Christ can be spoken ill of so often and by so many.

Angelology and Speculation

Speculation as an exercise in theological imagination has its place. However, such speculation needs to be acknowledged as such and not presented as dogma. Sergius Bulgakov serves as another case in point. He argues that there is an ontological unity between the celestial (heaven) and the terrestrial (earth). He contends, "Not only is a guardian angel found in personal correlation with the one whom it protects, but angels of fire, winds, and water are also found in an analogous correlation with a given region of creation."[76] He elaborates: "The angel of fire himself is fiery in the sense that he carries in his nature the noetic element of fire, just as the angel of waters has an aqueous nature."[77] He further claims that Mary the mother of Jesus has no guardian angel. He explains, "The Virgin Mary does not have her own guardian angels because her Son himself is her Guardian."[78]

How does Bulgakov know these things? I am reminded of Francis Bacon's (1561–1626) description of the men of dogma who "resemble spiders, who make cobwebs out of their own substance."[79] On his own admission, Bulgakov shows his debts to "platonic idealism."[80] He writes, "That world of the ideas, prototypes of being, which Plato gained sight of, only vaguely discerning its real place in God and even mixing it with Divinity, is in reality the angelic world in its relation to being."[81] He elaborates, "Platonic ideas are in reality angels of the Word, and Plato's sagacity, which compels us to recognize him as 'a Christian before Christ' (according to ecclesiastical literature) is that he recognized the necessity of grounding the earthly world in the heavenly, becoming in being, things in ideas."[82] The Westminster Confession of Faith (1646) displays an admirable alternative approach in its chapter 1, article 6:

> The whole counsel of God, concerning all things necessary for His own glory, man's salvation, faith and life, is either expressly set down in Scripture, or by

---

[76] Bulgakov, *Jacob's Ladder*, 26.
[77] Bulgakov, *Jacob's Ladder*, 31.
[78] Bulgakov, *Jacob's Ladder*, 98n24.
[79] Francis Bacon, *The New Organon*, book 1, http://www.antspiderbee.net/bacon/, accessed 7/5/2015.
[80] Bulgakov, *Jacob's Ladder*, 34.
[81] Bulgakov, *Jacob's Ladder*, 34.
[82] Bulgakov, *Jacob's Ladder*, 83.

good and necessary consequence may be deduced from Scripture: unto which nothing at any time is to be added, whether by new revelations of the Spirit, or traditions of men.[83]

An Enriched Christian Worldview

The dismissal of angelology leads to a diminished Christian worldview. Friedrich Schleiermacher (1768–1834), often called the father of liberal Protestantism, is representative of such a diminishment. In his classic *The Christian Faith*, both angelology and demonology are relegated to brief appendices. His rationale is that such discourse in Scripture belongs "to a time when our knowledge of the forces of nature was very limited, and our power over them at its lowest stage."[84] In his view, angelology and demonology are problematic subjects for dogmatic consideration and belong in the sphere of the private and the liturgical. What he is prepared to say is "that the question whether the angels exist or not ought to have no influence upon our conduct, and that revelations of their existence are now no longer to be expected."[85]

If the neglect of angelology may lead to an impoverished Christian worldview, then one that includes angelology cannot but be all the richer. To contemplate that heaven, seen as God's abode, is a place of never ceasing praise, joy, and love reminds us that, like the psalmist, we need to lift our eyes to the hills, to the God who made *heaven* and earth (Ps. 121:1–2). Heaven is indeed the place where God's declared will is done. Heaven is the place where God's kingly rule is not resisted, but rather is celebrated in speech and song (Rev. 4:11; 5:12–13). Barth was right to describe heaven as God's "distinctive sphere."[86] He was also right to point out that "In the first instance, it [the existence of the heavenly hosts] excludes any idea of a lonely God sitting on His heavenly throne in an empty or formless heaven."[87]

It is fair to ask whether many a Christian de facto operates as though God were indeed a lonely monad in need of our companionship. I recall being told the story of a beginning evangelist, who after his first evangelistic message was asked by one of his hearers if God was lonely and needed friends. Happily, my friend's preaching improved greatly after that.

An imaginative way into the richness of the Christian worldview in contrast to others is to picture the living room of a house with a person

---

[83] The Westminster Confession of Faith, http://www.reformed.org/documents/wcf_with_proofs/, accessed 7/5/2015.
[84] Friedrich Schleiermacher, *The Christian Faith*, ed. H. R. Macintosh and J. S. Stewart, various trans. (Edinburgh: T&T Clark, 1948), 159.
[85] Schleiermacher, *Christian Faith*, 159.
[86] Barth, *CD*, III/3 (432). There is merit in Barth's notion of the two spheres of created reality: heaven first, then earth. Heaven is first because it is from there that grace comes.
[87] Barth, *CD*, III/3 (448).

standing at the window. For the materialist, the window is partially boarded up. All above eye level is covered. Our materialist can see out at that level and below, but not up. As the saying goes, "seeing is believing," and so for this person that is all there is to reality.[88] In contrast, the Christian lives in a space with no coverings on the windows. The Christian standing at the window of being can look down, look out at eye level, and look all the way up. Karl Barth would add another feature to the house, and that is a skylight, so that the heavenly is not neglected.[89] In so doing, the whole of reality can be entertained, and that includes the *middle* of which Paul Hiebert wrote so insightfully.[90]

CONCLUSION

Angels are created spirits that serve God and God's images in a myriad of ways in heaven and on earth. They are hierarchically ordered, but the details are elusive. The angelic realm has attracted much metaphysical and theological speculation down through the ages.

There is no virtue in having a theology ignorant of angelology. Certainly, as a doctrine it ranks below Christology and soteriology. Even so, the evangelical theologian is committed to the *tota scriptura*, not some abridged version of it. Noll wisely says, "[A] case can be made that the Bible has an angelology, a consistent portrayal of angelic existence, character, and activity."[91] I concur. Blaise Pascal (1623–1662) rightly argued in his *Pensée* 121, "[Humanity] must not be allowed to believe that he is equal to animals or to angels, nor to be unaware of either, but he must know both."[92]

EXCURSUS: THE NATURE OF SPIRIT

Scripture asserts that angels are spirits. Scripture also asserts that God is spirit. But what is spirit? Does the word "spirit" (*pneuma*) mean the same thing in both cases? In this excursus we will discuss first the question of God as spirit before turning to the matter of angels as spirits. In doing so, metaphysics is unavoidable.[93]

---

[88] I was on one occasion challenged by someone with, "I will believe only what I can see!" I asked him if he had ever seen his own brain.

[89] Karl Barth, *Evangelical Theology* (London and Glasgow: Fontana, 1969), 151. In this context, Barth was referring to prayer.

[90] I owe the idea of this analogy to Huston Smith, "Postmodernism and the World's Religions," in *The Truth about the Truth: De-confusing and Re-constructing the Postmodern World*, ed. Walter Truett Anderson (New York: Tarcher Putnam, 1995), 206. I have developed the analogy in my own way.

[91] Noll, "Angels, Doctrine of," 45.

[92] Blaise Pascal, *Pensées*, trans. A. J. Krailsheimer (Harmondsworth, UK: Penguin, 1972), 60.

[93] The concept of metaphysics is an essentially contested one as to both its definition and its legitimacy as an enterprise of thought. Peter van Inwagen usefully defines "metaphysics" as an attempt "to get behind all appearances and to describe things as they really are" ("Metaphysics," in *The Oxford Companion to Christian Thought*, ed. Adrian Hastings, Alistair Mason, and Hugh Pyper (Oxford: Oxford University Press, 2000), 427. Van Inwagen is

God as Spirit

The classic text adduced to support the contention that God is spirit is John 4:24.[94] For example, it is the text that Thomas Aquinas (1225–1274) appealed to in his discussion of whether God is a body.[95] The context of this verse is Jesus's encounter with the woman by the well in Samaria (John 4:19–24):

> The woman said to him, "Sir, I perceive that you are a prophet. Our fathers worshiped on this mountain, but you say that in Jerusalem is the place where people ought to worship." Jesus said to her, "Woman, believe me, the hour is coming when neither on this mountain nor in Jerusalem will you worship the Father. You worship what you do not know; we worship what we know, for salvation is from the Jews. But the hour is coming, and is now here, when the true worshipers will worship the Father in spirit and truth, for the Father is seeking such people to worship him. God is spirit, and those who worship him must worship in spirit and truth."

Jesus had exposed the woman's marital history by his astute comments. She attempted to throw him off track by raising the issue of where true worship was to be located. The Jews and Samaritans had very different responses to that. Jesus was not fazed, and he gave her a lesson in the spirituality of God, who is not geographically constricted.

In the light of John 4:24, Princeton theologian A. A. Hodge (1823–1886) tackles the question of what it means to call God a spirit in a binary fashion. In this he follows the classic methods of *via negativa* and *via positiva*. He writes,

> When we say God is a Spirit we mean—
> 1st. Negatively, that he does not possess bodily parts or passions; that he is composed of no material elements; that he is not subject to any of the limiting conditions of material existence; and, consequently, that he is not to be apprehended as the object of any of our bodily senses.
> 2d. Positively, that he is a rational being, who distinguishes with infinite precision between the true and the false; that he is a moral being, who distinguishes between the right and the wrong; that he is a free agent, whose action is self-determined by his own will; and, in fine, that all the essential properties of our spirits may truly be predicated of him in an infinite degree.[96]

---

also helpful in arguing, "There would seem to be no good reason to insist that if one employs premises that one claims to know on the basis of revelation, then one is *ipso facto* not a metaphysician" (428).

[94] This is one of the "big three" Johannine texts that throws much light on the nature and character of God. John 4:24 speaks to the ontology of God (God's spirituality), 1 John 1:5 accents the purity of God as light (God's holy character), and 1 John 4:8 and 16 affirm that God is love. For a careful discussion of the claim that God is Spirit, see John S. Feinberg, *No One Like Him: The Doctrine of God* (Wheaton, IL: Crossway, 2001), 214–224.

[95] Thomas Aquinas, in Peter Kreeft, ed., *A Summa of the Summa: The Essential Philosophical Passages of St. Thomas Aquinas's Summa Theologica Edited and Explained for Beginners* (San Francisco: Ignatius, 1990), I, Q 3.1 (75).

[96] A. A. Hodge, *Outlines*, 140. Hodge assumes that the divine Spirit and the human spirit are immaterial realities. The substance dualism that Hodge espoused has been subject to much criticism both in philosophical and in some evangelical circles in recent years. Even so there is a contemporary stout defense of substance dualism to be found in John W. Cooper, *Body, Soul, and Life Everlasting: Biblical Anthropology and the Monism, Dualism Debate*

Another Reformed theologian, Louis Berkhof, likewise adduces John 4:24 as evidence for the spirituality of God.[97] He also adds to the picture, arguing that God as spirit has no extension in space, unlike a material object. Moreover, he deals with the anthropomorphisms in Scripture in a deft way: "It is true that the Bible speaks of hands and feet, eyes and ears, the mouth and nose of God, but in doing this it is speaking anthropomorphically or figuratively of him who transcends our human knowledge, and of whom we can only speak in a stammering fashion after the manner of men."[98]

Angels as Spirits

The proposition that an angel, like God, is a spirit also has a classic text in support (Heb. 1:14): "Are they [angels] not all ministering spirits sent out to serve for the sake of those who are to inherit salvation?" According to Aquinas, angels "are pure spirits; they are spirits with no admixture of matter in them."[99] Moreover, he contends that, since angels are pure bodiless spirits, unlike us who are embodied souls, they do not form a species. We do, because we humans have a substantial form in common. Thus, each angel is its own species.[100] That is to say, there are as many species of angel as there are angels. How this squares with the way Scripture puts angels into groups (e.g., cherubim) is not clear. What is clear is that, as spirits, angels do not have bodies. John S. Feinberg prefers to use "immaterial" of divine ontology.[101] He argues that "the basic characteristic of immaterial things is that they think."[102] That insight also applies to angel ontology, in my view.

Conclusion

There is solid biblical ground for asserting the spirituality of both God the Creator (John 4:24) and angels as his creatures (Heb. 1:14). Both are without materiality. Both are agents who think and act.

(Grand Rapids, MI: Eerdmans, 2000). This edition is the second printing and has an updated discussion of the *status questionis*, xv-xxviii. Cooper argues successfully, to my mind, that the traditional Christian doctrine of the intermediate state requires substance dualism. For an even more recent defense see Richard Swinburne, *Mind, Brain, and Free Will* (Oxford: Oxford University Press, 2013), esp. chapter 6.

[97] Louis Berkhof, *Systematic Theology* (London: Banner of Truth Trust, 1969), 65.

[98] Berkhof, *Systematic Theology*, 66.

[99] Thomas Aquinas, in Paul J. Glenn, ed., *A Tour of the Summa* (St. Louis and London: B. Herder, 1963), Ia, Q 50.1 (45).

[100] Aquinas, in Glenn, *Tour of the Summa*, I, Q 50.4 (45).

[101] Feinberg, *No One Like Him*, 223. For a useful, brief discussion of ontology, see Anthony C. Thiselton, *A Concise Encyclopedia of the Philosophy of Religion* (Oxford: Oneworld, 2002), 217–218.

[102] For the discussion and argument, see Feinberg, *No One Like Him*, 223–224.

ANGELS: THEIR ACTIVITY ON EARTH
WITH INDIVIDUALS AND NATIONS

In the previous chapter, we considered angels in the scheme of created things. Next we considered the angelic realm and its inhabitants, ranging from angels to seraphim. Then we explored questions concerning the nature of angels as created beings. Angelic activity in heaven was discussed next. In fact there is a long-standing distinction in angelology between the angels of heaven and their activity and the angels of earth and their activity.[1] In this chapter we continue the discussion of angels by focusing on the angels of earth and their activity. Next we consider the objects of that activity, both nations and individuals. One particular angelic figure is the next subject of interest: the angel of the Lord. There have been some landmark discussions of angels in the history of theology, and so Dionysius the Areopagite (c. AD 500) comes into view, followed by Aquinas and then Barth. To be practical, we consider the implications of our findings for belief and practice, before drawing the threads together by way of a conclusion. An excursus follows dealing with angelophanies.

ANGELIC ACTIVITY ON EARTH

A time-honored way of doing theology is to state what is not the case (*via negativa*), before stating what is the case (*via positiva*).[2] Barth does this in relation to angels when he argues,

> Angels cannot, then, speak words which as their own are the words of God. They cannot do works which as their own are divine works. They cannot save,

---

[1] Jean Danielou, *The Angels and Their Mission according to the Church Fathers*, trans. David Heimann (Notre Dame, IN: Ave Maria, 1957), 98. The distinction is useful but not to be over-pressed. The angel of a nation such as Israel is clearly concerned with earth, and the living creatures around the throne of God are clearly of heaven. However, the cherubim and seraphim can carry out earthly assignments, as this chapter will show.
[2] Karl Barth, *CD*, III/3 (369). For Barth, angels have four roles on earth. In general terms, they are "faithful servants of God." More specifically, they are messengers as God's ambassadors, witnesses to the divine revelation, and warriors "who victoriously ward off the opposing forms and forces of chaos." Barth is especially drawn to the idea of ambassadorship because the ambassador speaks and acts not in his or her own right, but in the place of the one they represent (*CD*, III/3 [512–513]). There is much truth in Barth's four descriptors.

redeem or liberate the earthly creature. They cannot forgive even the smallest sin, or remove even the slightest pain. They can do nothing to bring about the reconciliation of the world with God. Nor are they judges of the world. They did not create it. They can neither be wrathful nor gracious toward it. They did not establish the covenant between God and man, and they cannot fulfil, maintain, renew or confirm it. They do not overcome death. They do not rule the history of salvation, or universal history, or any history. Otherwise they would not be the angels of God.[3]

All this is admirably said, but it remains to ask what angels do, positively speaking, and to the positive witness of Scripture concerning angelic activity we now turn.

Bernard Ramm sums up angelic activity regarding the human sphere in terms of mediation. He argues,

> The communication between this great God and finite, limited man must thus always be a *mediated* communication.
>   This is not a judgment about the "impurity" of the world, which would force God to communicate indirectly lest he contaminate himself with the world. It is based upon the *transcendence* of Creator over the creature. Therefore, when God comes to humanity in revelation, He comes through *mediators*. The prophetic word is a *mediated* word. The theophany is a *mediated* manifestation of God. The Incarnation is the glory of God, *mediated* through the human nature of Christ. *Angels are part of the complex structure of the divine mediation.*[4]

What Ramm says about mediation particularly focuses on communication, but it applies *mutatis mutandis* to other ways in which God relates to our world. It is to those other ways as well as to the matter of divine communication that we now direct our attention.[5]

Guarding the Sacred

The story of Genesis 3 is one of catastrophe. The disobedient pair, Adam and Eve, find themselves estranged from God, each other, and the very environment in which they are to live. The paradise sacred zone has been forfeited.[6] The text speaks of their expulsion by the Creator (Gen. 3:24): "He drove out the man, and at the east of the garden of Eden he placed the cherubim and a flaming sword that turned every way to guard the way to the tree of life."

---

[3] Barth, *CD*, III/3 (460).
[4] Bernard Ramm, "Angels," in *Basic Christian Doctrines*, ed. Carl F. H. Henry (New York: Holt, Reinhart, & Winston, 1961), 66–67, emphases original.
[5] I am indebted here to Peter R. Schemm Jr.'s very helpful categories of angelic earthly activity ("The Agents of God: Angels," in *A Theology for the Church*, rev. ed., ed. Daniel L. Akin [Nashville: B&H, 2014], 253).
[6] See Gordon J. Wenham, *Genesis 1–15*, WBC (Dallas: Word, 2002), 67, for an excellent discussion of the nature of the "sacred zone" and Adam's priestly role within it.

This is the first biblical mention of such creatures, and their function is clear. They are guardians. Some suggest that their role is a merciful one. They are to prevent the primal pair from accessing the tree of life and as a consequence becoming locked into disobedience and pain.[7] Be that as it may, the garden has its guardians. That guardian function is most probably symbolized in the later placement of gold representations of them, one at each end, on the mercy seat. (Why the representations are made of gold and not of some other material is not explained in the text.) Here God will meet with the representative of his people (Ex. 25:17–22). It is important to note too that the cherubim not only relate adoringly to God. They have a role vis-á-vis humankind.

Bridging Heaven and Earth

Bernard Ramm's point about angels as *"part of the complex structure of the divine mediation"* is exemplified in the Genesis story of a dream Jacob had on his journey from Beersheba to Haran.[8] The incident took place at Bethel, about twelve miles north of Jerusalem. We read in Genesis 28:12–13,

> And he dreamed, and behold, there was a ladder set up on the earth, and the top of it reached to heaven. And behold, the angels of God were ascending and descending on it![9] And behold, the LORD stood above it and said, "I am the LORD, the God of Abraham your father and the God of Isaac."

Jacob's reaction is noteworthy (vv. 16–17): "Then Jacob awoke from his sleep and said, 'Surely the LORD is in this place, and I did not know it.' And he was afraid and said, 'How awesome is this place! This is none other than the house of God, and this is the gate of heaven.'" Sergius Bulgakov rightly sees this text as prototypical of the ultimate mediator who was to come.[10] John's Gospel supports Bulgakov's point in Jesus's response to Nathaniel in John 1:51: "Truly, truly, I say to you, you will see heaven opened, and the angels of God ascending and descending on the Son of Man."[11] Bulgakov comments, "This text has paramount importance for understanding the meaning which

---

[7] For this argument see Allen P. Ross, *Creation and Blessing: A Guide to the Study and Exposition of Genesis* (Grand Rapids, MI: Baker Academic, 1999), 149: "The story closes with the Lord's reasoned decision to prevent humankind from extending life in such a painful state."
[8] Ramm, "Angels," 66–67, emphases original.
[9] Were these the angels of earth (ascending) to meet the angels of heaven (descending), or was Rabbi Rashi (1040–1105) correct to suggest that they were the angels of Jacob's home meeting the angels of the place to which he was going? For the latter idea, see Gordon J. Wenham, *Genesis 16–50*, WBC (Dallas: Word, 1994), 221.
[10] Sergius Bulgakov, *Jacob's Ladder: On Angels*, trans. Thomas Allan Smith (Grand Rapid, MI and Cambridge: Eerdmans, 2010), 158. Terence E. Fretheim argues somewhat unconvincingly that angels are not mediatorial in this context, since they are silent ("Genesis," in *NIB*, 12 vols. [Nashville: Abingdon, 1993–2002], 1:540–544).
[11] Some of the early church fathers argued that the ascending angels were those entrusted with the care of the nations and who were rejoicing that definitive divine help had come to humanity in the Word made flesh, and the descending angels were those who had accompanied the Word from heaven for the task of salvation. See the discussion in Danielou, *Angels and Their Mission*, 24–33. There is no way to decide the truth value of these claims.

belongs to the incarnation in the establishment of relations between the angelic and human world."[12]

Guarding and Guiding God's People

The God of Abraham, Isaac, and Jacob promised that he would set his people
free from Pharaoh's grip and bring them to himself. The gathering of Israel at
Sinai bears witness to the God who keeps covenant. But what of the future?
What about the promises concerning the inheritance of a land? Once more
God makes promises (Ex. 23:20): "Behold, I send an angel before you to guard
you on the way and to bring you [sing., i.e., Moses] to the place that I have
prepared." This angel who both guards and guides has great authority (v. 21):
"Pay careful attention to him and obey his voice; do not rebel against him, for
he will not pardon your transgression, for my name is in him." The mention of
the divine name is highly significant. What does it mean? Walton, Matthews,
and Chavalas provide illumination:

> The "messenger" or angel sent by God is an extension of God himself, rep-
> resenting a continuous presence with the people of Israel. Since names and
> naming (see Gen 2:19; 17:5) were considered powerful in the ancient world
> (see Ex. 9:16; Lev 19:12), to say that Yahweh has invested his Name in this
> angel is to say that it is to be obeyed just as God is to be obeyed. All of God's
> presence and power is to be found in this messenger. He is to be trusted to do
> what God has promised.[13]

Clearly this authority, great though it may be, is not an independent one, as
reference to the divine name makes patent.

Israel is also warned through Moses that God will not accept his people
straying into false worship (Ex. 23:23–24):

> When my angel goes before you and brings you to the Amorites and the Hit-
> tites and the Perizzites and the Canaanites, the Hivites and the Jebusites, and I
> blot them out, you shall not bow down to their gods nor serve them, nor do as
> they do, but you shall utterly overthrow them and break their pillars in pieces.

Only one is to be worshiped (v. 25): "You shall serve the LORD your God, and he
will bless your bread and your water, and I will take sickness away from among
you." And again Israel is warned (vv. 32–33), "You shall make no covenant with
them and their gods. They shall not dwell in your land, lest they make you sin
against me; for if you serve their gods, it will surely be a snare to you." Sadly,
those gods did become a snare.

[12] Bulgakov, *Jacob's Ladder*, 158.
[13] John H. Walton, Victor H. Matthews, and Mark W. Chavalas, *The IVP Bible Background Commentary: Old Testament*, electronic ed. (Downers Grove, IL: InterVarsity Press, 2000), 119 (comment on Ex. 23:21).

Our passage is significant for angelology at a number of levels. An angel may carry great authority. In this instance the angel's voice is to be obeyed. Even so, angels are not to be worshiped. Only the living God is to be worshiped. Once more we see God working providentially through the mediation of creatures he has made. He did so in providing the quail and the manna in the wilderness, and he will do so again through an angelic agent (cf. Exodus 16 and 23:20–33).

The Communication of the Law

It is popular these days to construe the scriptural testimony and its theology as a drama.[14] In theater terms, then, angels are "bit players." The main actors on the stage are God and ourselves. After all, Scripture is not addressed to angels but to us. Even so, they do come on to the stage at significant junctures in salvation history (*Heilsgeschichte*). Sinai is one of those highpoints in the unfolding drama of redemption. God has done as he had promised. His people have been delivered from Egyptian bondage and have been brought to him at Sinai. The Lord now declares his will for his covenant people. Paul comments (Gal. 3:19), "Why then the law? It was added because of transgressions, until the offspring should come to whom the promise had been made, and it was put in place through angels by an intermediary ["*en cheiri mesitou*"; "by the hand of a mediator" is better]."[15] In the apostle's mind, angelic activity was part of the causal story of the giving of the law. Jean Danielou sees the role of angels in the communication of the law as emblematic of their general role in the OT as preparers of the coming incarnation of Christ, who is the fulfillment of the law.[16] The role of the angelic order in communicating the divine mind in revelation did not end with the giving of the law. At the beginning of the very last book of the canon, John the seer writes (Rev. 1:1–2),

> The revelation [*apokalypsis*] of Jesus Christ, which God gave him to show to his servants the things that must soon take place. He made it known by sending his angel to his servant John, who bore witness to the word of God and to the testimony of Jesus Christ, even to all that he saw.

Delivering Messages

The angelic role of messenger should be unsurprising, for that is what "angel" means. This role is easily evidenced from Scripture. Paul was on his way to

---

[14] For example, Kevin J. Vanhoozer, *The Drama of Doctrine: A Canonical Linguistic Approach to Christian Doctrine* (Louisville: Westminster John Knox, 2005). The drama idea has heuristic value, but if pressed too far it can distort the reading of Scripture through the use of a category brought to the biblical testimony rather than derived from it.

[15] Moses was the covenant mediator that Paul had in mind (R. Alan Cole, *Galatians*, TNTC [Downers Grove, IL: InterVarsity Press, 1989], 149).

[16] Danielou, *Angels and Their Mission*, 3–13.

Rome by ship when bad weather threatened. He was under arrest and under guard. The storm worsened. The Mediterranean can be deadly. There was panic on board, especially among the sailors, who could read the weather and understood the significance of the soundings. The sailors planned to flee the ship for land using the lifeboat. Paul took action and spoke in such a way to ensure that none would leave the ship. He declared (Acts 27:23–24), "For this very night there stood before me an angel of the God to whom I belong and whom I worship, and he said, 'Do not be afraid, Paul; you must stand before Caesar. And behold, God has granted you all those who sail with you.'" The ship was lost but the ship's company, including Paul, was saved. Paul acted because an angel delivered a message.

Interpreting Divine Messages

As we have seen, angels deliver messages, according to biblical testimony. However, they can do more than that. In the third year of King Belshazzar, Daniel has a vision of a ram and a goat. The complexity of the vision need not detain us.[17] What is of interest for our purpose is the role of Gabriel. Daniel 8:16 relates, "And I [Daniel] heard a man's voice between the banks of the Ulai, and it called, 'Gabriel, make this man understand the vision.'" The angel obeys, and the angelophany overwhelms Daniel (v. 17): "So he came near where I stood. And when he came, I was frightened and fell on my face. But he said to me, 'Understand, O son of man, that the vision is for the time of the end.'" This is no mere passing on of a message, but its interpretation. Even so, Daniel has difficulty absorbing all of its significance (v. 27): "And I, Daniel, was overcome and lay sick for some days. Then I rose and went about the king's business, but I was appalled by the vision and did not understand it." Clearly, encountering Gabriel was not necessarily a pleasant experience.

Rescuing God's Servants

Both in the Old Testament and in the New, on occasion angels were involved in rescuing the servants of God in hostile situations.

In Babylon, Darius the king had great plans for Daniel (Dan. 6:3): "Then this Daniel became distinguished above all the other high officials and satraps, because an excellent spirit was in him. And the king planned to set him over the whole kingdom." However, Daniel became the victim of a conspiracy on the part of those jealous of his status in the king's eyes (v. 4): "Then the high officials and the satraps sought to find a ground for complaint against Daniel

---

[17] For a helpful discussion of the text see John E. Goldingay, *Daniel*, WBC (Dallas: Word, 2002), 213.

with regard to the kingdom, but they could find no ground for complaint or any fault, because he was faithful, and no error or fault was found in him." The conspirators managed to get the king to agree to a decree that made it punishable by death if a person prayed to anyone but the king over a thirty-day period (vv. 6–9). Despite the king's decree, Daniel prayed three times a day, facing Jerusalem and in a place which could be seen by others. Consequently, Daniel found himself in the lions' den. The God to whom Daniel prayed delivered him, just as the king had hoped. Daniel explained to the king what had transpired in his deliverance (v. 22): "My God sent his angel and shut the lions' mouths, and they have not harmed me, because I was found blameless before him; and also before you, O king, I have done no harm."[18] The narrator sums up the situation (v. 23): "So Daniel was taken up out of the den, and no kind of harm was found on him, because he had trusted in his God." As for the plotters and their families, Persian justice was merciless.[19] They became meals for the ravenous lions (v. 24).

The NT has an angelic deliverance story of its own to tell. Peter is imprisoned by King Herod Agrippa. This king was particularly cruel. He had James, the brother of John, executed by sword (Acts 12:1–2). Next, he had Peter arrested. The apostle was bound in chains and had to sleep between two guards. An angel intervenes. The angel awakens Peter. Peter's chains fall off, the other guards offer no resistance, doors miraculously open, and the angel conducts him to safety (vv. 7–10). After initial confusion, Peter is in no doubt as to what has taken place (v. 11): "When Peter came to himself, he said, 'Now I am sure that the Lord has sent his angel and rescued me from the hand of Herod and from all that the Jewish people were expecting.'" This was no mere vision. A real supernatural rescue had been carried out.[20]

The God of the Bible is the God of means as well as ends. Over and over again in the biblical narrative, God uses agents (divine and human) to carry out his will and further his purposes.

---

[18] Shadrach, Meshach, and Abednego were also delivered miraculously—probably by an angel. In Daniel 3, the three men find themselves in the fiery furnace at the command of a wrathful pagan king, Nebuchadnezzar. As in the case of Daniel 6, the issue was idolatry. The three men survived the fire, and the king observed a fourth figure in the furnace (Dan. 3:24–25): "Then King Nebuchadnezzar was astonished and rose up in haste. He declared to his counselors, 'Did we not cast three men bound into the fire?' They answered and said to the king, 'True, O king.' He answered and said, 'But I see four men unbound, walking in the midst of the fire, and they are not hurt; and the appearance of the fourth is like a son of the gods.'" The phrase "a son of the gods" on the lips of a pagan most probably means in this context what Goldingay, *Daniel*, 70. It is unlikely that a preincarnate appearance of Christ is on view, in the light of the reference to "angel" in verse 28.

[19] The ancient Greek historian Herodotus noted such punishments in Persian history involving whole families, as Joyce G. Baldwin notes (*Daniel*, TOTC [Downers Grove, IL: IVP Academic, 2016], 145).

[20] For a discussion of various attempts by some commentators to remove the supernatural dimension from the account, see Ajith Fernando, *Acts*, NIVAC (Grand Rapids, MI: Zondervan, 1998), 364–366. Fernando is rightly critical of attempts at demythologizing the text.

Directing God's Human Agents

Angels not only deliver messages, according to the biblical testimony; they also give directions. Another NT account illustrates the role. Philip is given precise directions to follow (Acts 8:26): "Now an angel of the Lord said to Philip, 'Rise and go toward the south to the road that goes down from Jerusalem to Gaza.'" Philip is obedient and follows the direction. So he sets out from Jerusalem to Gaza. On the way he meets the Ethiopian eunuch and is directed now by the Holy Spirit to evangelize this dignitary. A celebrated conversion is the consequence. Interestingly, this account includes roles for both an angel and the Spirit of God, with Philip as the evangelist.

Caring for God's People

Angels appear in seventeen OT books. First Kings is one of them. After the victorious encounter on Mount Carmel between Elijah and the prophets of Baal, Elijah flees to Horeb, the mountain of God. He seems exhausted. Certainly he is afraid. Jezebel has not been deterred by the death of her prophets. Perhaps that was the source of what appears to be Elijah's deep depression. In that context we learn (1 Kings 19:5–6), "And he lay down and slept under a broom tree. And behold, an angel touched him and said to him, 'Arise and eat.' And he looked, and behold, there was at his head a cake baked on hot stones and a jar of water. And he ate and drank and lay down again." The angelic care does not end there (v. 7): "And the angel of the LORD came again a second time and touched him and said, 'Arise and eat, for the journey is too great for you.'"[21] Angels can serve as agents of divine care.[22]

Reconnoitering the Earth

In Zechariah's first vision, he sees a man on a red horse among myrtle trees. Behind the rider stand other horsemen on horses of various colors. The man explains their identity (Zech. 1:10): "So the man who was standing among the myrtle trees answered, 'These are they whom the LORD has sent to patrol [lit., "walk"] the earth.'" In the next verse (v. 11), the rider on the red horse and the angel of the Lord appear to be identified: "And they answered the angel of the LORD who was standing among the myrtle trees, and said, 'We have patrolled [lit., "walked"] the earth, and behold, all the earth remains at rest.'" The result of their inspection is reassuring. The earth is tranquil. There is then a space and

---

[21] This text (1 Kings 19:5–7) shows that, although angels are bodiless spirits, like the divine Spirit, they can effect actions in the physical world such as touch.

[22] John 5:1–15 is the story of a lame man healed by Jesus. There is a strange reference to angelic involvement in healings at this pool. These verses (vv. 3–4) are to be found in some manuscripts, but not the best ones. See the discussion in Bruce Milne, *The Message of John*, TBST (Leicester, UK, and Downers Grove, IL: InterVarsity Press, 1993), 94.

a time for the temple to be rebuilt and for Jerusalem to prosper (vv. 16–17).[23] Although, as indicated, the literal translation is "walk," the ESV's "patrol" seems a safe surmise and suggests a military tone. The idea of "reconnoitering" or "reconnaissance" may be even more accurate in the context.

Administering Judgment

Angels in Scripture also serve as agents of divine judgment. These judgments may be on a group or an individual. In the OT, 2 Samuel 24 provides an example of judgment of a group. David takes a census of his fighting men. The story is puzzling in many ways. The Lord incites David to do so and then judges him for it.[24] What is important for our present point is that the judgment is carried out by an angel (v. 17): "Then David spoke to the LORD when he saw the angel who was striking the people [70,000 died from plague], and said, 'Behold, I have sinned, and I have done wickedly. But these sheep, what have they done? Please let your hand be against me and against my father's house.'" A case of judgment on an individual is found in the NT account of the death of Herod Agrippa I. This king had executed James, the brother of John (Acts 12:2). His demise, however, is attributed to his arrogance in refusing to give praise to God (v. 23): "Immediately an angel of the Lord struck him down, because he did not give God the glory, and he was eaten by worms and breathed his last." The God of the Bible will not share his glory with another.[25]

Serving the Christ

The burden of Scripture is the story of the Christ. Christology—the person and work of Christ—constitutes the heart of the Bible's witness. As Jesus said concerning the OT (John 5:39–40), "You search the Scriptures because you think that in them you have eternal life; and it is they that bear witness about me, yet you refuse to come to me that you may have life." Paul famously concurs, in writing to Timothy (2 Tim. 3:14–15): "But as for you, continue in what you have learned and have firmly believed, knowing from whom you learned it

---

[23] See Ralph L. Smith, *Micah–Malachi*, WBC (Dallas: Word, 2002), 188.

[24] For an attempt to account for this puzzle and how the 1 Chronicles 21 story, which attributes the incitement to Satan, fits with it, see Walter C. Kaiser Jr., *Hard Sayings of the Bible* (Downers Grove, IL: InterVarsity Press, 1997), 240. For a Jewish perspective see Shaul Bar, "The Destroying Angel," *Jewish Biblical Quarterly* 42/4 (2014): 255–261. In this interesting article, Bar argues that in the parallel passage in 1 Chronicles 21:15, it should be assumed that the angel is acting as Yahweh's agent even though Yahweh is not mentioned (255–256). He also sees, albeit somewhat tentatively, the destroying angel as the angel who brings death in the tenth plague in Exodus 12:12–13, 256–257. Importantly, there appears to be no specific angel who is to be identified as the angel of death in either the Old Testament or the New. On the basis of Exodus 11:4; 12:12, 13, 23, and 29, Jewish scholar Richard Elliott Friedman is emphatic: "There is no such thing as an 'angel of death' in the Hebrew Bible." See his *The Disappearance of God: A Divine Mystery* (Boston: Little, Brown, 1995), 14.

[25] See I. Howard Marshall, *Acts*, TNTC (Downers Grove, IL: InterVarsity Press, 1980), 225. Marshall helpfully comments, "Luke ascribes the sudden onset to *an angel of the Lord*; here the phrase is applied to the ultimate divine origin of a natural disease, and it shows that Luke is not thinking of a visible appearance of a human or heavenly figure (contrast verses 7–11). The point is that God himself acts against those who usurp his position and claim divine honours for themselves" (emphasis original).

and how from childhood you have been acquainted with the sacred writings, which are able to make you wise for salvation through faith in Christ Jesus." So our question concerns the relation between Christology and angelology.[26]

Angels come into view at both the beginning and end of Christ's earthly life. In the beginning, for example, it is the angel Gabriel who informs Mary of her role in the Christ story. He comes not at his own initiative. He is divinely sent (Luke 1:26–27): "In the sixth month the angel Gabriel was sent from God to a city of Galilee named Nazareth, to a virgin betrothed to a man whose name was Joseph, of the house of David. And the virgin's name was Mary." His message is a stunning one (vv. 30–31): "And the angel said to her, 'Do not be afraid, Mary, for you have found favor with God. And behold, you will conceive in your womb and bear a son, and you shall call his name Jesus.'" The coming into the world of the Savior of the world is angelically announced.[27] The story does not end there. As the Lukan account unfolds, we soon read of angelic hosts appearing to humble shepherds. The coming into the world of its Savior is announced by one angel (Luke 2:8–11), and a whole host of them suddenly appear, praising God for what has taken place in Bethlehem (vv. 13–14). The shepherds go to the city of David to see for themselves. Soon, they too glorify and praise God (v. 20). Both heaven and earth are united in praise. No other biblical personage, apart from God himself, is so celebrated and so praised. Abraham wasn't. Moses wasn't. Samuel wasn't. David wasn't. Jesus was.

Years later and now a grown man, Jesus is baptized at the Jordan by John the Baptist. Next he is tempted by the devil in the wilderness for forty days and nights but does not deviate from the path of obedience (Matt. 4:1–10). And so, unlike Adam and unlike Israel, he does not fall to the temptation. The devil, discomfited, leaves him, but angels attend him (v. 11). The next angelic appearance occurs much later in the Christological story. Jesus is praying in the garden of Gethsemane. The cross awaits him. It is the Passion Week. It is an ordeal, and in that context we read (Luke 22:43), "And there appeared to him an angel from heaven, strengthening him." After his atoning death, it is an angel who announces Christ's victorious resurrection (Matt. 28:5–6): "But the angel said to the women, 'Do not be afraid, for I know that you seek Jesus who was crucified. He is not here, for he has risen, as he said. Come, see the place where he lay.'" The return of Jesus to heaven likewise has an angelic accompaniment (Acts 1:10–11). Bulgakov sums up the biblical testimony well: "The gospel story witnesses to the service of angels to Christ over the course of the whole history of the divine incarnation; in the annunciation, in His nativ-

---

[26] The relation between Christology and demonology will be addressed in a later chapter.

[27] Interestingly, the return of the risen Christ will also be announced by an angel (1 Thess. 4:16).

ity, baptism, temptation, in the sufferings and resurrection and in the glorious second coming."[28]

ANGELIC DEALINGS WITH INDIVIDUALS AND NATIONS

Hebrews 1:14 describes angels as ministering spirits.[29] Angelic ministry in the biblical witness extends to both individuals and peoples.[30]

Angelic Dealings with Individuals

An early example of angelic dealings with individuals comes from the patriarchal period and a story involving Abraham's servant. Abraham charged his chief servant that, when the servant went to secure a wife for Isaac, Abraham's son, that wife was not to be a Canaanite (Gen. 24:1–3). The sought-for woman needed to be a relative from Abraham's country and kindred. But how would this commission be successfully accomplished? Abraham was confident (v. 7): "The LORD, the God of heaven, who took me from my father's house and from the land of my kindred, and who spoke to me and swore to me, 'To your offspring I will give this land,' he will send his angel before you, and you shall take a wife for my son from there." That angel would prosper the servant's way; and indeed he did, and Rebekah became Isaac's wife.

Angelic Dealings with Nations and Peoples

In the Torah there is some evidence that the angelic order is involved in the supervision of nations. The key text is Deuteronomy 32:8: "When the Most High gave to the nations their inheritance, when he divided mankind, he fixed the borders of the peoples according to the number of the sons of God." The ESV offers this alternative as a footnote: "Compare Dead Sea Scroll, Septuagint [some later versions]; Masoretic Text *sons of Israel*." Michael S. Heiser maintains, "'Sons of God' is the terminology found in the Dead Sea Scrolls, the oldest manuscripts of the Bible. The ESV has it right."[31] Most scholars are on Heiser's side in this discussion, arguing that the alternative is an attempt to

---

[28] Bulgakov, *Jacob's Ladder*, 157.

[29] Ministry or service is a role that angels and humankind have in common, according to Revelation 22:9. The angel admonishes the seer not to worship him in these terms: "Don't worship me! I am a servant [*sundoulos*; "fellow slave/servant"] like you and your brothers the prophets. I am a servant like all those who obey the words in this book" (my paraphrase).

[30] Some might argue, given Revelation 2–3, where we read seven times, "to the angel of the church . . ." that churches too have angels (Rev. 2:1, 8, 12, 18; 3:1, 7, 14.). However, there is debate among exegetes as to whether a spiritual being is on view, or a church leader. For example, D. Broughton Knox, in *D. Broughton Knox Selected Works: Volume II, Church and Ministry*, ed. Kirsten Birkett (Kingsford, Australia: Matthias Press, 2003), 106, argues that the angel "probably means God's messenger to the congregation, that is their minister." See also the discussion in Scot McKnight, *The Hum of Angels: Listening for the Messengers of God around Us* (New York: Waterbrook, 2017), 170–172.

[31] Michael S. Heiser, *Supernatural: What the Bible Teaches about the Unseen World—and Why It Matters* (Bellingham, WA: Lexham, 2015), 49; see also his *The Unseen Realm: Recovering the Supernatural Worldview of the Bible* (Bellingham, WA: Lexham, 2015), 113.

remove the embarrassment of a reference to "God" or "gods."[32] This is plausible, if not definitive. If correct, then God put in place "a system of [delegated] divine oversight."[33]

Daniel contains intriguing references to the archangel Michael which fall in line with the interpretation of Deuteronomy 32:8 suggested above. In Daniel 10:13 the angelic speaker explains his delay in terms of the opposition from the "guardian angel" of the Persian Empire: "The prince of the kingdom of Persia withstood me twenty-one days." However, there is an angelic champion fighting for God's people: "But Michael, one of the chief princes, came to help me, for I was left there with the kings of Persia." God's people have their guardian too (see also Dan. 12:1).[34] It is important to note that whole peoples are on view, not individuals, in the Danielic text.

The conflict between good and evil is not reducible to that between God and rebellious humankind. There is, as Matthias Henze argues with reference to Daniel 10:20–11:1, ". . . a celestial conflict between the angelic princes that is currently raging, in which each prince represents a nation: the 'prince of Persia' and the 'prince of Greece' are fighting against Michael, the warrior and defender of Israel (12:1; 1 En 9:1; Rev 12:7; see also the War Scroll from Qumran)."[35] This conflict between angelic forces will be addressed in more detail in a later chapter.

The Mysterious Angel of the Lord

Stanley J. Grenz accurately describes the "angel of the Lord" as "the divine messenger par excellence, for he is the one supremely sent by God with a commission to fulfill."[36] The OT references to the mysterious figure of the angel of the Lord are numerous (e.g., Gen. 16:7–14; 21:17; 22:11, 15; 31:11; Ex. 3:2; 14:19; Num. 22:22–27, 31–35, to look no further than the Torah). The last references are in the postexilic prophet Zechariah (e.g., Zech. 1:11–12; 3:1, 5; 12:8). So who or what is this personage? Answering the question is challenging because there are OT passages in which the angel of the Lord and the Lord

---

[32] For an example, see John W. Rogerson, "Deuteronomy," in *ECB*, ed. James D. G. Dunn and John W. Rogerson (Grand Rapids, MI, and Cambridge: Eerdmans, 2003), 172.

[33] According to Rogerson, a Qumran manuscript [4QDeut] has "sons of God," and other ancient manuscripts, "sons of gods" (Rogerson, "Deuteronomy"). In either case, angels would be on view. The LXX has "angels of God [*angelōn theou*]."

[34] See the comments by Lawrence M. Wills, "Daniel," *JSB* (Oxford: Oxford University Press, 2004), 1662, 1665.

[35] Matthias Henze, "Daniel," in *The New Interpreter's Bible, One Volume Commentary*, ed. Beverley Roberts Gaventa and David Petersen (Nashville: Abingdon, 2010), 490. Some, however, claim that the opposition is from a human ruler and not from an angelic figure. Calvin, for example, argued that the opposition to Michael came from Cambyses, the son of Cyrus. See his *Commentaries on the Book of the Prophet Daniel* (Edinburgh: Calvin Translation Society, 1852), 252. Others argue for an unnamed human ruler. See David E. Stevens, "Daniel 10 and the Notion of Territorial Spirits," in *Bibliotheca Sacra* 157/628 (October 2000): 410–431. I find it hard to see how a mere human ruler can withstand an archangel of God, especially Michael, who according to Revelation 12:7–9 defeats Satan in battle.

[36] Stanley J. Grenz, *Theology for the Community of God* (Grand Rapids, MI: Eerdmans, 2000), 220.

seem to be one and the same (e.g., cf. Gen. 31:11 and 13). However, other passages seem to make a distinction, as in Genesis 16:11. The association with Yahweh is so close in some of the OT texts that Grenz rightly asserts, "As a result of this association, humans who witness the appearance of the angel of Yahweh often cry out, 'I have seen God and still live.'"[37]

According to Millard Erickson there are three main interpretations of the OT witness.[38] The first one is that the angel of the Lord is simply an angel with a special divine commission to carry out. The second is that the angel of the Lord is the Lord appearing temporarily in human guise. The final one is that the angel of the Lord is the preincarnate Christ, as the Logos temporarily appearing as human. Erickson maintains that none of the three interpretations is compellingly persuasive. Furthermore, he suggests that the second and third approaches are more satisfactory than the first. The first approach, he argues, can simply be a case of the Lord referring to himself in the third person, as in Genesis 16:11, in the story of Hagar.

In contrast to Erickson, Wayne Grudem is confident that "[t]hese are clear instances of the angel of the Lord or the angel of God appearing as God himself, perhaps more specifically as God the Son taking on a human body for a short time in order to appear to human beings."[39] Grudem has early church support for his view. Very early in Christian literature, Jesus was sometimes described as "the great angel." For example, Justin Martyr (c. 100–165) identified Jesus as such in a number of places. In chapter 34 of his *Dialogue with Trypho* he provides this impressive list of descriptors of Jesus: "For Christ is King, and Priest, and God, and Lord, and *angel*, and man, and captain, and stone, and a Son born, and first made subject to suffering, then returning to heaven, and again coming with glory, and He is preached as having the everlasting kingdom: so I prove from all the Scriptures."[40] Justin's scriptural source for the "angel" descriptor was Isaiah 9:6, as can be seen in chapter 72 of the dialogue: "And when Isaiah calls Him the Angel of mighty counsel, did he not foretell Him to be the Teacher of those truths which He did teach when He came [to earth]?" Justin is using the Septuagint, which translates the Hebrew of Isaiah 9:6 as, "For to us a child is born. . . . And his name will be called 'Angel of Great Counsel.'"[41] Justin did not believe that Jesus was an angel per se. After all, "angel" could simply mean "messenger." He knew that. Tertullian is explicit: "He [Jesus] has been, it is true,

---

[37] Grenz, *Theology for the Community of God*, 220.

[38] I am indebted to Millard J. Erickson, *Christian Theology*, 3rd ed. (Grand Rapids, MI: Baker, 2013), 413, for much of this paragraph.

[39] Wayne Grudem, *Systematic Theology: An Introduction to Biblical Doctrine* (Grand Rapids, MI: Zondervan, 1995), 401.

[40] For a detailed discussion of Justin Martyr's view and that of other early church figures, see Günther Junker, "Christ as Angel: The Reclamation of a Primitive Title," *Trinity Journal* 15/2 (Fall 1994): 224–235.

[41] I am following David Albert Jones, *Angels: A Very Short Introduction* (Oxford: Oxford University Press, 2011), 55.

called 'the angel of great counsel,' that is, a messenger, by a term expressive of official function, not of nature."[42] However, as David Albert Jones points out, "In the early centuries of Christianity there were some people who thought that Jesus was a saviour sent by God, but they did not believe he was really a human being. They thought he only appeared to be human, but really he was like an angel. They were called docetists, because Jesus was not really human but only seemed to be (in Greek *dokeo*)."[43]

A way of posing the question is whether the angel of the Lord's appearances are theophanies, Christophanies (i.e., preincarnate appearances of Christ), or angelophanies. In a most helpful journal article, Réne López offers a battery of convincing arguments for not identifying the angel of the Lord with either God per se or the preincarnate Christ. He pays particular attention to the book of Judges, which contains the most references to this OT personage. He carefully considers the case for theophany or Christophany before offering his alternative. He concludes that the OT evidence, especially those passages which distinguish the Lord and the angel of the Lord, are crucial for deciding the argument (e.g., cf. 1 Chron. 21:15; 2 Samuel 24; and Zech. 1:12). In his view, "The evidence adduced from grammar, linguistic distinction, ANE custom, and Scripture all points to understanding this angel as a representative of God rather than a theophany."[44] He judges the Christ-angel reading as "at worst patently anachronistic."[45] He rightly concedes that the angel-Christ view is logically possible, but even so, he agrees with Ronald F. Youngblood that "such an interpretation dilutes the uniqueness of Jesus' incarnation and undercuts the teaching of Hebrews 1:3–14, where God's Son is said to be superior to all the angels."[46]

Overall, I am more persuaded by López's arguments than by those of Grudem or Erickson. Indeed, I have two additional difficulties with identifying the angel of the Lord with the preexistent Christ. The first difficulty is well expressed by Scot McKnight:

---

[42] Tertullian, *On the Flesh of Christ*, chapter 14. In this work Tertullian is opposing Gnosticism. For angels, Satan, and demons in Gnostic literature, see Willis Barnstone and Marvin Meyer, eds., *The Gnostic Bible* (Boston and London: Shambhala, 2003).

[43] Jones, *Angels: A Very Short Introduction*, 56. The idea of some that Jesus was an angel may lie behind Gaius Marius Victorinus's (4th century) dilemma: *aut deus aut malus angelus* ("either god or a bad angel") which he posed in his debates with Arians. Gaius Marius Victorinus (also known as Victorinus Afer) was a converted Platonic philosopher. Technically speaking, the notion that Jesus was an angelic being or the incarnation of one or a human being exalted to the status of an angel is "angel Christology." See the discussion in Matthias Reinhard Hoffmann, *The Destroyer and the Lamb: The Relationship between Angelmorphic and Lamb Christology in the Book of Revelation* (Tübingen: Mohr Siebeck, 2005), 26. Hoffmann argues that the book of Revelation presents an angelmorphic Christology: namely, Christ is portrayed in angelic terms without implying that he is one (*Destroyer and the Lamb*, 28, 249–253).

[44] See René A. López, "Identifying the 'Angel of the Lord' in the Book of Judges: A Model for Reconsidering the Referent in Other Old Testament Loci," *Bulletin for Biblical Research* 20 (2010): 15.

[45] López, "Identifying the 'Angel of the Lord' in the Book of Judges," 16.

[46] Ronald F. Youngblood, *Exodus*, Everyman's Bible Commentary (Chicago: Moody, 1983; repr. Eugene, OR: Wipf & Stock, 2000), 32, quoted in López, "Identifying the 'Angel of the Lord' in the Book of Judges," 18.

But one thing surely disproves that Jesus appeared in the form of an angel-like human in the Old Testament. The same thing disproves that manifestations of the Angel of the LORD are Christophanies: no one in the New Testament suggested that Jesus of the New Testament was the Angel of the LORD of the Old Testament. Consider how many texts, figures, and images of the Old Testament are understood to have been fulfilled in Christ. Now consider that among these, not one suggests that he was the Angel of the LORD. We are left to conclude that the Angel of the LORD was not a Christophany.[47]

As for my second difficulty, according to Maxwell J. Davidson, "[G]eneral similarities between the Gospel nativity narratives and certain OT passages which mention the Angel of the Lord suggest that the angel in the nativity accounts is to be identified with the Angel of the Lord of the OT."[48] Given that conclusion, which Davidson convincingly argues for, a reason for my caution in too readily identifying the angel of the Lord with the preexistent Logos lies in the NT witness. In Matthew 1:24 there is a reference to the angel of the Lord's (*ho angelos kuriou*) dealings with Joseph. Mary was carrying Jesus at the time (cf. Matt. 1:18–20 and 1:24).[49] How could this be, if the angel of the Lord was the Son of God in Mary's womb?

A PATRISTIC ERA ELABORATION: DIONYSIUS THE AREOPAGITE

When Paul preached to the intelligentsia in Athens (the Areopagus) there was a convert worthy of naming, Dionysius the Areopagite (Acts 17:34). Around five centuries later, some ten letters and four treatises purporting to be from this convert surfaced.[50] One of the treatises became immensely influential: *The Celestial Hierarchy*. In it the order of angelic beings is explored in concert with the Neoplatonism of the day.[51]

Chapter 6 of the *Celestial Hierarchy* introduces the triad of first, middle, and last celestial beings.[52] Each of these forms a triad too. The first order consists of seraphim, cherubim, and thrones. The second is made up of dominions,

[47] McKnight, *Hum of Angels*, 84. I think "disproves" is a tad too strong. Hence I call it a "difficulty."
[48] Maxwell J. Davidson, "Angels," in *DJG*, ed. Joel B. Green, Jeannine K. Brown, and Nicholas Perrin, 2nd ed. (Downers Grove, IL: InterVarsity Press, 2013), 8.
[49] R. T. France, *Matthew*, TNTC (Downers Grove, IL: IVP Academic, 2008), 412, identifies the "angel of the Lord" mentioned in Matthew 28:2 with the one so-named in 1:24: "*The angel of the Lord* now appears for the first time since the two opening chapters of the Gospel" (emphasis original).
[50] Barth, *CD*, III/3 (385). Barth describes Dionysius the Areopagite's *Celestial Hierarchy* as "one of the greatest frauds in Church history." He is also severely critical of its speculative nature. Even so, he acknowledges that the work is "an epoch-making climax in the angelology of the Early Church" and "a remarkable and instructive enterprise" (385 and 388, respectively).
[51] For a useful brief treatment of Dionysius the Areopagite see Andrew Louth, "Dionysius the Areopagite," in *The Dictionary of Historical Theology*, ed. Trevor A. Hart (Grand Rapids, MI: Eerdmans, 2000), 161–162. In some ways an even greater theological speculator was Origen. Influenced by the Platonism of his day, Origen posited that human beings were once preexistent angelic souls now encased in bodies for their pre-mundane sins. Demons likewise had such an origin but had fallen even further. See the account in John Anthony McGuckin, *The Westminster Handbook of Patristic Theology* (Louisville and London: Westminster John Knox, 2004), 12–13.
[52] Dionysius the Areopagite, *Celestial Hierarchy*, chapters 6–10.

powers, and authorities. The last is composed of principalities, archangels, and angels. The order is important because the nine names are in descending order. The highest order is nearest to God; the lowest order is nearest to humankind. On this scheme, seraphim are the highest of the choir of heaven, whose role is to adore the triune God. Angels are the lowest of the celestial beings because they bring the divine message to us terrestrial creatures. C. S. Lewis puts it well: "The activity of both these hierarchies [the first and the middle ones] is directed towards God; they stand, so to speak, with their faces to Him and their backs to us. In the third and lowest Hierarchy we at last find creatures who are concerned with Man."[53] In reading the *Celestial Hierarchy*, I find myself over and over again asking, How does he know that this is so? The almost complete absence of specific references to Scripture shows a prodigious imagination adrift from biblical controls.[54] Calvin was astonished by the *Celestial Hierarchy*: "If you read the book, you would think a man fallen from heaven recounted, not what he had learned, but what he had seen with his own eyes."[55] Anthony C. Thiselton is blunt: "*This [Celestial Hierarchy] marks a departure from biblical doctrine to medieval speculation.*"[56]

The historical importance of the *Celestial Hierarchy* is undoubted. As we shall see next, Thomas Aquinas (1225–1274) was informed by it, but so too were Dante and Milton.[57] It is difficult to understand Eastern Orthodox angelology and Roman Catholic angelology without some knowledge of it.[58]

A MEDIEVAL ERA ELABORATION: AQUINAS

Thomas Aquinas gave considerable attention to angelology and came to be known as *doctor angelicus* with good cause.[59] His discussion of angelology makes frequent reference to both Dionysius the Areopagite and Scripture. He expounds the Dionysian hierarchy and finds it a reasonable one.[60] However

---

[53] C. S. Lewis, *The Discarded Image: An Introduction to Medieval and Renaissance Literature* (Cambridge: Cambridge University Press, 1984), 72.
[54] Dionysius the Areopagite does refer to Scripture in the abstract (e.g., "in the Scriptures") in a number of places and even thematizes Isaiah 6 in his chapter 13. He needs to discuss Isaiah 6 at length because, prima facie, in the biblical text a seraphim directly relates to the prophet. This is not allowed in Dionysius's theory. On his theory this is the job of the lowest rank of celestial beings, namely, angels. So he needs a way of explaining the prima facie away.
[55] John Calvin, *Institutes of the Christian Religion*, 1.14.4 (*CJCC*). Calvin contrasts the *Celestial Hierarchy*'s loquaciousness with the Pauline reticence expressed in 2 Corinthians 12:4.
[56] Anthony C. Thiselton, *A Concise Encyclopedia of the Philosophy of Religion* (Oxford: Oneworld, 2002), 111, emphasis original.
[57] Jones, *Angels: A Very Short Introduction*, 83.
[58] Writing from a Roman Catholic perspective, Peter Kreeft, *Angels and Demons: What Do We Really Know about Them?* (San Francisco: Ignatius, 1995), 58–59 and 74–75, follows Dionysius the Areopagite closely but he adds, "The scheme is not official dogma, but it is a beautiful work of art, a reasonable work of philosophical speculation, an inspiring work of faith, and an enduring work of tradition." What he fails to mention is that, biblically speaking, the Areopagite's schema is a text-free zone.
[59] Barth describes Aquinas's extensive treatment of angels as "the other great climax in the history of angelology" after Dionysius (*CD*, III/3 [390]).
[60] Thomas Aquinas, *ST*, I, Q 108.6. He finds that Gregory the Great offers a reasonable suggestion as to the nature of the hierarchy as well.

he goes far beyond the *Celestial Hierarchy* in pursuing, in his usual rigorous manner, the philosophical questions he sees as arising in angelology. And so he explores, in the first part of his *Summa Theologica*, questions involving the substance of angels (Q 50), their relation to bodies (Q 51), their location (Q 52) and movement (Q 53), their intellect (Qs 54–58), their will (Qs 59–60), their origins (Qs 61–64), and how one angel might affect another (Qs 106–107), among other topics. A good example of how Aquinas pursues the philosophical rather than the exegetical is seen in his treatment of angels and substance. Since angels do not have bodies, each angel is its own species and hence no two angels are essentially alike.[61]

Peter Kreeft in his recent work on angels shows that the influence of Aquinas, and before him Dionysius, is far from over. His debts to Aquinas are patent when he writes. He begins with the first of the triads: seraphim, cherubim, and thrones. The seraphim he describes as "the highest choir" since they comprehend God "with maximum clarity."[62] He suggests that Lucifer was once one of them. Cherubim likewise contemplate God, "but less in himself than in his providence, his wise plan for creatures." The thrones contemplate "God's power and judgments." This triad sees and adores God directly. The middle triad is "like middle management personnel." The dominations or dominions are in charge of the angels ranked below them. The virtues are under the command of the dominations and run the universe, as it were. The powers fight against any that oppose the plans of the virtues. The lowest triad "directly order human affairs." The principalities look after nations and kingdoms. The archangels convey "God's important messages to man." The "ordinary" angels are the guardian angels, and thus there is one for each human person.

Kreeft acknowledges that this scheme is not official dogma of the Roman Catholic Church, of which he is a member. Even so, as previously noted, he describes the work of Dionysius as "a beautiful work of art, a reasonable work of philosophical speculation, an inspiring work of faith, an enduring work of tradition."[63] Interestingly, he does not describe his analysis as a biblically grounded work of constructive theology. It isn't. As with Dionysius the Areopagite and Thomas Aquinas, the question must be put to Kreeft concerning the biblical anchorage of his theological claims. How does he know that his analysis is true?

One can reasonably argue that archangels and angels by definition stand in some kind of hierarchy. Indeed Michael, the archangel, is also described in Daniel 12:1 as a "great prince" (Hb. *sar gāgdōl*, LXX *ho angelos ho megas*).[64]

---

[61] Aquinas, *ST*, I, Q 50.4.
[62] For the substance of this paragraph I am indebted to Peter Kreeft, *Angels and Demons*, 75.
[63] Kreeft, *Angels and Demons*, 75.
[64] Barth unconvincingly tries to deconstruct any suggestion that "archangel" denotes rank (*CD*, III/3 [457]). His case in point is Michael.

But what of the rest: seraphim, cherubim, and the others? Isaiah 6:6–7 is particularly problematic for ancient, medieval, and even contemporary hierarchical approaches. A seraphim—the putative highest of the celestial beings, who supposedly relates only to God—flies to the prophet and touches the prophet's mouth.[65] Like Karl Barth and Millard Erickson, I find myself skeptical about the attempt to construct an overly elaborate celestial hierarchy.[66] Even so there is a certain attractiveness in T. C. Hammond's suggestion that "They are graded into at least three 'ranks'—Archangels, Cherubim and Seraphim, and Angels."[67]

WISDOM FROM BARTH

Dionysius the Areopagite certainly knew how to speculate in a way undisciplined by divine revelation. Thomas Aquinas took Scripture seriously, but in the area of angelology his philosophical interest predominated. Peter Kreeft follows Aquinas closely. By way of contrast, there is much wisdom in Karl Barth's contention that

> Holy Scripture gives us quite enough to think of regarding angels. And it is something positive. We have only to consider what it says in its distinctiveness, and try to assess it without pre-judgment. Nor does it do so in such a way that we can quickly leave the problem on the pretext that it is merely peripheral. If we wholeheartedly accept angels in the position and role assigned to them in the Bible, in their own place and way they make themselves so important that we can no longer ignore them when we consider the centre and substance of the biblical message. Again, the Bible is not so obscure in respect of angels that we cannot responsibly draw out certain notions and concepts which are quite adequate for a Christian understanding. All that is required is a firm resolve that the Bible should be allowed both to speak for itself in this matter, i.e., in the course of its message, as a witness of what it understands by the revelation and work of God, and also to be very impressively, and in its own way very eloquently, silent.[68]

One may take issue with Barth's less than evangelically robust doctrine of Scripture. But his caution here is exemplary.[69] But caution is not skepticism.

---

[65] Barth notes the issue that Isaiah 6 raises but does not develop it (*CD*, III/3 [387]).

[66] Barth, *CD*, III/3 (456–459); and Erickson, *Christian Theology*, 411–412. For a different view see C. Fred Dickason, *Angels: Elect and Evil*, rev. and expanded ed. (Chicago: Moody, 1995), 92–93, who suggests ranking angels by class (e.g., cherubim are the highest) or title (e.g., archangel) or sequence (e.g., thrones comes before powers in biblical lists).

[67] T. C. Hammond, *In Understanding Be Men*, 5th ed. (London: Inter-Varsity Christian Fellowship, 1956), 63. Seraphim and cherubim do seem to stand in a class apart, given their biblical descriptors.

[68] Barth, *CD*, III/3 (410). Ironically, it seems to me that Barth does not heed his own cautions when he deploys his very speculative notion of *Das Nichtige* ("the nothingness") in describing demons, even though he claims that "nothingness is not nothing" ("*Das Nichtige ist nicht das Nichts*"). There is little exegetical grounding for such an idea, as Thomas A. Noble rightly comments in his "The Spirit World: A Theological Synthesis," in *The Unseen World: Christian Reflections on Angels, Demons, and the Heavenly Realm*, ed. Anthony N. S. Lane (Grand Rapids, MI: Paternoster/Baker, 1996), 206n39. See also the helpful discussion and critique of Barth's view in Gregory A. Boyd, *Satan and the Problem of Evil: Constructing a Trinitarian Warfare Theodicy* (Downers Grove, IL: IVP Academic, 2001), 284–290.

[69] Kreeft shows no such caution as he speculates on the numbers of angels. He argues that there are more than five billion angels, "for everyone has a guardian angel," and such angels populate only one level in the celestial hierarchy

Again Barth puts it well: "At this point, again, we must err neither *in exessu* nor *in defectu*, i.e., neither in the direction of misplaced speculation nor in that of an equally misplaced scepticism."[70]

IMPLICATIONS FOR BELIEF AND PRACTICE

We turn now to drawing out some of the implications of our examination of angelic activity for our belief and practice.

Is It Wrong to Pray to Angels?

Angels are not deity, but may the Christian pray to such exalted beings that stand in the presence of God? In Roman Catholic angelology, angels may indeed be prayed to. Since the Roman Catholic OT includes the Apocrypha, there is a text to base this idea on.[71] In *Tobit* 12:11–22, Raphael reveals his angelic identity to Tobit and his son Tobias. In the encounter, Raphael explains how it is he who read the record of Tobias's and his wife Sarah's prayers "before the glory of the Lord" (NRSV). Raphael, it seems, can act as an intermediary. It is hard not to see how, in this light, others might so act, like departed saints and, of course, Mary the mother of Jesus.

Pope Leo XIII (1810–1903) provides an example of prayer addressed to an angel. He called upon Michael, the Archangel, in the following way:

> Saint Michael Archangel, defend us in battle!
> Be our protection against the wickedness and snares of the devil.
> My God rebuke him, we humbly pray;
> And do thou, O Prince of the heavenly hosts, by the power of God,
> Thrust into hell Satan and all the evil spirits
> Who roam through the world seeking the ruin of souls.[72]

Leo XIII prayed this at the end of the nineteenth century, and soon, of course, "the war to end all wars" began. Peter Kreeft in that light comments, "So the Pope was given a warrior's prayer for the Church in the coming century."[73]

As we saw in the "Introduction" to this volume (ch. 1), according to J. C. Ryle one of the ways that the gospel may be "spoiled" is by interposition.

(Kreeft, *Angels and Demons*, 91). How does he know this? What we do know from Scripture is that angels are very numerous. For example, Daniel 7:10 depicts the presence of angels in the heavenly court in these terms: "A stream of fire issued and came out from before him; a thousand thousands served him, and ten thousand times ten thousand stood before him; the court sat in judgment, and the books were opened."

[70] Barth, *CD*, III/3 (443).

[71] Anthony C. Thiselton argues correctly that the major difference between Protestant angelology and Roman Catholic angelology is the difference in their respective canons of Scripture. There are references to angels which Roman Catholics draw on in *Tobit*, *Bel and the Dragon*, *1 Maccabees*, and *4 Maccabees*. See Anthony C. Thiselton, *Systematic Theology* (Grand Rapids, MI: Eerdmans, 2015), 109: "Roman Catholic and Orthodox include the Apocrypha in their canon, which *explains much of the difference from Protestant angelology*" (emphasis original).

[72] Quoted in Kreeft, *Angels and Demons*, 126.

[73] Kreeft, *Angels and Demons*, 125.

Praying to angels appears to clearly exhibit this very danger. Indeed there is one letter in the NT that argues in such a way as to make any such interposition problematic in the extreme. Hebrews argues for the superiority of the Son over any angelic being (Heb. 1:4–14), and more to the point, that in his role as our great high priest he is the one to whom we go with our prayers:

> Since then we have a great high priest who has passed through the heavens, Jesus, the Son of God, let us hold fast our confession. For we do not have a high priest who is unable to sympathize with our weaknesses, but one who in every respect has been tempted as we are, yet without sin. Let us then with confidence draw near to the throne of grace, that we may receive mercy and find grace to help in time of need. (Heb. 4:14–16)

In fact it is this high priest after the order of Melchizedek who ever lives to intercede for us (Heb. 7:25). What then is so deficient in Christ's high priestly office that other intermediaries are needed? Surely nothing!

Is It Wrong to Pray to God for Angelic Assistance?

There are no recorded prayers in Scripture addressed to angels. However, Jesus did entertain the possibility of praying for angelic assistance. The relevant context is a Matthean one (Matt. 26:47–54). Jesus is confronted by Judas and a mob sent by the Jewish authorities. He commands Peter to put away his sword. (Peter had just struck off the ear of the servant of the high priest.) Jesus elaborates (v. 53): "Do you think that I cannot appeal to my Father, and he will at once send me more than twelve legions of angels?" Even so, Jesus stays on his messianic course (v. 54): "But how then should the Scriptures be fulfilled, that it must be so?" Clearly, in Jesus's mind, there is another possible world in which he would be rescued if he so desired. A prayer to the Father would give him command of angelic legions. How pitiful is a mere sword in the light of that! Now, not all of Jesus's actions are imitable. Only *his* death, for example, provides atonement. The intriguing question is whether praying to the Father in Jesus's name for angelic protection for this person or that, this church or that, this missionary or that, although not demanded by Scripture, may be consistent with Scripture. I do not see why not. Luther (1483–1546) had no qualms about this practice. In his *Small Catechism* he wrote this evening prayer:

> [S]ay this little prayer: I thank Thee, my Heavenly Father, through Jesus Christ, Thy dear Son, that Thou hast graciously kept me this day, and I pray Thee to forgive me all my sins, where I have done wrong, and graciously keep me this night. For into Thy hands I commend myself, my body and soul, and

all things. Let Thy holy angel be with me, that the Wicked Foe may have no power over me. Amen.

His next instruction is practical: "Then go to sleep promptly and cheerfully."[74]

Are There Guardian Angels?

The short answer is yes. The cherubim of Genesis 3 are clearly guardians of sacred space and the tree of life. Even the devil knows that angels are guardians, as can be seen in his misuse of Psalm 91 in his attempt to tempt Jesus in the wilderness to deviate from the path of messianic obedience (Matt. 4:5–7). This psalm does speak of this angelic role. The issue is not whether angels guard. They clearly do. The issue is whether a specific angel is assigned guardianship of a specific human person. The great early church Bible translator Jerome (347–419) certainly thought so. He wrote with regard to Matthew 18:10, "The dignity of human souls is great, for each has an angel appointed to guard it."[75] In the medieval period, Aquinas, following Jerome, whom he quotes, certainly thought so. In fact, according to Aquinas not only does each person on earth have his or her guardian angel, but once in heaven each man or woman will have a companion angel who will reign with him or her. Furthermore, there is a hellish mirror image of this. In hell, each human person will have a fallen angel assigned to punish them.[76] Kreeft amplifies the tradition: "There are twice as many persons as we see in every place, every kitchen or classroom, every hospital or nursery. Only half are *human* persons. There is an angel standing next to each bag lady."[77] Sergius Bulgakov maintains that "[a]ccording to the doctrine of the Church [the Orthodox Church] the guardian angel stands before our death bed and receives our soul."[78]

The putative biblical warrant for the doctrine of guardian angels in the main rests on Jesus's words in Matthew 18:10: "See that you do not despise one of these little ones. For I tell you that in heaven their angels always see the face of my Father who is in heaven." Much has been built on little. For example, Greek Orthodox theologian Philip Kariatlis argues, "The Orthodox tradition also claims quite emphatically that, upon Baptism God assigns each person a guardian angel to guide and protect human beings throughout their

---

[74] Martin Luther, *Small Catechism*, http://bookofconcord.org/smallcatechism.php, accessed 1/26/2015.

[75] Quoted by Aquinas in Paul J. Glenn, *A Tour of the Summa* (St. Louis: Herder, 1963), 93. Jerome does not quote chapter and verse. They weren't invented at that stage. Glenn locates the quote in Jerome's comments on Matthew 8:10, but the relevant Gospel text is actually Matthew 18:10.

[76] Aquinas, *ST*, I, Q 113.1–7.

[77] Kreeft, *Angels and Demons*, 93, emphasis original.

[78] Bulgakov, *Jacob's Ladder*, 71. His putative biblical evidence for this claim is found in the parable of Lazarus and the rich man. Upon the death of Lazarus, angels bring him to Abraham's bosom (Luke 16:22). However, it *is* a parable, which makes it difficult to know how far to press the imagery. And, the reference is to angels (*angeloi*, plural), not to just one, and there is no hint that these angels are guardians of any kind.

life on earth."[79] The proof text he offers is Matthew 18:10. In contrast, Herman Bavinck contends,

> Most support for the doctrine of guardian angels comes from Matthew 18:10, a text undoubtedly implying that a certain class of angels is charged with the task of protecting "the little ones." However, there is here not even a hint that every elect person is assigned his or her own angel. This idea is found only in the apocryphal book of Tobit. But by that very fact this doctrine of guardian angels also betrays its origin.[80]

Donald A. Hagner agrees: "This passage falls short of describing 'guardian' angels . . . assigned to each individual Christian, who attempt to keep her or him out of danger. A more general idea is in view, namely, that angels represent the 'little ones' before the throne of God." His application is on target too: "The point here is not to speculate on the *ad hoc* role of angels in aiding disciples of Jesus but rather simply to emphasize the importance of the latter to God. If the very angels of God's presence are concerned with the 'little ones,' how much more then should also fellow Christians be for one another! They are to be received and esteemed; special care must furthermore be taken not to cause them to stumble."[81] On analysis, the idea that each person has an assigned guardian angel is a text-less doctrine. However, the idea of angels having "a corporate guardianship" responsibility does have biblical warrant, as Psalm 91:11–12 suggests.[82]

The importance of disciples to God is reinforced by Jesus's language in Matthew 18:10, which suggests so strongly that disciples are represented at the divine court. Michael Green puts it well:

> It [Matthew 18:10] is a delightful way of expressing the unceasing love and care of the Creator for his creatures, and there is a strong note of accessibility as well. The "face" of the eastern ruler was hard to approach. He was a busy and important person. But the angels always see God's "face." They have unrestricted access to his presence. God cares very much for the little members, the stray sheep of his flock. . . . That is the thrust of this passage.[83]

It is quite a stretch to use this Matthean text in constructing a doctrine of guardian angels. For as Green and others point out, the accent in the text is not on guardianship but on representation before God.[84]

[79] Philip Kariatlis, "God-Creator of the Heavenly World," www.greekorthodox.org.au/general/resources/publications/articledetails.php?page=187article_id=10, accessed 3/30/2015.
[80] Herman Bavinck, *Reformed Dogmatics, Volume 2: God and Creation*, trans. John Vriend, ed., John Bolt (Grand Rapids, MI: Baker Academic, 2004), 467.
[81] Donald A. Hagner, *Matthew 14–28*, WBC (Dallas: Word, 2002), 526.
[82] Both Calvin and Barth make this point. See Thiselton, *Systematic Theology*, 103.
[83] Michael Green, *The Message of Matthew: The Kingdom of Heaven* (Leicester, UK, and Downers Grove, IL: InterVarsity Press, 2000), 193.
[84] For one of the others who agree, see D. A. Carson, "Matthew," in *EBC*, comment on Matthew 18:10–14.

The other key text adduced for the idea of individual guardian angels is Acts 12:15.[85] In the context, Peter has miraculously escaped imprisonment and now stands at the door of the house of Mary, Mark's mother, where Christians are gathered. He knocks and speaks. Rhoda, the servant girl, recognizes his voice and declares that it is Peter. The reaction of the rest is the key, in verse 15: "They said to her, 'You are out of your mind.' But she kept insisting that it was so, and they kept saying, 'It is his angel!'" In their minds, Peter was still in prison, so who else could it be? Most commentators interpret their reaction as expressing the popular Jewish belief at the time that indeed each Jew had a guardian angel.[86] Even if this is so, and a popular Jewish belief is being expressed, then importantly, from a hermeneutical point of view, we need to observe that Acts 12:15 is descriptive, not prescriptive. In other words, a narrative description should not be turned too facilely into doctrine, which by nature is prescriptive.[87]

What Are We to Make of New Age Angelology?

Chris Maunder sums up the "New Age" in this way: "New Age denotes the various beliefs in the non-material and supernatural that do not belong formally to any mainstream religious tradition, and the practices that are based upon them."[88] Those practices include the use of crystals, divinatory techniques of various kinds, and addressing angels by name. No one person speaks for the New Age, but a belief in angels as spirit guides is common.

Doreen Virtue is a prolific New Age author known especially for her writings on angels.[89] She offers this advice on how to see angels: Angels can appear in photographs as orbs of light. They can appear in dreams. Seeing sparkles or flashes of light can signify angelic presences. Clouds looking like angels may

---

[85] For the Roman Catholic commentator, *Tobit* is part of the canon of Scripture and much can be made therefore of the angel Raphael's role in the believer's life (e.g., esp. *Tobit* 5:4–22). The *Catholic Bible Dictionary* (ed. Scott Hahn [New York: Doubleday, 2009], 921) is eloquent on the point: "The narrative offers one of the greatest examples of angelophany in Scripture." As an example of a story of alleged angelophany, there is no dispute about the *Tobit* text. That it is part of Scripture is another matter for both the Protestant and the Orthodox Jew. During the intertestamental period, Jewish angelology became highly developed (see Hagner, *Matthew 14–28*, 526; and Maxwell John Davidson, "Angel," in *NIDB*, ed. Katharine Doob Sakenfeld, 5 vols. [Nashville: Abingdon, 2006], 1:148–155). *Tobit* is a good example, having been written around 200 BC and having been preserved in complete form only in Greek.
[86] See Kaiser, *Hard Sayings of the Bible*, 526: "Interesting as this passage is, it simply witnesses to the beliefs of the Christians in that house. The author of Acts reports rather than endorses their views." D. A. Carson, following B. B. Warfield, offers a different interpretation of both passages. The angel is the spirit of the deceased believer in both Matthew 18:10 and Acts 12:15, those in the house thought that Peter was dead and that this was his spirit speaking (Carson, "Matthew," comment on Matthew 18:10–14). This line of interpretation is possible but is the minority report. Hagner is dismissive, finding the Carson and Warfield view "unconvincing," but his reasons are sketchy (Hagner, *Matthew 14–28*, 526). Grudem (*Systematic Theology*, 400n7), gives good reasons at length for rejecting the Warfield-Carson interpretation.
[87] On the hermeneutical challenges in constructing doctrine from narrative, see my *He Who Gives Life: The Doctrine of the Holy Spirit* (Wheaton, IL: Crossway, 2007), 203–207.
[88] Chris Maunder, "New Age," in *The Oxford Companion to Christian Thought*, ed. Adrian Hastings (Oxford: Oxford University Press, 2000), 470.
[89] For this summary of her views I am drawing on Doreen Virtue, "How to See Angels," http://www.angeltherapy .com/blog/how-see-angels, accessed 9/6/2016.

indeed be an angelic communication. Signs such as flickering lights in one's home may indicate an angel is present.

In sharp contrast to this New Age advice, when one turns to the Scriptures it is striking to observe that God has to open a person's eyes to see angelic presences. The Syrian king wanted Elisha the prophet seized. He sent his army to Dothan to get the job done. Elisha knew what was happening and was relaxed. His servant was not. The story is instructive (2 Kings 6:15–17):

> When the servant of the man of God rose early in the morning and went out, behold, an army with horses and chariots was all around the city. And the servant said, "Alas, my master! What shall we do?" He said, "Do not be afraid, for those who are with us are more than those who are with them." Then Elisha prayed and said, "O LORD, please open his eyes that he may see." So the LORD opened the eyes of the young man, and he saw, and behold, the mountain was full of horses and chariots of fire all around Elisha.

Elisha knew the angels were there. The servant did not, until Elisha prayed that the servant's eyes would be opened. God must open eyes to see the otherwise invisible realm.[90] Unlike Doreen Virtue, the Bible offers no technique by which angelic presence may be seen.

New Age teaching on angels is eclectically constructed from Christian, Gnostic, and Hindu sources. The movement does testify to the spiritual nature of humankind and the quest for the divine as well as the rejection of materialistic reductionism. However, if one can "look for love in all the wrong places," the same is true of guidance for life. Paul the apostle has a salutary warning to offer. He writes out of concern for the Galatians (1:6–9):

> I am astonished that you are so quickly deserting him who called you in the grace of Christ and are turning to a different gospel—not that there is another one, but there are some who trouble you and want to distort the gospel of Christ. But even if we or an angel from heaven should preach to you a gospel contrary to the one we preached to you, let him be accursed. As we have said before, so now I say again: If anyone is preaching to you a gospel contrary to the one you received, let him be accursed.

The gospel test applies to claims about angelic guidance and encounters that are to be found in New Age literature, and on this score the New Age is found wanting.[91] Their quest is not for the forgiveness of sins through the atoning

---

[90] In another OT account we see a similar phenomenon. God has to open the eyes of Balaam to see the angel. See Numbers 22:31.

[91] For a sharp critique of New Age angelology, see the discussion in Robert P. Lightner, "Angels, Satan, and Demons: Invisible Beings That Inhabit the Spiritual World," in *Understanding Christian Theology*, ed. Charles R. Swindoll and Roy B. Zuck (Nashville: Thomas Nelson, 2003), 547–549. For angelology according to a New Age advocate, see the many books of Doreen Virtue, e.g., *How to Hear Your Angel* (Carlsbad, CA: Hay, 2007).

sacrifice of Christ but the actualization of one's inner divinity and the bliss it supposedly brings.[92]

What Are We to Do with Contemporary Angel Stories?

Understandably, given New Age love of angels, evangelicals can be rightly wary of contemporary angel stories. However, there are testimonies that are impossible to ignore, although interpreting them is challenging. A case in point is the story of Martin Pistorius that appeared in *Christianity Today*.[93] The account was written by Pistorius himself and so is a firsthand account.

Born in South Africa, Pistorius had a normal childhood until the age of twelve. In 1988, he developed a sore throat. Soon he could not speak and he lost the use of his limbs. Doctors concluded that he was suffering from a degenerative neurological disease and would soon pass away. For the next four years he was unaware of his environment, then at age sixteen, awareness began to return. However he was entombed in his body, unable to communicate. In his own words, "I had awoken as a ghost." At that point he had a profound experience. He writes,

> One night I suddenly "awoke" from sleep. It felt as if I were floating far above my bed. I knew I was not breathing. I could see angels with me, a male and a female. They were comforting and guiding me, and although we did not speak, I could hear their voices. They wanted me to come with them.[94]

He chose not to, and so began a dawning awareness that God was with him. Over time he became a Bible-believing Christian, a married man, a lecturer, and a web designer with his own business.

The testimony is impressive, but what is to be made of the role of angels in it? I would argue that, like Pistorius, we give thanks for his experience and enjoy his moving testimony. However, impressively, Pistorius does not turn his experience into theology. In other words, he does not make it normative, as though all genuine Christians should have similar stories. The apostle Paul in 1 Corinthians 14 thanked God that he spoke in tongues more than any of the readers. Even so, he did not turn his testimony into a norm. In fact, 1 Corinthians 12 makes it plain that he did not expect every Christian to speak in

---

[92] Gospel truth content mattered more to Paul than honorable motives. In Galatia, the "Judaizers" may have been sincere in serving God, but their gospel substituted Moses for Christ. In Philippians, Paul states that his imprisonment was made worse by others preaching the gospel out of wrong motives, but since it was the right gospel Paul rejoiced (cf. Gal. 1:6–9 and Phil. 1:15–18).

[93] Martin Pistorius, "I Couldn't Move or Speak for 12 Years: In My Enforced Silence Another Voice Spoke," *Christianity Today* (June 15, 2015), 79–80.

[94] Pistorius, "I Couldn't Move or Speak for 12 Years," 79. Bulgakov tells his own story of an angelic encounter in the context of severe illness. He claims it was his guardian angel whom he met. He heard an inner voice, but unlike Pistorius's claim, he saw no angelic form (*Jacob's Ladder*, 19). Like Pistorius's experience, it was a profound life-changing experience.

tongues, only some. His example is instructive. It is one thing to testify to and give thanks for an extraordinary experience of divine grace. It is quite another to turn such an experience into a normative one.

Discernment is needed. On the matter of prophetic speech, Paul counsels the Thessalonians to examine all things and to hold to the good and avoid the evil (1 Thess. 5:19–22). His open but discerning approach is worthy of emulation in today's church.

Conclusion

Angels are active creatures, whether they are the angels of heaven or the angels of earth. They worship their Creator, guard the sacred, bridge heaven and earth, guide God's people, communicate the Law, deliver and interpret messages, direct human agents, care for believers, reconnoiter the terrestrial sphere, administer judgment, and above all, serve the Lord Christ. They influence individuals and nations. There is much more to angelology that remains to be explored and to be made aware of and so it is to the infernal kingdom that we now turn our attention. A dark shadow has fallen over the good creation. There is a spoiler at work.

Excursus: Angelophany

In theological discourse, appearances of God in Scripture are termed theophanies (*theos*, "God"; and *phaneros*, "appearance"). At times such appearances are in human form. A case in point is that of Jacob wrestling with a mysterious "man" at the brook in Genesis 32. The narrative begins with a reference to a man (v. 24), but ends with Jacob's declaration (v. 30), "For I have seen God face to face, and yet my life has been delivered." Such theophanies can usefully be called "anthropomorphic theophanies."[95] God accommodates himself to the limitations of human understanding by such revelatory stooping. The most dramatic was at Mount Sinai, to Israel as a people and to Moses as an individual (cf. Ex. 20:18–21 and 34:5). The mysterious "commander of the army of the Lord" may be another example of an anthropomorphic theophany, or perhaps an angelophany (cf. Josh. 5:13–15 and Num. 22:23, 31).[96]

Sergius Bulgakov boldly states, "One of the most important features of the theophanies in the Old Testament is that God appears to people in

---

[95] I owe the term "anthropomorphic theophany" to James Barr. See my *The God Who Became Human: A Biblical Theology of Incarnation* (Downers Grove, IL: InterVarsity Press, 2013), 23.

[96] Carol Meyers, "Joshua," *JSB*, 472, points to Jewish tradition (*Aggadat Bereshit* 32.64), which identifies the commander of the army of the Lord with the archangel Michael. Joshua's obeisance before the figure can be read as the proper response either in the presence of deity (theophany) or to a superior (angelophany). For an impressive argument that it is a theophany, see Richard S. Hess, *Joshua*, TOTC (Downers Grove, IL: IVP Academic, 2008), 139.

the form of an angel, or, the other way around, that an angel represents the person of God."[97] Technically speaking, angelophanies are appearances of angels (*"angelos,* "angel"; and *phaneros,* "appearance"). This may not apply to every theophany in the OT, despite Bulgakov's claim that it does (e.g., Ex. 20:18–21).[98] He is certainly right, however, to draw attention to Stephen's speech before a hostile audience in the book of Acts. Stephen twice interprets the burning bush of Exodus 3 in angelophany terms (Acts 7:30–35):

> Now when forty years had passed, an angel appeared to him in the wilderness of Mount Sinai, in a flame of fire in a bush. When Moses saw it, he was amazed at the sight, and as he drew near to look, there came the voice of the Lord: "I am the God of your fathers, the God of Abraham and of Isaac and of Jacob." And Moses trembled and did not dare to look. Then the Lord said to him, "Take off the sandals from your feet, for the place where you are standing is holy ground. I have surely seen the affliction of my people who are in Egypt, and have heard their groaning, and I have come down to deliver them. And now come, I will send you to Egypt."
>
> This Moses, whom they rejected, saying, "Who made you a ruler and a judge?"—this man God sent as both ruler and redeemer by the hand of the angel who appeared to him in the bush.

Stephen's identifying the role of the angel in the burning bush event should not surprise. There is an analogy between appearances of God and appearances of angels, his servants. Angels, like their God, are spirits. On occasion, they may take on a sensible form. Moreover, angels are the messengers of the divine.

The account of the three visitors to Abraham in Genesis 18 reveals another anthropomorphic theophany (cf. Gen. 18:2, 10). The incident may also be described as an anthropomorphic *angelophany,* as the next chapter, set in Sodom, presents the remaining two visitors as angels in human form (Gen. 19:15).[99] This too is an example of celestial accommodation. However, there is another kind of angelophany, in which the presence of symbolism is patent. Some of these angelophanies are a mix of zoological and anthropomorphic features. The cherubim of Ezekiel 10:11–14 have a human face as well as that of a cherub, a lion, and an eagle: these may be usefully called "composite angelophanies." Finally, some angelophanies are visionary, as in Zechariah's first vision (Zech. 1:8–9). And so we have three categories to work with: anthropomorphic

---

[97] Bulgakov, *Jacob's Ladder,* 129.
[98] Bulgakov, *Jacob's Ladder,* 131. For Bulgakov there is only one theophany, i.e., the incarnation: "Christ coming into the world, His becoming human, was a single, authentic, perfect theophany which forever has abrogated all preliminary theophanies." Those preliminary theophanies, he argues, are in fact "theophanic angelophanies" (133).
[99] Heinz-Dieter Neef argues concerning angels, "The Bible is silent about their appearance." See his "The Angels of God in the Bible," in *Comfortable Words: Essays in Honor of Paul F. M. Zahl,* ed. John D. Koch Jr. and Todd H. W. Brewer (Eugene, OR: Pickwick, 2013), 78. This is hardly accurate.

angelophany, composite angelophany, and visionary angelophany. Ezekiel 10 presents a visionary composite angelophany.[100]

In some places in Scripture, the presence of an angel is affirmed but there is no suggestion of any perception of the celestial being on the part of people (e.g., Ex. 14:19). So there can be angelic presence without an angelophany. Again, a spirit need not take on a sensible form.

---

[100] For further definition of these categories, see the glossary.

FOUR

SATAN, THE MALEVOLENT SPOILER

Years ago I had occasion to speak to a youth audience about the Christian faith. Afterwards, a young woman came up to me, clearly keen to have a conversation. She had been an atheist. However, a friend had invited her to play around with a Ouija board as a laugh. Her experience on that night had so frightened her that she began to believe in the devil. Once she had made that move, logically the next one was to believe in God. Now that she had heard about Christ, she was ready to go even further and commit her life to him. Her story is evidence of the rediscovery of the occult and the resurgence of interest in things Satanic that took place in the 1960s and the "Age of Aquarius." In fact, the Church of Satan in the USA was officially founded in 1966 by Anton Szandor LaVey.[1]

Psychiatrist M. Scott Peck tells a similar story in the sense of his moving from skepticism to belief in the devil. Over the years, he had come to a belief in a benign divine being and in the reality of human evil. But as for the devil, he relates, "In common with 99 percent of psychiatrists and the majority of clergy [I assume he means mainline clergy], I did not think the devil existed." Being an open-minded scientist, Peck was prepared to change his mind, if he "could see one good old-fashioned case of possession." After many years, he claims that he saw that very thing: "I now know Satan is real, I have met it.[2]"

Up until the mid-eighteenth century, belief in God and belief in the devil were part and parcel of Western thought. The Enlightenment, with its appeal to reason among the literate elites, dismissed the idea of a personal devil. Since then the devil has been a marginal element in the mind-set of

---

[1] http://www.churchofsatan.com/, accessed 9/28/2015. It must be noted that the LaVey group is actually atheistic, and Satan for the group is merely a symbol. However, there are other sorts of Satanists. The other sort is on view when Nigel Wright, *The Satan Syndrome: Putting the Power of Darkness in Its Place* (Grand Rapids, MI: Zondervan, 1990), 11, usefully points out the difference between witchcraft and Satanism: "Whereas witchcraft is essentially pre-Christian in its understanding of the supernatural world, Satanism is explicitly anti-Christian. Satan is acknowledged as the ruler of the world and as Son of God. The church is hated and feared. . . . They are a growing force."

[2] M. Scott Peck, *People of the Lie: The Hope of Healing Human Evil* (New York: Simon & Schuster, 1983), 182–183. See also his more recent *Glimpses of the Devil: A Psychiatrist's Personal Account of Possession, Exorcism, and Redemption* (New York: Free Press, 2005).

the educated West. From the first half of the nineteenth century, Friedrich Schleiermacher provides evidence of the change in Zeitgeist after the Enlightenment in some church circles. In his *The Christian Faith*, which some judge the most important dogmatic work after Calvin and before Barth, he argues concerning the devil, "The idea of the Devil, as developed among us, is so unstable that we cannot expect anyone to be convinced of its truth."[3] However, the Western world is becoming a "reenchanted" place for some. For historian of ideas Philip C. Almond, the movie *The Exorcist*, released in 1973, signaled the beginning of the entertainment industry's reengagement with the demonic. And so he writes, "The Devil now has new domains and new borders."[4]

In biblical perspective, a rupture has taken place in the created order, and it is Satan who stands revealed in Scripture as the great spoiler. There is rebellion in the angelic order. As a consequence, the created order in which we now live is a dramatic one. That is to say, there is a great conflict underway between good and evil. In this chapter, the nature and names of Satan are discussed. Next, Satan's role in the great rupture is examined and the exact nature of his condemnation discussed. Hints in the OT as to Satan's sin will be brought into view as well as the much fuller NT revelation concerning him. The progressive nature of biblical revelation is to the fore in this chapter, and we shall see how the NT picture is so much more expansive than the OT one when it comes to delineating Satanic activity.[5] Even so, the wise words of T. Desmond Alexander should be heeded:

> We catch but occasional glimpses of this shadowy opponent. This should not surprise us. As divine revelation, the Bible exists to give us a deeper understanding of God. It is not designed to promote knowledge of the enemy, beyond what is necessary for comprehending the world in which we live and our own experience of it. Consequently, many questions remain unanswered when we collate what the Bible says about the devil or Satan.[6]

What it means for the NT to describe Satan as the god of this world will also be discussed, as we consider the sphere of Satanic influence.

---

[3] Friedrich Schleiermacher, *The Christian Faith*, ed. H. R. Macintosh and J. S. Stewart, various trans. (Edinburgh: T&T Clark, 1948), 161. The editors describe the work as follows: "In the opinion of many competent thinkers the *Christian Faith* of Schleiermacher is, with the exception of Calvin's *Institutes*, the most important work covering the whole field of doctrine to which Protestant theology can point" (v). They wrote this before Barth's great impact on Anglophone theology.
[4] Philip C. Almond, *The Devil: A New Biography* (Ithaca, NY: Cornell University Press, 2014), 221. For the substance of this paragraph, see xiii-xviii, 220–222.
[5] Walter C. Kaiser Jr., *Tough Questions about God and His Actions in the Old Testament* (Grand Rapids, MI: Kregel, 2015), 116, offers an interesting explanation for the paucity of explicit references to Satan in the OT. He argues, "In order to keep any incipient dualism or polytheism from rearing its head [in Israel], his name is held back in reserve in the Old Testament, but his work is often seen nevertheless."
[6] T. Desmond Alexander, *From Eden to the New Jerusalem: An Introduction to Biblical Theology* (Grand Rapids, MI: Kregel, 2008), 100. Kaiser, *Tough Questions*, 103, makes a similar point in a very helpful chapter on Satan when he writes, "Of all the major personalities in the Bible, Satan is perhaps the most enigmatic."

THE NATURE OF SATAN

In terms of nature, Satan is a creature.[7] Christopher J. H. Wright is accurate when he states, "He [Satan] is an active agent, with powers of intelligence, intentionality, and communication."[8] He is a spirit like other angels, albeit now a fallen angel.[9] The Council of Braga in AD 563 summed up earlier church teaching on Satan in canon 7 in these terms: "If anyone believes that the devil was not at first a (good) angel created by God, and that his nature was not the work of God, but (if he) claims that he emanated from chaos and darkness and had no author of his being, but that he is himself the principle and substance of evil, as stated by Manes and Priscillian, let him be anathema"[10] Moving to the present, *The Catechism of the Catholic Church* puts it pithily: "He is only a creature, powerful from the fact that he is pure spirit, but still a creature."[11] How such a celestial being could fall away from its Creator is not illumined by Scripture, although some see hints in Isaiah 14 and Ezekiel 28 (more anon).[12] One might say that, as an angel, Satan was created by God, but as a fallen angel, as Satan, he is self-made.[13] Was he an archangel now gone wrong? Was he one of the cherubim now gone wrong?[14] Given the biblical testimony, the idea that Satan was once an archangel makes some sense because he not only opposes God but also opposes the archangel Michael (Jude 9). But that would seem a little strange if, given the view of some, the highest angels (a cherubim), now fallen, can

---

[7] According to Bruce Baloian, "Satan" in Hebrew (LXX *diablos*) "basically means adversary or in a legal sense, accuser" ("Satan," in *The New International Dictionary of Old Testament Theology and Exegesis*, ed. Willem A. VanGemeren, CD-Rom version, 3 vols. [Grand Rapids, MI: Zondervan, 1997], 3:1231). Darren Oldridge (*The Devil: A Very Short Introduction* [Oxford: Oxford University Press, 2012], 21), goes too far when he argues that the angel of the Lord who blocked Balaam's path in Numbers 22:22 is "a Satan figure" because the angel obstructs Balaam's progress.

[8] Christopher J. H. Wright, *The God I Don't Understand: Reflections on Tough Questions of Faith* (Grand Rapids, MI: Zondervan, 2008), 37. Wright's treatment of the nature of Satan is puzzling in places. On the one hand he predicates personal attributes of Satan, but then on the other hand, he qualifies his account by describing Satan as "quasi-personal." It seems that for him only God and his image, that is to say humans, are persons (cf. 37 and 38).

[9] Tertullian, *Apology*, chapter 22: "Every spirit is possessed of wings. This is a common property of both angels and demons. So they are everywhere in a single moment; the whole world is as one place to them; all that is done over the whole extent of it, it is as easy for them to know as to report." Western art has taken its cue from statements such as this, and angels with wings have been in evidence ever since. For a fascinating suggestion involving an appeal to quantum physics as to how angels might move, see Peter Kreeft, *Angels and Demons: What Do We Really Know about Them?* (San Francisco: Ignatius, 1995), 69–70.

[10] http://www.vatican.va/roman_curia/congregations/cfaith/documents/rc_con_cfaith_doc_19750626_fede-cristiana-demonologia_en.html, accessed 3/20/2015. This canon is a clear rejection of metaphysical dualism. "Manes" is the "Mani" of Manichaeism, and Priscilian was Bishop of Avila (380–381), who seemed to have embraced similar ideas.

[11] *CCC* (Liguori, MO: Liguori, 1994), 99. Some readers may find it difficult that Catholic sources are quoted in places in the present work, but I follow the wisdom that says, "Have many teachers but only one Master."

[12] Philosophically some argue, for example Kreeft, that the misuse of free will (libertarian) is the reason for the angelic fall (*Angels and Demons*, 116).

[13] Some appeal to a free-will argument (libertarian) at this point to address the how question. See Kreeft, *Angels and Demons*, 116. The question of how it was possible for an unfallen angel to fall has attracted some philosophical interest in recent times. See Michael Barnwell, "*De Casu Diaboli*: An Examination of Faith and Reason via a Discussion of the Devil's Sin," *The Saint Anselm Journal* 6/2 (Spring 2009): 1–8; and William Wood, "Anselm of Canterbury on the Fall of the Devil: The Hard Problem, the Harder Problem, and a New Formal Model of the First Sin" (*Religious Studies* 52/2 [June 2016]: 223–245).

[14] This is C. Fred Dickason's view (*Angels: Elect and Evil*, rev. and expanded ed. [Chicago: Moody, 1995], 124), based on Ezekiel 28:14 and 16.

be countered and defeated by one of the lowest, the archangel Michael (see Rev. 12:7).[15] Interestingly, there are anthropomorphic theophanies, where God appears in human form (e.g., Genesis 18), and anthropomorphic angelophanies, where angels appear in human form (e.g., Genesis 19); however, there is no biblical account of an encounter with the devil, where the devil is described as appearing in human form. The famous encounter between Jesus and the devil in the wilderness offers no such description (cf. Matt. 4:1–11 and Luke 4:1–13). As an incorporeal spirit, however, he can enter into, in some sense, a human creature, as in the case of Judas (John 13:27), or even a serpent, as in the Genesis account (cf. Gen. 3:1 and 2 Cor. 11:3).

THE NAMES AND DESCRIPTORS OF THE DEVIL

Thus far we have employed some of the better-known names for the Great Spoiler, such as "Satan" and the "devil." There is in fact a plethora of names and descriptors predicated of this chief of evil spirits in the canonical Scriptures. Millard J. Erickson provides a handy summary of most of them. He writes,

> Several other terms are used of him less frequently: tempter (Matt. 4:3; 1 Thess. 3:5), Beelzebul (Matt. 12:24, 27; Mark 3:22; Luke 11:15, 19), enemy (Matt. 13:39), evil one (Matt. 13:19, 38; 1 John 2:13; 3:12; 5:18), Belial (2 Cor. 6:15); adversary (1 Peter 5:8), deceiver (Rev. 12:9), great dragon (Rev. 12:3), father of lies (John 8:44), murderer (John 8:44), sinner (1 John 3:8).[16]

J. I. Packer adds "Apollyon" (Rev. 9:11), meaning destroyer.[17] However, Charles H. H. Scobie takes a different view.[18] Apollyon is an evil angel, but there is no suggestion in Revelation 9:1–11 that this figure is the devil. Not much hangs on this difference in theological opinion.

THE MYSTERY OF INIQUITY

That evils exist in our world is an inescapable fact. The twenty-four-hour news cycle brings reports of evils from around the globe into our homes and onto our phones. From a Christian perspective, humanity is living in a new normal because of a cataclysmic event that lies in the past. That

---

[15] Kreeft, *Angels and Demons*, describes somewhat loosely Satan as "top guy next to God" (*Angels and Demons*, 118). How he knows this is not clear. What is clear is that Satan and his horde can be defeated by an archangel and his angelic forces. Satan is no rival, then, to Almighty God.

[16] Millard J. Erickson, *Christian Theology*, 3rd ed. (Grand Rapids, MI: Baker, 2013), 417.

[17] J. I. Packer, *Concise Theology: A Guide to Historic Christian Beliefs* (Wheaton, IL: Tyndale, 1993), 69. Others distinguish Apollyon from Satan and argue that Apollyon is a great demon ruler but an underling of Satan. See Merrill F. Unger, *Biblical Demonology: A Study of Spiritual Forces Today* (Grand Rapids, MI: Kregel, 1994), 73–74, for this view.

[18] Charles H. H. Scobie, *The Ways of Our God: An Approach to Biblical Theology* (Grand Rapids, MI, and Cambridge: Eerdmans, 2003), 254.

event has much to do with Satan, as we shall see as we now consider the "great rupture."

The Fall

From a literary perspective, the canon of Scripture presents a divine comedy. Leland Ryken makes the point well:

> It is a commonplace of literary criticism that comedy rather than tragedy is the dominant narrative form of the Bible and the Christian gospel. The overall shape of the biblical story is that of a U-shaped comedy plot. The story begins with the creation of a perfect world. It descends into the tragedy of fallen human history. It ends with a new world of total happiness and victory over evil.[19]

In the plotline of the biblical narrative, from Genesis to Revelation we observe the U-shaped structure: the creational harmony of Genesis 1–2 (the unity of heaven and earth) gives way to the disharmony of Genesis 3—the rupture of harmony—caused by the fall (the disunity of heaven and earth) through to Revelation 20, with creational harmony restored with Christ as the key character as seen in Revelation 21–22. The garden of God has become the city of God, set within a new heavens and a new earth.

In Genesis 3:1 and without explanation, the serpent enters the U-shaped narrative curve.[20] He comes armed with questions about the Creator: "Now the serpent was more crafty than any other beast of the field that the Lord God had made." T. Desmond Alexander notes the significance of the phrase "beast of the field":

> The serpent is elevated above every other "beast of the field," that is, the wild animals. This comment is likely to have had a negative connotation in the minds of the first readers or listeners to this story. Wild animals presented a threat to human beings. Ezekiel 34:8 describes, for example, how a flock of sheep without a shepherd could become "meat to every beast of the field." For this reason, the introduction of the serpent as the craftiest of the wild animals has an ominous ring to it.[21]

[19] Leland Ryken, *A Complete Handbook of Literary Forms in the Bible* (Wheaton, IL: Crossway, 2014), 46–47. Ryken's suggestion that the canon of Scripture be viewed in literary terms as a comedy should be treated as heuristic reading strategy. As such, the key question is whether such a perspective aids the reading of Scripture or impedes it. In my view it aids it.
[20] Stephen H. Webb, *The Dome of Eden: A New Solution to the Problem of Creation and Evolution* (Eugene, OR: Cascade, 2010), 147–148, offers an explanation for the lack of detail in the text of Genesis 3 about the serpent when he writes, "Throwing Satan into the beginning of the creation narrative [Genesis 1–2, presumably] would have given him a starring role, and given Satan's association with pride, it would have fallen into Satan's plan, not God's. Genesis was right to be discrete [*sic*] about Satan."
[21] T. Desmond Alexander, *From Eden to the New Jerusalem*, 102–103. Walter C. Kaiser Jr., *The Promise-Plan of God: A Biblical Theology of the Old and New Testaments* (Grand Rapids, MI: Zondervan, 2008), 42, argues that "Satan's form and shape are no more implied by his appellation 'the serpent' than by his name 'dragon.' Nor is the curse on him determinative for setting his morphology." Prima facie, the serpent is compared to other beasts

The serpent said to the woman, "Did God actually say, 'You shall not eat of any tree in the garden'?"[22] Dietrich Bonhoeffer (1906–1945) correctly points out that "The serpent's question was a thoroughly religious one. But with the first religious question in the world evil has come upon the scene. . . . This is the question that appears innocuous but through it evil wins power in us, through it we become disobedient to God."[23]

After the harmony of Genesis 1–2 has been narrated, we find a creature that becomes the catalyst for what Augustine termed the fall and for what more recently Jacques Ellul described as the Rupture.[24] Patently, the catastrophe that follows has its source neither in God nor in humankind. For our purposes, the terms of both Augustine ("fall") and Ellul ("rupture") capture a real aspect of the Genesis 3 story. The former term suggests that humanity has fallen away from its uprightness before God (traditionally understood as original righteousness). The latter accents the breaking of a network of relationships. Some argue that the Genesis 3 account is not referring to a space-time fall or rupture but that the ancient writer used a literary device for speaking of the condition of humankind as alienated from God under the guise of the story of one man and one woman. OT scholar M. D. Guinan, for example, takes this approach: "The man and woman of Genesis 2–3, as well as other characters of the primal stories, are intended to represent an Everyman and Everywoman."[25] There is a logical difficulty with this line of argument. If the Adam and Eve story is true of every one of us, then it was true of the very first of us, so we are back to some notion of a primal space-time fall.

I find Ellul's idea of the great rupture particularly illuminating. The relationship with God is ruptured. Fear and flight replace intimacy and fellowship (Gen. 3:8–10). The banishment from the garden dramatically shows the rupture, and the presence of the cherubim who bar reentry to Eden underline the seriousness of what had taken place (vv. 23–24). Death has come to the paradise of God.[26] Death in Scripture is the severing of relationship. Indeed, one of the vivid

---

of the field, which counts against Kaiser's argument. However, Kaiser argues that the translation could run, "any of the beasts of the field," which allows for his interpretation. This is possible. The ESV, NIV, NRSV, and *JSB* translators render the Hebrew (*mikkōl*, "than any") in such a way as to make a comparison between the serpent and other beasts of the field. As for the curse, which states, "on your belly you shall go," Kaiser argues that this is the language of humiliating a fallen opponent and need not imply a change in morphology.

[22] It is interesting to note that in Scripture there are only two accounts of talking animals. Both are in the OT. In Numbers 22 a donkey speaks to Balaam and in Genesis 3 the serpent speaks to Eve. In both stories angels are involved. In Numbers 22 it is the angel of the Lord behind the speech, and in Genesis 3 it is the fallen angel, Satan. However, if Kaiser is right about the serpent in Genesis 3 (see previous note), there is only one such account.

[23] Dietrich Bonhoeffer, *Creation and Fall, and Temptation: Two Biblical Studies*, trans. John C. Fletcher (New York: Simon & Schuster, 1997), 73.

[24] Augustine, *The City of God*, abridged and trans. G. G. Walsh, D. B. Zema, G. Monahan, and D. J. Honan (Garden City, NY: Image, 1958), 269. See also Jacques Ellul, *The Humiliation of the Word* (Grand Rapids, MI: Eerdmans, 1985), chapter 7. In literary terms, Satan is the great antagonist, who opposes God the great protagonist, who is the central character in the narrative: see Ryken, *Complete Handbook*, 23, for these categories.

[25] M. D. Guinan, "Adam, Eve, and Original Sin," http://www.americancatholic.org/Newsletter/CU/ac0507.asp, accessed 6/10/2008.

[26] Is it this fact that informs Jesus's statement in John 8:44 about the devil: "He was a murderer from the beginning"?

OT ways of capturing the idea with regard to physical life is that of being cut off from the people (*kāraṯ*; e.g., Ex. 31:14) for a capital sin.[27] Man and woman have died in this sense, just as the divine warning had said. There is now a self-consciousness that betrays a sense of shame (cf. Gen. 3:7 and 2:25). The relationship between male and female becomes difficult, as does the relationship to the environment. The man shifts blame to the woman, and to God for giving him such a companion (3:12). God's good creation has been spoiled. Satan in serpent guise comes before the reader as the great disuniter. Frank Thielman rightly argues, "from the time of the woman's encounter with the deceitful serpent in the garden, Satan has been on a rampage against God's people."[28]

The Primal Temptation

The nature of the primal sin of humankind has been variously explained. Henri Blocher provides a formidable list of suggestions, including pride, sensuousness, selfishness, unbelief, greed, violence, and inertia.[29] Each item on the list suggests a possible temptation: temptation to pride, temptation to sensuousness, temptation to selfishness, etc. In the Genesis narrative as it stands, pride does not seem to be the sin of Adam, let alone Eve. The serpent misrepresents God's word and Eve is deceived. The serpent draws Eve's attention to the tree of the knowledge of good and evil. Its fruit seems so inviting, so good to eat. Moreover, it delights the eyes, and it can make one wise (Gen. 3:6). The tree of the knowledge of good and evil seems to address many human needs: the need for food, the need to experience beauty, and the need for knowledge (cf. Gen. 3:6 and 2 Cor. 11:3). Adam listened to his wife and followed her example (cf. Gen. 3:17). Both Adam and Eve disobeyed God's command. Think of the serpent's opening gambit posed in question form: "Did God actually say, 'You shall not eat of any tree in the garden'?" (Gen. 3:1). Informing the disobedience was not so much pride as it was unbelief in God's word of command and in God's goodness. The serpent targeted both the command and character of God (vv. 1–5). As D. B. Knox argues, "The problem Adam faced was, could God be trusted?"[30] The Genesis 3 narrative reveals the serpent to be the enemy of the word of God, a slanderer against the good character of God by insinuation, and a deceiver of the innocent.[31]

---

[27] The idea of separation also applies to unbelievers in the spiritual realm (e.g., Matt. 25:41–46 and 2 Thess. 1:9). For believers, however, separation from the body does not mean a break in relationship with the Lord (e.g., Phil. 1:23–24).
[28] Frank Thielman, *Theology of the New Testament: A Canonical and Synthetic Approach* (Grand Rapids, MI: Zondervan, 2005), 634.
[29] H. A. G. Blocher, "Sin," in *New Dictionary of Biblical Theology* (Downers Grove, IL: IVP Academic, 2000), 783.
[30] D. B. Knox. *Justification by Faith* (London: Church Book Room, 1959), 9. Knox is not alone in singling out unbelief and its pivotal role in the Genesis 3 story. Luther, Calvin, and John Wesley for that matter each regarded unbelief, rather than pride, as the great sin in the garden. See Kenneth J. Collins, *John Wesley: A Theological Journey* (Nashville: Abingdon, 2003), 250–251. For a fuller account of these matters see my *God the Peacemaker: How Atonement Brings Shalom* (Downers Grove, IL: InterVarsity Press, 2009), 58–59. I draw from this monograph at a number of points.
[31] See Allen P. Ross, *Creation and Blessing: A Guide to the Study and Exposition of Genesis* (Grand Rapids, MI: Baker Academic, 1999), 130–138, for the serpent's attacks on the word of God and the character of God. The de-

The apostle Paul is the great interpreter of Genesis 3. Importantly for our purposes, when Paul addresses the sin of Adam in Romans 5, he writes of Adam's "breaking a command" (*parabaseōs*, v. 14 NIV), and of Adam's "disobedience" (*parakoēs*, v. 19). The great contrast that Paul draws out between Adam and Christ is not between pride (Adam) and humility (Christ) but the disobedience of Adam as opposed to the obedience of Christ (*parakoēs* versus *hypakoēs*, Rom. 5:19). Jesus lived by every word that proceeds out of the mouth of God (Matt. 4:4; cf. Deut. 8:3). Adam didn't.

The tempter targets the word of God. Gordon J. Wenham offers this comment on the Genesis account: "Genesis 2–3 may also be read as a paradigm of every sin: it describes what happens every time someone disobeys God. The essence of sin is rejecting God's commands, preferring human wisdom [or devilish wisdom] to his."[32] Paul Copan adds to the picture:

> In their primal sin, humans foolishly abused their freedom, resorting to *stealing* what wasn't theirs. Though unaware of the profound ramifications of their choice, they should have trusted God's reliable character instead of an imposter. The consequences were momentous. God's co-ruling, worshiping image-bearers, despite their dignity, entered into exile—alienation—from their *God and Maker*.[33]

We all now live in a new normal, which actually in biblical terms is a new abnormal. Normalization will require nothing less than a reclaimed creation.

Satan and the Identity of the Serpent

The serpent in the ancient Near East could stand as a symbol suggesting either wisdom or death. The serpent of Genesis 3 certainly brings death. The fittingness of the serpent figure in the narrative is well captured by Wenham:

> Within the world of OT animal symbolism a snake is an obvious candidate for an anti-God symbol, notwithstanding its creation by God. In one way, a dead animal, which is even more unclean than any living creature, would be a better anti-God symbol, yet it would be quite absurd to have a corpse talk. So for any Israelite familiar with the symbolic values of different animals, a creature more likely than a serpent to lead man away from his creator could not be imagined.[34]

---

ception of Eve is interesting. Given the narrative, she was not present when the command was given to Adam not to eat. Prima facie, she depended on Adam's instruction to know what the command was. When she replies to the serpent, she mentions not touching the tree, which was not part of the command. She seems to have an imprecise knowledge of the divine will, which may have given the serpent its opening (cf. Gen. 2:16–17 and 3:2–3). Adam was with her but was apparently silent (Gen. 3:6).

[32] Gordon J. Wenham, "Genesis," in *ECB*, ed. James D. G. Dunn and John W. Rogerson (Grand Rapids, MI, and Cambridge: Eerdmans, 2003), 41. Of course, logically speaking if this is paradigmatic of all, it was true of the first, Adam and Eve.

[33] Paul Copan, *Loving Wisdom: Christian Philosophy of Religion* (St. Louis: Chalice, 2007), 124, emphasis original.

[34] Gordon J. Wenham, *Genesis 1–15*, WBC (Dallas: Word, 2002), 73.

As a consequence of the temptation that Adam and Eve embraced, they find themselves cut off from the divine presence. Such cutting off, such severing of relationship, is the essence of death in biblical perspective. In fact, as we have seen, one of the vivid OT ways of capturing the idea is that of being cut off from the people (*kārat*; e.g., Ex. 31:14). As for wisdom, this crafty, wild reptile is anti-wisdom in the Genesis setting, leading Adam and Eve into deadly foolishness.[35]

The serpent of Genesis 3 is not identified in that context as Satan in serpent guise or as Satan using a serpent as a vehicle for addressing the primal pair, although this is a common view, as Sydney H. T. Page points out.[36] However, later biblical texts do make that identification either by contextual implication or quite explicitly. An example of the former is found in Paul's second letter to the Corinthians.[37] The context is Paul's warning to his readers about false teachers (2 Cor. 11:1–3):

> I wish you would bear with me in a little foolishness. Do bear with me! For I feel a divine jealousy for you, since I betrothed you to one husband, to present you as a pure virgin to Christ. But I am afraid that as the serpent deceived Eve by his cunning, your thoughts will be led astray from a sincere and pure devotion to Christ.[38]

Later in the same context, with deception on view, Paul maintains (vv. 13–14), "For such men are false apostles, deceitful workmen, disguising themselves as apostles of Christ. And no wonder, for even Satan disguises himself as an angel of light." Again Paul in 1 Timothy 2:12–14 makes use of the Genesis 3 story to make a point about male and female relations in the church at Ephesus: "I do not permit a woman to teach or to exercise authority over a man; rather, she is to remain quiet. For Adam was formed first, then Eve; and Adam was not deceived, but the woman was deceived and became a transgressor."[39] An explicit identification of Satan with a serpent is found in Revelation 20:1–2: "Then I saw an angel coming down from heaven, holding in his hand the key to the bottomless pit and a great chain. And he seized the dragon, that ancient serpent, who is the devil and Satan, and bound him for a thousand years . . ."

---

[35] J. Oliver Buswell Jr., "The Origin and Nature of Sin," in *Basic Christian Doctrines*, ed. Carl F. H. Henry (New York: Holt, Reinhart, & Winston, 1961), 105, rejects the notion that any kind of actual biological serpent is on view in Genesis 3. Rather he argues that "the Serpent" (LXX *ho ophis*) is a proper name for Satan, who is "evil personal intelligence." What then does Buswell do with Genesis 3:14 and its reference to the serpent eating dirt? He argues that this is an ancient metaphor for humiliating an enemy and is not to be taken literally. He offers no evidence to support this contention, however,

[36] Sydney H. T. Page, "Satan, Sin, and Evil," in *Fallen: A Theology of Sin*, ed. Christopher W. Morgan and Robert A. Peterson (Wheaton, IL: Crossway, 2013), 221. In my view, since Satan is a spirit creature, the view that Satan used a real serpent as his tool makes the better sense. Genesis 3:1 makes it clear that the serpent was a "beast of the field."

[37] Puzzlingly, Philip Almond (*Devil*, 34) claims that Justin Martyr (c. 100–c. 165) was the first to identify the serpent with Satan.

[38] Curiously, the very fine *Commentary on the New Testament Use of the Old Testament* (ed. G. K. Beale and D. A. Carson [Grand Rapids, MI: Baker Academic, 2007]) provides no commentary on this passage.

[39] For a judicious discussion of the issues attending this passage, see Derek Tidball and Dianne Tidball, *The Message of Women: Creation, Grace, and Gender* (Downers Grove, IL: InterVarsity Press, 2012), 249–268.

Charles H. H. Scobie rightly comments with regard to the NT understanding of the OT, "Retroactively it is recognized that Satan has been at work in the world since the beginning, being identified with the Serpent of Gen 3 (cf. 2 Cor 11:3) as well as the dragon/sea monster symbol of the powers of evil."[40]

The identification of the serpent of Genesis 3 with Satan raises key hermeneutical questions that must be addressed. Without a robust understanding of divine inspiration and the role of the Holy Spirit in Scripture production, these later NT identifications seem facile. After all, the Genesis 3 text makes no such identification, as we have already observed. However, armed with such a robust understanding, literary scholar Leland Ryken's observation concerning Scripture makes great sense. He writes,

> Although biblical literature is a collection of diverse works, it must also be regarded as possessing a high degree of unity. There is unity of national authorship [I would prefer to say "ethnic authorship"], with only two books in the whole Bible (Luke and Acts) not having been written by Jews. There is unity of subject matter, consisting most broadly of God's ways with people and the relationship of people to God and fellow humans. There is a unity of world view and general theological outlook from book to book. There is unity of purpose underlying all biblical literature—the purpose of revealing God to people so that they might know how to order their lives. There is, finally, a unity of literary texture based on allusion. Various biblical writers allude to earlier works in the same canon, or to the same historical events, or to the same religious beliefs and experiences, or to the same cultural context. The resulting unity of reference is immediately evident when one consults a modern Bible containing cross references in the marginal notes. *No other anthology of literature possesses the unified texture of allusions that biblical literature displays.*[41]

I believe that Ryken's observation is correct and makes most sense *ex hypothesi* on the basis of the kind of inspiration that Paul writes about in 2 Timothy 3:14–17, where he describes Scripture as "God-breathed" (*theopneustos*). Scripture has human authorship patently, but divine authorship as well, working concursively.[42] Kevin J. Vanhoozer rightly comments, "Canonization, we might say, is 'the providence of God put into writing.'"[43]

Regarding the reading of the OT in the light of the fuller NT revelation, Ellen F. Davis and Richard B. Hays offer useful insights when they argue,

---

[40] Scobie, *Ways of Our God*, 252.

[41] Leland Ryken, *The Literature of the Bible* (Grand Rapids, MI: Zondervan, 1980), 15–16, emphasis mine.

[42] The term "concursus" belongs in the doctrine of providence along with *conservatio* ("preservation") and *gubernatio* ("government"). The doctrine of Scripture, I would argue, may usefully be located within the doctrine of special providence. It is a crucial element in God's provision for his people, their preservation and government. To use the suitcase analogy (see chapter 2), the label on the doctrine suitcase is Special Providence and in it are *conservatio, gubernatio,* and *concursus.*

[43] Kevin J. Vanhoozer, *The Drama of Doctrine: A Canonical Linguistic Approach to Christian Theology* (Louisville: Westminster John Knox, 2005), 230.

Against the increasingly common contention that Christians should interpret "the Hebrew Bible" only in categories that were historically available to
Israel at the time of the composition of the biblical writings, we affirm that
a respectful rereading of the Old Testament in light of the New discloses
figurations of the truth about the one God who acts and speaks in both [and
I would add, "discloses figurations of the truth of the enemy of God who acts
and speaks in both"], figurations whose full dimension can be grasped only
in light of the cross and resurrection.[44]

They go on to argue, "The authors and editors of the canonical texts repeat-
edly gave new contexts and sense to earlier traditions, thereby initiating the
process of discerning multiple senses within the text."[45] A statement like this,
for some evangelicals, might seem like the proverbial nose of wax that could be
bent irresponsibly into any shape..[46] Perhaps a better way to describe the later
readings of the OT writings by NT authors is that the latter draw out a fuller
significance from an OT text than an OT-era reader might have seen.

The Condemnation of the Devil

There is a luminous statement in Paul's first letter to Timothy. He is laying out
the defining characteristics of an overseer in the church and issuing a warning
in so doing. He writes in 1 Timothy 3:6, "He [the overseer] must not be a recent
convert, or he may become puffed up with conceit [typhōtheis; "puffed up,"
"beclouded with," with the idea of conceit or pride understood] and fall into the
condemnation [krima, "judgment"] of the devil."[47] His point is to warn against
appointing a recent convert [neophytos] to an oversight role. The idea that the
temptation to pride would be too strong for a new convert seems to fit the context. Donald Guthrie comments, "Pride gives a false sense of altitude, making

---

[44] Ellen F. Davis and Richard B. Hays, eds., The Art of Reading Scripture (Grand Rapids, MI: Eerdmans, 2003), 2.
[45] Davis and Hays, Art of Reading Scripture, 3. In a more recent work, Hays describes this mode of reading as "figural reading" (Reading Backwards: Figural Christology and the Fourfold Gospel Witness [Waco, TX: Baylor University Press, 2014], 93). "The hermeneutical key to this intertextual dialectic is the practice of figural reading: the discernment of unexpected patterns of correspondence between earlier and later events or persons within a continuous temporal stream." Hays has Christ in mind, but his stimulating approach could be usefully applied to the correspondence between the serpent (earlier) and Satan (later).
[46] For example, Walter C. Kaiser Jr., "Single Meaning, Unified Referents: Accurate and Authoritative Citations of the Old Testament by the New Testament," in Three Views on the New Testament Use of the Old Testament, ed. Stanley N. Gundry, Kenneth Berding, and Jonathan Lunde (Grand Rapids, MI: Zondervan, 2008), 45–89. A classic and much earlier affirmation of the single meaning notion—albeit from a liberal theological perspective—is found in Benjamin Jowett (1817–1893). He wrote, "Scripture has one meaning—the meaning which it had to the mind of the Prophet or Evangelist who first uttered or wrote, to the hearers or readers who first received it" (quoted by David C. Steinmetz in his essay, "Uncovering a Second Narrative: Detective Fiction and the Construction of Histori-cal Method," in Art of Reading Scripture, 61–62). Steinmetz offers an intriguing analogy between detective novels and Scripture. In both, the sprawling narrative comes together at the end when a character (the lead detective, for example, or an apostle, respectively) is able to give a second narrative that solves the mystery. This character can see significance in the story that participants at earlier stages could not see. Steinmetz rejects the single meaning position.
[47] William Shakespeare (d. 1616) had his own idea: "I charge thee, fling away ambition: By that sin fell the angels" (King Henry VIII, act 3, scene 2). Shakespeare's contemporary Christopher Marlowe (d. 1593), in his play Doctor Faustus, makes both pride and insolence the cause of Lucifer's fall from heaven (Doctor Faustus [Leipzig: Bernard Tauchnitz, 1917], 34). See also Dorothy L. Sayers, "The Faust Legend and the Idea of the Devil" (The Whimsical Christian: Eighteen Essays [Boston: G. K. Hall, 1979], 491–524).

the subsequent *fall* all the greater."[48] The devil is exhibit A. Before returning to this NT hint, there are some key passages in the OT that are cited by some as throwing light on the origins of this angel's fall that need exploration.

The Old Testament Light on Satan: Isaiah 14:3–23 and Ezekiel 28:2–19

The key passages are found in two of the major prophets of Judah. Both passages are well described by Walter C. Kaiser Jr. as, "loaded with sarcasm and exaggerated metaphor."[49] The first is Isaiah 14:3–23, which is a taunt song directed against the king of Babylon but which includes words in verses 12–14 that seem too extravagant for just a human figure:

> How you are fallen from heaven,
>   O Day Star, son of Dawn!
> How you are cut down to the ground,
>   you who laid the nations low![50]
> You said in your heart,
>   "I will ascend to heaven;
> above the stars of God
>   I will set my throne on high;
> I will sit on the mount of assembly
>   in the far reaches of the north;
> I will ascend above the heights of the clouds;
>   I will make myself like the Most High."

The pride of self-will on view is patent. In the ESV translation the phrase "I will" occurs over and over. The egocentricity is staggering in its baldness. The fall is spectacular (v. 15): "But you are brought down to Sheol, to the far reaches of the pit." Can these descriptors apply only to an earthly ruler? Is this simply ancient Near Eastern hyperbolic speech?

The second passage is in Ezekiel 28. It too uses exaggerated language. In the first part of the chapter God makes it clear that, although the ruler of Tyre sees himself as a god, in fact he is a mere man (vv. 2 and 9). Then a lament follows (vv. 12–16) with this stunning depiction:

> You were the signet of perfection,
>   full of wisdom and perfect in beauty.
> You were in Eden, the garden of God;
>   every precious stone was your covering,

---

[48] Donald Guthrie, *The Pastoral Epistles*, TNTC (Downers Grove, IL: IVP Academic, 1990), 97, emphasis original.
[49] Kaiser, *Tough Questions*, 113.
[50] The King James Version (1611) renders this verse, "How art thou fallen from heaven, O Lucifer, son of the morning! how art thou cut down to the ground, which didst weaken the nations!" From this translation, wedded with the view that Satan is the intended referent, some arrive at the claim that Lucifer is one of the names of the devil. The first person in the early church period to make that identification was Origen, in his *On First Principles*, 1.5.5. Origen colorfully also describes Satan as an "apostate dragon."

sardius, topaz, and diamond,
  beryl, onyx, and jasper,
sapphire, emerald, and carbuncle;
  and crafted in gold were your settings
  and your engravings.
On the day that you were created
  they were prepared.
You were an anointed guardian cherub.
  I placed you; you were on the holy mountain of God;
  in the midst of the stones of fire you walked.
You were blameless in your ways
  from the day you were created,
  till unrighteousness was found in you.
In the abundance of your trade
  you were filled with violence in your midst, and you sinned;
so I cast you as a profane thing from the mountain of God,
  and I destroyed you, O guardian cherub,
  from the midst of the stones of fire.

On the surface of it, how could the king of Tyre have been in the paradise garden of God? How can this king be described as a cherub (vv. 14 and 16)?

C. Fred Dickason is one theologian who sees in Isaiah 14 and Ezekiel 28 a double reference.[51] His argument, based on his reading of Ezekiel 28, is as follows.[52] In his view the unusually exalted language cannot be simply explained away in terms of Canaanite Ugaritic mythology. Two persons are addressed in the passage. The first is a human leader (vv. 1–10); the second is the superhuman leader, Satan, standing behind the earthly one (vv. 11–19). The first leader is described as a man (vv. 2 and 9); the second is characterized as a "cherub" (vv. 14 and 16). Superlatives are used of the second figure such as "full of wisdom," "perfect in beauty," and "blameless." He concludes, "For these reasons we take Ezekiel 28:12–19 to refer to Satan, not to a human."[53] In arguing this, Dickason stands in a long line of interpreters. Origen (185–254) argued, "We find in the prophet Ezekiel two prophecies written to the king of Tyre. . . . The second is clearly of such a kind that it cannot be at all understood about a man."[54] As for Isaiah 14, which Dickason treats next, he sees a parallel with Ezekiel 28: first the human leader is addressed, then the superhuman one standing as the power behind him. The depiction of the earthly king has all the hallmarks of the antichrist to come, he argues, especially the five "I will" statements in verses 13–14, which are true of Satan as well. Dickason is persuaded

[51] See Dickason, *Angels: Elect and Evil*. Not all agree with this line of interpretation. For example, Sydney H. T. Paige sees this traditional interpretation as "unlikely" (*Powers of Evil: A Biblical Study of Satan and Demons* [Grand Rapids, MI: Baker, 1995], 37–42). I find Paige unconvincing.
[52] For the details of Dickason's argument, which I have condensed, see *Angels: Elect and Evil*, 135–145.
[53] Dickason, *Angels: Elect and Evil*, 136.
[54] Quoted in *DECB*, ed. David W. Bercot (Peabody, MA: Hendrickson, 1998), 593.

on the basis of Ezekiel 28 that Satan is a rebellious cherub. If Dickason is correct, then how ironic that a cherub, whose role is to guard the interests of God, began to attack those very interests.

Michael Green, however, translates the key verses of Ezekiel 28—verses 14 and 16—differently than Dickason. In verse 14 he translates the key sentence, "With an anointed guardian cherub I placed you," and in verse 16, "And the guardian cherub drove you out." This translation distinguishes the King of Tyre from the cherub.[55] The New Revised Standard Version reads similarly. Green gives no explanation, and his work does not state which translation he used or whether he translated it himself, which is quite possible. Supporting Green's translation is the LXX, which translates Ezekiel 28:14 "with the cherub" (*meta tou cheroub*).[56] Like Dickason, Green believes, following D. M. Lloyd-Jones, that the depiction of the human ruler represents "a foreshadowing of something bigger which is to come."[57] He does not give any details beyond this, though. Charles C. Ryrie offers a speculative suggestion that goes further than that of Lloyd-Jones: the King of Tyre was actually indwelt by Satan. He argues, "The king of Tyre was one whom he [Satan] indwelt in the past, as Antichrist will be the final one he [Satan] will indwell in the future."[58] However, he goes on to qualify the boldness of his statement: "And in describing this king, Ezekiel also gives us glimpses of the superhuman creature, Satan, who was using, if not indwelling, him."[59]

These Old Treatment passages are intriguing. Clearly they are referring to a foreign ruler and doing so in an extravagant way. The extravagance is so suggestive that these descriptors are not exhausted by reference to the king of Babylon (Isaiah 14) or the king of Tyre (Ezekiel 28). Even if the descriptors do not definitively prove the contention that there is a double reference here—one human and one suprahuman—such a contention is consistent with these passages, although not demanded by them in any undeniable way. Hence, there is debate. Even so, this is the sort of sin leading to a great fall that could indeed have been the case with Satan.

I am greatly attracted to Allen P. Ross's suggestion that biblical stories can

[55] As does Leslie C. Allen's translation of Ezekiel 28:14: "14*With a winged (?) guardian cherub I set you*" (Allen, *Ezekiel 20–48*, WBC (Dallas: Word, 1998), 89.

[56] For an argument for the Green and NRSV translation, see Leslie C. Allen, *Ezekiel 20–48*, WBC (Dallas: Word, 1998), 94. It must be noted that Allen rejects any suggestion of a double reference: "The application of vv 11–19 to Satan by third- and fourth-century AD Church Fathers, Tertullian, Origen, John Cassian, Cyril of Jerusalem and Jerome, and thence in some modern popular conservative expositions, is based on MT's equation of the king and cherub and on comparison with Isa 14:12–15. It is a case of exegeting an element of Christian belief by means of Scripture and so endeavoring to provide it with extra biblical warrant and to fit the passage into the framework of the Christian faith. However, it is guilty of detaching the passage from its literary setting (Ellison 108–9)." I am not convinced by Allen.

[57] Michael Green, *I Believe in Satan's Downfall* (London: Hodder & Stoughton, 1999), 40 (footnote indicated by an asterisk).

[58] Charles C. Ryrie, *Basic Theology: A Popular Systematic Guide to Understanding Biblical Truth* (Colorado Springs: ChariotVictor, 1997), 141.

[59] Ryrie, *Basic Theology*, 142.

work at two levels: the literal and the archetypal.[60] For example, Genesis 3 is the *literal* story of sin's entry into the world and the *archetypal* story of the process of temptation. Applying this approach to the passages in Isaiah and Ezekiel, I would argue that, at a literal level, they are about the two kings (of Babylon and of Tyre, respectively), but at the archetypal level they reveal the sort of arrogant sin that is true of Satan.[61]

Christopher J. H. Wright offers a nuanced reading worth noting. He maintains that it is:

> . . . a dubious exercise to try to build detailed doctrinal statements about the devil or the "underworld" upon them. Nevertheless, we may discern the fingerprints of Satan in what is described in these poems [Isaiah 14:4–21 and Ezekiel 28:1–17], since it is clear that these arrogant human beings [the kings of Babylon and Tyre, respectively] were brought low because of their blasphemous pride and boasting against God. Indeed, they are portrayed as usurping God's throne. In the poem, such claims are probably metaphorical for the human being's *hybris*, but they have a spiritual counterpart that is recognizably satanic.[62]

Wright has scriptural support for the "spiritual counterpart" contention. Returning to the 1 Timothy 3:6 text, it shows that pride (Lat., *superbia*)—the sort of pride seen in Isaiah 14 and Ezekiel 28—and the devil go together, as Augustine (354–430) believed, as did Origen (c. 185–c. 254), Ambrose (c. 333–397), Chrysostom (c. 347–407), and Jerome (347–419). In fact, that pride was the devil's sin was the majority report in the early church period.[63] I believe these fathers got it right.

To my mind, the presence of such exaggerated language in Isaiah 14 and Ezekiel 28, the NT identification of pride as the devil's sin, with the support of the majority of early church fathers, combine to strengthen the contention that Isaiah 14 and Ezekiel 28 contain a double reference: earthly rulers and the devilish usurper.

Other possibilities have been offered by way of explanation for the devil's fall. The apocryphal book *Wisdom of Solomon*, which belongs to the third century before Christ, posits envy as the cause of the devil's downfall (Wisd. 2:23–24 NRSV): "for God created us for incorruption, and made us in the

---

[60] Ross, *Creation and Blessing*, 130. It is important to note that "literal" is not to be confused with "literalistic." The literal recognizes differences in genre. The literalistic does not. I met a man years ago who argued that unless the parable of the good Samaritan (Luke 10:25–37) was based on actual historical reportage he could not believe in Jesus. Why? He argued that, if the story were not reality-based, Jesus would have been attempting to teach truth through a lie. He was reading Scripture in a literalistic way.

[61] Ryken, *Literary Forms*, 27–28, helpfully defines an archetype as a recurring pattern that refracts universal experiences. It could be a process, an activity, a character, an image, or a setting. Archetypes, he claims, are "the building blocks of the imagination."

[62] Christopher Wright, *God I Don't Understand*, 40.

[63] Peter King, "Angelic Sin in Augustine and Anselm," http://individual.utoronto.ca/pking/articles/Angelic_Sin.pdf, accessed 2/18/2015.

image of his own eternity, but through the devil's envy death entered the world, and those who belong to his company experience it." Not long into the Christian era, Irenaeus (c. 135–c. 202) took the same view—that the devil's sin is his envy of mankind. In his *Against Heresies* he writes,

> Just as if any one, being an apostate, and seizing in a hostile manner another man's territory, should harass the inhabitants of it, in order that he might claim for himself the glory of a king among those ignorant of his apostasy and robbery; so likewise also the devil, being one among those angels who are placed over the spirit of the air, as the Apostle Paul has declared in his Epistle to the Ephesians, becoming envious of man, was rendered an apostate from the divine law: for envy [Lat. *inuidia*] is a thing foreign to God.[64]

A number of the Patristic writers were of the same view as Irenaeus—that the devil's sin was envy—including Justin Martyr (c. 100–c. 165), Tertullian (c. 155–c. 220), and Cyprian (c. 210–258). This, however, was the minority report in the early church.[65]

The New Testament Light on Satan: Luke 10:17–20; Revelation 12:7–9; and 2 Peter 2:4

There are three more important NT texts to consider, besides 1 Timothy 3:6. The first of these is Luke 10:17–20:

> The seventy-two returned with joy, saying, "Lord, even the demons are subject to us in your name!" And he said to them, "I saw Satan fall like lightning from heaven. Behold, I have given you authority to tread on serpents and scorpions, and over all the power of the enemy, and nothing shall hurt you. Nevertheless, do not rejoice in this, that the spirits are subject to you, but rejoice that your names are written in heaven."[66]

These disciples are overjoyed at their victory over the demonic. However, they need to be reminded of an even more joy-worthy reality: their names are written in heaven. In the course of drawing their attention to their spiritual security, Jesus cryptically speaks of a fall of Satan. The question arises as to what is on view here.

---

[64] Irenaeus, *Against Heresies*, book 5, chapter 24, paragraph 4.
[65] Peter King, "Angelic Sin," in Webb, *Dome of Eden*, 142, offers an intriguing suggestion as to Satan's attitude that led to his fall. Positing that the incarnation would have taken place irrespective of the fall, he writes: ". . . he [Satan] could not abide . . . the fact that there were creatures that were granted an intimacy with the Son that he would never know." He argues, "Jealousy, then, is the root of all evil, not power, pride, or greed." In this stimulating work, Webb also offers a nuanced version of the much criticized Gap Theory of Creation but without a concomitant commitment to a reconstruction of the earth (142–147).
[66] Maureen Mullarkey sees in this NT reference the idea that Satan was beautiful: "Consider how beautiful the devil must be. A fallen angel is an angel still. Jesus likened the plunge to 'lightning from heaven.' (Luke 10:18). Lucifer appears a pulsing field of light, a flash of pure spirit. All luminous intelligence, he is bright as the morning star, radiant as dawn" ("Lucifer, Patron of the Arts," *First Things*, http://www.firstthings.com/blogs/mullarkey/2014/09/Lucifer-patron-of..., accessed 9/11/2014). However, Jesus may have simply meant that Satan's fall was sudden.

The traditional view is that Jesus is speaking retrospectively. He is referring to a primordial fall of Satan from heaven. More recently others, such as Charles H. H. Scobie, suggest that Jesus is seeing in the success of the mission of the seventy-two a proleptic event, anticipating the defeat of Satan on the cross or the final eschatological fall of Satan.[67] Hence it is prospective. Michael Green canvases the same ground as Scobie but is uncertain as to which of the interpretations to embrace. However he helpfully draws attention to the key points: "It indicates that Satan's home was in heaven with God. It tells us that Satan fell from that happy estate. It reveals that there is a war on."[68]

The mention of war above brings us to a second relevant text, Revelation 12:7–9, which speaks of opposing armies:

> Now war arose in heaven, Michael and his angels fighting against the dragon. And the dragon and his angels fought back, but he was defeated, and there was no longer any place for them in heaven. And the great dragon was thrown down, that ancient serpent, who is called the devil and Satan, the deceiver of the whole world—he was thrown down to the earth, and his angels were thrown down with him.

Angel is at war with angel. Michael and his angels fight the dragon—which in the book of Revelation is the devil—and his angels as identified in our passage. The movement is from heaven to earth. The earth becomes the setting for the dragon's infernal operations. Some, like Michael Green, see this as a reference to a premundane fall.[69] Others argue, like Charles H. H. Scobie, that this apocalyptic text refers to the counterpart in the heavenly realm to Christ's victory over the devil on earth on the cross.[70] Dickason argues that the battle between Michael and Satan will take place in the Great Tribulation and before the return of Christ for his millennial reign.[71] This variety of interpretations shows the difficulty in building a doctrine on an apocalyptic

---

[67] See the discussion in Scobie, *Ways of Our God*, 253.
[68] Green, *I Believe in Satan's Downfall*, 35.
[69] Green, *I Believe in Satan's Downfall*, 36. Green sees Revelation 12 as "a very plain hint . . . given of the fall of Satan from his original state as one of the angels of God." Thomas A. Noble mentions this view, but without endorsement ("The Spirit World: A Theological Synthesis," in *The Unseen World: Christian Reflections on Angels, Demons, and the Heavenly Realm*, ed. Anthony N. S. Lane [Grand Rapids, MI: Paternoster/Baker, 1996], 204). Peter G. Bolt, "Towards a Biblical Theology of the Defeat of Evil Powers," in *Christ's Victory over Evil: Biblical Theology and Pastoral Ministry*, ed. Peter G. Bolt (Nottingham, UK: Inter-Varsity Press, 2009), 61, rejects the idea of a premundane fall of Satan, arguing, "Despite its popularity, however, the theory [a premundane Satanic fall] is derived from the pseudepigrapha, and not from the Bible itself." In his view, we cannot go back before Genesis 3 (63). His treatment of the origins of Satanic and demonic beings leaves one devoid of an explanation as to how a creature can come from the outside of the sacred garden zone, malevolently intent on casting aspersions on the goodness of God, attempting to undermine the integrity of the word of God, and flatly contradicting God. In my view, the traditional idea of a premundane fall of Satan still merits belief. Moreover, Bolt freely uses the term "mythological," as in his treatment of Isaiah 14:4–20 and Ezekiel 28:11–19 (61, and on 69n97), where he describes the serpent as "a mythological figure." Some definition is in order, as "mythological" is widely interpreted in secondary literature.
[70] Scobie, *Ways of Our God*, 254.
[71] Dickason, *Angels: Elect and Evil*, 232. Unger takes a similar view (*Biblical Demonology*, 53).

text, and how one's eschatological frame of reference comes into the hermeneutical picture. Some wisdom from Calvin is apposite here:

> Some persons grumble that Scripture does not in numerous passages set forth
> systematically and clearly that fall of devils [and by definition that of the
> devil], its cause, manner, time, and character. But because this has nothing
> to do with us, it was better not to say anything, or at least to touch upon it
> lightly, because it did not befit the Holy Spirit to feed our curiosity with empty
> histories to no effect.[72]

Calvin goes on to note, "And we see that the Lord's purpose was to teach
nothing in his sacred oracles except what we should learn to our edification."[73]
Again, we need to observe that Scripture is addressed to humankind and not
to the angelic realm. Hence, we have hints in places rather than extensive pre-
sentations in the biblical witness.

The third text is 2 Peter 2:4, which speaks of the fate of rebellious angels:
"God did not spare angels when they sinned, but cast them into hell and committed them to chains of gloomy darkness to be kept until the judgment." The
sin is not explained. Does Peter have in mind Genesis 6:1–4 understood as an
angelic sin? A number of commentators think so. Michael Green comments,
"He [Peter] begins with the fallen angels of Genesis 6, but does not specify their
sin. In Genesis 6:1–4; Jude 6 and Revelation 12:7 it is made clear that rebellion
was the prime cause of their fall, though lust is also mentioned." Green is aware
that other commentators see borrowings here from *1 Enoch*, but he is cautious:
"But if Peter alludes to this apocryphal book at all, he does so with the utmost
discretion (as he does in 1 Pet. 3:19; 4:6 where again he *may* be familiar with
apocryphal material, but it is impossible to prove it)."[74] Richard Bauckham
does not think that Peter is necessarily drawing on *1 Enoch* directly but knows
the tradition of the Watchers of Genesis 6 that was part of the thought life of
the Judaism of the time.[75]

What is clear from the Petrine text is that some angels sinned and those
angels fell. Moreover, they were judged by their Creator and face further judgment to come. Importantly, Satan is not in their number, which leads Sydney
Page rightly to argue that, for both this text and the one analogous to it in Jude
(v. 6), "there is good reason to think that they refer to a fall subsequent to the

---

[72] John Calvin, *Institutes of the Christian Religion*, 1.14.16 (CJCC).
[73] Calvin, *Institutes*, 1.14.16 (CJCC).
[74] Michael Green, *2 Peter and Jude*, TNTC (Downers Grove, IL: IVP Academic, 1987), 121, emphasis original.
[75] Richard J. Bauckham, *2 Peter, Jude*, WBC (Dallas: Word, 1983), 50. We shall return to *1 Enoch* and other intertestamental texts such as *Jubilees* in the next chapter, on demons. A key question to consider is what role, if any, should
extracanonical sources play in constructive evangelical theology. This important question will also be addressed
in the next chapter. Philip Jenkins, *Crucible of Faith: The Ancient Revolution That Made Our Modern Religious
World* (New York: Basic, 2017), 69, is off the mark and overreaches the evidence when he states, ". . . the New
Testament Epistle of Jude cites 1 Enoch as scripture." Jenkins cites no actual verse from Jude to support his claim.

fall of Satan."[76] This is a matter to which we shall return in the next chapter, on the origin, nature, and activities of demons.

As to when the defection from God took place, Erickson is correctly cautious: "Just when this rebellion took place we do not know, but it must have occurred between the time when God completed the creation and pronounced it all 'very good,' and the temptation and fall of the humans (Gen. 3)."[77] What is clear from texts like those considered above is that some angels have fallen from the divine favor and are now condemned, and that Satan is chief among them. Tertullian (c. 155–c. 220) speaks for many in the early church when he writes,

> We are instructed, moreover, by our sacred books how from certain angels, who fell of their own free-will, there sprang a more wicked demon-brood, condemned of God along with the authors of their race, and that chief we have referred to. It will for the present be enough, however, that some account is given of their work. Their great business is the ruin of mankind.[78]

That ruinous work, particularized in that of Satan, will next occupy us.

THE ACTIVITIES OF SATAN

In the flow of redemptive history, it is striking how little Satan figures in the old covenant story in contrast to how much he rises to prominence in the new covenant one. We consider the Old Testament witness first, then that of the New.

The Old Testament Testimony

We now turn our attention to the activity of Satan according to the OT testimony. Thus far, we have noted his activity as the tempter that has been in evidence right from the beginning of the biblical canon in his guise as the serpent of Genesis 3.[79] In that Genesis 3 context we also saw his opposing the word of God, his slander against the good character of God, and his deception of Eve. He stands revealed as tempter, opponent, slanderer, and deceiver. But Genesis 3 does not exhaust the OT witness, as we shall now see concerning his activities when we consider Job.

Job is an extraordinary book of the OT. Its structure is a microcosm of the biblical canon as a whole.[80] Job the righteous sufferer begins in prosperity and happiness. This blameless, upright, and pious man has many sons and

---

[76] Page, "Satan, Sin, and Evil," 220n6.
[77] Erickson, *Christian Theology*, 416.
[78] Tertullian, *Apology*, chapter 22.
[79] Regarding the serpent, Nigel Wright, *Satan Syndrome*, 33, as we shall see, is right to observe that, in the biblical testimony, "It is true to say that the devil is pictured as a serpent, but it is more usual for the activity of the devil to come into view."
[80] See Ryken, *Literature of the Bible*, 109. From a literary theory point of view, Job displays the U-shape structure of comedy, from harmony through disharmony to harmony again.

daughters, much and varied livestock. He is described as "the greatest of all the people of the east" (Job 1:3). However, for the bulk of the book he suffers loss and indignity, and criticism from putative friends. However, by the end of the book he is vindicated by God and his fortunes more than restored. In fact he lives twice the expected lifespan (140 years) and dies "full of days" (42:17).

For our purpose it is the role of the Satan in Job that is of interest. After the prologue, which introduces Job, we are introduced to a heavenly scene in Job 1:6: "Now there was a day when the sons of God came to present themselves before the LORD, and Satan [Hb. "the Satan"; LXX "the devil," *ho diabolos*] also came among them."[81] "Satan" does not appear to be a personal name in this context but descriptive of a role, that of adversary and/or accuser.[82] In the setting of the divine council, the Satan reports of his roaming the earth, and God responds by drawing attention to the outstanding person of Job. It is then that the Satan raises the question of Job's motivation (1:9): "Does Job fear God for no reason?" Interestingly, the Satan cannot see into Job's heart, whereas the NT's testimony is that Jesus *did* have such insight (e.g., Mark 2:8). A test is set up. The Satan afflicts Job mightily in two phases. In the first phase Job loses family—except for his wife—and servants and flocks. Job remains blameless (Job 1:13–22). In the second phase his own body is assaulted with afflictions. Job remains blameless in his speech (2:4–10). In each phase God sets limits. In the first phase, Job's person is not to be touched (1:12). In the second phase, his life is to be spared (2:6). This is no metaphysical dualism of equal forces of good and ill opposed to each other. What takes places does so within the sovereign control of God.[83] This is the God who can take away, as Job declares (1:21), and who can restore, as the last chapter shows (42:12–17). Page rightly suggests, "The author of Job expresses this distinction [the asymmetry between God's causal relation to the good and to the evil] by portraying God as one who gives permission that Job suffer, rather than afflicting him directly, and by portraying Satan as one who acts out of malice, whereas God mercifully sets limits on the harm he can afflict."[84] The book of Job reveals the Satan to be an adversary, an accuser, and a tormentor.[85]

---

[81] Note that "sons of God" is another name for these celestial beings.

[82] Is there a parallel with "Christ," which in the NT can be both a title for a role and a personal name (cf. 1 Cor. 11:3, "the Christ" [in the Greek]; and 1:1, "apostle of Christ Jesus")? This is not only a phenomenon in ancient languages. Think of a first name in English like "Hunter," or a last name like "Baker."

[83] Almond, *Devil*, 53–56, terms this "the demonic paradox," because Satan can be both the opponent of God and the enforcer of the divine will at the same time.

[84] Page, "Satan, Sin, and Evil," 231. Page also correctly points out how mysterious the ways of God are in the book of Job.

[85] The Jewish scholar Mayer Gruber distinguishes "the Satan" from "Satan" as a personal name, as in 1 Chronicles 21:1. He writes, "Later, the idea of Satan developed into the devil, but these associations were not present at the time of our story" ("Job," *JSB* [Oxford: Oxford University Press, 2004], 1506). How does he know this? The Christian theologian, who works with a *tota scriptura* that includes the NT witness, need not hesitate to identify the figure of Job 1 with that of 1 Chronicles 21 with that of Matthew 4. Furthermore, there is a parallel in *modus operandi* between the serpent of Genesis 3 and the Satan of Job 1–2. Both raise questions about character and motive. In Genesis 3 it is God's character. In Job 1–2 it is Job's character.

The next OT text of interest concerns King David. David was an exemplary ruler in so many ways. A man after God's own heart, we read. Yet he did sin. His sin with Bathsheba was as though he had a Ten Commandments checklist that he systematically broke: coveting, adultery, lying, and murder (2 Samuel 11). He also took a census of his people, which displeased the Lord. According to 1 Chronicles 21:1–2, it was Satan who incited him to do so: "Then Satan [Hb. *śātān*, LXX *diabolos*] stood against Israel and incited David to number Israel. So David said to Joab and the commanders of the army, 'Go, number Israel, from Beersheba to Dan, and bring me a report, that I may know their number.'" Joab knew the danger (v. 3): "Why then should my lord require this? Why should it be a cause of guilt for Israel?" To the modern reader the problem in David's kingly action may seem obscure. However, Joab's reaction is a clue. What problem did he see? Some suggest that David's action was the prelude to a draft of under-aged males for his army. Others consider David's action as prideful. After all, God had promised numerous descendants, so why take these steps? Still others see David's move as not only prideful but also ambitious.[86] What is clear in the passage is that Satan is now the personal name for the opponent of God's good purposes.[87] Even though God and his people have an opponent, there is no suggestion that Satan stands on the same metaphysical plane as God.[88]

The last OT passage to consider is in Zechariah. The prophecy of Zechariah presents a vision of Joshua the high priest clothed in filthy garments and the object of the Satan's accusations (Zech. 3:1–5). Joshua is blameworthy, but in the mercy of God his filthy garments are removed and he is clothed with pure ones. He is indeed "a brand plucked from the fire" (v. 2). As Stephen F. Noll points out, Satan has, as it were, had his license to accuse revoked. The high priesthood in the postexilic period as represented by Joshua is now to be restored as integral to God's covenant dealings with his people. The condemnation that was appropriate before the exile is now removed.[89] In this context the evil accuser is referred to by role, "the Satan" [Hb. *haśśātān*; LXX *ho diabolos*, "the devil"] rather than by a personal name.[90]

The appearances of Satan in the OT may be few and far between, but they

---

[86] These options are well discussed in Walter C. Kaiser, *Hard Sayings of the Bible* (Downers Grove, IL: InterVarsity Press, 1997), 240. Kaiser opts for pride and ambition. He also usefully discusses the issue of divine action and permission in the light of the parallel passage in 2 Samuel 24, which attributes the incitement directly to God.

[87] In the light of 1 Chronicles 21:1, David Albert Jones, *Angels: A Very Short Introduction* (Oxford: Oxford University Press, 2011), 103, is mistaken when he writes, "Satan is not a proper name in Hebrew, like David or John, it is always a title or description. It is not Satan but always *the* Satan" (emphasis original).

[88] Almond builds too much on too little when he claims, "Here we have the beginnings of a cosmic dualism— of Satan representing evil and God representing good" (*Devil*, 19).

[89] Stephen F. Noll, *Angels of Light, Powers of Darkness: Thinking Biblically about Angels, Satan, and Principalities* (Eugene, OR: Wipf & Stock, 1998), 105.

[90] Mike Butterworth, "Zechariah," in *NBC*, comment on Zechariah 3:1, who comments, "This section describes how Joshua the high priest is accused by 'the Satan.' The word 'satan' in Hebrew means 'adversary' and occurs as a proper name only in 1 Ch. 21:1. The only other place in the OT where it means a superhuman adversary is in Jb. 1–2. Otherwise it indicates human adversaries, either personal or national. The Adversary's function here and in Job is to accuse one of God's servants."

are highly significant when the objects of the attacks are considered. Adam and Eve were the fountainhead of the race according to the biblical plotline, Job was the outstanding exemplar of God-fearing piety, David the paragon of kingship, and Joshua, God's high priest. By the time the OT draws to a close, Satan is revealed as tempter, adversary, slanderer, accuser, tormentor, and inciter to evil.

The New Testament Unveiling

In the unfolding story of redemptive history, the NT displays a quantum leap in three areas at least. First, God is on view in the NT as Father in ways far beyond the paucity of references in the OT might suggest. Second, the Holy Spirit assumes a prominence far greater in the NT than the OT presents. Lastly, Satan takes on a profile far beyond anything seen in the older Scripture. Why is this so? In brief, the Christ has come.

There are continuities that need noting. Satan is still the tempter. He tempts Christ in the wilderness (cf. Genesis 3 and Matt. 4:1–11). He can tempt believers to abandon the faith through the experience of persecution for the faith (e.g., 1 Thess. 3:1–5). Indeed, the devil can cast believers into prison, as the risen Christ's words to the church at Smyrna show in Revelation 2:10: "Behold, the devil is about to throw some of you into prison, that you may be tested, and for ten days you will have tribulation."[91] He is still the adversary against the word of God (cf. Gen. 3:1 and Mark 4:15). He is still the deceiver (cf. Genesis 3; 1 Tim. 2:14; and 2 Cor. 11:3). He is still the seducer (cf. Genesis 3 and 2 Cor. 11:3). He is still the tormentor (cf. Job 2:6 and Luke 13:16).[92]

There is also in the NT fresh information about Satan's nefarious activities. Jesus describes Satan as a murderer (John 8:44). This is perhaps because Satan's seduction ultimately leads to the primal pair being cut off from God (cf. Gen. 2:17; 3:24). Or is it a reference to Cain's slaying of Abel, his brother (Genesis 4)? Jesus teaches that petitionary prayer ought to include an expressed need for deliverance from the evil one (Matt. 6:13). Interestingly, some bystanders who witnessed an exorcism performed by Jesus misidentify Jesus as "Beelzebul, the prince of demons" (Luke 11:15). In their minds, the devil has a domain and commands a force of demons. He has an army, as it were. Jesus himself describes Satan as "the ruler of this world" (John 12:31). He too affirms that Satan has a domain. We find in the famous foot-washing scene in John 13 that Satan can enter into a human being. He enters into Judas Iscariot, and the betrayal of Jesus soon follows (John 13:27). The apostle Paul adds key

---

[91] It is worth observing that, regarding the seven churches described in Revelation 2–3, there are four references to "Satan" (Rev. 2:9, 13, 24; and 3:9) and one to "the devil" (Rev. 2:10) as the opponent of the churches. The evil one is viewed as the personage or domain from whom the opposition emanates.

[92] We shall return to some of these texts when in a late chapter we relate Christology, Satanology, and demonology.

descriptors to the NT picture. On Cyprus, Paul was confronted by a sorcerer named Elymas (Acts 13:6–11). Elymas opposed Paul and sought to subvert the proconsul Sergius Paulus's interest in the gospel. Filled with the Spirit, Paul describes Elymas as a child of the devil and a perverter of the right ways of God. Elymas is full of trickery and deceit. He is an enemy of what is right. The phrase "son of the devil" (v. 10) suggests that in Paul's mind Elymas was exhibiting the character of Satan: trickster, deceiver, and enemy. Like father, like son. Later in the Acts account, Paul explains his apostolic commission to King Agrippa in terms of his turning the Gentiles "from darkness to light and from the power of Satan to God" (Acts 26:18). He could frame his apostolic commission in terms of opposing Satan. In fact, according to Paul and in language similar to Acts 26:18, Satan blinds unbelievers to prevent their seeing the light of the gospel. In this, Satan is the god of this world (2 Cor. 4:4). Of a piece with this, Paul in Ephesians 2:2 describes the devil as "the prince of the power of the air."[93] Peter compares the devil to a lion ravenous for meat, that prowls around looking for prey (1 Pet. 5:8). In 1 John 5:19 we learn that the whole world is under the sway of the evil one. There is then a consistent claim found in Jesus, Paul, Peter, and John that this world is the devil's domain. C. S. Lewis was right, then, in NT perspective, to describe this world as "enemy-occupied territory."[94] The book of Revelation is particularly illuminating when it speaks of war in heaven, with Michael and his angels fighting the dragon and his angels (Rev. 12:7). The dragon leads an army. Moreover, the devil is at his usual game. Revelation 12:9 describes him as "the deceiver of the whole world."

THE STRANGE THESIS OF KARL BARTH

A surprising claim made by Karl Barth is that the devil and demons are not fallen angels. He describes the doctrine of the fall of the angels as "one of the bad dreams of the older dogmatics."[95] He concludes that the devil was never an angel.[96] Barth's biblical proof text for this contention is John 8:44, where Jesus characterizes the devil as a murderer from the beginning: "You are of your father the devil, and your will is to do your father's desires. He was a murderer from the beginning, and does not stand in the truth, because there is no truth in him. When he lies, he speaks out of his own character, for he is a

[93] The NIV translation unhelpfully imports the idea of a kingdom into the text: "the ruler of the kingdom of the air." There was a great deal of speculation in the medieval era as to how Satan exercised his malice in the air beneath heaven and above the earth's surface. For a discussion see Almond, *Devil*, 61–67. Bolt, "Towards a Biblical Theology of the Defeat of Evil Powers," 54, argues that the "air" on view is "an 'after-life' space." Once again, it is important to note the reserve of the NT on such matters. What should be avoided is any attempt to turn such phrases as "prince of the power of the air" into cosmology. The point of the biblical language may be as simple as this: Satan exercises power in the same environment in which we find ourselves, with the air blowing in our faces.
[94] C. S. Lewis, *Mere Christianity* (New York: Collier, 1960), 46.
[95] Karl Barth, CD, III/3 (531).
[96] Barth, CD, III/3 (531). How does Barth know this?

liar and the father of lies." The reference to "from [the] beginning" (*ap archēs*) appears to mean for Barth that there was never a time when the devil stood for truth, from which he then fell. Hence, the devil was never a good angel who fell. However, John 8:44 may simply be asserting that the devil was a murderer from the beginning of the human story.

Barth has a defender in Thomas A. Noble, who contends that Barth is working with the Bible and its concepts of chaos or evil. Moreover Barth, he argues, does believe that demons exist, but wants to preserve an asymmetry between angelic existence and demonic existence. However, Noble does concede that "Barth's treatment is highly speculative, and. . . . must be seen as an opinion somewhere on the border of Christian doctrine."[97] Noble is most generous here. Also generous to a degree is Nigel Wright. He rightly points out that Barth's concept of "nothingness" needs to be located within the sweep of Barth's theology. Wright explains,

> Here Barth is at his most novel. Nothingness, he argues, has its origins in the "No" of God which is implied by his original creative "Yes." In other words, in saying "Yes" to the creation and calling it into being, God uttered an implied "No," a rejection of that which is evil, and this "No," being also a powerful word of God, has created the realm of nothingness.

Wright, however, is critical too. Barth's use of Scripture is question-begging despite all the richness of his ideas. Nor can the idea of an angelic fall be cavalierly dismissed. Wright concludes, "We are compelled to conclude that Barth's concept does not stand up to scrutiny."[98] I would add that surely Barth has failed to heed his own advice about the need to work with the biblical text in an exegetically responsible way, rather than to indulge in metaphysical speculation.[99]

IMPLICATIONS FOR BELIEF AND PRACTICE

The biblical presentation of the devil raises a number of matters for belief and practice: the question of whether the devil is a person, the question of evil and Satan's relation to it, the question of theodicy in contradistinction from defense, the need for epistemic humility, and yet the importance of knowledge of the devil's wiles.[100]

---

[97] Noble, "Spirit World," 207.
[98] Nigel Wright, *Satan Syndrome*, 36–42, esp. 42.
[99] Barth's apparent lack of interest in Satan and the demonic can be seen in the disproportionate amount of space given to angels as opposed to that given to the demonic. He gives 150 pages to his discussion of angels and 12 pages to that of the demonic. He justifies this lack of attention in this way: "It does not make the slightest impression on the demons if we do so [i.e., pay them attention], and there is the imminent danger that in so doing we ourselves might become just a little or more than a little demonic" (Barth, *CD*, III/3 [519]).
[100] The classic work that explores the devil's wiles is from the Puritan nonconformist Thomas Brooks (1608–1680), *Precious Remedies against Satan's Devices* (Lexington, KY: Feather Trail, 2010). I thank my colleague Greg Scharf for drawing my attention to this work.

Is the Devil Personal?

Nigel Wright boldly asserts that "[t]he use of *personal language* about the devil is problematic. It personalizes the devil and therefore gives a dignity to him which he does not deserve."[101] For Wright, the language predicated of persons ought only to be used of God and those made in the image of God, namely, humankind. He maintains that "it would be more accurate to think of the devil as a non-person, as sub-personal rather than personal. It would be more accurate and satisfying if we were able to refer to the devil as 'it.'"[102] Satisfying for whom?, one might ask. His own preference is to use the phrase "power of darkness" of this biblical figure.[103]

I have some sympathy with not giving the evil one too much dignity. Even so, to deny that the evil one is a person and at the same time to assert intelligence, will, and moral accountability of this figure is confusing, to say the least. Like God and like us, the devil is a speech agent who can use "I" and "me" language, according to Scripture, as in Matthew 4:9 ("I will give," *dōsō*; and "me," *moi*). Is not this a sufficient condition to predicate personal language of the devil?

Evil and Satan

For many years I taught the philosophy of religion as well as theology. I was surprised to find encyclopedias of philosophy with no entry on "evil," except when discussing objections to theism. However, since 9/11 and the sight of the burning Twin Towers, the wider problem of the existence of evil, especially moral evil, has become inescapable.[104] The human will can do unfathomably wicked things. Now, one can find secular philosophical discussions of a topic that a biblically informed Christian has never neglected.

When it comes to accounting for the palpable evils we experience, the great spoiler needs to be taken with sober seriousness. The devil is not to be reduced to "essentially a metaphor. . . . a conflux of influences—social, political, biological, and psychological—that promote destruction and pain."[105] In contrast, Michael Green does take the devil seriously.[106] He argues forcefully, if somewhat loosely,

---

[101] Nigel Wright, *Satan Syndrome*, 28, emphasis original.

[102] Wright, *Satan Syndrome*, 28.

[103] Wright, *Satan Syndrome*, 29.

[104] It is commonplace in philosophical discourse to distinguish between natural evils, where an intelligent will, prima facie, is not involved, and a moral evil, where an intelligent will is involved. A disease that kills penguins in the Antarctic would be an example of the former; the dreadful Holocaust or Shoah of the Nazi years is an example of the latter. C. S. Lewis, *The Problem of Pain* (London, Great Britain: Geoffrey Bles, 1965), 123, speculates that natural evils such as animal pain have a Satanic cause: "If there is such a power . . . [Satan], it may well have corrupted the animal creation before man appeared."

[105] Oldridge, *Devil: A Very Short Introduction*, 2. Oldridge is describing what he assumes to be the view of "many readers" of his book (2).

[106] Schleiermacher does not. Dismissively he argues, "The poetic use [of the idea of the devil] is therefore the freest and least harmful. For in poetry personification is quite in place, and no disadvantage is to be feared from an

Some of the reasons which have led to and supported this belief [belief in a "good, personal, transcendent God"] are the marks of design in our world; the existence of moral qualities such as beauty, truth and goodness; and the uniformity of nature, which suggests care of a beneficent Creator and Sustainer. But do not similar considerations lead us to infer the existence of Satan? Are there no marks of design in the forces of evil which form our daily news coverage?[107]

Green rightly points out that his line of thinking does not lead to a dualism of good and evil, which the biblical testimony disallows. And the question he raises is a good one. How do we account for apparent dysteleological features of the world we experience?[108] Less abstractly put, how do we account for the massacre at Columbine High School in 1999, when two adolescents murdered twelve fellow students and a teacher? Philosopher Gordon Graham uses this example to argue that humanistic and scientific attempts at explanation fail in such a case.[109]

Theodicy or Defense?

Following some lines of thinking from philosopher Alvin Plantinga, let me suggest, with regard to the origin of Satan, that all that may be offered is a defense rather than a theodicy.[110] A theodicy gives *the* reason God allows or does X. It was the philosopher Gottfried Leibniz (1646–1716) who coined the term "theodicy" (Lit., *theos* = "God"; *dikē* = "justice"). He famously argued that in order to create the "best possible" world, evil is a necessity. Of course, God could have chosen not to create, but if it were to be the best possible world, then evil was unavoidable.[111] A defense offers a more modest proposal. It recognizes its epistemological limitations.[112] A strong defense would give reasons

emphatic use of this idea in pious moods. It would therefore be inexpedient and in many ways unjustifiable to wish to banish the conception of the devil from our treasury of song." See his *Christian Faith*, 170.
[107] Green, *I Believe in Satan's Downfall*, 19–20. I say "loosely" for a number of reasons. Is beauty a moral quality or an aesthetic value? Is truth a moral value or an intellectual one? Would it have been better to draw attention to design-like features in the world rather than beg the question that the marks we see are design? Strictly speaking, there needs to be an argument *to* design before an argument *from* design may be mounted.
[108] Oldridge, *Devil: A Very Short Introduction*, 4, goes beyond the evidence in suggesting, "It is possible to argue that the devil emerged for this purpose."
[109] I am drawing on the account of Oldridge here (*Devil: A Very Short Introduction*, 93). See Gordon Graham, *Evil and Christian Ethics* (Cambridge: Cambridge University Press, 2001). Some argue that no explanation is possible. Evil is a surd. And although human beings have a need to understand and explain, when it comes to evil, making sense does not work. Instead, Christopher Wright, *God I Don't Understand*, 42, says, "Evil is not there to be understood, but to be resisted and ultimately expelled." Richard Beck, *Reviving Old Scratch: Demons and the Devil for Doubters and the Disenchanted* (Minneapolis: Fortress, 2016), 175, takes a similar tack: "Our response to suffering isn't *intellectual* but *behavioral*. Our response to suffering isn't theological debate and mental rumination—a big pile of questions, doubts, and existential breakdowns. . . . our response must be *action*. Resistance is our only theodicy" (emphases original). Thanks to my colleague Kevin J. Vanhoozer for drawing my attention to Beck's book.
[110] Alvin Plantinga, *God, Freedom, and Evil* (Grand Rapids, MI: Eerdmans, 1980), 10–11, 26–29. I have adapted this paragraph from my *God the Peacemaker*, 241–242. For a careful though brief discussion of the difference between theodicy and defense, see John S. Feinberg, *The Many Faces of Evil: Theological Systems and the Problem of Evil*, rev. and expanded ed. (Wheaton, IL: Crossway, 2004), 29. The appendix in his book dealing with theodicy and defense-making is especially valuable (489–490).
[111] See Anthony C. Thiselton, *A Concise Encyclopedia of the Philosophy of Religion* (Oxford: Oneworld, 2002), 168.
[112] A great strength of Paul Copan's treatment of the problem of evil in his *Loving Wisdom*, 128, is his sensitivity to epistemological limitations, as can be seen in his careful distinction between gratuitous evils (without reason) and inscrutable ones (the reason for their existence is not disclosed).

for trusting in God's moral integrity (for example, the love of God expressed through the cross, as found in Rom. 5:6–8) and would also offer a theory of how that integrity is not compromised by the existence of evils, and with them, Satan. A moderate defense would likewise give reasons for trusting in God's moral integrity (for example, the love of God expressed through the cross), but unlike the strong defense, a moderate one would offer no account of how the existence of evils—and with them, Satan—comport with that integrity. I would argue that, because of the limitations in scope of special revelation—not all has been revealed (Deut. 29:29, "the secret things belong to the Lord")—at the most only some kind of strong defense is possible. And in such a defense, some reference to Satan would figure.[113]

Epistemic Humility

We live in a society in which there is much available by way of "entitlements." In such a culture, it is easy to feel that we are entitled to know much more than Scripture reveals. To use C. S. Lewis's image, we have put God "in the dock," and we are asking our questions of him like prosecuting attorneys. The reality, however, is that the *world* is on trial, and the Holy Spirit is the prosecutor.[114] This is a major part of the argument of the Gospel of John, as A. A. Trites rightly has maintained.[115] As we have noted before, the secret things belong to the Lord (Deut. 29:29). Not all has been revealed. Moreover, there are many hints in Scripture that the human story is being played out on a much bigger stage. Job and his friends did not know that. They were unaware of the heavenly backdrop to Job's suffering.[116] Paul makes an intriguing claim in Ephesians 3:8–10:

> To me, though I am the very least of all the saints, this grace was given, to preach to the Gentiles the unsearchable riches of Christ, and to bring to light for everyone what is the plan of the mystery hidden for ages in God,

---

[113] Gregory A. Boyd takes a stronger view in arguing for a Trinitarian warfare theodicy that "is *the* explanation of evil" (*Satan and the Problem of Evil: Constructing a Trinitarian Warfare Theodicy* [Downers Grove, IL: IVP Academic, 2001], 430, emphasis mine). The strength of Boyd's account is his taking supernatural evil so seriously. However, I think his claim is a reach. For an excellent treatment of the problem of evil that is an older one but still most valuable, see Bernard L. Ramm, *The God Who Makes a Difference: A Christian Appeal to Reason* (Waco, TX: Word, 1972), 119–155. The strength of this work lies in its engagement with the biblical testimony and with the notions of Christological alleviation and eschatological vindication.

[114] See C. S. Lewis, *God in the Dock: Essays on Theology and Ethics*, ed. Walter Hooper (Grand Rapids, MI: Eerdmans, 1970).

[115] Alison A. Trites, *The New Testament Concept of Witness* (Cambridge: Cambridge University Press, 2004), 78–127.

[116] Feinberg, *Many Faces of Evil*, 479–480, sees a possible reason in the divine permission to allow Job's suffering: "God allowed Job's afflictions at least in part to *demonstrate true or genuine faith to Satan*. Satan claimed that the only reason Job served God was that it was worth Job's while. . . . Through Job's afflictions and through his faithfulness to God, Satan saw that there are those who serve God out of genuine love, not because 'it pays to do so.'" He elaborates: "Likewise, God may use afflictions in our life to accomplish some purpose *for us*, and at the same time use our response to show Satan and his cohorts that there are still those who love and serve God regardless of their personal circumstances in life" (emphases original).

who created all things, so that through the church the manifold wisdom of God might now be made known to the rulers and authorities in the heavenly places.

The mystery now revealed is that God is bringing both Jewish and Gentile believers jointly into the one new man/human (Eph. 2:14–16), into the one temple of the Spirit (vv. 19–22), and into the one body of Christ (3:6). In so doing, a point is being made to spiritual beings in the heavenly places ("the rulers and authorities"). In other words, redemptive history is not only about us. How much more we would like to know about this! But hints are all we have. This is epistemologically humbling.

The Importance of Knowledge

In a classic work about the loss of the Christian mind to secular thinking, Harry Blamires articulates the defining characteristics of the Christian mind in terms of its supernatural orientation, its conception of truth, its acceptance of authority, its concern for the person, and its sacramental cast ("sacramental" broadly understood).[117] Significantly, Blamires also lists its awareness of evil. He is on good NT ground especially with regard to the awareness of evil. The apostle Paul serves as a case in point. Of all the Pauline writings, it is 2 Corinthians that contains the most explicit references to Satan per se and the need for Christians to be aware of his evil. There are four passages in this letter that are of particular interest. The first of these is 2 Corinthians 2:10–12, where impressively Paul claims knowledge of the devil's designs: "Anyone whom you forgive, I also forgive. Indeed, what I have forgiven, if I have forgiven anything, has been for your sake in the presence of Christ, so that we would not be outwitted [*pleonekteō*, "to take advantage of"] by Satan; for we are not ignorant of his designs [lit., *noēmata*, "thoughts"]." In the Corinthian context, it would appear that a device of the devil is to somehow influence Christians in such a way that forgiveness is withheld. The devil attacks in the realm of the interpersonal. Without forgiveness, relationships that have been broken or strained cannot even begin to be repaired. There was a pastoral need at Corinth for a reaffirmation of love for the offender who had caused pain not only to Paul but to others as well (2 Cor. 2:5–8). Colin G. Kruse suggests another possibility that to my mind is complementary. If the offending member is lost permanently to the congregation through the devil's wiles, then the Corinthians would in effect have been successfully defrauded by the evil one.[118] What is important for our purposes is to note that, in Paul's mind,

[117] Harry Blamires, *The Christian Mind* (London: SPCK, 1966), v.
[118] Colin G. Kruse, *2 Corinthians*, TNTC (Downers Grove, IL: IVP Academic, 2015), 84.

the devil can work his mischief by sowing discord within the body of Christ and not just outside it, in the world.

Another design of the devil may be seen in 2 Corinthians 4:3–5. In this context it is not the church on view, but the world outside the church. Paul writes,

> And even if our gospel is veiled, it is veiled to those who are perishing. In their case the god of this world [lit., the god of this age, *aiōnos toutou*] has blinded the minds [*ta noēmata*, "the thoughts"] of the unbelievers, to keep them from seeing the light of the gospel of the glory of Christ, who is the image of God.[119]

The devil's sphere of influence is the world, but again this is not a metaphysical dualism on view, but a moral one, as Murray J. Harris points out.[120] Once more we see the devil as the opponent of the word of God as crystallized in the gospel. He is the blinder. How the blinding works Paul does not elaborate. Significantly, he does locate the problem in the human mind, not the human emotions.[121] I recall spending months with a friend at university going through the gospel and the evidence for it. Eventually he told me that he now believed that Jesus really is the Son of God and alive from the dead. I was thrilled and said to him, "You are going to become a Christian!" He replied, "No!" "Why not?" I asked. He answered that God might want him to give up his medical studies and become a missionary.

Yet another 2 Corinthians text may shed light on the devil's designs. Paul is worried that the Corinthians will be led astray by the serpent's cunning. Their devotion to Christ will be undermined by his seduction. He expresses his concern this way in 2 Corinthians 11:2–3:

> For I feel a divine jealousy for you, since I betrothed you to one husband, to present you as a pure virgin to Christ. But I am afraid that as the serpent deceived Eve by his cunning, your thoughts [*ta noēmata*, "the thoughts"] will be led astray from a sincere and pure devotion to Christ.

What would such a seduction look like? Paul explains (v. 4): "For if someone comes and proclaims another Jesus than the one we proclaimed, or if you receive a different spirit from the one you received, or if you accept a different gospel from the one you accepted, you put up with it readily enough." Clearly, for Paul, the serpent's stratagem is to work through plausible human agents,

---

[119] Paul worked within a two-age framework: the present evil age, and the age to come. In Galatians 1:4 he describes the present age as evil presumably because it is Satan's sphere of influence.

[120] Murray J. Harris, "2 Corinthians," in *EBC*, comment on 2 Corinthians 4:4, writes, "If dualism is found in Paul, it is an ethical and temporal dualism, not a material or metaphysical one. Satan is not the god of 'the age to come.'"

[121] A point well made by Paul Barnett, *The Message of 2 Corinthians*, TBST (Leicester, UK, and Downers Grove, IL: InterVarsity Press, 1988), 82, who comments, "The Achilles' heel of man is his mind, since he is so prone to intellectual pride, especially in matters to do with religion. It was with unerring judgment about human vulnerability, therefore, that Satan *blinded*, not the emotions, or the will, but the *mind* of man" (emphasis original).

claiming to be gospel people. Later in the same chapter (v. 13) he describes such people as "false apostles, deceitful workmen, disguising themselves as apostles of Christ." Their nefarious work has a sinister precedent (vv. 14–15): "And no wonder, for even Satan disguises himself as an angel of light. So it is no surprise if his servants, also, disguise themselves as servants of righteousness."

Paul's second letter to Corinth lastly shows that Satan's attacks could get very personal (2 Cor. 12:7). Writing of his apostolic hardships, he becomes autobiographical in a most self-revealing way: "So to keep me from becoming conceited because of the surpassing greatness of the revelations, a thorn was given me in the flesh, a messenger of Satan [lit., "an angel of Satan"] to harass me, to keep me from becoming conceited." What that thorn was we simply do not know for sure.[122] What we do know is how the apostle places the experience, quite possibly a physical one ("in the flesh"), within a larger frame of reference. The experience keeps him humble, as a man who had been caught up into the third heaven with rare access to the heavenly realm for someone still in this world (2 Cor. 12:1–6). He is being ironic and rhetorically clever. He is opposing the so-called "super-apostles" (hyperlian apostolōn) who are so full of boasting and so critical of Paul's apparent lack of gravitas in person (cf. 2 Cor. 12:11 and 10:10).

Paul's Corinthian correspondence shows a Satan who is at work both inside and outside the church, and who can attack God's servants personally.

CONCLUSION

According to the biblical testimony, the devil or Satan is a fallen angel. Angels, as glorious beings, do not evolve into even more glorious ones. However, the fall of Satan shows that some angels have *devolved* into inglorious beings.[123] Satan's intent is evil. The Puritan Thomas Brooks captures that intent well:

> Beloved, Satan being fallen from light to darkness, from felicity to misery, from heaven to hell, from angel to devil, is so full of malice and envy that he will leave no means unattempted, whereby he may make all others eternally miserable with himself; he being shut out of heaven, and shut up "under the chains of darkness until the judgment of the great day" (Jude 6), makes use of all his power and skill to bring all the sons of men into the same condition and condemnation with himself.[124]

Satan's origins are mysterious, and although there are hints in the biblical testimony, caution is in order. In canonical perspective, Satan makes a first ap-

---

[122] Kruse, *2 Corinthians*, 199. Kruse offers a useful discussion of the three main suggestions: spiritual harassment, persecution, or physical ailment, which is the most common view.
[123] The fact that there is no evidence in Scripture that angels can become even more glorious shows a difference between angelology and anthropology. The believer will be glorified (Rom. 8:30; Phil. 3:20–21).
[124] Thomas Brooks, *Precious Remedies*, 4.

pearance as the seductive serpent of Genesis 3. In that guise the Satanic *modus operandi* is laid bare. The serpent is revealed as the enemy of the word of God, the enemy of the integrity of God, and the enemy of the people of God. At times, this spiritual being of immense power and cunning works his mischief as an angel of light. Other times he is like a ravenous lion on the prowl. He is a spoiler. He is a disuniter. He is the enemy of the interpersonal. Temptation is his specialty from the beginning. Christians need to have a worldview that takes the devil seriously in its awareness of evil. Calvin wrote wisely in saying,

> It seems to me, therefore, that I have accomplished what I meant to do, namely, to equip godly minds against such delusions [that devils don't really exist], with which uneasy men confound themselves and others more simple-minded than they. But it was worth-while to touch upon this point, also, lest any persons entangled in that error, while thinking themselves without an enemy, become more slack and heedless about resisting.[125]

However, importantly, Satan does not work alone. He is also the leader of the pack. Eric L. Mascall captures this well: "Devils are fallen angels . . . and the Devil with a capital D is only the leader of a self-frustrating and hatred-ridden rabble."[126] To this hatred-ridden rabble, the demons, we now turn our attention.

---

[125] Calvin, *Institutes*, 1.14.19 (*CJCC*). The idea of resisting the devil we shall return to in the chapter on spiritual warfare.
[126] E. L. Mascall, *The Christian Universe* (London: Darton, Longman, & Todd, 1967), 111.

CHAPTER

FIVE

DEMONS, THE DEVIL'S ENTOURAGE

According to Scripture, Satan is not alone as an agent of evil. He has company, his own entourage.[1] His demons do his nefarious work. I have never knowingly encountered a demon. However, in a parish in which I served I met an ethnically Dutch couple who had immigrated to Australia from Indonesia, which had been a Dutch colony. They told me an alarming story. They had fled from their families, who were deeply entrenched in the occult. Once in Australia, they started to explore the Christian faith. They told me of seeing the walls of their bedroom writhe with demons. From their exploration of the gospel they had learned that the evil one is overcome by the blood of the Lamb (Rev. 12:11), and they prayed to Jesus that his blood would prevail. Once they did that, there were no more such visions and they both came to faith in Christ for themselves. They struck me as sober people whose testimony was not to be dismissed.[2]

In this chapter we consider the demonic. We start with the biblical testimony before moving into an examination of Amos Yong's "emergence" thesis. We also examine Walter Wink's controversial theology of the principalities and powers that has spurred much new interest in angelology. A host of questions then arise concerning Christian belief and practice, such as whether a believer can be demon-possessed. An excursus is added, dealing with methodological questions arising from very different exegeses of the same passage.

SATAN IS NOT ALONE

As we saw in the previous chapter, Jesus was on one occasion misidentified as "Beelzebul, the prince [*archonti*, "ruler"] of demons" (Luke 11:15). However, such a descriptor *is* accurate of *Satan*, according to the biblical witness. In

---

[1] Karl Barth uses the metaphor, with emphasis, of an "entourage" of angels (*CD*, III/3.3 [493]). It is a useful one to describe Satan's celestial followers.
[2] See Sharon Beekmann and Peter G. Bolt, *Silencing Satan: Handbook of Biblical Demonology* (Eugene, OR: Wipf & Stock, 2012), xvii–xx. In this extremely helpful work, Beekmann shares her own story of deliverance from the demonic. I find impressive in her story, and that of others related in the book, that deliverance came instantly when Jesus was called upon to save. This seems much more like the NT accounts, rather than some of the stories of a protracted process that some tell today.

his magisterial parable of the sheep and the goats, Jesus establishes the asymmetry between the kingdom of heaven and the eternal fire. The kingdom is for the righteous (Matt. 25:34). The righteous end up in the place designed for them. In contradistinction, for the unrighteous there is only the eternal fire (v. 41), which was "prepared for the devil and his angels." The unrighteous end up in a place not made for them. Paul also describes Satan as a prince. In Ephesians 2 he reminds the readers that once they were under the thrall of the prince [*archonta*, "ruler"] of the power [*exousias*, "authority"] of the air, when they were his followers as "the sons of disobedience" (vv. 2–3). Princes are rulers, and rulers have servants. Revelation 12 is relevant once more, as it speaks of war in heaven, and of the dragon and his angels.[3] Not only was the dragon thrown down from heaven, so too were his angels (vv. 7–9). There is an evil sphere of influence, which Paul calls "the domain [*tēs exousias*, "the authority"] of darkness" (Col. 1:13). This is where the devil and his demons are at work.

The Nature of Demons

Demons are fallen angels who are now malicious spiritual beings. Their malevolence is seen in phrases such as "evil spirits" (Luke 8:2, *pneumatōn ponērōn*) and "unclean spirit" (9:42, *tō pneumatic tō akathartō*). Luke 8:2 shows that "demons" and "evil spirits" have the same referent. Mary Magdalene is described as one who had been cured of evil spirits and also as someone from whom seven demons (*daimonia*) had been cast out. Demons still have some of the characteristics of unfallen angels. They are persons who are speech agents and can use the language of "I" and "us" (Mark 1:24). They are intelligent, as shown in their recognition of Jesus's true identity as the "Holy One of God" (Luke 4:34). Their knowledge has limitations, however. The evil spirit that the seven sons of Sceva confronted at Ephesus knew Jesus and Paul but had to ask who the sons of Sceva were (Acts 19:13–15). They can express emotion-like behavior best described as fear (Luke 8:28). They can enter into and possess the human body and personality, either singly (arguably, Mark 1:26) or in enormous numbers in some cases (Mark 5:9). They can cause physical effects involving human subjects (Luke 4:35). They are unlike the unfallen angels in moral character (holiness), and there is no suggestion in Scripture that an unfallen angel ever possesses God's image bearers as some kind of vehicle.[4]

---

[3] Beekmann and Bolt, *Silencing Satan*, 140, take a different view. They contend that Satan's kingdom is chaotic and not hierarchical. However, it seems to me that Revelation 12:7–9, with its reference to Satan and "his angels" in pitched battle with Michael and "his angels," strongly suggests otherwise.

[4] Peter G. Bolt, "Towards a Biblical Theology of the Defeat of Evil Powers," in *Christ's Victory over Evil: Biblical Theology and Pastoral Ministry*, ed. Peter G. Bolt (Nottingham, UK: Inter-Varsity Press, 2009), 49–57, distinguishes between lower demons ("dirty demons"), who are from below, and higher demons ("pasty principalities"), who are from above, at work in "celestial realms." Very suggestive, very speculative. One may also ask what "pasty" means. It seems an odd adjective to use.

THE PROVOCATIVE THESIS OF AMOS YONG

We saw in an earlier chapter that Amos Yong offers a breathtakingly provocative thesis concerning the nature of angels as "emergent" realities. He is equally provocative on the subject of demons. He contends, "Demonic spirits, then, are divergent (as opposed to *emergent*) malevolent realities that oppose the salvific grace of God in human lives."[5] How and when did the "emergence" take place? He argues,

> But just as the human spirit emerges from the socially and environmentally embedded brain and body, and just as angelic spirits emerge as supervenient upon the concreteness and complexity of our interpersonal, social, and cosmic relations, so also, I suggest, do demonic spirits emerge from and supervene upon the human experience of alienation that disintegrates lives and destroys human relationships in general and human well-being as a whole.[6]

The demonic manifests itself in a myriad of ways: "archetypally as the primeval chaos (Gen. 1:2)," "antipersonally as various destructive powers," "socially, historically, politically, and economically in terms of the domination systems" (à la Walter Wink), "regionally, geographically, terrestrially, or cosmically as forces of chaotic destruction . . ." (e.g., . . . "tsunamis"), and "anticelestially as fallen angels."[7] Once the demonic spirit has emerged, then it has a "top-down" influence on lesser creatures. Yong is more comfortable in describing demons as "antipersonal" than as "personal." In this he adopts Augustine's privative view of evil, and the idea that evil is parasitic on the good.[8] The antipersonal is parasitic on the personal.

Yong acknowledges that his thesis on the nature of demons is speculative, and he offers it tentatively.[9] Even so, it is difficult not to be critical. He assumes both a macroevolutionary framework and that "emergence" is the true characterization of the origins of the human spirit. Both claims need much more argument. Particularly question-begging is the sequence his view appears to assume: first the material body and brain, next the emerged human spirit, then the derivative angelic spirit, lastly the deformation (?) of the angelic spirit to emerge as a demonic one. His speculative "emergentist cosmology" seems adrift from careful exegesis of the biblical text. Biblical texts are cited and placed in brackets, in the traditional *dicta probantia* method of prooftexting, but left unengaged with in any meaningful way. This is a great weakness, because Scripture as *norma normans* (the norming norm) is not allowed

---

[5] Amos Yong, *The Spirit of Creation: Modern Science and Divine Action in the Pentecostal-Charismatic Imagination* (Grand Rapids, MI, and Cambridge: Eerdmans, 2011), 217 (emphasis original).
[6] Yong, *Spirit of Creation*, 217–218.
[7] Yong, *Spirit of Creation*, 218–219.
[8] Yong, *Spirit of Creation*, 219–220.
[9] Yong, *Spirit of Creation*, 213.

to provide the control beliefs—as Nicholas Wolterstorff has taught us to say—
that act as gatekeepers on what is an acceptable theological proposition and
what is not.[10] For example, Aquinas saw the strength in Aristotle's argument
for the eternity of the world. However, Genesis 1:1 taught him *creatio ex nihilo*
and thus Aristotle's argument did not prevail with him. I am left wondering
just what control beliefs are operative in Yong's theologizing.

THE SATANIC AND DEMONIC DISORDER

What are the origins of the demonic? When did the demonic disorder begin?
What was the motive?[11] Did it begin when Satan fell, or after?

In my view, the Scriptures do not give us access to information as to when
the demonic disorder began.[12] Millard Erickson is accurate in claiming, "The
Bible has little to say about how evil angels came to their current moral character and even less about their origin."[13] As with Satan's fall, the safest surmise is
that it took place between Genesis 1:1 and Genesis 3:1. Peter Kreeft speculates
that their fall took place within moments after their creation.[14] How one de-
cides this question is beyond me.

Some, however, have seen the account in Genesis of the sons of God bed-
ding the daughters of men as the key to answering such a question. To this
possibility we now attend. In Genesis 6:1–4 we learn of a puzzling episode in
the unfolding OT story, and one which has few, if any, parallels in the ancient
Near Eastern world.[15] The interpretation of the passage has generated a great
diversity of scholarly opinion. Walter Kaiser accurately says, "Few texts in
the history of interpretation have aroused more curiosity and divergence of
opinion than Genesis 6:1–4. It is at once tantalizing and deeply puzzling."[16] He
points out the chief difficulty: "What is most difficult is the identification of
the main participants in this short narrative—the 'sons of God,' the 'daughters
of men' and the 'Nephilim' (or 'giants')."[17] This strange story illustrates the

---

[10] Nicholas Wolterstorff, *Reason within the Bounds of Religion*, 2nd ed. (Grand Rapids, MI: Eerdmans, 1984), chapter 9.

[11] Sergius Bulgakov, *Jacob's Ladder: On Angels*, trans. Thomas Allan Smith (Grand Rapid, MI and Cambridge: Eerdmans, 2010), 111, synthesizes the Patristic witness and argues that self-love rather than love for God was the motive, and it issued in carnal lusting after the daughters of men (Genesis 6), pride, and envy. In his view, Satan infected some of the other angels when they were drawn to his example (112).

[12] Job 4:18 (ESV) reads, "Even in his servants he puts no trust, and his angels he charges with error." Some may think that this text throws light on demonic disorder. However, as Francis I. Anderson points out (*Job*, TOTC [Downers Grove, IL: InterVarsity Press, 1976], 123), "The meaning of the word translated *error* in verse 18b, which occurs only here, is quite unknown, and has occasioned much guesswork and emendation." One can hardly start building doctrine on such uncertainty.

[13] Millard J. Erickson, *Christian Theology*, 3rd ed. (Grand Rapids, MI: Baker, 2013), 416.

[14] Peter Kreeft, *Angels and Demons: What Do We Really Know about Them?* (San Francisco: Ignatius, 1995), 119. Kreeft judiciously acknowledges how difficult the time question is.

[15] See Terence E. Fretheim, "Genesis," in *NIB*, 12 vols. (Nashville: Abingdon, 1993–2002), 1:382–384.

[16] Walter C. Kaiser Jr., *Hard Sayings of the Bible* (Downers Grove, IL: InterVarsity Press, 1997), 106. See also his discussion in his *The Promise-Plan of God: A Biblical Theology of the Old and New Testaments* (Grand Rapids, MI: Zondervan, 2008), 49–51.

[17] Kaiser, *Hard Sayings of the Bible*, 106.

deleterious entailments of the primal sin delineated in Genesis 3. It follows the story of murderous Cain, who slew his own brother (Gen. 4:1–8), and that of Lamech, a descendant of Cain, who was even more murderous (vv. 23–24). In Genesis 6:1–4 we read,

> When man began to multiply on the face of the land and daughters were born to them, the sons of God saw that the daughters of man were attractive. And they took as their wives any they chose. Then the LORD said, "My Spirit shall not abide in man forever, for he is flesh: his days shall be 120 years." The Nephilim were on the earth in those days, and also afterward, when the sons of God came in to the daughters of man and they bore children to them. These were the mighty men who were of old, the men of renown, [lit., "men of the name"].

Next we read (vv. 5–6), "The LORD saw that the wickedness of man was great in the earth, and that every intention of the thoughts of his heart was only evil continually. And the LORD regretted that he had made man on the earth, and it grieved him to his heart." Prima facie, the wickedness of men and the story of the sons of God and the daughters of men seem connected.

There are three main lines of interpretation of the Genesis 6 passage, only one of which involves celestial beings and human ones.[18] The first interpretative approach has been labeled "the sociologically mixed races view" (despotic male aristocrats and beautiful female commoners).[19] It understands "the sons of God" to be sons of princes. There is some ancient Near Eastern evidence for such a usage. The issue, on this view, is that royals married women beneath their station. Some ancient Jewish interpreters took this approach (e.g., *Targum Onkelos* and *Midrash Rabbah*), as well as some modern scholars. For example, Meredith G. Kline and John Walton advocate different versions of it.[20] Kaiser also argues for this interpretation and concludes,

> Genesis 6:1–4, therefore, is best understood as depicting ambitious, despotic and autocratic rulers seizing both women and power in an attempt to gain all the authority and notoriety they could from those within their reach. Their progeny were, not surprisingly, adversely affected, and so it was that God was grieved over the increased wickedness on planet Earth. Every inclination of the hearts and thoughts of humanity was evil. Thus the flood had to come

---

[18] For what follows in this section I am drawing on the particularly helpful discussion in Peter R. Schemm Jr., "The Agents of God: Angels," in *A Theology for the Church*, rev. ed., ed. Daniel L. Akin (Nashville: B&H, 2014), 260–263, which covers the interpretative possibilities and their advocates. The discussion in Philip C. Almond, *The Devil: A New Biography* (Ithaca, NY: Cornell University Press, 2014), 1–6, is also useful. A fourth view, but not one widely held, is that demons possessed men, who then took wives. For this view, see Willem VanGemeren, "The Sons of God in Genesis 6:1–4 (An Example of Evangelical Demythologization)," *WTJ* 43/2 (1981): 320–348.

[19] Kaiser, *Hard Sayings*, 107. "Race" is hardly the right word here. See my comments in the excursus.

[20] For Meredith G. Kline, see *Kingdom Prologue: Genesis Foundations for a Covenantal Worldview* (Overland Park, KS: Two Age Press, 2000), 185–189; and for John Walton see his piece, "The Sons of God in Genesis 6:1–4," in *The Genesis Debate*, ed. Ronald Youngblood (Eugene, OR: Wipf & Stock, 1999),184–209.

to judge humankind for the perversion of authority, the state, justice and human sexuality.[21]

As for the Nephilim, he argues, "[T]here is no reason to consider the Nephilim to be giants. It is more likely that the term describes heroic warriors, perhaps the ancient equivalent of knights errant."[22] However, as Peter R. Schemm Jr. points out, there is little in the language of the passage that suggests royal personages are on view.[23]

The second interpretation has been described as "the cosmologically mixed races view (angels and humans)."[24] This interpretation identifies the "sons of God" as fallen angels.[25] After all, in Job 1:6–12 "sons of God" refers to angels. Gordon J. Wenham contends that this is the natural sense of the passage, extraordinary though it may be to "modern secular readers." He draws on Canaanite literature for a similar understanding of "sons of God" as referring to angels. Further, he argues that it is the oldest interpretation found in Jewish writers. Second Peter 2:4 and Jude 6–7 provide further evidence. He points out that the ancient world believed that divine beings mated with humans to produce "supermen."[26] Presumably he has the Nephilim in mind. One could buttress his account by highlighting how 2 Peter 2 speaks of a fall of angels (v. 4) before going on to the flood story (v. 5) and that of Sodom and Gomorrah (vv. 6–8). Is it not plausible to think that the Petrine text is following the narrative sequence in Genesis? Traditionally, the chief problem with Wenham's approach is metaphysical. How can celestial spirits have intercourse with terrestrial flesh? A further difficulty is Jesus saying that, in the world to come, believers are like the angels in heaven in that they "neither marry nor are given in marriage" (Matt. 22:30).[27]

The third approach is the "religiously mixed races view" (godly Sethites and worldly Cainites)."[28] It identifies the sons of God with godly Sethite men

---

[21] Kaiser, *Hard Sayings*, 108. In his *Promise-Plan of God*, 51, Kaiser adduces several lines of evidence in support: ancient Targums rendered "sons of God" as "sons of nobles," Symmachus (late second century) translated the phrase "the sons of kings or lords," and *'elohim* in Scripture could refer to "magistrates" or "judges" (Ex 21:6; 22:8; Ps 82:1, 6).

[22] Kaiser, *Promise-Plan of God*, 51.

[23] Schemm, "Agents of God: Angels," 261.

[24] Kaiser, *Hard Sayings*, 107. Again, "race" is not the right term. "Creatures" would be a better word. Not even "species" would work here if Aquinas is right in arguing that each angel is a species of one. See Thomas Aquinas, *ST*, I, Q 50.4.

[25] In the early church period Justin Martyr (c. 100–160) took this view, and its last great Patristic representative was Lactantius (c. 250–c. 318). See the account in Almond, *Devil*, 10–13.

[26] Gordon J. Wenham, *Exploring the Old Testament, Volume One: A Guide to the Pentateuch* (Downers Grove, IL: InterVarsity Press, 2003), 25–27. Augustine takes the view that the giants were simply very tall human beings and gives an example of a woman in Rome who was so tall that she attracted crowds of gawkers (Augustine, *City of God*, chapter 23.

[27] John H. Sailhamer claims that the apparent contradiction between Genesis 6:1–4 and Matthew 22:30 is the primary reason why the angels and women view is not the common one ("Genesis," in *EBC*, comment on Genesis 6:1–4). However, it could be argued that this is where the sin of these angels lies. They married women in defiance of the divine intent for angels. This is not my view.

[28] Kaiser, *Hard Sayings*, 107.

who have intercourse with ungodly Cainite women.[29] This approach appeared early on in church history with Julius Africanus (c. 160–240) and climaxed with Augustine (354–430) in the fifth century.[30] Augustine argued that in his day many viewed the sons of God as angels, but in the light of his two-cities distinction he maintains that the sons of God were Sethites, who as citizens of the City of God "formed a connection" with daughters of men, who were of the City of Man (i.e., Cainites).[31] As for the reference to the Nephilim, it can be argued that the presence of the Nephilim, and the marriage between the sons of God and the daughters of men, are not logically connected in the text but are juxtaposed to give some indication of the setting. As for the men of renown, according to this view they are the ten great men referred to in Genesis 5. The Nephilim could be they. However, a connection with the Nephilim is assumed, not shown, according to Schemm.[32] Further, regarding 2 Peter 2:4 and Jude 6, there is no compelling reason for thinking that these texts are alluding to Genesis 6:1–4, unless extrabiblical literature is used to decide the exegesis. This third line of interpretation is the one that Schemm takes. He concludes, "This [interpretation] fits well the larger context of Genesis 1–11 in which there is a constant tension between the progress of God's blessing on mankind and threats to that blessing."[33] However, he does not deal with any objections to his view. For example, Walter Kaiser maintains that his third view fails to meet the test of consistency with the biblical data and context. It understands the term "men" in verses 1 and 2 in two different senses: in verse 1 "men" is used to indicate humanity generically, while in verse 2 it is understood to refer to the Cainite line specifically. He suggests that such an abrupt change in meaning without any indication in the text is unwarranted. This is the problem of equivocation. Moreover, how could a union of mere men and mere women produce physical giants, if the Nephilim are understood to be such?[34]

The contrast in scholarly opinion concerning the meaning of Genesis 6:1–4 raises the question of what the way forward is, when the experts disagree. In the excursus at the end of this chapter, I will address this important question and give my own view of the best understanding of the Genesis 6:1–4 passage and suggest that the method of "comparative difficulties" constitutes the best methodological way forward in dealing with difficult texts.

---

[29] Kaiser, *Hard Sayings*, 25. Wenham notes a fourth suggestion in the scholarly literature. According to L. Eslinger, the sons of God are the sons of Cain who marry the daughters of Seth. See Gordon J. Wenham, *Genesis 1–15*, WBC (Dallas: Word, 2002), 139.

[30] Almond, *Devil*, 13–15.

[31] Augustine, *City of God*, chapter 23.

[32] So Schemm, "Agents of God: Angels," 261, argues. Barnabe Assohoto and Samuel Ngewa ("Genesis," *ABC*, ed. Tokunboh Adeyemo [Grand Rapids, MI: Zondervan, 2006], 20), rightly argue, in my opinion, "all that the text seems to say is that *Nephilim* existed at the time."

[33] Schemm, "Agents of God: Angels," 263.

[34] These are the criticisms of Kaiser, *Hard Sayings*, 107.

THE BIBLE, EXTRABIBLICAL SOURCES, AND
DOING EVANGELICAL THEOLOGY

Some of these lines of interpretation of Genesis 6:1–4, as we have noted, look to ancient Near Eastern background or to later Jewish commentary to throw light on the passage. Other scholars work mainly within the canonical Scriptures. John H. Sailhamer, for example, argues regarding the book of Genesis, "In the final analysis, an understanding of the book and its message comes from reading the book itself. No amount of historical and literary scholarship can replace the simple reading of the text as the primary means for determining the book's nature and purpose."[35]

I am sympathetic to Sailhamer's contention. Importantly, his contention does not rule out the value of historical background information. What it does do is make the Bible reader cautious lest background information be given such a weight that the authority of Scripture as God's word written is undermined by it. Andrew Naselli offers much wisdom here. Although he is writing about the NT, his concerns apply *mutatis mutandis* to the OT too. He offers a cautious yes to the appeal to background information but with this caveat:

> I can't overstate how important this is. You can discover so much about the historical-cultural context by simply reading the text carefully. Never lose your anchor to this one text: the Bible. Everything else is supplementary. So in your zeal to understand the historical-cultural context, don't neglect the one text that matters most. Give it preeminence. Read the text more often than you read any other. Let this text be supreme over all others.[36]

A high view of biblical inspiration and authority demands nothing less.

Instead of working in generalities, let's consider what has been described as "the first great landmark in Jewish demonology."[37] *First Enoch* was written over a long period of time, from the fourth century BC to the start of the early church period. Chapters 1–36, which were complete in the third century BC, deal with "The Watchers." These spiritual beings fall into sin, and Genesis 6:1–4 tells the story. There are two versions.[38] One version (*1 Enoch* 6:4–6) has one Shemihazah leading two hundred watchers in a rebellion against God in their lust for women, whom they not only bedded but to whom they also taught

---

[35] Sailhamer, "Genesis," in *EBC*, section 1 of introduction, comment on background.

[36] Andrew David Naselli, *How to Understand and Apply the New Testament: Twelve Steps from Exegesis to Theology* (Phillipsburg, NJ: P&R, 2017), 174. See also Jason S. DeRouchie, *How to Understand and Apply the Old Testament: Twelve Steps from Exegesis to Theology* (Phillipsburg, NJ: P&R, 2017), part 3.

[37] Elaine Pagels, quoted in Almond, *Devil*, 4. For the substance of this paragraph I am indebted to Almond's excellent account (3–6). For the actual text of *1 Enoch* in translation, see http://www.sacred-texts.com/bib/boe/, accessed 12/19/2017.

[38] The 2014 movie *Noah*, starring Russell Crowe, offers its own take on this tradition. Noah and his family are hunted by Tubal-Cain. They find refuge with the Watchers, who are fallen angels turned into stone giants (*nephilim*) for helping Adam and Eve in the garden. By fighting for Noah and his family, the watchers when killed in battle return to their heavenly glory.

sorcery. These women bore the Nephilim, who were ruthless, homicidal giants. The other version (*1 Enoch* 8:1–2) has one Asael teaching men metal working and magic. Asael was a sub-chief under Shemihazah (*1 Enoch* 6:8). Men make instruments of war as a result. These fallen watchers also have sexual relations with women, who bear them "half-breed giants." Archangels Michael, Sariel, Raphael, and Gabriel carry out the divine judgment on the watchers, including both Shemihazah and Asael, whom they imprison under the earth awaiting the great day of final judgment. The giants are killed. However, out of their corpses come their evil spirits. These evil spirits go on to torment humankind (*1 Enoch* 15:9–12). As disembodied spirits, they escape the waters of the flood.

The present work is one of systematic theology. How do background studies and a source like *1 Enoch* fit with an evangelical systematic theology? Interestingly, Augustine wrestled with the question of extrabiblical sources when considering the meaning of Genesis 6:1–4. He argued,

> Let us omit, then, the fables of those scriptures which are called apocryphal, because their obscure origin was unknown to the fathers from whom the authority of the true Scriptures has been transmitted to us by a most certain and well-ascertained succession. For though there is some truth in these apocryphal writings, yet they contain so many false statements, that they have no canonical authority.[39]

I have sympathy with Augustine's position. My rule of thumb as a systematic theologian who uses an evidence-based approach—and where that evidence is the biblical text—is that I may draw on background studies insofar as the biblical text is illuminated by them. The scholar wants to know everything about something. So the Pauline scholar, for example, wants to know the primary texts from Paul, their interpretation, the history of scholarly discussion about those texts, and all the NT background that is relevant to Pauline studies. The systematic theologian, on the other hand, wants to know something about everything.[40] In other words, the systematic theologian's scholarly interests are typically far broader than that of the New Testament specialist. But that desideratum brings with it certain limitations.

With the above in mind, and returning to *1 Enoch*, to be sure it is a fascinating book, as are many of the later Gnostic documents in the early church period. However, the biblical testimony stands out for its reserve on such matters, whether the question is the origin of demons or the physics of resurrection.[41]

---

[39] Augustine, *City of God*, chapter 23.

[40] This distinction, if I recall rightly, is found in the writings of Cambridge theologian Nicholas Lash, but I no longer remember where.

[41] As an undergraduate, I recall sitting in a large lecture theater in the University of Sydney, listening to the renowned classicist professor Edwin A. Judge. He was lecturing on the Jesus of myth and legend. He spent almost the entire hour expounding Gnostic literature. At the end of it he said that if, by way of contrast, you wish to read ancient documents written by those who believe that the events narrated actually happened in history, then read Matthew,

This systematic theologian works within the parameters set by such reserve, as did both Calvin and Barth, as we have noted previously.[42] This should not hinder the curiosity of the biblical scholar.[43] Nor should it restrain the historian of ideas.[44]

THE ACTIVITY OF DEMONS

The activity of fallen angels depends on their present state of being. Some of these angels appear at present to be bound (2 Peter 2:4; Jude 6) as they await the day of final judgment. Others are at present bound but will be released at the eschatologically appropriate moment (Rev. 9:14).[45] Still others are at work in our own created context, and it is these that concern us now.[46]

What, then, are demons up to?[47]

Demons and False Worship

Humankind has been created to worship the living God. The OT makes that clear in the story of Israel's redemption from Egyptian bondage. They were rescued from Pharaoh and from Egypt's gods (Ex. 2:22–25 and 12:12, respectively) and rescued for the worship of the God of Abraham, Isaac, and Jacob (Ex. 10:3). Jesus in the NT told the woman of Samaria that the Father is seeking those who will worship him in spirit—that is, in a way that accords with his nature—and in truth—that is, in a way that accords with what is revealed through Jesus (John 4:23–24). Indeed, one way to characterize the *missio dei* (mission of God) in a broken world is the divine quest to restore true worship.

It is no accident, then, that Satan in his pride seeks to be the object of the worship due the Creator. So his last temptation directed at Jesus is the offer

---

Mark, Luke, and John. As for the other literature, it is the work of the religious imagination attempting to fill in the gaps. I have that same sense when I read *1 Enoch*. The text of *1 Enoch* can be read at http://www.hermetics.org/pdf/bookenoch.pdf, accessed 2/25/2015.

[42] Peter Bolt, "Towards a Biblical Theology of the Defeat of Evil Powers," 49, wisely counsels, "The willingness to live with the Bible's own restraint is an important step towards a truly biblical theology."

[43] John H. Walton of Wheaton College has wisdom to offer here. He noted, in a conference session I moderated and in which he was a panelist, that ancient Israel was embedded in a stream of ancient Near Eastern culture but "embeddedness" did not necessarily translate into "indebtedness." By that he seemed to mean that the exegete should not jump too quickly into thinking that a given biblical text (e.g., Genesis 1) borrowed from extrabiblical sources. Walton made it plain that Israel could swim against the stream as well as with it (the Dabar Conference at Trinity Evangelical Divinity School, Deerfield, Illinois, June 9, 2016).

[44] For example, Philip Jenkins, *Crucible of Faith: The Ancient Revolution That Made Our Modern Religious World* (New York: Basic, 2017), argues that the era from 250 to 50 BC produced a plethora of speculations about the devil, demons, and angels which Christianity (and Islam) inherited. A bold and stimulating thesis. However, it makes the restraint of the NT writers all the more remarkable, in my view. For a distillation of his book, see Philip Jenkins, "The Crucible Era," *Christian Century* (October 11, 2017), 36–39.

[45] See Schemm, "Agents of God: Angels," 257.

[46] Erickson, *Christian Theology*, 416, takes a different view and concludes, "Though cast into the nether gloom, the fallen angels have sufficient freedom to carry out their evil activities." Wayne Grudem, *Systematic Theology: An Introduction to Biblical Doctrine* (Grand Rapids, MI: Zondervan, 1995), 412–413, argues similarly.

[47] C. Fred Dickason discusses the activities of demons under the chapter heading "Duties of Demons" (*Angels: Elect and Evil*, rev. and expanded ed. [Chicago: Moody, 1995], 181). This seems rather odd. It is as though "demon" is a job that can be applied for. Be that as it may, his chapter is insightful.

of kingdom authority and splendor if only Jesus would make Satan the object of worship (Matt. 4:8–9). Jesus would have none of it (v. 10): "Be gone, Satan! For it is written, 'You shall worship the Lord your God and him only shall you serve.'" Given this devilish machination, it is not surprising that there are hints in both the Old Testament and the New that demons, Satan's entourage members, are inciters of false worship.[48]

There are three important passages in the OT that relate the demonic to false worship.[49] The first of these is Leviticus 17:7: "So they [Israel] shall no more sacrifice their sacrifices to goat demons [satyrs], after whom they whore. This shall be a statute forever for them throughout their generations." Clearly there is something very wrong about demons being the objects of worship. The language of prostitution is very strong. But just who or what are these "goat demons"? They appear to be demons thought to appear as goats in wilderness areas. John E. Hartley comments, "The worship of such spirits was a tyrannical force, binding the people in the chains of fear and superstitions. These laws were designed to guard the Israelites from becoming enslaved by such evil practices."[50] The second text criticizes Israel ("Jeshurun") for growing fat like a beast and forgetting God (Deut. 32:15). Israel's religious impulse turned elsewhere, to strange gods. Idols captured their allegiance (v. 16). They even offered sacrifices to demons (v. 17): "They sacrificed to demons [šēdîm, a rare word; LXX daimoniois, "demons"] that were no gods." Using stunning feminine imagery, Moses declares (v. 18): "You were unmindful of the Rock that bore you, and you forgot the God who gave you birth."[51] The third text is Psalm 106:35–37. Here the psalmist recalls how Israel indulged at one stage in child sacrifice. In other words, God's people acted like the nations around them. In so doing, "They served their idols, which became a snare to them. They sacrificed their sons and their daughters to the demons" (v. 37). Thus Israel had played the whore (v. 39). In this text demons are clearly linked to death, as the language of sacrifice shows.[52]

---

[48] "Hints" is the operative word. In a number of places in the scriptural testimony there are hints that there are spiritual forces at work that cannot be reduced to a contest between simply the human and the divine. The judgment on Pharaoh was also a judgment on Egypt's gods (Ex. 12:12), Israel sacrificed to demons in the wilderness (Deut. 32:17), and through the church God is making a point to the principalities and powers (Eph. 3:10—11). These references are few but intriguing.

[49] Fascinatingly, the early church fathers argued that it was the mission of angels to lead pagans to worship the one true God, but demons corrupted that task. Demons became the source of idolatry. For Eusebius, Romans 1:21–23 provided biblical evidence for this contention. See the discussion in Jean Danielou, The Angels and Their Mission according to the Church Fathers, trans. David Heimann (Notre Dame, IN: Ave Maria, 1957), 14–23.

[50] John E. Hartley, Leviticus, WBC (Dallas: Word, 1992), 272.

[51] Deuteronomy 32 is remarkable in using masculine and feminine descriptors of Yahweh (cf. v. 6, "Father," and v. 18, "mother" implied). The God of the Bible is never addressed in feminine terms, but his activities are described in places using feminine terms. Probably, to have addressed God in feminine terms would have all too easily, in that ancient context, led to reframing Israel's God in earth mother categories.

[52] The devil too is linked to death ("a murderer," John 8:44). With regard to the secondary literature, Bolt, "Towards a Biblical Theology of the Defeat of Evil Powers," 67, observes, "The fact that so many views on demonology overlook, ignore or deny the connection between the evil powers and death is a serious distortion of the biblical

An OT-like connection between idols and the demonic comes into view in the NT in Paul's Corinthian correspondence. Paul warns the Corinthians in 1 Corinthians 10 to flee from idolatry (v. 14). To eat the bread and to drink the wine in the Lord's Supper is to participate in the body and blood of Christ, respectively (v. 16). Paul draws out the implications: Idols are nothing (v. 19). Even so, the one who offers a sacrifice (i.e., a worshiper) at the pagan altar is actually worshiping demons and not God (v. 20). God is jealous when it comes to worship, hence the warning. The aptness of the contrast between the table of the Lord and that of demons is well brought out by W. Harold Mare, who writes,

> To make it clearer, Paul speaks of "The Lord's table"—a term that the Corinthian converts from paganism would readily associate with "tables" used for pagan idol meals. In the Oxyrhynchus Papyrus CX there is a revealing sentence that says, "*Chairemon invites you to a meal at the table of the lord Serapis* in the Serapeum, tomorrow the fifteenth from nine o'clock onwards." So Paul is teaching that a Christian cannot at the same time participate in the meal at the table of the pagan god and the table of the Lord.[53]

"Possession" of Individuals

Interestingly, there are no unequivocal OT examples of "demon-possession" or exorcism.[54] Some, for example Josephus, have suggested that King Saul was afflicted by a demon ("a harmful spirit from the LORD," 1 Sam. 16:14). Be that as it may, once Jesus walks the earth there are a number of such stories. As J. Keir Howard rightly says, "Exorcism was an undisputed feature of the ministry of Jesus."[55] There are six such stories in the Synoptic Gospels.[56] Fascinatingly, there are none in the Fourth Gospel and only two specific examples in the Acts of the Apostles (Acts 16:16–18 and 19:11–19). Surprisingly, there are no references to demon-possession or exorcism in the remainder of the NT. Indeed, of the ministries bestowed by the ascended Christ on his church, it is important to note that "exorcist" is not one of them in Ephesians 4:10–11.[57]

Mark's Gospel has the longest account of demon-possession and exor-

---

picture." This is not to suggest that human death in every instance has a demonic cause. For example, in 1 Corinthians 11:30, Paul explains that bad behavior at the Lord's Supper led to the death of some of the Corinthians.
[53] W. Harold Mare, "1 Corinthians," in *EBC*, comment on 1 Corinthians 10:21, emphasis original.
[54] J. Keir Howard, "Exorcism," in *Oxford Guide to the Bible*, ed. Bruce M. Metzger and Michael D. Coogan (Oxford: Oxford University Press, 1993), 216. I am using ordinary Christian language here. Whether such a phrase as "demon possession" is accurate shall be discussed later in this chapter.
[55] Howard, "Exorcism," 217.
[56] Mark has four such stories (1:21–28; 5:1–20; 7:24–30; 9:14–29), with parallels in Matthew and Luke. Matthew has two stories of his own: Matthew 9:32–33 and 12:22. Howard goes far beyond the evidence to suggest that Matthew, Mark, and Luke limited the exorcisms of Jesus and the twelve to Jesus's lifetime (Howard, "Exorcism," 217). How does he know this? And what does he make of Acts 5:16?
[57] Bolt, "Towards a Biblical Theology of the Defeat of Evil Powers," 43, asks, "Why do we keep on talking about Jesus doing 'exorcisms,' when the NT never once calls him an exorcist, nor is the exorcism language used for his driving out spirits?" However, the idea of exorcism may be present even if the exact term is not. Bolt himself writes of Jesus's "driving out spirits" (43) and "casting out unclean spirits" (78). Perhaps he has a very narrow definition of exorcism, such that exorcism must involve some formal ritual. See his footnote (43n18).

cism, and it is particularly illuminating. It is also, as Craig A. Evans suggests, "the eeriest episode in the life of Jesus."[58] In Mark 5:1–20, we read of an exorcism that took place in the country of the Gerasenes (v. 1). In typical Markan style, the event occurs "immediately" (*euthys*) upon Jesus's arrival (v. 2). A man confronts him. The man lived among tombs and was super strong (v. 3). He also did self-harm and was a howling mess (v. 5). Jesus commands the numerous unclean spirits to leave the man, and they do (vv. 8–13). He gives permission for the unclean spirits to enter the unclean pigs, which then rush to their doom (v. 13). The demons are still causing harm. The pigs drown.[59] The demons call themselves "Legion" because of their number (v. 9). Jesus is clearly in charge as he gives permission for the unclean spirits to enter the nearby herd of pigs (v. 13). The man, now demon-free, is restored to his right mind and tranquility (v. 15). The man becomes an enthusiastic herald (v. 20, *kēryssein*) of Jesus in the region of Decapolis. He has been restored to a purpose for living. This is one amazing before-and-after story.

This gospel story is full of interest. Demon-possession had cut this man off from his community. He dwelt alone among the tombs. Demon possession attacked his body, even though that body could display amazing strength. He could break chains. He cut himself with stones. He suffered violence from these spirits. Demon-possession also attacked his mind. Origen, in the early church period, regarded such an attack as one of two main operations of demons: "Sometimes they take complete and entire possession of the mind, so as not to allow their captives the power of either understanding or feeling."[60] The demons in Mark 5 were many, as the name "Legion" suggests. A legion was up to around six thousand Roman soldiers. There is no record of Jesus's commanding the demons to leave the man in this account. Instead he gives permission for their leaving (v. 13). (In a later Markan story of demon-possession, there is a dominical command that the demon leave [Mark 9:25].)[61] Exorcism restored the man's sanity and his clothing.[62] Exorcism led to calm. He now sat still, rather than crying out night and day. He could conduct a sensible conversation with Jesus. After the exorcism he could think of his future. He wanted to

[58] Craig A. Evans, "Mark," in *ECB*, ed. James D. G. Dunn and John W. Rogerson (Grand Rapids, MI, and Cambridge: Eerdmans, 2003), 1077.
[59] This is a case of animal "demon possession."
[60] Quoted in *DECB*, ed. David W. Bercot (Peabody, MA: Hendrickson, 1998), 204. The other line of attack, according to Origen, was through temptations, persuading an individual to do evil. Judas is his example (204).
[61] The Gospel accounts stand in stark contrast with an apocryphal text like *Tobit*, where defeating a demon seems more like magic. The angel Raphael directs Tobias to protect himself and his bride along these lines in *Tobit* 6:17–18 (NRSV): "When you enter the bridal chamber, take some of the fish's liver and heart, and put them on the embers of the incense. An odor will be given off; the demon will smell it and flee, and will never be seen near her anymore." Apparently demons have sensitive "noses." See Beekmann and Bolt, *Silencing Satan*, 34–35, for a helpful analysis of the Tobit story.
[62] Jesus's miracles and exorcisms all seem to be works of restoration that anticipate the restoration of all things. He restores the sea to order (Mark 4:35–41). He restores a woman's health (5:25–34). He restores a child to life (5:35–43). He restores the demoniac to his right mind. In some of these cases the miracles also enable—one might reasonably infer—the restoration of the healed person to their community by dealing with an uncleanness (5:25).

accompany Jesus. As for the demons, they recognized Jesus as "the Son of the Most High God" (Mark 5:7). They sought post-exorcism reembodiment. In the Lukan version the demons appear to fear being cast into the abyss (Luke 8:31).[63] As we have seen, the unclean spirits were given permission to enter the unclean pigs. Sometimes blame is laid at Jesus's feet for the drowning of the pigs. However the narrative makes it clear that this is what the demons themselves did with their reembodiment. The people of both town and countryside begged Jesus to leave. They were afraid. Clearly, something out of the ordinary had taken place. The story also shows that "demon" and "unclean spirit" have the same referent.

Deceiving Believers

The church at Ephesus was a troubled church, as the many references to false teachers and false teaching in it make clear. Paul's first letter to Timothy about the situation at Ephesus begins and ends on those notes (cf. 1 Tim. 1:3–7 and 5:20–21). An important part of Paul's response to the pastoral need at Ephesus is found in 4:1–5. He informs Timothy of a Spirit-revealed aspect of the present situation (v. 1): "Now the Spirit expressly says that in later times some will depart from the faith by devoting themselves to deceitful spirits and teachings of demons." What is the teaching that Paul deems so unacceptable? It seems to be some form of deviant asceticism (vv. 2–3): ". . . through the insincerity of liars whose consciences are seared, who forbid marriage and require abstinence from foods that God created to be received with thanksgiving by those who believe and know the truth." The antidote to such teaching is to appreciate the goodness of creation (vv. 4–5): "For everything created by God is good, and nothing is to be rejected if it is received with thanksgiving, for it is made holy by the word of God and prayer." What is of interest for our purposes is how Paul frames the problem in terms of demonic deceit (v. 1). Walter Liefeld rightly sees the significance of Paul's words: "This text [v. 1] gives us a behind-the-scenes glimpse and reveals that the real perpetrators of heresy are not only the heretics but the evil spiritual forces that deceived and taught them."[64] The teaching of demons comes through those human teachers whom they have deceived. John Stott makes the point with his usual admirable clarity: "Thus in the same verse Paul refers both to the Holy Spirit and to evil spirits or demons. For behind the false teachers he sees the activity of demonic forces. Speaking himself under the influence of the Spirit of truth he declares the false teachers to be under the influence of deceiving spirits."[65]

[63] Merrill F. Unger, *Biblical Demonology: A Study of Spiritual Forces Today* (Grand Rapids, MI: Kregel, 1994), 74, describes the abyss as "an intermediate place of detention for evil spirits."
[64] Walter L. Liefeld, *1 and 2 Timothy, Titus*, NIVAC (Grand Rapids, MI: Zondervan, 1999), 149.
[65] John Stott, *Guard the Truth: the Message of 1 Timothy and Titus* (Downers Grove, IL: InterVarsity Press, 1996), 111.

Warring against Other Angels

Revelation 12:7–9 is a text that has been highlighted a number of times already in this work. In this discussion of the demonic it is important once again. This time we find in these verses that the war in heaven between Michael and his angels, and the dragon and his angels, shows that the demons are part of Satan's army and as such are not only the opponents of humankind but also of angel-kind. Leon Morris helpfully comments, "This little vision teaches that we are caught up in a wider conflict than the one we see. The thought is not quite that of Paul who spoke of wrestling 'against the spiritual forces of evil in the heavenly realms' (Eph. 6:12). John is speaking of spiritual forces indeed, but the conflict is not simply one between demons and men. Angelic forces are also engaged. Our struggles are not to be shrugged off as insignificant. They are part of the great conflict between good and evil."[66]

The Principalities and Powers Revisited

In biblical perspective, sin takes many forms. Sin can be exhibited by individuals (e.g., Cain in Genesis 4). Sin can take root in groups (e.g., the Benjaminites of Judges 19). And sin can lodge in societal structures (e.g., Nebuchadnezzar mandated idolatry by law in Daniel 3). This last category of sin has come to be termed "structural sin."

The theologian who has brought structural sin and demonology together is Walter Wink. In a trilogy of very influential books he reframed the discussion of angels in a fresh way.[67] He wrote,

We are living at the juncture of two ages, when a senescent worldview [Enlightenment materialism] is contending with its upstart successor. . . . We cannot simply revive [the] ancient worldview [which for Wink, as for Bultmann, includes the assumptions of the Bible] without jettisoning much of what humanity has gained in the interval since. But we can reinterpret [the powers] . . . as symbolic of the "withinness" of institutions, structures, and systems. People may never again regard them as quasi-material beings flapping around the sky, but perhaps they will come to see them as the actual spirituality of actual entities in the real world.[68]

The older liberal theology (nineteenth century) eliminated the supernatural from Scripture. Wink's postmodern approach reinterprets the scriptural

[66] Leon Morris, *Revelation*, TNTC (Downers Grove, IL: IVP Academic, 2009), 156.
[67] Walter Wink, *Naming the Powers: The Language of Power in the New Testament* (Philadelphia: Fortress, 1984); *Unmasking the Powers* (Philadelphia: Fortress, 1986); and *Engaging the Powers: Discernment and Resistance in a World of Domination* (Minneapolis: Fortress, 1992). Wink has distilled much of his work in his *The Powers That Be: Theology for a New Millennium* (New York: Doubleday, 1998). Wink is still influential. For example, Richard Beck's *Reviving Old Scratch* (Minneapolis: Fortress, 2016) shows its indebtedness to Wink in many places and at times explicitly (115).
[68] Quoted in Stephen F. Noll, *Angels of Light, Powers of Darkness: Thinking Biblically about Angels, Satan, and Principalities* (Eugene, OR: Wipf & Stock, 1998), 24–25. The insertions are Noll's.

testimony and has done so in such a way as to renew the discussion of angelol-ogy in general and demonology in particular, even in liberal theological circles.

According to Wink, what then are the powers at work in the structures of human life? Wink answers the question as follows:

> All of us deal with the Powers That Be. They staff our hospitals, run city hall, sit around tables in corporate boardrooms, collect our taxes, and head our families. But the Powers That Be are more than just the people who run things. They are the systems themselves, the institutions and structures that weave society into an intricate fabric of power and relationships. These Powers surround us on every side. They are necessary. They are useful. We could do nothing without them. Who wants to do without timely mail delivery or well-maintained roads? But the Powers are also the source of unmitigated evils.[69]

For Wink there is a human dimension to the Powers That Be, and a "system" is one such example. For him, systems can take on a personality of their own. So too can a church, in his view.[70] These Powers That Be can be either Jekyll or Hyde.

In an interview given in 2010 Wink provides a clear illustration of what he calls the powers deleteriously at work—the Mr. Hyde side. When he was in South Africa he heard a phrase from black South Africans that he still remem-bered, despite his dementia. He put it this way: "When I was in South Africa, I actually heard South African people use the phrase, 'The system is at the door. Sneak out the back.'"[71] Apartheid had a corporate spirit about it. This spirit was a power working an inhuman injustice in white-dominated South African society. How does an institution become demonic? "When a particular Power becomes idolatrous, placing itself above God's purposes for the good of the whole, then that power becomes demonic."[72] In his book *Engaging the Powers*, Wink argues that the way to respond to such a corporate spirit is nonviolent resistance.[73] Wink believes that in this way the powers may be redeemed. As for Satan, Wink contends, "Perhaps in the final analysis Satan is not even a 'personality' at all, but rather a function in the divine process, a dialectical movement in God's purpose which becomes evil only when humanity breaks off the dialectic by refusing creative choice."[74]

At one level, Wink may have rejected Bultmann, but at another this seems

[69] Wink, *Powers That Be*, 1.
[70] In fact the catalyst for Wink's theology of the powers was his reflection on the angels of the churches in Revela-tion 2 and 3. He concluded that the angel was the corporate spirit of each church (Wink, *Powers That Be*, 3–4). Others argue that these angels are church leaders.
[71] Walter Wink, interviewed by Steve Holt http://www.guildsf.org/news/confronting-powers-interview-walter-wink-and-june-keener-wink-interview-steve-holt, accessed 3/6/2015.
[72] Wink, *Naming the Powers*, 5.
[73] Cited in Noll, *Angels of Light*, 24.
[74] Quoted in Noll, *Angels of Light*, 123.

his own kind of demythologization.[75] Be that as it may, he has an important point that needs hearing. N. T. Wright is one NT scholar who has heard the point and gives a nuanced response, in his commentary on Colossians 1:16. With regard to thrones, dominions, rulers, and authorities he writes,

> As to their referent, in our modern age it has often been taken for granted that Paul's language about supernatural power-structures needs to be demythologized, to be turned into language about (say) international power politics or economic "structures." This is quite legitimate, since for Paul spiritual and earthly rulers were not sharply distinguished. In his view, earthly rulers held authority (in the sense intended by John 19:11; Rom. 13:1-7) only as a trust from the creator. At the same time, we should not ignore the supernatural or 'demonic' element in these 'powers.' Anything to which human beings offer the allegiance proper only to God is capable of assuming, and exerting, a sinister borrowed power. For Paul, the 'powers' were unseen forces working in the world through pagan religion, astrology, or magic, or through the oppressive systems that enslaved or tyrannized human beings.[76]

Even so, for all of Wink's creativity at the level of ideas, and the helpful accent on how institutions can instantiate evil—structural sin is real—far too much of the biblical testimony is reinterpreted away and so much is built on so little biblical testimony.

IMPLICATIONS FOR BELIEF AND PRACTICE

In this section we attend to a number of important matters pertaining to belief and practice. The questions include: Can believers be influenced by the demonic? (The category of "the demonic" includes the Satanic, given that Satan is the prince of demons.) Can believers be oppressed by the demonic? Can believers be possessed by the demonic? Are there genuine exorcisms today? Is there a relation between structural sin and the demonic? Is there a relation between superstition and the demonic? Is there a relation between demon-possession and mental illness? Demons are "believers" (cf. James 2:19), so why aren't they saved? Is belief the same as trust?

Can Believers Be Hindered by the Demonic?

Given the biblical witness, it is reasonable to believe that Satan may hinder believers. By "hinder" I mean cause believers to pay attention to that which

---

[75] Thomas A. Noble, "The Spirit World: A Theological Synthesis," in *The Unseen World: Christian Reflections on Angels, Demons, and the Heavenly Realm*, ed. Anthony N. S. Lane (Grand Rapids, MI: Paternoster/Baker, 1996), 231, accurately argues that demythologization of the principalities and powers may not be Wink's intent. However, according to Noble, Wink does so in effect. Noble effectively critiques Wink's Jungianism (210–214).

[76] N. T. Wright, *Colossians and Philemon*, TNTC (Downers Grove, IL: IVP Academic, 2008), 76.

otherwise they might not, or make difficult the pursuit of godly goals. Temptation would be the key stratagem, and one as old as the Genesis 3 story. Such influence would be indirect and would be done through the flesh and the world, to use two traditional categories.[77] The apostle Paul writes of Satanic hindrance in 1 Thessalonians 2:17–18: "But since we were torn away from you, brothers, for a short time, in person not in heart, we endeavored the more eagerly and with great desire to see you face to face, because we wanted to come to you—I, Paul, again and again—but Satan hindered [*enekopsen*] us."[78] Paul does not elaborate on the exact nature of the hindrance. Michael W. Holmes judiciously comments, "How Paul was blocked is not stated. In view of Acts 17:9, it is possible that there were legal barriers to his return. On the other hand, if the 'thorn in the flesh' of 2 Corinthians 12:7 was an illness, it may be that poor health prevented Paul from traveling."[79] Here is another case of our listening in, as it were, to one end of the telephone conversation, and ignorance needs to be admitted, as Holmes wisely does: "Timothy no doubt informed the Thessalonians about the circumstances that made it impossible for Paul to visit them, but we must acknowledge that Paul's letter leaves us without a clue."[80]

Can Believers Be Oppressed by the Satanic and/or the Demonic?

If by "oppress" is meant "cause distress," whether physical or mental, the answer biblically speaking is yes. If Satan was able to harass Paul with a thorn in the flesh, then the question may be asked, why not other believers, through his minions?

John Wesley (1703–1791), the great evangelist, believed that the devil could cause believers distress. He wrote, "I am persuaded none that has faith can die before he is made ripe for glory. . . . True believers are not distressed hereby, either in life or in death: unless in some rare instance, wherein the temptation of the Devil is joined with a melancholy temper."[81] For Wesley, the distress could be caused by the devil's old trick of using temptation.[82] However he also believed that such a phenomenon would be rare, and that some psychological malady afflicting the subject needed to be present.

---

[77] "World" (*cosmos*) used in this sense refers to the lifestyle of humankind lived in God-displeasing ways (e.g., 1 John 2:15–17), and "flesh" (*sarx*) is that sinful nature of the human person that shows itself in God-dishonoring behaviors (e.g., those listed in Gal. 5:19–21).

[78] In Romans 15:22 Paul also writes of being hindered (the same Greek word as in 1 Thess. 2:18) in coming to a group of Christians, but for very different reasons. In the case of the Romans, it had to do with not preaching Christ where he had already been named. The hindrance was nothing sinister but instead had to do with missionary strategy.

[79] Michael W. Holmes, *1 and 2 Thessalonians*, NIVAC (Grand Rapids, MI: Zondervan, 1998), 95.

[80] Holmes, *1 and 2 Thessalonians*, 95.

[81] Quoted in Kenneth J. Collins, *John Wesley: A Theological Journey* (Nashville: Abingdon, 2003), 173.

[82] Kreeft, *Angels and Demons*, 114–116, argues that temptation is one of three ways that demons can influence humankind today: "There are three levels of demonic influence on men: (1) temptation, (2) oppression, and (3) possession." He does not tackle the question of whether a regenerated child of God could be possessed by a demon.

Can Believers Be Possessed by the Demonic?

Some scholars reject "demon-possession" as a phrase. For example, C. Fred Dickason and Wayne Grudem take this view. Dickason argues as follows: "Translating this word [*daimonizomenos*] as demon-possessed has caused confusion. Some take it to mean ownership. This cannot be. The demons own nothing. They are intruders and usurpers. The New Testament regards them as squatters and invaders of property that does not belong to them."[83] So what does Dickason propose instead? He argues, "From the etymology and the usage of the word *daimonizomenos*, its meaning is better understood as the inhabiting of a human by one or more demons who exercise various degrees of control with resultant physical, psychological, and spiritual manifestations."[84] As evidence he cites Luke 13:10–17 as an example of "mild" control. This is the case of the woman with the bent back. And he cites Luke 8:26–39 as one of "wild" control. This applies to the Gerasene demoniac. Dickason, like Grudem, prefers the term "demonization."[85]

What can be said about the issue of terminology? I am sympathetic to Dickason and Grudem's positions. Interestingly, the RSV and the NRSV avoid the phrase "demon-possessed" in Mark 5:15–16. However, Jesus compared the presence of a demon in a person's life to home occupancy (Matt. 12:43–45). Moreover, the NT language is of Satan entering in (John 13:27, *eisēlthen*) or of a demon coming out (Matt. 12:43, *exēlthon*). This suggests, albeit metaphorically, movement into and out of space. So whether "demon-possessed" is the preferred phrase or "demonized" is the preferred term, careful explanation is needed. The explanation would need to point out that usurped, destructive control of whole or part of another is the key, together with the idea of a continued demonic presence (Luke 8:26–39 and 13:10–17, respectively). Perhaps "demon inhabited" is an even better phrase to capture the idea of an indwelling demon or indwelling demons. Demons are squatters.

With all that said above, we can now consider the question itself. There are no examples in Scripture of believers who are possessed by the demonic. In fact, the Pauline teaching is that the individual believer is a temple of the Holy Spirit (1 Cor. 6:19–20): "Or do you not know that your body is a temple of the Holy Spirit within you, whom you have from God? You are not your own, for you were bought with a price. So glorify God in your body." This reality makes the demonic possession of the Christian highly dubious. Moreover, 1 John 4:4

---

[83] Dickason, *Angels: Elect and Evil*, 197.

[84] Dickason, *Angels: Elect and Evil*, 198. The problem with the word "control" is that it is, philosophically speaking, a vague term, like "hot," "cold," or "bald." A qualifier is needed to add precision (e.g., "very hot" or "partially bald").

[85] Grudem, *Systematic Theology*, 423–425, especially the lengthy footnote 19, rejects the expression "demon possession" as inaccurately capturing the meaning of the Greek verb *daimonizomai*, which he argues should be translated, "under demonic influence" or "to be demonized."

states, "Little children, you are from God and have overcome them, for he who is in you is greater than he who is in the world." Those who are overcome by believers appear to be the false prophets mentioned in 1 John 4:1, and "he who is in you" in context is the Holy Spirit, who is mentioned in verse 2. As for "he who is in the world," this is the antichrist of verse 3.

It seems extremely doubtful to me that such a possession can happen. A scenario in which there is both the indwelling Holy Spirit and a demon resident in the same human person seems a theological surd.[86] Brian Borgman and Rob Ventura argue similarly from Matthew 12:43–45: "It appears from this text that an unclean spirit cannot take up residence in a place already occupied. Therefore, since the Holy Spirit permanently indwells the believer, this can never happen (Rom. 5:5)."[87] However, regarding believers one may speculate that demonic oppression may reach such intensity in some cases that the line between oppression and possession may be hard to distinguish.[88]

Looking again at 1 John, we see that 1 John 4:1–6 distinguishes between the Spirit of truth and the spirit of error (v. 6). The Spirit of truth expresses himself through the writer of the letter (v. 6). The spirit of error is found in false prophets (v. 1). Their falsehood is seen in their Christology. They deny the incarnation (v. 2). This denial reveals the spirit of antichrist (v. 3). As for the readers, John is clear about their status (v. 4): "Little children, you are from God and have overcome them, for he who is in you is greater than he who is in the world." Stephen S. Smalley rightly identifies the one in the world: "The 'one who is in the world' is the evil one, or the devil (cf. 2:13–14; 3:12; 5:18–19), whose relative power (he in *you* is μείζων, "*more* powerful") is assumed."[89] The one identified as greater than the devil is either God or Christ or the Spirit.[90] Again, it is hard to imagine how a believer, described in these Johannine terms, could be possessed by an evil spirit.

Clinton E. Arnold rejects the idea of believers being demon-possessed. He writes emphatically: "Christians cannot be demon-possessed if one means by that expression ownership of a believer by Satan or demons. Believers are the property of God and belong exclusively to him."[91] So what does he propose instead? He argues that, "Christians can be inhabited by demons, but only if they provide the spirits with the space to occupy through protracted sin

---

[86] Jesse Penn-Lewis, of the 1904 Welsh Revival, had a very different point of view and argues that believers may indeed be possessed by the demonic (*War on the Saints* [New York: Thomas Lowe, 1973]).

[87] Brian Borgman and Rob Ventura, *Spiritual Warfare: A Biblical and Balanced Perspective* (Grand Rapids, MI: Reformation Heritage, 2014), 119.

[88] There is a useful discussion of the difference between demon-possession and demonization with reference to the Christian in Gregory A. Boyd and Paul R. Eddy, *Across the Spectrum: Understanding Issues in Evangelical Theology*, 2nd ed. (Grand Rapids, MI: Baker Academic, 2009), 313–314.

[89] Stephen S. Smalley, *1, 2, 3 John*, rev. ed., WBC (Dallas: Word, 2007), 227.

[90] Smalley, *1, 2, 3 John*, 227.

[91] Clinton E. Arnold, *Three Crucial Questions about Spiritual Warfare* (Grand Rapids, MI: Baker, 1998), 138.

or by inviting their presence."[92] But is this a distinction without a difference, assuming that believers can be under such control? Arnold is sensitive to the fact that the spatial imagery of inhabiting is metaphorical. Once more, I find 1 Corinthians 6:19–20 and 1 John 4:1–6 hard to square with his proposal.[93] I also note that there is no suggestion in any of the epistles of the NT that Christians can be inhabited by demons.[94] Instead, we find that the disobedient believer described in 1 Corinthians 5:1–5 is to be handed over to Satan (v. 5), and likewise the troublesome pair Hymenaeus and Alexander of 1 Timothy 1:20. To be handed over to Satan in these contexts appears to refer to expulsion from the fellowship of believers. Michael S. Heiser explains, with reference to 1 Corinthians 5:5, "Since God indwells believers today through his Spirit, each church—each gathering of believers—is holy ground. This is why Paul, when sadly telling the Corinthians to expel an unrepentant Christian who was living in sin, instructed them to 'deliver this man to Satan.' . . . The church was holy ground. Outside the fellowship of believers was the domain of Satan. That was where sin and its self-destruction belonged."[95] From these texts it appears that Satan is an external force in the believer's life, not an internal one.

Are There Exorcisms of Demons Today?

There is no debate that there were exorcisms conducted in the early church period after the close of the NT. For example, mid-second century, Justin Martyr wrote, "Throughout the whole world, and in your city, many of our Christian men have healed numerous demon-possessed persons, exorcising them in the name of Jesus Christ."[96] The Church in Rome mid-third century provides an important example. Stephen Neill points out that the most precise statistics for any church in the early church period are those of Rome in AD 251.[97] Bishop Cornelius of Rome writes to Bishop Fabius of Antioch as follows: "[I]n it [Rome] there were forty-six presbyters, seven deacons, seven sub-deacons, forty-two acolytes, fifty-two exorcists, readers and door-keepers, over 1500 widows and persons in distress, all of whom the grace and loving kindness of

---

[92] Arnold, *Three Crucial Questions*, 138.
[93] Nigel Wright, *The Satan Syndrome: Putting the Power of Darkness in Its Place* (Grand Rapids, MI: Zondervan, 1990), 125, acknowledges that the NT does employ "the spatial model of being indwelt by the Holy Spirit." Even so he contends that there are other models in the NT, such as "that of the Christian as a battle zone where the Spirit of God and the sinful nature confront each other in hostility. This holds open the possibility that the Spirit of God may on occasion not co-exist with but confront an evil spirit across a frontier drawn across a human life." How this comports with Paul's use of temple imagery in his pneumatology is left unaddressed and hence unexplained.
[94] According to Danielou, *Angels and Their Mission*, 79–81, the early church fathers took the view (e.g., Origen and Athanasius) that within every person is both a good angel and an evil one. The promptings toward virtue come from the good angel and the promptings to evil from the demon. The NT provides no support for this contention.
[95] Michael S. Heiser, *Supernatural: What the Bible Teaches about the Unseen World—and Why It Matters* (Bellingham, WA: Lexham, 2015), 84.
[96] Quoted in *DECB*, 268.
[97] Stephen Neill, *A History of Christian Missions*, 2nd ed. (London: Penguin, 1991), 30.

the Master nourish."[98] Significantly, "exorcist" is an official role according to the list.

In today's world, the Roman Catholic Church takes exorcism so seriously that there is a rite to observe in conducting an exorcism.[99] A Roman Catholic "rite of exorcism" dated 1999 is very lengthy, at 6,295 words, and involves numerous prayers and appeals to God, Mary, and the saints. The subject to be exorcised is also addressed more than once, and the evil spirit commanded to depart from him or her.[100] Pope Francis frequently refers to the devil in his speeches, and in 2014 a conference (the ninth) was convened in Rome at the Pontifical Athenaeum Regina Apostolorum to encourage the training of more exorcist priests.[101] There are 250 trained exorcist priests in Italy alone at present.

Since the fourth century, the Orthodox Church has regarded the priest as the successor of the early church exorcist. Orthodox prayer books contain prayers of exorcism drawn from the early church fathers. In the Orthodox Book of Prayers (*Euchologion to Mega*), there are three such prayers from Basil of Caesarea and four from John Chrysostom. The prayers are to be prayed on behalf of "those who suffer from demonic possessions and every other malady."[102] Orthodox theologian George C. Papademetriou writes, "Through these prayers, the devil is exorcised (renounced) 'in the name of God Almighty and the Lord Jesus Christ,' and commanded to come out of the victim." It is important to note that, for Papademetriou, "Christ is the *exorcist par excellence* for it is He who won the victory over the power of the devil."[103] Priests follow Christ's example as exorcists. Pentecostals, then, aren't the only Christian group that is rightly sober-minded concerning Satanic evil.[104]

As a non-cessationist, who does not think that the Spirit-given gifts of the NT writings ended with the closure of the biblical canon, I am open to there being demon-possession and exorcisms today.[105] Indeed, "[testing] the spirits," as commanded in 1 John 4:1, may reveal the need for exorcism. (The excursus at the

[98] Neill, *History of Christian Missions*, 31.

[99] It is worth noting that the *Catechism of the Catholic Church* makes it clear that, in Roman Catholic theology, baptism is a form of exorcism. See Philip Jenkins, "Speak of the Devil," *Christian Century* (September 27, 2017): 45.

[100] "Rite of Exorcism," http://www.catholicdoors.com/prayers/english/p01975b.htm, accessed 3/6/2015.

[101] Yasmine Hafiz, "Exorcism Conference at Vatican Addresses the Need for More Demon-Fighting Priests," http://www.huffingtonpost.com/2014/05/13/exorcism-conference-rome-priests_n_5316749.html, accessed 3/6/2015.

[102] George C. Papademetriou, "Exorcism in the Orthodox Church," http://www.goarch.org/ourfaith/ourfaith7079, accessed 3/31/2015.

[103] Papademetriou, "Exorcism in the Orthodox Church."

[104] In an interesting article, Craig S. Keener looks at anthropological studies of spirit possession from diverse places in today's world, including Nigeria, Nepal, and Sri Lanka. He acknowledges that the explanations for the phenomena—superhuman displays of strength, knowledge, and trances—vary from neurological and social (in the West) to possession by ancestral spirits or other supernatural explanations (outside the West). His aim is to show that these phenomena and NT descriptions are analogous, which suggests that the NT may be embodying eyewitness testimony. See Keener's "Spirit Possession as a Cross-cultural Experience," *Bulletin for Biblical Research* 20/2 (2010): 215–236.

[105] On the debate between cessationists and continuationists, see my discussion in my *He Who Gives Life: The Doctrine of the Holy Spirit* (Wheaton, IL: Crossway, 2007), 248–258.

end of chapter 7 deals with this text and the question of testing the spirits.) How an exorcism might be conducted today is beyond the purview of this work. This is a work of systematic theology and not a manual of pastoral theology. However, one observation is in order: NT exorcisms appear to have required a brief word of command appealing to Jesus's name. Arguably, there are no NT examples of protracted prayer to effect an exorcism. Acts 16:18 is no exception if the NIV translation is correct, which reads, "At that moment the spirit left her." The text literally reads that the spirit came out at Paul's command in Jesus's name ". . . in the same hour" (*autē tē hōra*). The ESV and NRSV translate the Greek literally ("that very hour"). The NIV takes the phrase as idiomatic and renders the Greek accordingly. The idea of the need for protracted praying to conduct a successful exorcism may go back to the King James translation, which renders Mark 9:28–29 as follows: "And when he was come into the house, his disciples asked him privately, Why could not we cast him out? And he said unto them. This kind can come forth by nothing, but by prayer *and fasting*. The mention of fasting suggests strongly an elapse of time connected to praying. However, the phrase "and fasting" appears to be an addition and not part of the original text.[106]

A Caveat (Matthew 7:21–23)

To exorcise a demon would be an unforgettable experience. One might think that surely such ability would say something about the noble spiritual stature of the exorcist. Not so, according to Jesus. His sober warning to those listening to him in the context of the Matthean Sermon on the Mount gives pause:

> Not everyone who says to me, "Lord, Lord," will enter the kingdom of heaven, but the one who does the will of my Father who is in heaven. On that day many will say to me, "Lord, Lord, did we not prophesy in your name, and cast out demons in your name, and do many mighty works in your name?" And then will I declare to them, "I never knew you; depart from me, you workers of lawlessness."

R. T. France comments, "Not only the profession of discipleship, but even miraculous activity in the name of Jesus, is not enough to prove a genuine disciple. . . . Prophecy, exorcism and miracles can be counterfeited. 'Charismatic' activity is no substitute for obedience and a personal relationship with Jesus."[107]

We recall once more Jesus's words to the seventy-two upon their return from mission (Luke 10:17–20):

---

[106]Craig A. Evans, *Mark 8:27–16:20*, WBC (Dallas: Word, 2001), 47, comments, "P⁴⁵ᵛⁱᵈ ℵ² A C D L W 33 and many later authorities add καὶ νηστείᾳ, 'and fasting.' The addition probably reflects the church's growing interest in fasting; cf. *TCGNT*, 101."

[107]R. T. France, *Matthew*, TNTC (Downers Grove, IL: IVP Academic, 2008), 153. France also points out that the book of Acts gives evidence of how the name of Jesus was used in attempted exorcisms by those outside the kingdom (Acts 19:13).

> The seventy-two returned with joy, saying, "Lord, even the demons are subject
> to us in your name!" And he said to them, "I saw Satan fall like lightning from
> heaven. Behold, I have given you authority to tread on serpents and scorpions,
> and over all the power of the enemy, and nothing shall hurt you. Nevertheless,
> do not rejoice in this, that the spirits are subject to you, but rejoice that your
> names are written in heaven."

Would not Judas have been in their number? And would not Jesus's words in
Matthew 7 have been applicable to him? The exercise of a spiritual ability or
authority is no *ipso facto* guarantee that one's name is written in heaven.

The dominical warning remains relevant to any who think that extraordinary experiences such as performing exorcisms provide grounds for the assurance that one is truly a child of God.

Is There a Relation between Superstition and the Demonic?

Stanley J. Grenz certainly thinks so. In an illuminating discussion, he argues
that there is a connection between the superstitious practices of humankind
dating back to antiquity and the demonic disorder.[108] He draws attention to
passages in the OT that warn against superstitious practices (e.g., Deut. 18:9–
13). Those practices included divination, sorcery, and consultation with me-
diums. The warnings were not heeded, though. Time and again Israel fell into
superstition (e.g., 1 Chron. 10:13, King Saul and the medium). God's judgment
came upon his people as a result (e.g., 2 Kings 17:16–17). Grenz maintains,
"As these texts [2 Kings 17:7–16 and 2 Chron. 33:2–5] indicate, involvement
in superstition was one dimension of that great evil plaguing the ancient people of God and against which the prophets of Yahweh contended—the sin of
idolatry."[109] These superstitious practices are also grounds for exclusion from
God's presence, as the depiction of the last judgment in the book of Revelation
shows (Rev. 21:8; 22:15; *pharmakoi*, "sorcerers").

Grenz ties these superstitious practices to idolatry in a way reminiscent of
Wink's argument about the "powers." "The powers," Grenz argues, "are real,
but they are evil and malicious."[110] The practices he lists include soothsaying or
necromancy, astrology, and divination. These practices he distinguishes from
those of traditional medicine (e.g., the use of herbs). He asks, "How then
should we approach superstitious beliefs and practices?" He answers, "Simply
stated—with great caution and vigilant discernment."[111]

What can be said of Grenz's concerns? He is right that superstitious prac-

---

[108] Stanley J. Grenz, *Theology for the Community of God* (Grand Rapids, MI: Eerdmans, 2000), 235–238.
[109] Grenz, *Theology for the Community of God*, 239.
[110] Grenz, *Theology for the Community of God*, 239.
[111] Grenz, *Theology for the Community of God*, 242. For practical guidance on how to address such beliefs and
practices, see Beekmann and Bolt, *Silencing Satan*, 193–226.

tices may indeed be demonic, but not in every instance. In that light, his call for discernment is a wise one. I think of a Roman Catholic lady I know who buries upside down in her garden the statuette of a saint when she is praying to God for something. This to me seems bizarre and foolish, but hardly demonic.

Is There a Relation between Mental Illness and the Demonic?

This is a difficult subject. In Britain, for example, there are many migrants who attend immigrant African churches. In fact, there are about 1.5 million African-born residents in the nation. Exorcism is a common practice in many of these churches. According to Philip Jenkins, "Such churches view apparent possession cases in terms of demonic activity rather than as a mental health issue treatable by secular means."[112] The British media has sensationalized these practices "as a form of primitive jungle savagery dressed in Christian guise."[113] In reaction, the British government has placed "far stricter rules for African clergy and minsters seeking to enter the United Kingdom."[114] Such controversy raises acutely the question of the relation between mental illness and demonic possession.

Roy Clements writes, "There are few forms of illness that cause more distress or generate more social stigma than those which derange the mind. That such mental illness is in some general sense an 'evil' no one can doubt. But what kind of 'evil' is it?"[115] And this is especially the case when one reads present-day accounts of attempted exorcisms that have led to the death of a subject who had been medically diagnosed with some form of mental illness. Were the NT writers misidentifying disease and the demonic because of the ignorance characterizing the times in which they lived?

There is NT evidence suggesting that the writers were not as naïve as some moderns might contend.[116] It is important to note that the NT writers appear to distinguish between disease and the demonic. For example, in Matthew 4:24, speaking of Jesus's mighty works, a number of categories are on view: "So his fame spread throughout all Syria, and they brought him all the sick, those afflicted with various diseases [*nosois*, "illnesses"] and pains [*synechomenous*, "torments"], those oppressed by demons [*daimonizomenous*, "demon-possessed"], those having seizures [*selēniazomenous*], and paralytics

---

[112] Philip Jenkins, "Speak of the Devil," 44. For the British data, Jenkins draws on Ben Ryan, *Christianity and Mental Health: Theology, Activities, Potential*, https://www.theosthinktank.co.uk/research/2017/07/03/christianity -and-mental-health-theology-activities-potential, accessed 9/28/2017.
[113] Jenkins, "Speak of the Devil," 44.
[114] Jenkins, "Speak of the Devil," 44.
[115] Roy Clements, "Demons and the Mind," http://www.courage.org.uk/article.asp?id=134, accessed 8/8/2015. This brief piece is outstanding.
[116] An example can be seen in Joseph, who did not believe the story about Mary's pregnancy until he had an encounter with an angel himself. His initial reaction was to end the relationship with Mary quietly (Matt. 1:18–25). Another example is how the apostles did not believe that the women had encountered the risen Christ (Luke 24:9–11). In both cases, some convincing needed to take place.

[*paralytikous*], and he healed them." According to D. A. Carson, "Those 'ill with various diseases' and 'those suffering severe' pain are divided into three overlapping categories: (1) the demon-possessed (cf. Mt. 8:28–34; 12:22–29); (2) those having seizures—viz., any kind of insanity or irrational behavior whether or not related to demon-possession (17:14–18; . . . *selēniazomenous* ['epileptics' . . .], which etymologically refers to the 'moonstruck' [i.e., 'lunatic']) . . . and (3) the paralyzed, whose condition also had various causes."[117]

It seems to me that when there is an alleged case of "demon-possession," the best way forward is a team approach: the pastor, the Christian psychiatrist, and a praying church.[118] The mood should be open, because demon inhabitation is biblically real, but discernment is needful.[119] Again Clements is wise: "Thus mental illness might be caused by faulty body chemistry (physical influence), dysfunctional family experience (social influence), demonic assault (spiritual influence) or unresolved guilt (personal sin)."[120] Misdiagnosis, however, may lead to a tragic outcome.[121] The story of Job should act as a caution here. His so-called friends got the diagnosis wrong with their simplistic moral calculus of "suffering means sin" (see Job 42:8). Similarly, when the disciples in John 9 asked about the man born blind, as to who sinned, whether it was the man or his parents, the dominical answer was "neither" (v. 3).

Theologians, when speaking of divine action, distinguish between God as the *causa remota* and the *causa propinqua*. As *causa remota* (remote cause) God is, metaphysically speaking, the ultimate cause of all events because he decided to create and thus there is a platform for events that came into existence and which the divine will holds in existence. As *causa propinqua*, he is the immediate cause of an event such as the raising of Jesus from the dead. Perhaps this holds true of the devil as well. As the introducer of evil (Genesis 3), he is the *causa remota* of all evil events befalling humankind. In some

---

[117] D. A. Carson, "Matthew," in *EBC*, comment on Matthew 4:24. David Instone Brewer, "Jesus and the Psychiatrists," in *The Unseen World: Christian Reflections on Angels, Demons, and the Heavenly Realm*, 148, offers a similar analysis of Matthew 4:24: 'He [Matthew] listed three types of healing: 'those who were demonized, those which were lunatic and paralytics." Philip Jenkins, *Crucible of Faith*, 149, appears to confuse categories in his reading of the evidence in the Gospels. He writes of the story of the expulsion of demons from the Gadarene demoniac in these terms: "Jesus' method of healing left readers in no option but to see the man's *illness* in terms of real, objective demonic forces rather than any inner or psychological condition" (emphasis mine). Which is it, illness or demonization?

[118] Roy Clements, "Demons," agrees that the way forward is "teams of Christian psychiatrists, psychotherapists, counselors and pastors working together on the same cases."

[119] Brewer, "Jesus and the Psychiatrists," 148, exemplifies this approach. Particularly impressive is the sober recounting by this NT scholar of his own experiences and the behavior of a subject in response to specific silent prayers—for example, for the demon to name itself/themselves—that Brewer prayed.

[120] Clements, "Demons." Clements proposes a holistic model of the human person that takes seriously physical, social, and spiritual influences. His model is predicated on a psychosomatic understanding of the human constitution. The model works also for those holding a dualistic understanding of the human person, when the person for all intents and purposes is encountered phenomenologically as a functioning whole.

[121] My colleague Greg Scharf, whose expertise is in pastoral theology, shared in private conversation that his pastoral rule of thumb when dealing with what could be construed as demonic possession is that, if the person claims they are demon-possessed, they probably aren't, and if a person claims not to be demon-possessed, maybe they are. Satan is a deceiver.

instances, however, he is also the *causa propinqua* (e.g., the seduction of Eve). The mistake is facilely to make the devil the *causa propinqua* for every ill. The comedian Flip Wilson's catchphrase, "The devil made me do it!," is illustrative. The biblical fact is that neither the devil nor demons are omnipresent. Only God is. Therefore, not every malady is to be laid unthinkingly at the devil's or the demonic door.

Demons Are Believers, So Why Aren't They Saved?

From James 2:19 we learn that demons are monotheists who believe the *Shema*: "You believe that God is one; you do well. Even the demons believe—and shudder!" However, a propositional belief that X is the case, and a personal saving belief that trusts in X, are two very different life stances. The demons have the first. Christian believers have both the first and second. Indeed for believers there is no tension between the propositional and the personal. Personal trust in X presupposes propositional belief about X. Logically speaking, I cannot trust X if I do not believe X is real or true. Think of the absurdity in saying I trust Jesus but I don't believe he existed or exists. John's Gospel understands the distinction. John 20:30–31 exhibits both the propositional and the personal aspects of biblical believing: "Now Jesus did many other signs in the presence of the disciples, which are not written in this book; but these are written so that you may believe that [*pisteuēte hoti*) Jesus is the Christ, the Son of God [the propositional], and that by believing you may have life in his name [the personal]." The very famous text John 3:16 also reveals the personal aspect: "For God so loved the world, that he gave his only Son, that whoever believes [*pisteuein eis*] in him should not perish but have eternal life." No trust, no salvation. The non-saving belief of the demons throws into sharp relief the nature of saving faith as trust in another.[122]

CONCLUSION

There are fallen angels led by Satan who are the demons of biblical record. They are malicious spirits who can hinder, harass, oppress, but not possess believers. Believers, after all, are temples of the Holy Spirit. However, demon inhabitation is still a real possibility in today's world and should not be dismissed as superstition. There appears to be the real possibility also that superstitious practices and even mental illness in some instances may have a demonic root. Great caution is needed here, though. The real answer to certain human

---

[122] In the era of the Protestant scholastics, both Lutheran and Reformed, it was thought that the demons had *fides historica* ("historical faith") but not *fides salvifica* ("saving faith"). For these categories see Richard A. Muller, *Dictionary of Latin and Greek Theological Terms: Drawn Principally from Protestant Scholastic Theology* (Grand Rapids, MI: Baker, 1986), 115. Muller states concerning *fides historica*, "[E]ven devils believe that Christ died to save the world from sin," but without spiritual benefit.

behaviors may be medication and psychiatric care. The question of discerning what is the case in a particular instance is very tricky. Discernment is needed because neither Satan nor demons are omnipresent. Some believers seem to overlook this fact and so the devil and demons are seen as present on every occasion and in every place. (More anon when in a later chapter spiritual warfare is on view.) As for demons, their theology of God is orthodox but such belief is propositional and not personal. They do not have saving faith.

EXCURSUS: GENESIS 6:1–4 AND THE METHODOLOGICAL QUESTION

Gordon J. Wenham describes Genesis 6:1–4 as "probably the most problematic in the whole of Genesis."[123] David Albert Jones adds to the chorus: "This short paragraph from the book of Genesis is possibly the strangest passage in the entire Hebrew Bible."[124] As we have seen, there are three major interpretations: "the sociologically mixed races view" (despotic male aristocrats and beautiful female commoners), or as I prefer to say, the sociologically mixed humans view; "the cosmologically mixed races view" (angels and humans), or as I prefer to say, the ontologically mixed creatures view; and "the religiously mixed races view," or as I prefer to say, the morally mixed humans view (e.g., godly Sethites and worldly Cainites).[125] Exploring the issues posed by the interpretation of Genesis 6:1–4 raises important methodological considerations. What is the way forward when exegetes disagree on the meaning of key passages or even, if they agree, then disagree on their continuing significance?

Philosopher D. Elton Trueblood offers sage advice in his concept of the method of "comparative difficulties." Trueblood claims this about philosophy: "The mood of philosophy is not that of the person who waits until he finds a solution utterly free from difficulties; it is rather the mood of one who knows very well that the best available is itself imperfect."[126] Again he argues, "Philosophy in this, as in so many intellectual decisions [note: not just in philosophy as a discipline], is the art of balancing imperfect alternatives."[127] On analysis, some alternatives have weightier difficulties or more numerous ones than the position under immediate discussion. Or an alternative may raise fewer questions but the questions raised are more profound.

What Trueblood contends concerning the intellectual discipline of phi-

---

[123] Wenham, *Exploring the Old Testament*, 25.
[124] David Albert Jones, *Angels: A Very Short Introduction* (Oxford: Oxford University Press, 2011), 110.
[125] Contra Kaiser (*Hard Sayings*, 107), I cannot see how royals and commoners constitute different races, nor can I see how Sethites and Cainites form two different races. And are angels a race? With the phrase, "the morally mixed humans view," I am following a suggestion offered by Glenn N. Davies, archbishop of Sydney, who pointed out in private conversation that the antithesis is between the righteous and the wicked, which is a pervasive biblical theme. Moreover, Sethites and Cainites were related, and therefore hardly different races.
[126] D. Elton Trueblood, *General Philosophy* (Grand Rapids, MI: Baker, 1976), 73. The section from which the quotation is taken is headed, "The Method of Comparative Difficulties."
[127] Trueblood, *General Philosophy*, 74.

losophy applies to the disciplines of exegesis and theology. And his approach could be refined further by combining it with the humble Anselmian mood of faith seeking understanding (*fides quaerens intellectum*) and a Chalcedonian strategy which seeks to set out the boundaries of an orthodox belief on a subject within which fruitful debate and differences of opinion may take place.[128] One such boundary would be the authority of Scripture. If a theory on the present subject undermined biblical authority (e.g., Gen. 6:1–4 is a relic of a fanciful mythological worldview, which no contemporary person could believe) then the theory is truant.

So as we enter some controversial areas of discussion, there is room indeed for debate, but in the end, if a judgment call is needed, then the method of comparative difficulties may help show where the probabilities lie. In the case of Genesis 6:1–4 and the story of the entanglement of the sons of God and the daughters of men, I would argue that the passage refers to men and women. I would find it easier to believe the angels and women thesis if only sexual relations were on view. However, although Gordon J. Wenham takes "the ontologically mixed creatures view" (angels and humans), he points out that the language of the passage does not imply rape: "Though v. 2 has been read as describing the rape of women, in fact the verbs imply perfectly *legitimate* marital relations."[129] If that is so, then that would comport better with "the religiously mixed humans view" (either the righteous and the unrighteous or the despotic rulers and commoner women or the godly Sethites and the worldly Cainites). It is hard to conceive, given their viciousness, *ex hypothesi*, of fallen angels wanting to marry rather than in some way ravish human women. Moreover, the offspring of the sexual union of the sons of God and the daughters of men are clearly human and not some kind of hybrid (Gen. 6:4).

What about the Nephilim and their identity? I take it that the Nephilim were humans—albeit mighty ones of renown. The text makes it plain that the Nephilim were present on the earth before the sons of God make their appearance in the text (Gen. 6:4): "The Nephilim [the meaning of "Nephilim" is obscure] were on the earth in those days, *and also afterward*, when the sons of God came in to the daughters of man and they bore children to them. These were the mighty men who were of old, the men of renown."[130]

Is this judgment call free of difficulties? No! However, the other approach

---

[128] The Chalcedonian Definition of AD 451 set out the boundaries of an orthodox Christology: one person in two natures, truly human and truly God. The Definition offered no theory as to how this was so, but set the boundary lines. For example, to deny the two natures was to cross the boundary, as Eutychianism had done.

[129] Gordon J. Wenham, "Genesis," in *ECB*, 42, emphasis mine.

[130] I owe this point about timing to Derek Kidner, *Genesis: An Introduction and Commentary*, TOTC (Downers Grove, IL: InterVarsity Press, 1982), 91. Could the Nephilim have been an exceptionally tall demographic? There were exceptionally tall humans in Israel's orbit and even among themselves (e.g., Goliath and Saul, respectively). So this is a possibility, but hard to prove. The LXX does use the term *gigantes* ("giants") for the Hebrew of Genesis 6:4. But the LXX is not the inspired word of God. The Israelite spies did report to Moses that they had seen Nephilim in the land of Canaan and made a point of their height (Num. 13:33). However, this was the report of

(angels and women) seems to have more weighty issues attached to it, as does the view that the Nephilim were giants produced by the union of angels and humans. Given the method of comparative difficulties, I favor the morally mixed humans view, but leave open the question as to *which* humans precisely.[131]

Erickson takes a similar view, although he does not call it the method of comparative difficulties. For him, the sticking point with the fallen angel approach is Jesus's teaching about the afterlife and the idea that believers would be like the angels in not being married nor given in marriage (Matt. 22:30). Erickson argues,

> In the light of this, the interpretation that understands the "sons of God" in Genesis 6:2 to be sons of Seth who mated with pagan descendants of Cain seems to present less difficulty than does the interpretation of "sons of God" as angels, although neither view can be held dogmatically. There simply is not enough evidence to justify using this passage as a source of information about angels. This should not be considered a case of "evangelical demythologizing," as some have suggested [namely, Willem A. VanGemeren]. It is simply a matter of remaining skeptical in the face of insufficient evidence.[132]

I take the stronger view—given the method of comparative difficulties—that Genesis 6:1–4 is not relevant to the fall of angels. What is not lost on this view? The idea of an angelic fall is not lost, because of NT texts such as 2 Peter 2:4 and Jude 6–7. What *is* lost is a putative explanation as to why some fallen angels are imprisoned until the Day of Judgment.

---

spies who were looking for every excuse not to go into the land, and so exaggeration and self-serving inaccuracy on their part is quite plausible.

[131] For arguments in support see Schemm, "Agents of God: Angels," 262–263; and Grudem, *Systematic Theology*, 413–414. Robert P. Lightner, "Angels, Satan, and Demons: Invisible Beings That Inhabit the Spiritual World," in *Understanding Christian Theology*, ed. Charles R. Swindoll and Roy B. Zuck (Nashville: Thomas Nelson, 2003), 589–591, adopts something like the method of comparative difficulties but comes to a different judgment than mine. He argues for the wicked angels view.

[132] Erickson, *Christian Theology*, 412.

SIX

JESUS, CHRISTUS VICTOR

Philip C. Almond accurately sums up the importance of Christology in relation to Satan and demons in the early church period "For the early Church Fathers, the life, death and resurrection of Christ was set within the context of the historical battle between God and the Devil that ranged from the fall of Satan, before the beginning of history, until its end."[1] Indeed the fathers argued that the victory of Christ and his triumphant ascension astonished the angelic realm. Jean Danielou sums up their view as follows: "Thus, to the wonderment of the heavenly forces, the human nature is exalted in the person of Christ, above every angelic nature, known or unknown."[2] More to the point, though, is that the early church fathers saw in Christ's coming, cross, and coming to life again, that the decisive blow had been struck against the darkness. Jesus, speaking of his coming passion on the cross, put it this way in John 12:31: "Now is the judgment of this world; now will the ruler of this world be cast out." And cast out he was. So in his letter John was right to sum up Christ's purpose in his coming into the world in this striking way (1 John 3:8): "The reason the Son of God appeared was to destroy the works of the devil." But how did—or how does—Christ destroy the works of the devil? Such destruction does not seem at all obvious in the light of the daily news and the cavalcade of horrors it reveals: war, murder, sexual and domestic violence, to name only a few of the evils reported.

In this chapter we explore the relation between Christology—our doctrine of Christ's person and work—and Satan and demons. It will do so within the framework set up by the promises found in Genesis 3:15. Philip Melanchthon (1497–1560), Luther's younger associate, recognized in this OT text ". . . the first promise, the first gospel, by which Adam was raised up and understood a certain hope of his salvation, indeed, he was justified."[3] Hence this text is

---

[1] Philip C. Almond, *The Devil: A New Biography* (Ithaca, NY: Cornell University Press, 2014), 49.
[2] Jean Danielou, *The Angels and Their Mission according to the Church Fathers*, trans. David Heimann (Notre Dame, IN: Ave Maria, 1957), 36–37.
[3] Philipp Melanchthon, *Loci Communes*, quoted in Martin Foord, "'A New Embassy': John Calvin's Gospel," in *Aspects of Reforming: Theology and Practice in Sixteenth Century Europe*, ed. Michael Parsons (Milton Keynes, UK: Paternoster, 2013), 140.

known as the *protevangelium* or "the first gospel." This exploration will examine Christ's encounters with Satan and his teaching on Satan and demons as well as his exorcisms. Special focus will be on the cross and its role in the defeat of the evil one. To consider the cross and what was achieved there brings in atonement theory, especially early church speculations as to how Christ's cross and his resurrection defeated the devil. Atonement theories that see Christ's defeat of the devil as central to his atoning work are *Christus Victor* theories. There are difficult NT passages that also must be brought into purview, including the Petrine text about the spirits in prison and the vexed question of their identity.

THE PROTEVANGELIUM

John Calvin made this comment on Genesis 3:15: "That God might revive the fainting minds of men , . . . it became necessary to promise them, in their posterity, victory over Satan."[4] He was right. The promise made by God in Genesis 3:14–15 ramifies through the biblical narrative, and our Christology needs to give due weight to it. This text is found within the context of the divine judgments pronounced by the Creator in the light of the Adamic rebellion. The Creator addresses the deceiving serpent:

> Because you have done this,
>> cursed are you above all livestock
>> and above all beasts of the field;
> on your belly you shall go,
>> and dust you shall eat
>> all the days of your life.
> I will put enmity between you and the woman,
>> and between your offspring and her offspring;
> he shall bruise your head,
>> and you shall bruise his heel.

Gordon J. Wenham argues, "'Hostility' . . . ['enmity,' ESV and NIV]: Both in this context and other passages suggest that long-lasting enmity is meant (cf. Num. 35:21–22; Ezek. 25:15; 35:5)."[5] In biblical perspective, the conflict will not end quickly, but end it will.

James Hamilton in his treatment of Genesis 3:15 and of its echoes throughout the rest of Scripture states, "from the moment God uttered his judgment against the serpent, the seed of the woman (the collective of those who trust God) were hoping for *the* seed of the woman (the man who would achieve the ultimate victory over the serpent.)"[6] As I have written elsewhere,

---

[4] John Calvin, *Calvin's Commentaries, Genesis* (Grand Rapids, MI: Baker, 2003), 169.

[5] Gordon J. Wenham, *Genesis, 1–15*, WBC (Dallas: Word, 2002), 79.

[6] James Hamilton, "The Skull Crushing Seed of the Woman: Inner-Biblical Interpretation of Genesis 3:15," *SBJT* 11 (2006): 43, emphasis original. There is scholarly debate about whether "seed" refers to all the descen-

How the serpent's fortunes are to be reversed is not revealed in any depth in Genesis 3. A male descendant of the woman will be involved. That is clear. Suffering will be involved for both the male offspring and the serpent: "he will crush your head, and you will strike his heel" Gen. 3:15). That too is clear. The serpent will lose definitively, a crushed head versus a struck heel. Both Jewish translators and early Christian commentators saw in the progeny of the woman a messianic hope.[7]

Without some understanding of the programmatic nature of the *protevangelium* of Genesis 3:15 and its accent on the victory of the male offspring over the serpent, the canon of Scripture loses its narrative coherence and its storyline becomes opaque. That male offspring turns out to be none other than Jesus Christ, and the defeat of the serpent, the devil, will involve Christ's coming, his cross, and his coming again.

DEFEATING THE DEVIL

So then why, according to the NT writers, did God become human or, to use the famous title of Anselm's classic work, *Cur Deus Homo?*[8] Thomas Oden captures the many-sided biblical testimony to the reason for the incarnation by offering five reasons.

> To reveal God to humanity (John 1:18; 14:7–11).
> To provide a high priest interceding for us able to sympathize with human weaknesses (Heb. 4:14–16).
> To offer a pattern of the fullness of human life (1 Pet. 2:21; 1 John 2:6).
> To provide a substitutionary sacrifice for the sins of all humanity (Heb. 10:1–10).
> To bind up the demonic powers (1 John 3:8).[9]

Oden's last point is particularly germane to this project. Jesus did not embrace the blind spot identified by Hiebert. He had no difficulty in recognizing that evil cannot be reduced to the bad behavior of humankind. So then how does Jesus defeat the devil? We start with Christ's active obedience; that is

---

dants of the woman or one particular one. T. Desmond Alexander argues cogently for an individual descendant (*From Eden to the New Jerusalem: An Introduction to Biblical Theology* [Grand Rapids, MI: Kregel, 2008], 105–106).

[7] Graham A. Cole, *God the Peacemaker: How Atonement Brings Shalom* (Downers Grove, IL: InterVarsity Press, 2009), 92.

[8] Anselm intentionally wrote his work as though he knew nothing of Christ. He expounds what he sees as the human predicament and how an incarnation and atonement provided by a God-man can remedy the problem that reason without divine aid has uncovered. Anselm's work contrasts, then, with the present one, which seeks to discover how the Bible itself answers his question. The methodology could not be more different. For a useful treatment of Anselm's appeal to reason, see J. L. González, *A History of Christian Thought: From the Beginnings to the Council of Chalcedon*, vol. 1, rev. ed. (Nashville: Abingdon, 1987), 158–167.

[9] Thomas C. Oden, *Classic Christianity: A Systematic Theology* (New York: HarperCollins, 1992), 271, emphasis original. By "biblically defensible" I mean claims that have exegetical grounding rather than being the products of theological speculation. Oden's list is not exhaustive. One could add Hebrews 2:14–15, which links specifically the incarnation of Jesus to his death in the defeat of the devil.

to say, his perfect doing of the will of the Father. It was an obedience that was soon tested.

Jesus Stays True despite Temptation

The first explicit reference in the Gospels to devilish opposition to the messianic mission of Jesus comes immediately after his baptism at the hands of John the Baptist in the Jordan River.[10] In Mark, the language is breathlessly forceful: "The Spirit immediately drove [better, "drives"; *ekballei*] him out into the wilderness" (Mark 1:12). There Jesus is tempted by Satan. He was with the wild beasts and ministered to by angels (v. 13). The reference to "the wild animals" is suggestive of a restored harmony between the new Adam and the previously estranged animal kingdom—estranged because of the fall.[11] The Markan account is tantalizingly brief. Matthew enlarges the story considerably. We learn of Jesus's hunger and the precise nature of the temptations. The devil attempts to lure Jesus into pursuing a different will from that of the Father by providing for himself in the wilderness (Matt. 4:3), by putting God to the test by leaping from the temple top (vv. 5–7), and by worshiping none other than the tempter himself to gain the world with its kingdoms (vv. 8–9). There is a great irony in this last temptation. The devil offers Jesus the chance to become the ruler of the world, and in refusing the temptation Jesus ensures that he *will* be, as Matthew 28:18–20 will show.[12] And so Jesus stays fully aligned with the Father's will throughout the ordeal. And in this longer account the angels come at the end of the ordeal to minister to Jesus (Matt. 4:1 and 11). He subsequently leaves the scene of his triumph "in the power of Spirit" (Luke 4:14). Gerald F. Hawthorne rightly suggests, "Thus at the outset of his ministry Jesus is depicted as overcoming the evil one who stands in opposition to the work of the kingdom ([Luke] 11:19, 20) through the all-sufficient energizing power of the Spirit of God."[13] More recently, N. T. Wright makes the same point: "But where did Jesus' victory over the powers of evil begin? All three synoptic gospels provide an answer: in a dramatic battle at the outset of Jesus' public career."[14]

---

[10] "Explicit" is the key word. Revelation 12:1–6 strongly indicates that there was murderous opposition from Satan as "a great red dragon" even before the birth of Mary's child (v. 4): "And the dragon stood before the woman who was about to give birth, so that when she bore her child he might devour it." Exegetes differ as to whether the woman is Mary or Israel or the church. There is general agreement, though, that the child is the Messiah of Israel. Stephen H. Webb, *The Dome of Eden: A New Solution to the Problem of Creation and Evolution* (Eugene, OR: Cascade, 2010), 151, argues that Revelation 12 ". . . gives as the reason for Satan's fall his jealousy of the woman 'clothed with the sun' . . . and her child." However, the text actually gives no reason. This is eisegesis.

[11] See George T. Montague, *The Holy Spirit: Growth of a Biblical Tradition: A Commentary on the Principal Texts of the Old and New Testaments* (New York: Paulist, 1976), 243.

[12] A point well made by Anthony J. Saldarini, "Matthew," in *ECB*, ed. James D. G. Dunn and John W. Rogerson (Grand Rapids, MI, and Cambridge: Eerdmans, 2003), 1011.

[13] Gerald F. Hawthorne, *Presence and Power: The Significance of the Spirit in the Life and Ministry of Jesus* (Dallas, London, Vancouver, and Melbourne: Word, 1991), 139.

[14] N. T. Wright, *Jesus and the Victory of God* (Minneapolis: Fortress, 1996), 457. Wright strikingly argues that for Jesus it was Satan not Rome that was the ultimate enemy of God's people: "The pagan hordes surrounding Israel

The Matthean and Lukan accounts are highly suggestive. Given the genealogy that opens Matthew, with its Abrahamic starting point (Matt. 1:1–17), and given the Jewish thrust of this Gospel, it is not too fanciful to see in Jesus's triumph in the temptations the very reverse of Israel's experience. Israel, God's son (Ex. 4:22), was tested in the wilderness also but failed.[15] If only Israel had lived the theology of Deuteronomy, which Jesus so strategically quotes in his encounter with the devil, it would presumably not have fallen. The Lukan presentation of the temptations is also preceded by a genealogy (Luke 3:23–38). This time the genealogy goes all the way back to Adam. It is not too fanciful to see here an allusion to Adam's test in the paradise of God and subsequent failure, in contrast to the testing of this Son of Adam, Jesus, who in a very different setting—not a garden but a wilderness—does not fail. In the power of the Spirit, Jesus is all that Israel should have been as God's son, and all that Adam should have been as God's son. In other words, Jesus is the true Israel and the true Adam. Here is the one person who lives by every word that proceeds out of the mouth of God.

Jesus Teaches the Truth about the Devil and the Demons

One of the most common ways that Jesus was addressed was "teacher," and so he was.[16] Indeed he endorsed "teacher" as a self-designation in John 13:13 during the Upper Room discourse: "You call me [the] Teacher [*ho didaskalos*, "the teacher"] and Lord, and you are right, for so I am." From the outset of Jesus's public ministry (Mark 1:14–15), the theme of his teaching was the kingdom of God. In teaching about the kingdom he taught an awareness of evil. There is an enemy of God and humanity. That enemy needs to be known. For example, in the famous parable of the farmer and the seed, it is Satan who snatches away the kingdom seed before it can take root in a hearer's life (Mark 4:15). Again, in the parable of the weeds in Matthew 13:24–30, Jesus speaks of an enemy who sows weeds among the wheat, and in his explanation in verses 36–43 Jesus identifies the enemy as "the evil one," "the devil" (especially Matthew 13:38–39). In the parable of the sheep and the goats we find that the eternal fire (*to pur to aiōnion*) is for the devil and his angels (Matt. 25:41). But Jesus could teach more straightforwardly than by

---

were not the actual foe of YHWH. Standing behind the whole problem of Israel's exile was the dark power known in some Old Testament traditions as the satan, the accuser" (451). Wright famously argues that first-century Judaism was still in exile until the victory of the cross, which was also a key part of the return of YHWH to Zion in the person of Christ (463).

[15] William J. Dumbrell, in *The Search for Order: Biblical Eschatology in Focus* (Eugene, OR: Wipf & Stock, 2001), 163, provides a fine account. See also Donald A. Hagner, *Matthew 1–13*, WBC (Dallas: Word, 1993), 60–70 (comment on Matthew 4:1–11).

[16] The Gospel of John recounts this form of address in more than one place. "Rabbi" (*rabbi*) is found in John 1:38, 49; 3:2; 6:25; and "teacher" in John 3:2 (*didaskalos*). "Teacher" was used often in Matthew's account of Jesus during the Passion Week. The Pharisees and the Herodians in Matthew 22:16 addressed Jesus as "teacher" (*didaskale*); so too the Sadducees in Matthew 22:24; and again the Pharisee scribe in Matthew 22:36.

parable. According to N. T. Wright, Jesus had Satan in mind when he warned the twelve in Matthew 10:28, "And do not fear those who kill the body but cannot kill the soul. Rather fear him who can destroy both soul and body in hell."[17] However, this seems unlikely. Although Jesus refers to Beelzebul and his minions in Matthew 10:25, he also instructs his disciples in verse 26 not to fear them. It is God who is to be feared.[18] On one occasion Jesus described a group of the Pharisees and teachers of the law as "a wicked and adulterous generation" (Matt. 12:39 NIV). He warned that their fate could become far worse than at present. He spoke of a man out of whom a spirit came. But the departed spirit was replaced by seven others even more wicked than itself. He compared the situation to that of a house that had been left empty only to be further occupied by worse inhabitants (Matt. 12:43–45).[19]

Individuals also learn from Jesus that they are the objects of Satanic mischief. Peter is a case in point (Luke 22:31–32): "Simon, Simon, behold, Satan demanded [*exētēsato*; "requested," "demanded"] to have you [*hymas*, plural], that he might sift you like wheat, but I have prayed for you [*sou*, singular] that your faith may not fail. And when you have turned again, strengthen your brothers."[20] The old adage is *lex orandi lex credendi*. That is to say, the law of praying is the law of believing. What we really believe shows in our prayer life. Our espoused theology may say one thing but our operational theology (our godly practices or lack of them) may say another. Jesus taught the awareness of evil in the Lord's Prayer (Matt. 6:13): "And lead us not into temptation, but deliver us from evil [*apo tou ponērou*, "the evil one"; cf. NIV text and ESV mg.]." In either case, the awareness of evil is on view. In praying for the preservation of Peter's faith, Jesus practiced what he preached (Luke 22:31–32). Jesus also practiced what he preached in the garden of Gethsemane. And in his "high priestly" prayer, in John 17, he prayed for his disciples (v. 15), "I do not ask that you take them out of the world, but that you keep [*tērēsēs*, "keep" or "protect" or "preserve"] them from the evil one [*ek tou ponērou*, "from the evil one"]." Jesus knew that his followers needed divine protection, and as the great high priest he ever lives to intercede for them (Heb. 4:14–16 and 7:23–25).

Jesus Despoils the Strong Man

Frank Thielman rightly argues, "One of the most important elements in the vocation of Jesus, the apostles, and other evangelists is the deliverance of Sa-

---

[17] N. T. Wright, *Jesus and the Victory of God*, 454–455.

[18] For this view see R. T. France, *Matthew*, TNTC (Downers Grove, IL: IVP Academic, 2008), 189.

[19] N. T. Wright, *Jesus and the Victory of God*, 456, argues that the house on view is the temple. Revolutionary movements such as that of the Maccabeans cleansed the house (the temple) for a while, but it proved only one of many such attempts. A fascinating suggestion, but it is not that convincing in the end.

[20] It is interesting to observe that Satan must ask God for permission to sift Peter like wheat. Satan's power is circumscribed. Indeed, Jesus's words reveal that God is the object of a *demand* from Satan and a *prayer request* from Jesus.

tan's victims from his power."[21] The very first Gospel in the NT canon bears
Thielman out. In Matthew's account, on one occasion Jesus healed a demon-
oppressed blind and mute man and the Pharisees took great offense (Matt.
12:22–24). In a dramatic statement, Jesus explained what he had just done in
both kingdom and pneumatological terms (vv. 28–29): "But if it is by the Spirit
of God that I cast out demons, then the kingdom of God has come upon you.
Or how can someone enter a strong man's house and plunder his goods, unless he first binds the strong man? Then indeed he may plunder his house." In
response to the criticism that his power came from the dark side, Jesus argued
in classic reductio ad absurdum terms (vv. 25–26): "Every kingdom divided
against itself is laid waste, and no city or house divided against itself will
stand. And if Satan casts out Satan, he is divided against himself. How then
will his kingdom stand?"[22] Thus he compared the devil to a strong man. Before a strong man can be despoiled, he needs to be bound. Jesus saw his work
in exorcism in those terms (Matt. 12:29). He was despoiling the strong man
by liberating those in Satan's grip. What Tremper Longman III and Daniel G.
Reid argue concerning Mark's Gospel is also true of the Matthean account:
"From an eschatological perspective, Jesus was carrying out a new Exodus and
Conquest, routing the enemy that had occupied the land and held individuals
in his thrall."[23] Jesus comes before the reader of both Matthew and Mark as
"the incarnate divine warrior."[24]

One of Peter's sermons in Acts is particularly apposite. He preached to the
Gentile Cornelius and in the course of his sermon summed up Jesus's public
ministry in this striking way:

> You know the message God sent to the people of Israel, telling the good news
> of peace through Jesus Christ, who is Lord of all. You know what has hap-
> pened throughout Judea, beginning in Galilee after the baptism that John
> preached—how God anointed Jesus of Nazareth with the Holy Spirit and
> power, and how he went around doing good and *healing all who were under
> the power* [katadynasteuomenous, "being oppressed"] *of the devil*, because
> God was with him. (Acts 10:36–38 NIV 1984)

This Petrine statement brings so many themes together: the ministry of John
the Baptist, the messianic commissioning at the Jordan, the role of the Holy
Spirit, the message of peace (the shalom of OT hope), and most significantly

---

[21] Frank Thielman, *Theology of the New Testament: A Canonical and Synthetic Approach* (Grand Rapids, MI:
Zondervan, 2005), 634.
[22] The great antithesis in Scripture is not between faith and reason but between faith and fear (Mark 4:40), faith
and unbelief (John 20:27; *apistos*, i.e., "faithless"), and faith and sight (2 Cor. 5:7). Some of the other forms of
reasoning used in Scripture include a fortiori (e.g., Matt. 7:11) and hypothetical stepped syllogisms (e.g., 1 Cor.
15:12–20).
[23] Tremper Longman III and Daniel G. Reid, *God Is a Warrior* (Grand Rapids, MI: Zondervan, 1995), 109.
[24] I owe the phrase "the incarnate divine warrior" to my colleague Dana Harris.

for our purposes, Jesus's successfully combating the devil ("healing all who were under the power of the devil"). The strong man was bound indeed.

The Incarnation, the Cross, and the Evil One

At least two of the NT writers explain the purpose of the incarnation of the Son of God in terms of defeating the devil. The first is the writer to the Hebrews. We find in Hebrews 2:14–15, "Since therefore the children share in flesh and blood, he himself likewise partook of the same things, that ["with this purpose in mind," *hina* of purpose] through death he might destroy [*katargeō*, "to render inoperative or ineffective"] the one who has the power of death, that is, the devil, and deliver all those who through fear of death were subject to lifelong slavery." The devil exploits the very real human fear of death to enslave humankind, but God does not abandon us to such malevolence. The divine response is incarnation and atonement. Indeed, the atonement has more than one purpose. Christ not only takes on himself our just judgment; in so doing he also defeats the evil one.[25]

The second text is 1 John 3:7–8: "Little children, let no one deceive you. Whoever practices righteousness is righteous, as he is righteous. Whoever makes a practice of sinning is of the devil, for the devil has been sinning from the beginning. The reason the Son of God appeared [*ephanerōthē*; "manifested," aorist] was to destroy the works of the devil." The idea of "manifested" locates the incarnation solidly in space-time. One of the false ideas that John is combatting in this letter is the denial of a real incarnation in history, as 1 John 4:2–3 shows: "By this you know the Spirit of God: every spirit that confesses that Jesus Christ has come in the flesh is from God, and every spirit that does not confess Jesus is not from God." Jesus was no phantom from an ethereal realm.

Christ's coming and cross are connected by divine intentionality. Calvin articulates the connection admirably:

> In short, since neither as God alone could he feel death, nor as man alone could he overcome it, *he coupled human nature with divine* that to atone for sin he might submit the weakness of the one to death; and that, wrestling with death by the power of the other nature, *he might win victory for us*. . . . But we should especially espouse what I have just explained: our common nature with Christ is the pledge of our fellowship with the Son of God; *and clothed with our flesh he vanquished death and sin together that the victory and triumph might be ours.*[26]

---

[25] David G. Peterson rightly argues, "We can only be released from Satan's power and freed to serve God by the forgiveness or cleansing made possible by Jesus' death (*cf.* 9:14–15, 27–28; 10:19–22). He removes the threat of judgment and condemnation for those who trust in him and gives the assurance of life in the world to come" ("Hebrews," in *NBC*, quoted in Graham Cole, *The God Who Became Human: A Biblical Theology of Incarnation* [Downers Grove, IL: InterVarsity Press, 2013], 133n34).

[26] John Calvin, *Institutes of the Christian Religion*, 2.12.3 (*CJCC*), emphases mine.

THE CROSS, THE RESURRECTION, AND THE SPIRITS IN PRISON

The idea that Christ on Holy Saturday descended to the realm of the dead, preached, and set some free has a long history in Christian thought.[27] This is the "harrowing of hell" doctrine. The Orthodox Church in particular makes much of it, as can be seen in this description by Richard Beck:

> The Harrowing of Hell is so important to the Eastern Orthodox Church that they reenact it during their Easter liturgy. The priest exits the church with a cross held high, and the congregation remains inside. The church doors are locked and the lights are turned off. The darkened church becomes hell, the Devil's jail. The priest then pounds on the doors of the church—symbolizing Christ assaulting the gates of Hades—proclaiming "Open the doors to the Lord of the powers, the king of glory!" Inside the church the people make a great noise of rattling chains, the resistance of hell to the coming of Christ. Eventually the doors are opened, the cross enters, and the church is lit and filled with incense.[28]

Beck rightly identifies the *Christus Victor* theology that informs this practice: "For the Orthodox, Easter is all about how Jesus defeats the power of death. And the Harrowing of Hell is a critical part of this."[29]

Certainly tradition is prima facie on the side of the doctrine. After all, does not the ancient Apostles' Creed state that he descended into hell (Lat., *descendit ad inferos*)? In fact, belief in the harrowing of hell is very early. Hippolytus (170–236 AD): "The jailers of Hades trembled when they saw Him. And the gates of brass and the bolts of iron were broken. For look! The Only-Begotten, God the Word, had entered Hades with a soul—a soul among souls."[30] Importantly, very early on in the church's life two views developed on what Jesus did on Holy Saturday. The Alexandrian theologians, Clement and Origen, believed that Jesus raided hell or Hades to set free not only OT saints but also noble pagans. This was a minority view. In contrast, Augustine and Gregory the Great, while they accepted the idea of a raid on hell, believed that Christ did so only to set free those who looked for the Messiah to come. This was the majority view.[31] The key text appealed to in support in this period is the very difficult one of 1 Peter 3:18–20: "He was put to death in the body but made alive by the Spirit, through whom also he went and preached to the spirits in prison who disobeyed long ago when God waited patiently in the days of Noah while the ark was being built" (NIV 1984).

---

[27] Doubtless N. T. Wright speaks for many when he writes, "It's hard to know what to say about where Jesus was between the afternoon of Good Friday and the morning of Easter Day." See N. T. Wright, *Simply Good News: Why the Gospel Is News and What Makes It Good* (New York: HarperCollins, 2015), 53.

[28] Richard Beck, *Reviving Old Scratch: Demons and the Devil for Doubters and the Disenchanted* (Minneapolis: Fortress, 2016), 148.

[29] Beck, *Reviving Old Scratch*, 148.

[30] Quoted in *DECB*, ed. David W. Bercot (Peabody, MA: Hendrickson, 1998), 207.

[31] For a discussion of these views, see Almond, *Devil*, 56–61.

Some recent theology takes a different view when dealing with the biblical passages (e.g., Acts 2:27; Rom. 10:6–7; Eph. 4:8–9) adduced in support of the tradition, and especially with regard to the Petrine texts (1 Pet. 3:18–20; 4:6), which are the putative basis for the traditional view of an actual descent of Christ to the place of the dead. Robert Letham writes with specific regard to 1 Peter 3:18–22, "[A] growing appreciation seems to be developing on syntactic, structural, semantic and theological grounds that what Peter is teaching is that Christ pronounced judgment on the spirits in prison in his resurrection."[32] There is merit in this proposal. First Peter 3:19, on this reading, refers to Christ's announcement to the Satanic realm of his victory over the demonic.[33] Michael Green rightly argues that it is significant that, in the text, the word for Christ's activity in Hades is *ekēruxen* ("heralded" or "made a proclamation") and not "preached good news" (*euangelizein*).[34] This supports the view that Christ announced judgment and not salvation to the inhabitants of hell. This is a very different understanding of what happened on Holy Saturday when compared to the Eastern Orthodox practice described earlier, and to that of the early church fathers mentioned previously.

The question remains as to the identity of the "spirits in prison" (1 Pet. 3:19). Are they those flood generation humans to which the preincarnate Christ preached through Noah, the preacher of righteousness (2 Pet. 2:5)?[35] Or are they those imprisoned flood generation humans to whom the incarnate Christ preached after descending into hell? Or, as the *Catechism of the Catholic Church* suggests, are they the just who died before Christ's victory: "Jesus did not descend into hell to deliver the damned, nor to destroy the hell of damnation, but to free the just who had gone before him."[36] Or are they the Nephilim of Genesis 6:1–4?[37] Or are they those fallen angels imprisoned, as 2 Peter 2:4 has it?

What then is the interpretative way forward? To start with, "spirit" (*pneuma*) in the NT, when used without any qualification, appears to refer to either angels (e.g., Heb. 1:14), or demons (e.g., Mark 9:20), or to a human quality (e.g., 1 Cor. 14:14), or to the Holy Spirit of God (e.g., Rev. 22:17), but not to human beings per se. When used with a qualifier, a human being may indeed be the referent. Hebrews 12:23 furnishes an example: "the spirits of the righteous made perfect." Since there is no qualifier used of "spirits" in 1 Peter

---

[32] Robert Letham, *The Work of Christ* (Leicester, UK: Inter-Varsity Press, 1993), 150.

[33] The classic work on this theme is that of William J. Dalton, *Christ's Proclamation to the Spirits: A Study of 1 Peter 3:18–4:6*, 2nd ed., *Analecta Biblica* 23 (Rome: Pontifical Biblical Institute, 1989).

[34] Green, *I Believe in Satan's Downfall*, 214.

[35] For a robust defense of this view see John S. Feinberg, "1 Peter 3:18–20, Ancient Mythology, and the Intermediate State," *WTJ* 48 (1986): 303–336. This article is also very valuable for its insights into the benefits of analytic philosophy for biblical interpretation well before many others. Feinberg saw the value of the tools of analytic philosophy for biblical interpretation well before many others.

[36] CCC (Liguori, MO: Liguori, 1994), 164.

[37] Green, *I Believe in Satan's Downfall*, 213.

3:19, it is most likely that fallen spiritual beings are in Peter's mind. Only this last interpretation bears on angelology, and on balance it appears to me to be the best of the views.[38]

THE CROSS, THE DEVIL, AND *CHRISTUS VICTOR*

The early church fathers were especially attracted to the idea of victory over the devil, and some of them developed strange ways of elaborating the concept.[39] However, their speculations as to how the cross achieved such a victory were bizarre, to say the least. For example, Rufinus of Aquileia (c. 345–410) wrote,

> [The purpose of the incarnation] was that the divine virtue of the Son of God might be like a kind of hook hidden beneath the form of human flesh [. . .] to lure on the prince of this world to a contest; that the Son might offer him his human flesh as a bait and that the divinity which lay underneath might catch him and hold him fast with its hook.[40]

As I have written elsewhere, "One may applaud Rufinus of Aquileia for taking the defeat of Satan so seriously. But his imagination took him into the realm of the fanciful and the dubiously moral. Is such deception of Satan compatible with divine goodness? I think not."[41] Maybe this line of thinking should be called an "Entrapment Theory of the Atonement."

Rufinus's "fish hook" is one example of a *Christus Victor* atonement theory. Gregory the Great (c. 540–604) and Augustine (354–430) had their own spin on the theory. Gregory the Great saw the cross as a snare that trapped the devil like snares trap birds. Bizarrely, Augustine likened the cross to a mousetrap and the blood of Christ was the bait that the devil took.[42] The belief that, by deceiving Adam and Eve, the devil gained some right over their destinies

---

[38] For a defense of this view, see C. Fred Dickason, *Angels: Elect and Evil* (Chicago: Moody, 1995), 246–248. I am indebted to his argument. I would add that I can see a possible theological rationale in having some of the fallen angels imprisoned and some of them having judgment announced to them. If this were the case then the event was proleptic, pointing to the future overthrow of all fallen spiritual beings and the pronouncement of final judgment on them.

[39] It was the Swedish Lutheran theologian Gustaf Aulén, *Christus Victor*, trans. A. G. Herbert (London: SPCK, 1931), who made the phrase "*Christus Victor*" famous in theology. He argued that this understanding of the atonement was the classic view of the fathers of the early church and of Luther too. He may have overstated his thesis, but in so doing he recovered a key aspect of the NT witness. Jaroslav Pelikan, *The Christian Tradition: A History of the Development of Doctrine, Vol. 1: The Emergence of the Catholic Tradition (100–600)* (Chicago: University of Chicago Press, 1971), 149, offers this caution: "To be sure, other ways of speaking about the atonement were too widespread even among the Greek fathers to permit us to ascribe exclusive or even primary force to any one theory, but Christ as victor was more important in orthodox expositions of salvation and reconciliation than Western dogmatics has realized." Pelikan's observation is borne out by the amazing absence of the *Christus Victor* theme from Roman Catholicism's most recent official catechism (CCC [Liguori, MO: Liguori, 1994]), as both the table of contents and subject index show.

[40] Quoted in *The Christian Theology Reader*, 4th ed., ed. Alister E. McGrath (Southern Gate, Chichester, UK: Wiley-Blackwell, 2011), 292.

[41] Cole, *God the Peacemaker*, 125–126.

[42] For Gregory the Great's and Augustine's theories see Alan Richardson, *Creeds in the Making: A Short Introduction to the History of Christian Doctrine* (London: SCM, 1972), 103.

and those of their descendants was held by a number of prominent figures in the first millennium (e.g., Irenaeus, Origen, and Gregory of Nyssa, to name but few). However, because Christ died as an innocent, the devil exceeded his authority, and in so doing his power was broken. This appears to be the logic of this line of thinking. The devil forfeited his rights over humankind, having been trapped by the cross and the one who hung there.

A thousand years after Rufinus, Martin Luther (1483–1546) was also attracted to the cross as a trap for the devil theory. In his "Table Talk" he ruminated on the *protevangelium* of Genesis 3:15 in the following way: "I often delight myself with that similitude in Job, of an angle-hook that fishermen cast into the water, putting on the hook a little worm; then comes the fish and snatches at the worm, and gets therewith the hook in his jaws, and the fisher pulls him out of the water."[43] Luther then makes the comparison: "Even so has our Lord God dealt with the devil; God has cast into the world his only Son, as the angle, and upon the hook has put Christ's humanity, as the worm; then comes the devil and snaps at the (man) Christ, and devours him, and therewith he bites the hook, that is, the godhead of Christ, which chokes him, and all his power thereby is thrown to the ground." The argument is quaint and bizarre, but its accent on the victorious Christ is unmistakable and important.

Gregory A. Boyd is a contemporary proponent of *Christus Victor*. Boyd argues, "I believe the Christus Victor model of the atonement should be considered more foundational to our thinking about Jesus than other atonement models."[44] Interestingly, he can affirm a nuanced version of the "bait" theory as argued by the fathers.[45] He writes, ". . . Though a fair amount of fantasy was often interwoven into the conception, and though the way in which this 'outsmarting' was articulated at times expressed a less-than-ideal view of God (viz., God was deceptive), the core of the concept is biblical. God used Satan's evil to bring about Satan's own demise. This constitutes a central dimension of 'God's wisdom, secret and hidden.'"[46] Boyd's argument rests on a wide induction of biblical testimonies covering the warfare motif in Scripture and Christ's victory over the powers. How right is he? Is the Bible on his side?

The idea that one key aspect of the work of Christ on the cross is to deal with Satan and evil has firm biblical grounding. As we have already discussed,

---

[43] Martin Luther, "Table Talk," in *A Compendium of Luther's Theology*, ed. Hugh T. Kerr (Philadelphia: Westminster, 1974), 53.
[44] Gregory A. Boyd, "The Christus Victor View," in *The Nature of the Atonement: Four Views*, ed. James K. Beilby and Paul Rhodes Eddy (Grand Rapids, MI: Baker Academic, 2006), 46.
[45] Boyd, "Christus Victor View," 37.
[46] Gregory A. Boyd, *God at War: The Bible and Spiritual Conflict* (Downers Grove, IL: IVP Academic, 1997), 256. Michael S. Heiser, *Supernatural: What the Bible Teaches about the Unseen World—and Why It Matters* (Bellingham, WA: Lexham, 2015), 102, takes a similar view to that of Boyd. He writes, "The Devil and those with him . . . were *duped* into killing Jesus just as God had planned. They launched the series of events that would lead to their own demise. It was divinely designed misdirection" (emphasis original). Heiser's statement raises the divine deception issue more than Boyd's.

the *protevangelium* of Genesis 3:15 signals the divine intent to defeat evil. The cross constitutes the blow. Paul tells the Colossians,

> When you were dead in your sins and in the uncircumcision of your sinful nature, God made you alive with Christ. He forgave us all our sins, having canceled the written code, with its regulations, that was against us and that stood opposed to us; he took it away, nailing it to the cross. *And having disarmed the powers and authorities, he made a public spectacle of them, triumphing over them by the cross.* (Col. 2:13–15 NIV 1984)

The death of Jesus on the cross had more than one divine purpose. Christ's cross not only saves us but also disarms those forces arrayed against us. Jerome Murphy-O'Connor points out how Colossians 2:15 presents God like a Roman emperor who "awards a Roman triumph to Christ (his victorious general), who . . . stripped angelic beings of their power."[47] Daniel G. Reid sees an OT backdrop to verse 15 in that it shows Christ to be "the Jewish archetype of the divine warrior vanquishing his foes."[48] Both interpretations fit the context.

Paradoxically, in dying, Christ deprives the principalities and powers of their sway over humankind, now that "the written code, with its regulations, that was against us and that stood opposed to us" is cancelled, taken away, nailed to the cross (Col. 2:14 NIV 1984). These forces no longer have any grounds to accuse the Colossians and us who believe (cf. Col. 2:15).[49] In such accusation lay their power. Christ dying in our place robs them of their power. Indeed they were disarmed (Col. 2:15; *apekdysamenos*, "having disarmed," "having stripped").[50] I believe, however, that the *Christus Victor* theory needs the explanatory power of the idea of substitutionary atonement.[51] By standing in our place, Christ wins the victory on our behalf. The accusations have been decisively addressed (Rom. 8:31–34). French theologian Henri Blocher captures the divine *Christus Victor* strategy in a remarkable way in his book *Evil and the Cross*. He argues,

> At the cross evil is conquered as evil: corruption, perversion, disorder, a parasite. . . .

---

[47] Jerome Murphy-O'Connor, "Colossians," in *OBC*, 1195. I take the view that God is the subject and not Christ. For the alternative view, see D. G. Reid, "Triumph," in *DPL*, ed. Gerald F. Hawthorne and Ralph P. Martin (Downers Grove, IL: InterVarsity Press, 1993), s.v.

[48] Reid, "Triumph."

[49] Some have suggested that on view here are those spiritual intelligences that record human transgressions (cf. Isa. 65:6; *1 Enoch* 81:2–4). See Murphy-O'Connor, "Colossians," *OBC*, 1195. See also A. T. Lincoln, "Colossians," in *NIB*, 12 vols. (Nashville: Abingdon, 1993–2002), 11:625, who writes, "The accusatory book has in effect been ruled out of court. It was canceled and set aside by being nailed to the cross."

[50] The NRSV provides an alternative reading of *apekdysamenos* in the margin. Instead of Christ disarming the rulers and authorities, he divests himself of them. Morna D. Hooker, "Colossians," in *ECB*, 1408, comments, "But the margin [NRSV] may be correct in suggesting that Christ has stripped himself of these alien powers, so that it is they who are left hanging powerless on the cross." On either reading, Christ remains *Christus Victor*.

[51] A point well argued by Garry Williams, "Atonement, Creation, and Trinity," in *The Atonement Debate: Papers from the London Symposium on the Atonement*, ed. D. J. Tidball, D. Hilborn, and J. Thacker (Grand Rapids, MI: Zondervan, 2008), 187–188.

Evil is conquered as evil because God turns it back upon itself. He makes the supreme crime, the murder of the only righteous person, the very operation that abolishes sin. The manoeuvre is utterly unprecedented. No more complete victory could be imagined. . . . Evil, like a judoist, takes advantage of the power of good, which it perverts; the Lord, like a supreme champion, replies by using the very grip of the opponent. . . .

We have no other position than at the foot of the cross. . . . God's answer is evil turned back upon itself, conquered by the ultimate degree of love in the fulfillment of justice.[52]

Indeed, the very last book in the canon reveals that it is the slain Lamb whose shed blood enables martyrs to overcome (*enikēsan*) the devil (Rev. 12:11).[53]

PAYING OFF THE DEVIL

The New Testament presentation of the achievement of the cross is multifaceted: expiation, propitiation, exemplary, a manifestation of divine righteousness, and providing a ransom, to name some aspects. The latter idea of a ransom captured the imagination of Origen, the most speculative thinker in the early church period. In Matthew 20:28, Jesus described his mission in these terms: ". . . even as the Son of Man came not to be served but to serve, and to give his life as a ransom [*lytron*] for many." His death cost. For Origen, Jesus's words raised a question. In his comment on Matthew 16:8, Origen asks,

To whom was the ransom paid? Certainly not to God; can it be to the evil one? For he had power over us until the ransom was given to him on our behalf, namely the life of Jesus; and he was deceived thinking he could keep his soul in his power; not seeing that he could not reach the standard required so as to be able to keep it in his power.[54]

It seems for Origen that the cross broke the devil's power through a divine stratagem of deception.

Gregory of Nyssa (c. 335–394) had a more noble way of articulating the ransom theory. He believed, as we noted earlier in the chapter, that through the first humans' sin the devil acquired rights over humankind. So God was

---

[52] Quoted in Christopher J. H. Wright, *The God I Don't Understand: Reflections on Tough Questions of Faith* (Grand Rapids, MI: Zondervan, 2008), 68.

[53] David E. Aune, *Revelation 6–16*, WBC (Dallas: Word, 1998), 702–703 (comments on Revelation 12:11): "'And they conquered him through the blood of the Lamb.' The verb νικᾶν, 'to conquer, be victorious,' occurs seventeen times in Revelation; when Christ is the subject of this verb (5:5), it means that he conquered *through death*, and it means precisely the same thing when it is used eleven times of Christians, explicitly in 12:11 and implicitly in the other references (cf. 2:7, 11, 17, 26; 3:5, 12, 21[2x]. . . . There is a close parallel to 12:11a in 1 Cor 15:57, 'Thanks to God who gave us victory [νῖκος] through our Lord Jesus Christ,' where in the context of the entire chapter it is likely that the resurrection of Jesus is meant. Nevertheless, in both passages, one emphasizing Christ's death and the other his resurrection, victory is achieved by means of Christ's work (διά)."

[54] Origen, in *The Early Christian Fathers*, ed. and trans. Henry Bettenson (Oxford: Oxford University Press, 1979), 224. Why commenting on Matthew 16:8 raised the ransom question for Origen is a puzzle.

required to act justly to set human beings free. This God did by making over "to the master of the slave whatever ransom he may agree to accept for the slave in his possession."[55] The devil, captivated by Christ's miracles, chose Christ. However, he only saw Christ's flesh and not his veiled deity and thus tricked himself. Like a greedy fish, he was caught on the hook of Christ's deity hidden in the human flesh.[56]

These early church interpretations of Matthew 20:28 are puzzling to the modern reader since the text does not refer to the devil in any way. So what then does ransom mean in the context? Donald A. Hagner offers this comment on the meaning of Matthew 20:28:

> "Ransom," although drawn from the background of purchasing the freedom of a slave or captive (i.e., to free by payment), is here used in a metaphorical sense for a setting free from sin and its penalty at the cost of the sacrifice of Jesus. This is the service performed by the suffering servant of Isa 53 (see esp. Isa 53:10–12, where the servant [v 11] gives himself up to death as an offering for sin and bears the sin of "many" [v 12]).[57]

Early church figures such as Origen and Gregory of Nyssa were asking questions that the Scripture does not ask. Asking such questions requires caution and restraint, as the theological imagination can become unanchored from the biblical text all too easily. Origen, in particular, provides an instructive example.

A Different Angle of Vision: Girard on Violence, Jesus, and the Devil

In his influential theory of mimetic violence, René Girard argues that violence comes from rivalry.[58] Rivalry occurs in a community, state, or nation when more than one person pursues the same goal. Rivalry produces violence and becomes a contagion that leads to group violence. However, according Girard, if a scapegoat is found, the scapegoat becomes the object of that violence, and as a result communal catharsis takes place. Such peace is so tension-reducing that scapegoating becomes ritualized as a communal habit, even a matter of religion. Girard maintains that mimetic rivalry is found in every culture. What is unique about the story of Jesus is that God becomes the victim of the scapegoating mechanism. Because Jesus is an innocent, the false basis of the scapegoating mechanism is revealed. If a person embraces the story of Jesus, then, in that person's life the cycle of scapegoating is broken and the contagion stopped. Indeed, the object of scapegoating violence—Jesus—is innocent, not

---

[55]Gregory of Nyssa, in *The Later Christian Fathers*, ed. and trans. Henry Bettenson (Oxford: Oxford University Press, 1977), 141.

[56]Gregory of Nyssa, in *Later Christian Fathers*, 142.

[57]Hagner, *Matthew 14–28*, WBC (Dallas: Word, 2002), 582.

[58]In this paragraph I draw upon my discussion in *God the Peacemaker*, 251–253.

guilty, and this breaks the cycle of violence among those who imitate Christ. They become a good contagion.

Where does Satan figure in Girard's theory? Girard looks at Jesus's question in Mark 3:23, "How can Satan cast out Satan?" Here he comes up with a novel idea: Satan indeed casts out Satan![59] Satan keeps humanity locked into the cycle of mimetic violence with its scapegoating mechanism. But on the cross Jesus exposes the mechanism for what it is. Girard writes,

> Satan would not be the prince of this world if he were not, first of all, prince of darkness. The Christian revelation dissipates the darkness of the founding murder [think of Cain and Abel] by showing the innocence not only of one victim, Jesus, wrongly accused by Satan, but of all such victims. The Christian revelation undermines the power of Satan, slowly at first but then faster and faster.[60]

Girard appeals to Colossians 2:13–15 and 1 Corinthians 2:7–8 as the biblical basis for his contention. Colossians 2:13–15 "is a first attempt to say that the principalities and powers, in other words Satan, are defeated and even ridiculed by the Cross."[61] With regard to 1 Corinthians 2:7–8, he contends, "The rulers of this age, are the same thing as the powers of this world and Satan himself. Had they foreseen that the crucifixion would deprive them of the powerful tool with which they had been operating all along, their first order of business would have been the protection of the scapegoat mechanism, and they would have refrained from crucifying Jesus."[62]

How exactly did the cross work? Girard has his own version of the trap theory so popular in parts of the early church:

> The idea that the Cross was really a trap set by God himself in order to lure Satan flows logically from the preceding: Since Jesus, almost every time he opens his mouth, reveals the secret of Satan's power, he becomes, in the eyes of Satan, a most intolerable source of disorder; he must be silenced once and for all. In order to reach this goal, Satan only has to resort to his favorite trick which is exactly what is needed in this case, the very trick about which Jesus is talking so much, the traditional trick of mimetic murder and the scapegoat mechanism. Since this trick has always succeeded in the past, Satan sees no reason why it would not succeed in the case of Jesus.

So Jesus dies, but with an unintended consequence for Satan: "Everything turns out as anticipated by Satan except for one thing. With the help of the Paraclete, Jesus' disciples finally break away from the mimetic consensus and provide the

---

[59] René Girard, in *The Girard Reader*, ed. S. G. Williams (New York: Crossroad, 2003), 195–210.
[60] Girard, *Girard Reader*, 207.
[61] Girard, *Girard Reader*, 206.
[62] Girard, *Girard Reader*, 207.

world with a truthful account of what should remain hidden in this affair, at least from the perspective of Satan."[63]

By engineering the murder of Jesus, Satan defeats himself: Satan casts out Satan. Girard is offering his own version of a nonviolent *Christus Victor* theory: "This is the supreme theme regarding Satan, the most amazing and the most difficult to believe, the idea that the Cross is a decisive victory over Satan, the end of his power."[64] Since Jesus's death, the good contagion has spread. Girard argues, "Jesus' death is a source of grace not because the Father is 'avenged' by it, but because Jesus lived and died in the manner that, if adopted by all, would do away with scandals and the victimization that follows from scandals. Jesus lived as all men should live in order to be united with a God whose true nature he reveals."[65] In the light of this claim, Girard appears to hold not only a *Christus Victor* understanding of the cross, but moral influence and exemplarist ones as well. More and more, hidden victims of society's use of mimetic violence have come to light and liberation: slaves, oppressed women, and the lower classes. The meaning is this: "Our being liberated from Satan's bondage means that the supernatural power of Satan and his demons is an illusion, that Satan does not exist."[66] It is hard to pin Girard down as to whether there is a fallen angel known as Satan. In his theory, Satan is the cipher for the personification of the mimetic rivalry that leads to accusation and murder in society. He said in an interview, "Satan is the name of the mimetic process seen as a whole; that is why he is the source not merely of rivalry and disorder but of all the forms of lying order inside which humanity lives."[67]

The editor of *The Girard Reader*, S. G. Williams, argues that Girard ". . . bracketed and set aside the question of the 'existence' or 'reality' of Satan apart from human systems of order and the threat of disorder."[68] This suggestion leaves the impression that for Girard the existence of Satan is an open question. Charles K. Bellinger, however, is confident that for Girard "Satan is not an individual person but rather the entire complex process [of mimetic violence with its scapegoating]."[69] I find Girard's position on the reality of Satan as an ontologically real individual tantalizingly elusive.

Girard is a creative thinker and has offered a novel reading of the biblical testimony that has generated much scholarly activity and debate. Even so, much is conjecture and exhibits a cherry-picking of the biblical text. For

[63] Girard, *Girard Reader*, 207.
[64] Girard, *Girard Reader*, 205. "Nonviolent" in the sense that God is not a violent actor in the violent story of the cross. Girard's theory has informed a number of recent nonviolent atonement theories. See my *God the Peacemaker*, 247–257.
[65] René Girard, "Are the Gospels Mythical?" *First Things* 62 (April 1996): 30.
[66] Girard, *Girard Reader*, 209.
[67] Girard, *Girard Reader*, 161.
[68] S. G. Williams, *Girard Reader*, 194.
[69] Charles K. Bellinger, "The Joker Is Satan, and So Are We: Girard and *The Dark Knight*," *Journal of Religion and Film* 13/1 (April 2009), https://www.unomaha.edu/jrf/vol13.no1/JokerSatan.htm, accessed 1/6/2016.

anyone committed to the *tota scriptura* principle, Girard's theory falls far short of being persuasive (contra Wink), whatever other criticisms might be emanating from secular anthropologists and philosophers. In so many places it appears to be his theory of mimesis driving the exegesis, and not the other way around.

IMPLICATIONS FOR BELIEF AND PRACTICE

Christ as the defeater of the devil has some important implications for Christian belief and practice. We shall consider just five of them: the repopulation of heaven, a useful distinction between espoused and operational theology, the fear of death addressed, the accuser answered, and confidence in Christ.

The Repopulation of Heaven

Adam Johnson, in a fascinating piece, draws attention to how the atonement benefits the unfallen angels.[70] One of the benefits he sees is that heaven is repopulated, making up for the loss of the rebellious angels from the heavenly ranks. The defection of these rebels had left a gap. Augustine reflected on this gap:

> [S]ince it was not the whole company of angels that had perished by deserting God, those who had perished should remain in perpetual perdition, while those who had persevered with God . . . should have the joy of knowing that their future happiness was assured; as for . . . humankind, since they had totally perished by reason of their sins and punishments, . . . some of them should be restored to fill the gap left in the company of the angels by the devil's fall.[71]

This is speculative, but could be true. If it is, then a rationale is provided for the doctrine of definite atonement, which when usually formulated begs questions about divine arbitrariness. Christ's death atoned for the number that needed to be made up.

A Useful Distinction: Espoused versus Operational Theology

A point was made earlier in this chapter about how the law of praying is the law of believing. Our prayers reveal how deep or shallow our theology is. Put another way, our praying will show whether our espoused theology matches our operational theology. The Christian may believe all that the Bible teaches

---

[70] Adam Johnson, "Where Demons Fear to Tread: Venturing into an Obscure Corner of the Doctrine of the Atonement regarding the Un-fallen Angels," *Journal of Reformed Theology* 9/1 (2015): 37–55.
[71] Augustine, *The Augustine Catechism: The Enchiridion on Faith, Hope, and Love,* trans. Bruce Harbert (Hyde Park, N.Y.: New City Press, 1999). 59–60. Augustine supports this last point with Luke's claim that we will be equal to the angels (20:36).

about the devil and Christ's victory on the cross but his or her personal prayer life does not show it. Martin Luther was asked by his barber, Peter Beskendorf, for some guidance on how to pray. So, early in 1535, Luther wrote an open letter titled, "How One Should Pray: For Master Peter the Barber." Peter Beskendorf was not only Luther's barber but also an old friend. Luther suggested taking each statement in the Lord's Prayer as a prompt. He suggested this with regard to the sixth petition, "Lead us not into temptation":

> Say: "O dear Lord, Father and God, keep us fit and alert, eager and diligent in Thy Word and service, so that we do not become complacent, lazy, and slothful as though we had already achieved everything. In that way the fearful devil cannot fall upon us, surprise us, and deprive us of Thy precious Word or stir up strife and factions among us and lead us into other sin and disgrace, both spiritually and physically. Rather grant us wisdom and strength through Thy Spirit that we may valiantly resist him and gain victory. Amen."[72]

Luther had an acute awareness of evil, and his advice, if followed, would have helped foster that same awareness in his barber. A prayer life that exhibits no sense of the awareness of evil is in a cocoon removed from the anguish in the world and the Christ who wept over Jerusalem (Luke 19:41) and for his dead friend Lazarus (John 11:35). In Jesus's case, his espoused theology and his operational theology were a perfect match.

The Fear of Death Addressed

Scripture calls death the last enemy (1 Cor. 15:26). It is like a power that can exert an influence over us. The writer to the Hebrews sees the very human fear of death as the means by which the devil may enslave us (Heb. 2:14–15). How that works the NT does not explain. One can surmise, though, that it is what death brings, eschatologically speaking, that may be the answer. Again Hebrews is relevant, when the writer asserts that after death comes judgment (Heb. 9:27–28). On the cross, the Christ took our judgment. "In our place condemned he stood" is not only what the well-known hymn asserts; it is also NT teaching. To really believe that is to be at peace about the future.

The Accusations Answered

Conscience is the human capacity to experience guilt, either real or imagined. The devil is the accuser. Real guilt, whether felt or not, is our true moral state before a holy God as creatures who have fallen short of his glory (sin), have been morally bent out of shape (iniquity), and have defied the boundaries the

---

[72] Cited in John F. Thornton and Susan Varenne, eds., *Faith and Freedom: An Invitation to the Writings of Martin Luther* (New York: Random, 2002), 327.

divine will has set (transgression). All three of these are found in Psalm 51:1–2. We stand before the divine court, as it were. Justification is the verdict that we are deemed right with God in the divine court. This is the end-time verdict received now by the believer. This is all of grace, not merit. The devil may attempt to use our conscience as a means of spoiling our spiritual poise, but as Paul says, it is God who justifies, and he has (Rom. 5:1).

"My Angel": Jesus and High Christology

A high Christology does not view Jesus as a mere man but as God incarnate: one person in two natures. The incarnate Son of God is truly deity and truly human. This is the classic theological position as articulated in the Chalcedonian definition of AD 451. There is plenty of NT evidence to warrant this contention. John's Gospel, for example, begins as follows (John 1:1): "In the beginning was the Word, and the Word was with God, and the Word was God." Later in the same chapter we read (v. 14), "And the Word became flesh [*sarx*] and dwelt among us, and we have seen his glory, glory as of the only Son from the Father, full of grace and truth." The unfolding narrative makes it plain what kind of flesh the Word assumed. The woman of Samaria speaks plainly to her fellow Samaritans (John 4:28–29): "So the woman left her water jar and went away into town and said to the people, 'Come, see a man [*anthrōpon*] who told me all that I ever did. Can this be the Christ?'" Jesus became truly human, without surrendering his deity.

What has any of the above to do with Jesus and high Christology? The OT affirms that God has his angels, as in Psalm 148:1–2: "Praise the LORD! Praise the LORD from the heavens; praise him in the heights! Praise him, all his angels; praise him, all his hosts!" The Gospels affirm that Jesus has *his* angels. In Matthew 13:41–42 Jesus states, "The Son of Man will send his angels, and they will gather out of his kingdom all causes of sin and all law-breakers, and throw them into the fiery furnace. In that place there will be weeping and gnashing of teeth." In context, Jesus is clearly speaking of himself. Revelation 22:16 puts it emphatically: "I [*egō*], Jesus, have sent my angel [*ton angelon mou*, "my angel"] to testify to you about these things for the churches. I am the root and the descendant of David, the bright morning star." (Paul affirms the same point in 2 Thessalonians 1:7–8 when writing of judgment to come: ". . . when the Lord Jesus is revealed from heaven with his mighty angels [*met' angelōn dunameōs autou*, "with his angels of power"] in flaming fire, inflicting vengeance on those who do not know God and on those who do not obey the gospel of our Lord Jesus.") No other biblical character, God excepted, speaks of his or her angels. Leon Morris rightly argues concerning Revelation 22:16, "The emphatic *egō* stresses the fact that *Jesus* is the speaker. He tells us that the angel has spoken on his authority (cf. 1:1). That he can send an *angel* shows that his authority is great."[73] Matthias Reinhard Hoffmann likewise concludes, "Christ does . . . represent far more than an angel in Apc 22:16, because he is in command of angels (Apc 22:16a), and he is also the brightest of the stars, which further hints at a superior position."[74] A low Christology does not work, given such biblical witness. This is arguably further evidence that Jesus is God and not merely human.

Confidence in Christ

Given that the fear of death has been addressed and the accusations of the accuser met, there are grounds for the Christian's confidence before God even in a world exhibiting its anguish, but also a world that God will set to its rights. Paul the apostle had that confidence, as his letter to the Romans shows in this magnificent statement (Rom. 8:37–39):

> No, in all these things we are more than conquerors [*hypernikōmen*] through him who loved us. For I am sure that neither death nor life, nor angels nor rulers, nor things present nor things to come, nor powers, nor height nor depth, nor anything else in all creation, will be able to separate us from the love of God in Christ Jesus our Lord.

The angels, rulers, and powers of which Paul writes appear to be on the side of darkness, not light. Be that as it may, the love of Christ will not let us go. The language of conquering is used in a number of places in the NT in relation to Satan. For example, the young men mentioned twice in 1 John 2:13–14 are those who have overcome [*venikēkate*] the evil one [*ton ponēron*]. Revelation 12:11 likewise speaks of those who overcome [*enikēsen*] the devil. In this text Christology is crucial because the blood of the Lamb is referenced.

Martin Luther expressed something of that same apostolic confidence in one of his hymns, written in 1529 when the Reformation was still very young and opposition to it fierce:

> And tho this world, with devils filled,
> should threaten to undo us,
> we will not fear, for he hath willed
> his truth to triumph thro' us.
> The Prince of Darkness grim,
> we tremble not for him;

---

[73] Leon Morris, *Revelation*, TNTC (Downers Grove, IL: InterVarsity Press, 1987), 248 (emphasis original). Revelation 12:7 does not constitute a counterexample. In this text the angels that the archangel Michael commands are in battle with those of Satan. Importantly, Revelation 22 makes it plain that Jesus is greater than any angel. He is entitled to worship, but the mighty angel of Revelation 22 is not and knows it.
[74] Matthias Reinhard Hoffmann, *The Destroyer and the Lamb: The Relationship between Angelmorphic and Lamb Christology in the Book of Revelation* (Tübingen: Mohr Siebeck, 2005), 203.

his rage we can endure,
for lo, his doom is sure;
one little word shall fell him.

Luther's lyrics are further evidence of the Reformer's acute awareness of evil and of its supernatural aspect. He expected to experience Satanic hostility. Even so, he lived *sub specie aeternitatis* (Lat., "under the aspect of eternity"). The future does not belong to the evil one: "for lo, his doom is sure." We shall return to this theme when we explore the last battle and the destiny of the darkness in a later chapter.

CONCLUSION

There were many reasons for Christ's incarnation. A key one was to defeat the devil. Defeating the devil, as we have seen, involved both Christ's active obedience (his life) and his passive obedience (his death). The life he lived and the death he died are the keys to our salvation on the one hand and the defeat of the darkness on the other. Jesus did the Father's will. He resisted the devilish temptations in the wilderness and proved thereby to be the faithful Adam and the faithful Israel. Whereas those two sons had failed, this son remained obedient throughout. He lived by every word that proceeded out of the mouth of God. And he went on the offensive against the devil's darkness, practicing exorcism with the word of command. He also taught his hearers about the devil and the devil's ways. He made the darkness visible, as it were. When the light of the world came, the darkness rose up against him. Above all, on the cross, in his passive (suffering) obedience, he bore our condemnation for us and in so doing addressed our fear of death, which is, on analysis, about the judgment after it. There is no condemnation for those who are in Christ Jesus, as Paul taught the Romans (Rom. 8:1), nor is there separation from the love of Christ (vv. 38–39). Nor are there any grounds for devilish slander against God's elect (vv. 33–34). Christ in his substitutionary atoning death dealt with that too. Again, Paul makes that clear in both Romans and Colossians. But the final defeat of the devil and his demons awaits. The Christian lives between the cross and the coming again of the victor. And so the believer lives in between, and in between is the sphere of spiritual warfare to which we next turn.

SEVEN

SPIRITUAL WARFARE

In America, the entertainment industry is deeply invested in shows with a spiritual warfare theme. Good versus evil becomes a contest between Satan or demons and human subjects. At times God may intervene, but more often a good angel or two is humanity's helper or a fallen angel is a foe. A good example is provided by the TV show "Supernatural." Such is its appeal that this show, starring two fictional brothers battling supernatural foes, is in its twelfth season.

For the Christian who knows his or her Bible, the contest between good and evil, Satan and humanity is very serious and not a matter for entertainment. The believer lives this side of Christ's victory on the cross, between Christ's first coming and his return in glory. In other words, we live in the sphere of brokenness. An enemy is at work still. NT scholar Oscar Cullmann used an analogy that is most illuminating and which throws light on the structure of our existence. In June 1944 the Allies landed on Normandy's beaches. This was D-Day. It was the turning point in the European theater of World War II. However, victory did not come until 1945, with the death of Hitler and the German surrender on May 7 in France and May 8 in Germany. This was V-E Day. Cullmann argued that the Christian lives between D-Day and V-E Day, eschatologically speaking.[1] The cross was decisive, but much remains to happen before evil is finally extinguished. Put another way, our present setting is the groaning creation (Rom. 8:18–25) and these last days (Heb. 1:1–2). Paul describes our time frame in this life as "the present evil age" (Gal. 1:4). The contest between good and evil continues. Eric L. Mascall puts it this way: "Scripture, tradition and Christian experience combine in assuring us that the struggle against evil with which Christians on earth are concerned can be

---

[1] The present-day Christian's frame of reference is that of "inaugurated eschatology." That is to say, Christ is in some sense King over evil now, but there is so much more victory to come. This is the already–not yet tension that Gregory A. Boyd defines in his *Satan and the Problem of Evil* (Downers Grove, IL: IVP Academic, 2001), 417: It is, says Boyd, "The tension between those aspects of Satan's defeat and the coming of God's kingdom that are already accomplished and those aspects that remain to be achieved in the future (also sometimes labeled 'realized eschatology')." The description is right, although the label is wrong. Realized eschatology is the view famously espoused by C. H. Dodd, that NT passages referring to eschatology do not have a future reference but have been realized in the ministry of Jesus.

seen in its true proportions only against the background of a vaster and more mysterious conflict in the unseen world in which they are caught up."[2]

Just what is spiritual warfare, this "struggle against evil"? The phrase "spiritual warfare" is not a biblical one, but is it a biblical idea? How might it best be defined? What light does the NT throw on the practice of spiritual warfare? Why is the concept of spiritual warfare so controversial?[3] What implications does spiritual warfare have for Christian belief and practice? An excursus at the end of this chapter addresses the further question of how to "test" the spirits (see 1 Thess. 5:21) to see whether they are from God.

THE CHALLENGE OF DEFINITION

Definitional questions are among the most challenging, philosophically speaking. A strong definition would specify all the necessary conditions sufficient in totality to warrant a word's use in a given context. A weak definition specifies only some of the key conditions for such usage. When it comes to the phrase "spiritual warfare" we enter into a contested definitional area where only a weak—or better, a working—definition is manageable.

Clinton Arnold argues that spiritual warfare as a descriptive phrase does not refer merely to a specialized form of ministry: "exorcism, deliverance . . . , or certain types of intercession."[4] Instead he contends that the phrase should cover "*a way of characterizing our common struggle as Christians*" and that, "Whether we want to think about it or not, the truth is that we all face supernatural opposition as we set out to live the Christian life."[5] That common struggle is against three enemies: the world, the flesh, and the devil.[6] Arnold helpfully points out the way the apostle Paul clusters these three enemies together in Ephesians 2:1–3:

> And you were dead in the trespasses and sins in which you once walked, following the course of this world [*cosmos*], following the prince [*archōn*] of the power of the air, the spirit that is now at work in the sons of disobedience—among whom we all once lived in the passions of our flesh [*sarx*], carrying out the desires of the body and the mind, and were by nature children of wrath, like the rest of mankind.[7]

What is striking about the Pauline text is how the devil, as the prince of the power of the air, is at work in the disobedient.[8]

---

[2] E. L. Mascall, *The Christian Universe* (London: Darton, Longman, & Todd, 1967), 129.

[3] Peter R. Schemm Jr., "The Agents of God: Angels," in *A Theology for the Church*, rev. ed., ed. Daniel L. Akin (Nashville: B&H, 2014), 274, writes, "Perhaps there is no area of doctrine in the church today more readily abused and less biblically understood than that which is practiced in the name of 'spiritual warfare.'"

[4] Clinton E., Arnold, *Three Crucial Questions about Spiritual Warfare* (Grand Rapids, MI: Baker, 1998), 19.

[5] Arnold, *Three Crucial Questions*, 27, emphasis original.

[6] I have heard the evil triad summed up this way: The world says, "Conform to me!" The flesh says, "Satisfy me!" The devil says, "Worship me!"

[7] See Arnold, *Three Crucial Questions*, 32.

[8] When one reflects on it, humankind move in air, and that is the realm in which the evil one operates.

Whatever the understanding of spiritual warfare needs to be, the devil is an integral part of the story. So as a working definition, let me define spiritual warfare as that aspect of our common struggle as Christians against the machinations of malevolent spiritual creatures that are intent on thwarting God's redemptive plan for his human creatures. A broader definition would take into account the way that our passions can arise within us and conduct war, as in James 4:1–2: "What causes quarrels and what causes fights [*polemoi*, "wars"] among you? Is it not this, that your passions are at war [*strateuomenōn*, "warring"] within you? You desire and do not have, so you murder. You covet and cannot obtain, so you fight and quarrel [*polemeite*, "war"]." But given our angle of vision in this study on angelology, the narrower definition will suffice for our purposes.

SPIRITUAL WARFARE: THE BIBLICAL TESTIMONY

The NT offers a wide range of perspectives on spiritual warfare, from the need for prayer to the wisdom of wearing the armor of God in combat. We begin with Jesus.

According to Jesus

In the Gospel of Mark, both Jesus and his disciples perform exorcisms. In the very first chapter there is an exorcism story (Mark 1:21–28), and Christ's public ministry is summed up in these terms (v. 39): "And he went throughout all Galilee, preaching in their synagogues and casting out demons." Then in Mark 6:7–13, Jesus gives the twelve the authority to preach, heal, and cast out demons. However, in 9:14–29 we find a story of failure: Jesus returns from the Mount of Transfiguration with Peter, James, and John to a troubled crowd scene. A man with a son who was mute because of an unclean spirit had asked the remaining disciples for help (v. 17). But the disciples had failed (v. 18). Jesus is not pleased. He exclaims (v. 19), "O faithless generation, how long am I to be with you? How long am I to bear with you? Bring him to me." Jesus proceeds to cast the demon out, and the boy is healed (vv. 20–27). To the disciples' credit, they want to know—understandably, privately—the reason for their inability to help the demonized boy. Jesus is clear in his answer (v. 29): "This kind cannot be driven out by anything but prayer."[9]

A number of commentators point out the contrast between the disciples' success in Mark 6:13 and their later failure in Mark 9:18.[10] A key factor in the

---

[9] David E. Garland has a useful discussion of the variant reading that appears in some early manuscripts, which adds "and fasting" to verse 29. He offers some very good reasons for not embracing this variant (see his comment on Mark 9:28–29 in *Mark*, NIVAC [Grand Rapids, MI: Zondervan, 1996], 356–359). Recall also my brief mention of this phrase in chapter 5 at note 106.

[10] For example Garland, *Mark*, 354; and Walter W. Wessel, "Mark," in *EBC*, comment on Mark 9:28–29.

Mark 9 episode is their lack of faith (v. 19). The faith theme soon reappears in relation to the father of the troubled son. In verse 23 Jesus says to him, "'If you can'! All things are possible for one who believes." The father responds (v. 24), "I believe; help my unbelief!" And help Jesus does. In that light one can surmise that the disciples either had lost the faith that was needed on their part or they had a misplaced faith in their own authority. After all, they had cast out demons on an earlier occasion. Why not now? Why not here? Jesus refers to prayer. Prayer at the very least is an expression of dependence not on self but on God. Jesus is drawing the connection between faith and prayer. Walter W. Wessel comments, "Apparently they [the disciples] had taken for granted the power given them or had come to believe that it was inherent in themselves. So they no longer depended prayerfully on God for it, and their failure showed their lack of prayer."[11] Over a millennium later, Calvin was right to consider prayer as the principal exercise of faith.[12]

In terms of the Christian's stance toward spiritual warfare, the Markan story is instructive. Calling upon the Lord in prayer is clearly integral to a successful engagement with the destructive forces of evil. Jesus in the Lord's Prayer taught his disciples to pray for deliverance from the evil one. In the Markan case the disciples needed to pray for deliverance not for themselves but for the poor, afflicted lad before them. David E. Garland is right when he comments, "Jesus' positive example reveals that only a life governed by faith and prayer can repel the threat from the evil spirits."[13]

According to Acts

The Acts of the Apostles refers to Satan and evil spirits in several places. In the early stages of the Jesus movement in Jerusalem, the apostles relieved many of the torments from evil spirits (Acts 5:12–16). Philip, on mission in Samaria, likewise cast out evil spirits (8:4–8). Significantly, Philip's ministry shows that exorcisms were not confined to the apostles. In the Gentile world, Paul was involved in exorcisms (e.g., 16:16–18 and 19:11–12). This material is *descriptive*, in that it reports what Paul did. There is no suggestion that the reader is to do likewise. Similarly, Paul's account of his conversion and calling in Acts 26 is descriptive.

Under arrest and imprisoned, Paul mounts an apology before King Agrippa. He relates his Damascus road experience before the skeptical king. Of special interest are the remembered words from the lips of the ascended Christ (Acts 26:16–18):

---

[11] Wessel, "Mark."
[12] John Calvin, *Institutes of the Christian Religion*, 3.20 (CJCC). Calvin's heading is, "Prayer, Which Is the Chief Exercise of Faith, and by Which We Daily Receive God's Benefits."
[13] Garland, *Mark*, 357.

> But rise and stand upon your feet, for I have appeared to you for this purpose, to appoint you as a servant and witness to the things in which you have seen me and to those in which I will appear to you, delivering you from your people and from the Gentiles—to whom I am sending you to open their eyes, so that they may turn from darkness to light and from the power of Satan to God, that they may receive forgiveness of sins and a place among those who are sanctified by faith in me.

The apostolic task is set within the contest between light and darkness, God and Satan. The task involves opening the eyes of the spiritually blind (cf. Acts 26:18 and 2 Cor. 4:4). The proclamation of the gospel is the spearhead against the darkness. The gospel benefit that is thematized is forgiveness of sins, which is the very thing that Jesus made central to the good news in the Lukan "Great Commission" (Luke 24:45–47).

According to Paul's Letters

In the light of the testimony in Acts, however, we should expect to see the dominion of darkness, the kingdom of light, and God versus Satan thematized in the Pauline epistles, and indeed that is what we find (e.g., Col. 1:12–14, where "dominion," "darkness," "kingdom," "light," and "forgiveness of sins" are all mentioned). Paul was aware that the battle could not be waged with weapons of flesh. Divine power was needed to bring down the strongholds of opposition (2 Cor. 10:3–6). Arnold suggests that, in context, the stronghold to be pulled down is Christological error.[14] This is plausible. False apostles are at work preaching a different Jesus, Spirit, and gospel (cf. 2 Cor. 10:1–6 and 11:1–5). Paul, though, does not tease out what the weaponry is. However, in his letter to the Ephesians we may have clues.

Paul's letter to the Ephesians is particularly relevant to the practicalities of spiritual warfare. In Ephesians 4:26–27 he counsels the readers that, if they are angry, they are not to let the sun go down on their anger. Clearly there are contexts in which anger is the proper Christian response, but prolonged anger works mischief. Paul warns (v. 27): ". . . give no opportunity [*topos*, "place"] to the devil." This reference to the devil is found in a context where a number of sinful behaviors are on view (vv. 25–29; "falsehood," "[theft]," "corrupting talk"). In the contemporary world, one can imagine a number of scenarios in which the Christian may give a place to the devil to work his nefarious mischief. For example, a disturbing number of pastors are addicted to pornography.[15] Is this not giving a place to the devil? The great spoiler, it seems, knows how to work through human appetites to bring division and

---

[14] Arnold, *Three Crucial Questions*, 54–56.
[15] See http://www.expastors.com/how-many-pastors-are-addicted-to-porn-the-stats-are-surprising/, accessed 11/5/2015. This site discusses the troubling statistics.

hurt. Even so, giving a place to the devil and "demon-possession" ought not to be confused. The Christian may be ensnared by the devil, but repentance provides a way out of his traps, according to Paul (*pagis*, "snare" or "trap"; cf. 1 Tim. 3:7 and 2 Tim. 2:26).

It appears, then, that sinful behavior makes the Christian vulnerable. However, Paul knows of how the evil one may be defended against, as his famous description of the armor of God in Ephesians 6:10–20 shows.[16] I. Howard Marshall makes this astute comment:

> The whole section thus underlines the setting of the Christian life in the conflict between good and evil, conceived as the struggle between spiritual or supernatural powers. It reflects a realization that the power of evil is something that cannot be overcome by human resources, and that human beings can gain a more than human power to enable them to win in this struggle. This interpretation of the nature of the human situation may be uncongenial to materialists and even to some Christians, but it is so fundamental to Paul that it is difficult to see how it can be rejected without rejecting the heart of his religion.[17]

How then is the armor of God to be employed?

Craig S. Keener suggests, "Aspects of Paul's conclusion [in Ephesians 6:10–20] resemble the exhortations that generals gave to their armies before battle."[18] Significantly, Paul draws attention to the double-agency aspect of spiritual warfare (the divine and the human). The believer is to "be strong in the Lord and in the strength of his might" (v. 10). That is the divine element. And yet human responsibility is patent: "Put on the whole armor of God, that you may be able to stand against the schemes of the devil" (v. 11). The idea is to stand and withstand the enemy (vv. 11, 13–14). The ESV translation of verse 12 has the Christian "wrestling" with the enemy, and the enemy is not earthly ("the spiritual forces of evil in the heavenly places"). The NIV has the Christian "struggling" against the enemy. The NIV is to be preferred, since the imagery is military rather than athletic in the wider passage. Paul appears to be drawing on OT language about God's armor (e.g., Isa. 59:17) and the kind of armor a Roman soldier would wear.[19] Given such an opposition, the whole armor of God is needed: the belt (either metal or a leather apron), the breastplate, shoes

---

[16] Paul appears to have been comfortable with military imagery. In 1 Thessalonians 5:8 he encourages putting on faith and love as a breastplate, and hope as a helmet. In Romans 13:12 he refers to weaponry. The believer puts off the clothing of darkness and puts on the weaponry or armor (*hopla*) of light. In 2 Timothy 2:3–4 he writes of how the soldier endures hardship and avoids civilian entanglements out of a desire to please the commanding officer.
[17] I. Howard Marshall, "Ephesians," in *ECB*, ed. James D. G. Dunn and John W. Rogerson (Grand Rapids, MI, and Cambridge: Eerdmans, 2003), 1392–1393.
[18] For much in this paragraph I am indebted to Craig S. Keener's excellent discussion on this passage in *The IVP Bible Background Commentary: New Testament* (Downers Grove, IL: InterVarsity Press, 1993), comment on Ephesians 6:10–20.
[19] Interestingly, the apocryphal *Wisdom of Solomon* (first or second century BC) mentions the armor of God and four of the items in 5:17–20 (NRSV): "whole armor," "breastplate," "helmet," "shield," and "sword."

(probably a half boot is in mind), shield (probably of wood and leather), helmet (probably of bronze), and sword (Eph. 6:14–17). All of these items assume the believer is facing the enemy and standing his or her ground. There is no protection referenced for the back. Each item is qualified. The belt is the belt of truth. Presumably in this context gospel truth is in mind. The breastplate is of righteousness. That is to say, the gift of righteousness that comes through the gospel. The shoes enable the spread of the gospel. The shield of faith extinguishes the fiery darts of opposition. Temptation to sin would be one such dart, given the wider biblical testimony to the devil's wiles. Roman soldiers, as in the movie *Gladiator*, would drench their leather-covered wooden shields in water to put out flaming darts. The helmet of salvation protects the mind, and the sword of the Spirit provides the offensive weapon. Interestingly, no spear is mentioned.[20] This suggests that the contest with the principalities and powers is up close and personal, and not at a distance. The word of God, which is the sword of the Spirit, is the gospel in the Pauline epistles (see 1 Thess. 2:13). Prayer rounds out the presentation, and in a way it returns the reader to the beginning, that is, to God, in whom the believer is to be strong (Eph. 6:10). The practice of prayer is to suffuse the whole (v. 18): "praying at all times in the Spirit (*en pneumati*), with all prayer and . . . supplication for all the saints." Arnold is true to Paul when he writes, "Prayer is the essence of spiritual warfare and the most important means by which believers are strengthened by God."[21] Paul sought that strength. And in that light Paul becomes personal (vv. 19–20): ". . . and [pray] also for me, that words may be given to me in opening my mouth boldly to proclaim the mystery of the gospel, for which I am an ambassador in chains, that I may declare it boldly, as I ought to speak." The armor of God is not enough without the God of the armor, and prayer is the link.

According to James's Letter

When it comes to the practicalities of Christian obedience, the letter of James is outstanding. In his fourth chapter he shows his understanding of community life and how it can be riven by quarrels (James 4:1). Unfulfilled and thwarted desires are the problem (vv. 1–2). Prayer is not answered (vv. 2–3). How can it be when the attitudes, behaviors, and motivations are so wrong?

Believers' loyalty should be to God, but all too often they are worldly (James 4:4). A jealous God will not brook friendship with the world (v. 5). What, then, is the way forward? "Humility, humility, humility," as Augustine

---

[20] The Roman soldier's spear was the *pilum*. In offense, the spear would be thrown at the enemy before the soldier advanced with his short sword (*gladius*) for close-quarter combat. See http://www.bbc.co.uk/schools/primary history/romans/the_roman_army/, accessed 9/25/2016. The absence of a reference to the spear is consistent with the idea that defense is on view. The believer is not looking for a confrontation with the devil.

[21] Clinton E. Arnold, *Ephesians*, Zondervan Exegetical Commentary on the New Testament (Grand Rapids, MI: Zondervan, 2010), 474.

suggested in a different context.[22] God opposes the prideful, but for the humble there is grace (v. 6). And how does humility show itself? It submits to God first and resists the devil second (v. 7). The devil flees such resistance. James does not elaborate on what shape the resistance takes. However, the next verse may be a clue (v. 8): "Draw near to God, and he will draw near to you." J. A. Motyer correctly suggests, "The first element in the conflict is this central battle to live near God."[23] Such drawing near needs to be done with cleansed hands, purified hearts, and appropriate repentance (vv. 8–9). God exalts the humble (v. 10).

According to Peter's First Letter

There are affinities between James's advice on spiritual warfare and that of Peter. In 1 Peter 5:6 the humility theme surfaces once more, and with it the idea of the humble then being exalted by God: "Humble yourselves, therefore, under the mighty hand of God so that at the proper time he may exalt you." This is the God upon whom all care can be cast (v. 7). This was especially relevant to Christians in Asia Minor facing increased hostility from outsiders. Yet there was another dimension to the hostility (v. 8): "Be sober-minded; be watchful. Your adversary the devil prowls around like a roaring lion, seeking someone to devour." Like James's readers, the Petrine readers needed to show themselves part of the Christian resistance (v. 9): "Resist him, firm in your faith, knowing that the same kinds of suffering are being experienced by your brotherhood throughout the world." The future does not belong to the devil but to the people of God (v. 10): "And after you have suffered a little while, the God of all grace, who has called you to his eternal glory in Christ, will himself restore, confirm, strengthen, and establish you."

The roaring lion imagery is powerful. Lions are ferocious. So too is the prowling slanderer of God's people. Resistance is required. The OT witness also comes to mind on this point. One thinks of how Moses resisted the magicians of Egypt and their determined opposition in OT times.[24] Wayne Grudem gets the balance right: "While it is wrong to ignore the devil's existence, it is also wrong to cower before him in fear: Resist him!"[25] Interestingly, there are no NT texts that counsel attacking the devil, but there is more than one, as we have seen, that counsel resisting the devil. The form of that resistance is not specified, but clearly a firm faith is involved. Faith here appears to mean

---

[22] Quoted in Donald Demarco, "A Cardinal Virtue," http://www.catholiceducation.org/en/faith-and-character/faith-and-character/a-cardinal-virtue.html, accessed 4/16/2015.

[23] J. A. Motyer, *The Message of James*, TBST (Leicester, UK, and Downers Grove, IL: InterVarsity Press, 1985), 152.

[24] A point well made by Wayne A. Grudem, *1 Peter*, TNTC (Downers Grove, IL: IVP Academic, 1988), 203: "In both passages [James 4 and 1 Peter 5] the word *resist* implies active, determined opposition, often through confrontation (it is used of the Egyptian magicians who opposed Moses in 2 Tim. 3:8; *cf.* its use in Acts 13:8; Rom. 13:2; Gal. 2:11; 2 Tim. 4:15)" (emphasis original).

[25] Grudem, *1 Peter*, 203.

confidence in God despite circumstances that involve suffering. Living as I do in an affluent Western context with little to fear, I can only imagine how a text like this speaks so literally to believers undergoing persecution in other parts of the world.

According to John's First Letter

The contest between darkness and light comes to the fore in the very first chapter of 1 John. There are two ways to walk in this life: we walk either in the darkness or in the light (1 John 1:5–7). The first mention of the agent of darkness, the evil one, comes in the second chapter.[26] The "young men" are those who have overcome the evil one (1 John 2:13–14). How they overcame him is not articulated. John's third chapter gives insight into how those who are of the devil may be identified. Those who practice sinning belong to the devil, the archetypal sinner (1 John 3:8). The devil's children behave like the devil—for example, murderers like Cain (v. 12). Those who belong to God, who is light (1 John 1:5), practice righteousness (3:7). Moreover, they love their Christian brothers and sisters (v. 11) in contrast to the devil's progeny, who don't (v. 10). In the background of these contrasts lies the fact that the community to whom John is writing is in schism (1 John 2:19): "They went out from us, but they were not of us; for if they had been of us, they would have continued with us. But they went out, that it might become plain that they all are not of us." The last chapter in the letter gives the reader assurance that though the evil one is at work in the world, which lies in his thrall, there is divine protection for those born of God (5:18–19).[27]

According to Revelation

The book of Revelation provides an extraordinary end to the biblical canon. Like the OT canon, whether the Hebrew Bible or the Protestant one, it ends on the note of hope and expectation. In the Hebrew Bible, the hope is for a return to Jerusalem ("let him go up"; 2 Chron. 36:23). In the Protestant OT, it is the return of Elijah and the dawning of the day of the Lord (Mal. 4:1–6). Revelation is looking for the return of Jesus ("Come, Lord Jesus!"; Rev. 22:20). Before the return of the King there is much conflict described and mysterious personages surface, such as the beast of the sea and the beast of the earth (Revelation 13) and the false prophet (Rev. 16:13; 19:20). Satan is mentioned early in the book. For example, we read of the church in Pergamum, where Satan's throne is found (Rev. 2:13). Faithful Antipas was put to death there. The several

[26] This chapter of John's first letter also contains a reference to the coming of the antichrist (1 John 2:18). The antichrist will be discussed in our next chapter.
[27] The fourth chapter of 1 John contains an important passage about testing the spirits, which will be discussed in the excursus on discernment ("How to Test the Spirits").

mentions of Satan in the second and third chapters show John's keen awareness of evil (2:9, 13, 24; 3:9). Significantly too, promises are held out to those in each one of the seven named churches who overcome (2:7, 11, 17, 26; 3:5, 12, 21).

In terms of spiritual warfare and the Christian's engagement in it, a passage from later in Revelation is particularly relevant, and yet again the language of overcoming appears (12:10–11):

> And I heard a loud voice in heaven, saying, "Now the salvation and the power and the kingdom of our God and the authority of his Christ have come, for the accuser of our brothers has been thrown down, who accuses them day and night before our God. And they [*autoi*; emphatic, given the use of the personal pronoun] have conquered him by the blood of the Lamb and by the word of their testimony, for [*kai*; lit., "and"] they loved not their lives even unto death.

Martyrs are clearly on view, as Leon Morris argues.[28] What Christ achieved in his victorious dying, and the martyrs' testimony to it, discomfort the evil one.[29] Moreover, such a testimony can cost Christians the ultimate price of death for their words. In fact, in so dying, does not the Christian imitate his or her conquering Lord (cf. Rev. 3:21 and 12:11)? Indeed, as I write, there are places in the world where such imitations are happening.[30]

SPIRITUAL WARFARE: SEVEN CONTEMPORARY APPROACHES

James K. Beilby and Paul R. Eddy have provided a useful interactive discussion by four prominent writers in the area of spiritual warfare: Walter Wink, David Powlison, Gregory A. Boyd, and C. Peter Wagner—and Rebecca Greenwood, who is lesser known. The diversity of their views shows again how controversial the matter of spiritual warfare is in today's world.[31] In this section we consider these four models along with three additional ones: the very different one proposed by Timothy G. Gombis, a Catholic pastoral model proposed by Michael Scanlan and Randall Cirner, and a Protestant pastoral model advo-

---

[28] Leon Morris, *Revelation*, TNTC (Downers Grove, IL: IVP Academic, 1987), 157. The Greek is even more forceful than the ESV translation. These martyrs overcame the devil because (*dia*) of the blood of the Lamb and because (*dia*) of the word of their testimony.

[29] David E. Aune shows that the idea of martyrs conquering their opponents through their deaths has intertestamental Jewish precedents: "The motif of Jewish martyrs 'conquering' (νικᾶν) their besiegers and torturers by facing suffering and death nobly is emphasized in 4 Macc 6:10, 'And like a noble athlete the old man, while being beaten, was victorious [ἐνίκα] over his torturers.'" See David E. Aune, *Revelation 6–16*, WBC (Dallas: Word, 1998), 702. He maintains, "The same motif occurs in Christian martyrological literature. In *Mart. Perpetua* 10.13–14, the martyr states (tr. Musurillo, *Acts*, 119), 'Then I awoke. I realized that it was not with wild animals that I would fight [*pugnaturam*] but with the Devil, but I knew that I would win the victory [*uictoriam*].' Here, of course, *uictoria* means dying without renouncing faith in Christ."

[30] The fact that there are Christians suffering for the name of Christ today has implications for reading Scripture. There are places in the world where the biblical treatment of suffering for the faith makes the Bible speak with a directness of applicability that the affluent Western Christian reader simply may not appreciate. There are, for example, parts of Africa where there are Christian slaves. For them, 1 Peter 2:18–25 has immediate relevance. See, for Sudan, http://csi-usa.org/slave_liberation.html, accessed 4/10/2015.

[31] For this section I am heavily, though not exclusively, indebted to James K. Beilby and Paul Rhodes Eddy, eds., *Understanding Spiritual Warfare: Four Views* (Grand Rapids, MI: Baker Academic, 2012).

cated by Peter G. Bolt and Donald S. West.[32] I will also offer my own model before drawing out implications for belief and practice.

The Domination System Model: Walter Wink[33]

For Walter Wink, Satan is a symbol, and behind the symbol is real experience. It is an experience of evil. He argues, "Satan is an archetypal image of the universal human experience of evil."[34] For him, "Satan thus becomes the symbol of the spirit of an entire society alienated from God, the great system of mutual support in evil, the spirit of persistent self-deification blown large, the image of unredeemed humanity's collective life."[35] A great strength of Wink's position is his acute sense of the reality of institutionalized evil. However, he rejects the traditional view that Satan is a spiritual being characterized by intelligence and will. Instead, he offers a developmental view of the biblical story and argues that God becomes pure light over the biblical period, while Satan remains, throughout, God's servant who sifts the loyalty of God's people.[36] Wink provocatively states, "I shall labor even more, to rectify two millennia in which Satan has been so persistently maligned."[37] Even so, the language of "Satan" and "satanic" has its place, because some evils are so horrendous that they cannot be better named (e.g., a nuclear arms race).[38] The fundamentalist makes the error of turning Satan into a spiritual being, while the liberal Christian makes the mistake of being dismissive of the symbol.[39]

How then is Satan to be opposed? Wink sees similarities between his own theological position and that of some evangelicals and charismatics on the matter of spiritual warfare. He agrees with the idea that prayer should be aggressively directed against "the Powers," but disagrees as to how the demonic is to be understood. He says, "I do not believe that evil angels seize human institutions and pervert them. Rather, I see the demonic as arising within the institution itself, as it abandons its divine vocation for a selfish, lesser goal."[40] According to Wink, the key practice of spiritual warfare is intercession: "The act of praying is itself one of the indispensable means by which we engage the

---

[32] Beilby and Eddy, *Understanding Spiritual Warfare*, appear to use the terms "view" and "model" interchangeably. Neither term is defined by them but, given their usage, they appear to mean differing examples of an approach to spiritual warfare. I will follow their lead and use "model."

[33] Beilby and Eddy use the phrase "The World Systems Model" to describe Wink's position. However, Wink himself uses the phrase "the Domination System" (*Understanding Spiritual Warfare*, 71). This is his preferred phrase as can be seen in his book *The Powers That Be: Theology for a New Millennium* (New York: Doubleday, 1998). In that work Wink refers to the Domination System more than fifty times. On page 39, Wink defines the Domination System as an "overarching network of Powers. . . . It is characterized by unjust economic relations, patriarchal gender relations, hierarchical power relations, biased racial relations, and the use of violence in them all."

[34] Wink, "World Systems Model," 58.

[35] Wink, "World Systems Model," 57.

[36] Wink, "World Systems Model," 48–56.

[37] Wink, "World Systems Model," 56.

[38] Wink, "World Systems Model," 59–60.

[39] Wink, "World Systems Model," 60.

[40] Wink, *Powers That Be*, 197.

Powers."[41] And what is intercession? He argues, "Intercession is spiritual defiance of what is, in the name of what God has promised."[42] He rightly contends, "Unprotected by prayer, our social activism runs the danger of becoming self-justifying good works."[43] Wink clearly believes in the importance of prayer.

Wink also argues for the practice of nonviolent love as a way of engaging the Powers: "There is another power at work in the universe that, like water, cuts stone: non-violent love."[44] Jesus embodies this way in his actions.[45] The Jesus way constitutes a third way because it avoids the extremes of submissiveness and violence.[46] It is the way of nonviolent loving resistance. In modern times that third way has exemplars in Mohandas Gandhi and Martin Luther King Jr.[47] Particularly formative for Wink's theology of nonviolent loving resistance is the theory of René Girard about mimetic violence and scapegoating. As we saw in chapter 6, Girard argued that for society to cope with its violence a scapegoat must be found to which those at enmity can redirect their violence and form a stable society. In the ancient world this violence took a sacred form. It is on view in the OT, but Jesus, by becoming the innocent victim, exposed the scapegoating mechanism for what it is and broke the cycle of sacred violence. Put another way, God took the part of the victim and not that of the violent oppressor.[48] If we imitate Jesus, we walk in his third way of nonviolence even if it means our death. Wink writes, "Here also the cross is the model: we are liberated, not by striking back at what enslaves us—for even striking back reveals that we are still controlled by violence—but by a willingness to die rather than submit to its command."[49]

Wink finds both the book of Revelation and the book of Daniel particularly illuminating. In Revelation the Roman Empire is presented as an idolatrous world domination system that is opposed by God's intercessors.[50] The God of the Bible is no static construct made out of ancient Greek ontology. Prayers that articulate an alternative future to that envisaged by the world domination system open a space for change through the ones who so pray, and such intercession impacts upon God, no less. The God of the Bible is not frozen, but responsive to such intercession. Wink strikingly claims, in somewhat exaggerated anthropomorphic fashion,

---

41 Wink, *Powers That Be*, 181.
42 Wink, "World Systems Model," 61.
43 Wink, *Powers That Be*, 181.
44 Wink, *Powers That Be*, 80.
45 Wink, *Powers That Be*, 86.
46 Wink, *Powers That Be*, chapter 5.
47 Wink, *Powers That Be*, chapter 5.
48 Wink's debt to Girard can be seen in *Powers That Be*, 85–86 and 91–92. See René Girard, "Violence and Religion: Cause or Effect?" in *The Hedgehog Review: Critical Reflections on Contemporary Culture* 6/1 (Spring 2004): 8–20. In this essay Girard sums up his mimetic theory of violence and its relation to Christianity.
49 Wink, *Powers That Be*, 93.
50 Wink, *Powers That Be*, 181.

Praying is rattling God's cage and waking up God and setting God free and giving this famished God water and this starved God food and cutting the ropes off God's hands and the manacles off God's feet and washing the caked sweat from God's eyes and then watching God swell with life and vitality and energy and following God wherever God goes.[51]

However, Wink argues, the Powers can block divine action. The book of Daniel, in its own mythological way, reveals that God's response to intercession may be delayed. In Daniel's account it was delayed for twenty-one days as the angel of Persia stood opposed. Wink describes the delay as "an accurate depiction, in mythological terms, of the actual experience we have in prayer."[52] Ultimately God prevails, but it may take time.

Wink's rhetoric startles. But the God he so describes seems one of his own making. Wink seems to be arguing that God, so defined by him, acts by being believed on by us in the world. He maintains, regarding our praying, that, "A new force field appears that hitherto was only potential. . . . The change in one person thus changes what God can thereby do in the world."[53] Disturbingly, however, he argues, "Prayer is not a request made to an almighty king who can do anything at any time."[54] But for all of Wink's fondness for the book of Revelation, is not this in fact the God the book presents (e.g., 19:6, "For the Lord our God the Almighty reigns")? Wink appears to be cherry-picking the biblical text as it suits his thesis. David Powlison's critique is to the point: "He [Wink] controls the text rather than submitting to what the text actually says."[55] From an evangelical point of view, the theologian needs to take seriously the *tota scriptura*, not just parts of it.

The Classical Model: David Powlison

David Powlison notes that the classic creeds (Apostles', Nicene, and Athanasian) don't thematize the world, the flesh, and the devil. Baptismal liturgies do, however. The great Reformation era statements of faith don't focus on the devil either. He argues that both the early church and the Reformers observed the accents of Scripture in their emphases. He concludes that "God seems to think we don't need to know all the details."[56]

Powlison notes that the phrase "spiritual warfare" is not found in the Bible. So what are we to make of it? He contends that "It is a pastoral theological term for describing the moral conflict of the Christian life."[57] In contrast to

---

[51] Wink, *Spiritual Warfare*, 67.
[52] Wink, *Powers That Be*, 191.
[53] Wink, *Powers That Be*, 186.
[54] Wink, "World Systems Model," 67.
[55] David Powlison, "Response to Walter Wink," in *Understanding Spiritual Warfare*, 72.
[56] David Powlison, "The Classical Model," in *Understanding Spiritual Warfare*, 90.
[57] Powlison, "Classical Model," 92.

Wink, Powlison has a very broad understanding of spiritual warfare and how the Christian is to engage in it. He writes, "To win spiritual warfare is simply to live as light in a dark world."[58] He finds Ephesians 6:10–20 especially relevant to the task. The imagery of that passage, he argues, comes from Isaiah 11:1–12 and 59:1–21. He has no time for the usual explanation that Paul was inspired by the armor of the Roman soldier: "When Paul lists individual implements, the soldier we are to imagine is not Roman, but divine and messianic. We are to imagine the Lord God in person [clothed in his armor]."[59] In contradistinction to the usual interpretations, Powlison maintains that the armor is offensive and not defensive. God is on the move against the darkness, and so too is the Christian. For example, Powlison provocatively argues that the fiery darts (Eph. 6:16) are "return fire and counterattack."[60] He further argues that Paul the apostle is exhibit A of the Christian clothed in the whole armor of God and on the offense.

Powlison seems to be aware that his approach begs questions, and he deals with five in particular. First, he tackles the question of what spiritual warfare looks and feels like. His answer is that "It looks like the Christian life."[61] It is simply living Christianly in the light of temptations and troubles. Next, Powlison discusses the occult.[62] How are devotees of the occult to be helped? He sees Manasseh, the OT king, as a devotee whose ways were changed (2 Chronicles 33). And in the NT he explores Philip's encounter with Simon the practitioner of the dark arts (Acts 8:9–24). In both cases there is no mention of exorcisms. Instead, the "normal" ministry of the word is employed, with its call to repentance. Third is the matter of addiction. Again, there is no suggestion of deliverance from spirits in the biblical testimony. Instead, once again, it is the "normal" ministry of the word and a call for repentance that is to be deployed.[63] But what of the accounts of exorcisms in Matthew, Mark, Luke, and Acts? This is Powlison's fourth question, and he is very provocative at this point. Exorcisms are not part of spiritual warfare. Instead, they are expressions of mercy ministry. Therefore they are to be understood in the context of addressing human suffering, and not human sin. They are "a subset of the category of healing."[64] Powlison's last question is whether there is an affinity

---

[58] Powlison, "Classical Model," 98.
[59] Powlison, "Classical Model," 94. My difficulty with Powlison's argument at this point is that when God the warrior is presented in the OT, in texts such as the ones Powlison cites (e.g., Isa. 59:1–21), he is on the attack in judgment. This is hard to square with Paul's language of exhorting Christians to stand and withstand an attack, as in Ephesians 6:10–18.
[60] Powlison, "Classical Model," 96.
[61] Powlison, "Classical Model," 98. Peter G. Bolt, "Towards a Biblical Theology of the Defeat of Evil Powers," in *Christ's Victory over Evil: Biblical Theology and Pastoral Ministry*, ed. Peter G. Bolt (Nottingham, UK: Inter-Varsity Press, 2009), 43, says, "The 'spiritual warfare' in which the Christian is engaged is not a particular aspect of the Christian life, but is the Christian life itself."
[62] Powlison, "Classical Model," 101–103.
[63] Powlison, "Classical Model," 103–104.
[64] Powlison, "Classical Model," 105.

between the animist worldview (a universe filled with spirits) and deliverance ministry. He believes there are commonalities. To make his case he offers two stories. One involves a European missionary in West Africa. This missionary began with a theology "tilted towards Western rationalism."[65] The shock of meeting the African animist worldview then swayed him toward deliverance ministry. Over time, however, he became disillusioned with this move because people so "healed" did not change in character, and he returned to the "normal" ministry of the word and the call for repentance, with success. His second story involved a woman with bizarre behaviors who was ultimately helped not by an abortive deliverance attempt, but by "normal" Christian counseling.[66] Powlison knows that his anecdotes don't prove his thesis. But neither do other stories prove a different explanation—by which he means deliverance ones.[67]

There is much biblical wisdom in Powlison's discussion. The pastoral angle is especially helpful. There is much to learn from his discussion of the armor of God. However, why can't Paul be drawing upon the OT for the imagery, and also upon contemporary life, where Roman soldiers were highly visible? He was in chains, after all. Moreover, is all the armor for offense? Why then does Paul refer, in more than one place, to taking a stand? Could this not be a place for conjunctive rather than disjunctive theology—both/and, and not a simple dichotomous either/or? Still further, I wonder, regarding deliverance ministry (to use that phrase), whether there is a reductionism at work in Powlison's treatment. Are exorcisms reducible to subsets of healing, especially when Jesus connects them to the binding of the strong man? This may be another instance where conjunctive rather than disjunctive theology is needed. That is to say, an exorcism both expels a demon and heals the person. It is both spiritual warfare and a ministry of mercy. A final point is that there may be a theological elephant in the room. On the matter of spiritual gifts, is Powlison a cessationist? If so, that also may have contributed to the muting of certain biblical accents such as exorcism.

The Ground-Level Deliverance Model: Gregory A. Boyd

The approach of Gregory A. Boyd is very different from that of Powlison and shows some debts at points to that of Wink.[68] Boyd believes in deliverance ministry. The Christian lives in the midst of war, albeit a spiritual one. The war is between God and the gods. One such god is the prince of Persia, who in Daniel 10 opposes Michael the archangel. Boyd apparently prefers the term

---

[65] Powlison, "Classical Model," 108.
[66] Powlison, "Classical Model," 109–110.
[67] Powlison, "Classical Model," 111.
[68] Gregory Boyd, "The Ground-Level Deliverance Model," in *Understanding Spiritual Warfare*, 129n2. He has his criticism of Wink, especially over the personal nature of the devil, which Boyd believes in but Wink does not.

"god" to the more traditional phrase "fallen angel." He appeals to both the Old and New Testaments to make his case that "the motif of cosmic warfare runs throughout the biblical narrative."[69] Earthly spiritual conflict has its heavenly counterpart. Central to the victory of light over darkness is a *Christus Victor* Christology. Indeed, Boyd argues that Jesus's lifestyle was warfare. He writes,

> Framed within this apocalyptic framework, we can see that Jesus's unique countercultural life style was not merely a revolt against aspects of his culture but was also against the fallen powers that lay [*sic*] behind and fuel every aspect of society and creation that is inconsistent with the reign of God he came to inaugurate.[70]

The unique lifestyle features to which Boyd refers include Jesus's treatment of women, the poor, and the Samaritans.

Boyd goes on the attack when he considers the modern denial of the demonic, whether by Bultmann or David O'Connor or Hans Küng. He sees in the modern denials confusion between disbelief in the "mythic portrayals" of angels, Satan, and powers found in Scripture and denial of the ontological entities to which they nevertheless point. In Boyd's view, the biblical garb may be mythic but the realm to which it points is very real. He also sees these modern denials as predicated on a Western naturalism that is elitist in the light of global experience. Postmodern thought and anthropological studies challenge the privileging of the naturalistic worldview. He draws on cross-cultural studies and testimonies to argue for what he terms a "new democratized epistemology" which takes non-Western testimony seriously, not dismissively. He concludes, "I would argue that, whatever else we make of them [cross-cultural experiences], they provide empirical support for the New Testament view that spirits and 'demon possession' are real."[71]

How then is the Christian to engage at ground level in spiritual warfare? First, the Christian is to wake up to the fact of spiritual warfare. After all, the NT calls upon us to live like soldiers and please our enlisting officer (2 Tim. 2:4). And what does that life look like? Boyd argues, "We are to live with the singular mission of advancing God's kingdom by the unique way we live, the self-sacrificial way we love, the humble way we serve, and the power we demonstrate against oppressive forces."[72] Next, we are to "live a revolting lifestyle."[73] That is to say, we imitate Jesus in revolting against the powers. We do so by loving our enemies and refusing to use power against them, even to the point of our death. And we are to use both a deliverance approach to help the de-

---

Boyd, "Ground-Level Deliverance Model," 130.
Boyd, "Ground-Level Deliverance Model," 138.
Boyd, "Ground-Level Deliverance Model," 147.
Boyd, "Ground-Level Deliverance Model," 151.
Boyd, "Ground-Level Deliverance Model," 152.

monized and a therapeutic one to help the troubled. In some instances both approaches are needed. He says of his own church's ministry, "We pray warfare prayers and engage in counseling with everyone who comes in, regardless of whether we believe they're in need of deliverance or counseling."[74] His approach is conjunctive. He is skeptical, however, about those who move far beyond ground-level deliverance and speak of engaging "territorial spirits." He finds no biblical warrant for the latter model of deliverance.

Boyd writes with great verve and great learning. He articulates briefly his own open theism view of God, but it does not obscure his discussion. His emphasis on *Christus Victor* captures an important biblical truth. However, he seems to downplay the importance of the forgiveness of sins as a gospel benefit over against deliverance.[75] This is simply not true to the accents in the biblical text, whether it is God's self-description in the theophany on Sinai (Ex. 34:6–7) or the fact that in the Lukan "Great Commission" Jesus made the proclamation of the forgiveness of sins the heart of the gospel benefit—in Luke 24:45–49 and echoed throughout Acts, as in 2:38; 5:31; 10:43; 13:38 and 26:18. The great creeds also affirm this benefit of the forgiveness of sins (Apostles, Nicene, and Athanasian). The fathers knew their Bible. And it is strange that Boyd cites Ephesians 6:10–20 on occasion but the text plays no substantive role in his discussion. And this absence is especially noticeable when he discusses the Christian as a soldier.[76] His point that human combat against territorial spirits has no biblical precedent is very valuable.

The Strategic-Level Deliverance Model:
C. Peter Wagner and Rebecca Greenwood

There are family resemblances between Boyd's model and that proposed jointly by C. Peter Wagner and Rebecca Greenwood.[77] Both of the latter are proponents of deliverance ministry as integral to spiritual warfare. However, there is a difference. Wagner and Greenwood paint on a very large canvas compared to Boyd's ground-level approach.[78]

It is important to note that Wagner provides only "some introductory

---

[74] Boyd, "Ground-Level Deliverance Model," 155.
[75] Boyd, "Ground-Level Deliverance Model," 137.
[76] Boyd, "Ground-Level Deliverance Model," 151–152.
[77] C. Peter Wagner and Rebecca Greenwood, "The Strategic-Level Deliverance Model," in *Understanding Spiritual Warfare*, 176. Interestingly, Justin Lee argues that the bestselling novels by Frank Peretti, *This Present Darkness* and *Piercing the Darkness*, are "straightforward dramatizations of 'Strategic Level Spiritual Warfare,'" ("The Art of Spiritual Warfare," *First Things* (March 20, 2019), 58. According to Lee, *This Present Darkness* has sold more than 2.5 million copies since 1986.
[78] Their large canvas approach illustrates what Tony Payne, following Nigel Scotland, terms "expansive demonology," which had its rise within the charismatic movement in the 1970s (see Payne's "A Short History of Deliverance," in *Christ's Victory over Evil*, 14). Payne quotes Scotland: ". . . the expansives live in a world which is ruled by an exceptionally big and powerful devil, who at times appears almost as the evil equivalent to Jesus. The nations are believed to be ruled over by the prince of demons, and the skies and just about every human activity and relationship are infested with Satan's minions" (15).

material" to the overall discussion. In doing so he draws attention to the Fuller Theological Seminary Symposium on power evangelism held in 1988. He contributed a paper at this symposium entitled "Territorial Spirits" and indicated it was a fresh area of research in spiritual warfare.[79] He outlined his understanding of that phrase: "[n]amely, that satan [sic] delegates high-ranking members of the hierarchy of evil spirits to control nations, regions, cities, tribes, people groups, neighborhoods, and other significant social networks of human beings throughout the world."[80] To what end does Satan do this? Wagner suggests, "Their major assignment is to prevent God from being glorified in their territory, which they do through directing the activity of lower-ranking demons."[81] In 1988 Wagner offered this self-described thesis on territorial spirits as a working hypothesis.[82] Over the years his hypothesis has clearly become a firm theological position for some, as can be seen in his joint piece written with Greenwood, to whom we now turn.

Greenwood draws on her personal experience for much of her contribution.[83] She describes herself as "a prophetic warfare intercessor." She offers a definition of spiritual warfare in terms of "an invisible battle in the spiritual realm involving a power confrontation between the kingdom of God and the kingdom of darkness."[84] This battle takes place at three levels. First, there is ground-level spiritual warfare that consists of "the practice of deliverance ministry that involves breaking demonic influences in an individual."[85] Second, the occult-level spiritual warfare "deals with witchcraft, Satanism, freemasonry, New Age beliefs, Eastern religions."[86] Third, there is strategic-level spiritual warfare that battles "demonic entities . . . assigned to geographical territories and social networks."[87] It is this third kind of spiritual warfare which occupies most of her attention. She sees in Acts 16 and the account of Paul casting out a demon from the slave girl a biblical example of a power confrontation with demonic territorial spirits. She contends that Philippi, where this took place, was the home of Python, a territorial spirit, and this was the spirit cast out, causing a social uproar in the city. The city uproar is, for her, further evidence that a territorial spirit was involved.[88]

There are weapons to be used against territorial spirits, which include

---

[79] C. Peter Wagner inter alia, *Supernatural Forces in Spiritual Warfare* (Shippensburg, PA: Destiny Image, 2012), 78. The papers and responses to them have been reprinted because Wagner believes that the lessons of the late 80s and 90s about spiritual warfare need to be taught to a new generation (9).
[80] Wagner, *Supernatural Forces in Spiritual Warfare*, 78.
[81] Wagner, *Supernatural Forces in Spiritual Warfare*, 78.
[82] Wagner, *Supernatural Forces in Spiritual Warfare*, 76–79.
[83] The great bulk of their essay comes from the pen of Rebecca Greenwood.
[84] Wagner and Greenwood, "Strategic-Level Deliverance Model," 176.
[85] Wagner and Greenwood, "Strategic-Level Deliverance Model," 179.
[86] Wagner and Greenwood, "Strategic-Level Deliverance Model," 179.
[87] Wagner and Greenwood, "Strategic-Level Deliverance Model," 179.
[88] Wagner and Greenwood, "Strategic-Level Deliverance Model," 180–181.

spiritual mapping, identificational repentance, prophetic decrees, prophetic acts, power encounters, prayer walking (more anon), and prayer journeys.[89] She describes each in detail. For example, prayer mapping "is the practice of identifying the spiritual conditions at work in a given community, city, or nation."[90] These might include bloodshed, idolatry, sexual immorality, or broken covenants. Regarding the last of these, she cites the 371 broken treaties between the federal administration of the United States and native American Indians as a case in point.[91] On her view, the church has been given authority to reclaim territory and social networks from the devil and for God.

Drawing on her own experiences in particular, Greenwood discusses at length the spiritual warfare conducted against an abortion clinic in Kansas and its doctor, George Tiller. In the battle, she recalled a dream of years earlier that it was a demon called Lilith who was the principal force behind death and abortion at the clinic. Outside the clinic on one visit, she prayed, for example, "In the name of Jesus I bind the territorial spirit of death. I bind you, Lilith, and say you no longer will be able to execute bloodshed of the innocent and unborn from this location. You will no longer advance in your demonic strategies and agendas. You are bound." Now, who is Lilith, exactly? Here Greenwood draws on the Jewish Talmud for her understanding of the demon. At one point in the campaign against the clinic, an owl was caught in fishing line and was trapped in a tree near the church offices of some of Greenwood's colleagues. She connects that incident with the idea that Lilith is depicted traditionally as the screeching owl. The campaign lasted from 2005 to 2007 and involved a number of trips to Kansas. The clinic did close after Dr. Tiller was murdered by a pro-life activist. Greenwood distances herself from that event but clearly sees the closure of the clinic as success.[92]

The sincerity of Greenwood (and Wagner) is patent, but so is the lack of biblical grounding for her ideas. Indeed, what is one to make of using the Jewish Talmud as an authority? What is to be made of linking a dream and a trapped owl? In terms of the biblical text, the incident in Acts 16 where Paul casts out a demon from the slave girl who was persistently following him is not framed in territorial spirits language. In fact, Paul acts out of annoyance (v. 18). Moreover, as in other places in Acts, local people were afraid of the loss of income if their trade in idols, amulets, and so forth were harmed by apostolic ministry (cf. 16:19–21 and 19:23–27). In other words, the uproar can be explained contextually in a very different way than the one offered by Greenwood. Walter Wink is excoriating: "This is not spiritual warfare but archaic

---

[89] Wagner and Greenwood, "Strategic-Level Deliverance Model," 181–191 passim.
[90] Wagner and Greenwood, "Strategic-Level Deliverance Model," 182.
[91] Wagner and Greenwood, "Strategic-Level Deliverance Model," 186–187.
[92] For the substance of this paragraph I am indebted to Wagner and Greenwood, "Strategic-Level Deliverance Model," 193–197.

pagan religion dressed up as Christianity."[93] Powlison and Boyd are critical too, but softer in tone. For them—and for me as well—it is the lack of firm exegetical grounding, the use of personal anecdotes, and fantastic conjectures which constitute for them a major problem with this theology of spiritual warfare.

The Embodying the Divine Warrior Model: Timothy G. Gombis

The four models discussed above do not exhaust the possibilities. Recently Timothy G. Gombis has presented a very different approach to the question of spiritual warfare that draws upon Paul's letter to the Ephesians. In doing so he draws heavily, with acknowledgement, on Kevin J. Vanhoozer's drama approach to text and doctrine.[94] The opening words of his preface are indicative: "This book presents Ephesians as a drama—a gospel script that invites performances by communities of God's people."[95]

Gombis argues that Paul draws on the divine warrior tradition as found in OT texts such as Isaiah 59:15–19 in order to present the church in this striking way:

> Quite surprisingly, Paul situates the church as the divine warrior, carrying out spiritual warfare in the world. God showed up at various times throughout the Scriptures to wage warfare against Israel's enemies—and even against Israel when the nation was unfaithful. In the same way, the church is now the divine warrior, involved in intense spiritual conflict with the powers that rule the present evil age. Paul also reveals how the church is to carry out divine warfare, though it is far from what many of us anticipate in our spectacle-oriented culture.[96]

What is surprising, then, about the church as divine warrior? Gombis maintains, "As we shall see, the church embodies the divine warrior by undergoing constant community transformation through renewed imagination and practices."[97]

Ephesians 6:10–18 appears to be his point of departure for elaborating his thesis. He contends that this passage is the rhetorical conclusion to the letter to the Ephesians.[98] From this point on his argument becomes puzzling. He asks how spiritual warfare is to be conducted. He answers in terms of

---

[93] Walter Wink and Michael Hardin, "Response to Wagner and Greenwood," in *Understanding Spiritual Warfare*, 203.

[94] Timothy G. Gombis, *The Drama of Ephesians: Participating in the Triumph of God* (Downers Grove, IL: IVP Academic, 2010), 185, notes on chapter 1.

[95] Gombis, *Drama of Ephesians*, 9.

[96] Gombis, *Drama of Ephesians*, 155–156. Gombis believes that "Paul does not derive the armor of God from pondering the armor of a Roman soldier . . . but from a consideration of the Scriptures" (156). As in the case of David Powlison's approach, my difficulty with Gombis's argument is that when God the warrior is presented in the OT in texts such as the ones he cites (e.g., Isa. 59:15–19) he is on the attack in judgment. This is hard to square with Paul's language of exhorting Christians to stand and withstand an attack, as in Ephesians 6:10–18.

[97] Gombis, *Drama of Ephesians*, 156.

[98] Gombis, *Drama of Ephesians*, 157.

transformed community, as can be found set out in passages such as Ephesians 4:17–31; 5:6–14, 15–17, 18–21; and 5:22–6:9. The transformed community is characterized by resistance to compromising its holiness, by exhibiting the new humanity as opposed to the old, by transformative impact on the surrounding culture, by discerning what pleases the Lord, and by justice in relationships.[99] He sums up his findings in these terms: "Spiritual warfare against Satan and the powers of darkness, therefore, does not involve wild behavior or direct engagement with demonic entities. We do not rebuke Satan, nor do we command demons. Our warfare against the powers takes place on a mundane level."[100] That mundane level involves resisting "idolatrous and destructive patterns of life. We battle the powers when we refuse to participate in their corruptions of creation."[101] (There are affinities here between Gombis and Powlison. To live a robust Christian life is to engage in spiritual warfare.) The discussion is rich with insights, especially the recognition that Paul is addressing a community, not an individual. However, Ephesians 6:10–18 is never exegeted, and thus, though mentioned, is left largely unexplored. This is a serious lacuna.

A Catholic Pastoral Model: Michael Scanlan and Randall Cirner

Roman Catholic charismatic writers Michael Scanlan and Randall Cirner offer what they describe as a "pastoral model" of spiritual warfare. It is pastoral because spiritual warfare is to be conducted with a view to providing pastoral care.[102] The theological framework they employ is that of kingdom. The kingdom of God is at war with the kingdom of Satan.[103] How do they know this? They know it because of revelation: God has spoken on the subject. They know it from tradition (e.g., Justin Martyr, Irenaeus, Origen, Tertullian, and Cyprian). And as one would expect in a Roman Catholic work, they know it because the teaching office of the Church teaches that it is so.[104] In addition, they draw on their own experience of spiritual warfare.

These two writers use the category of "deliverance" as their way into the subject of spiritual warfare. They write, "The term 'deliverance' is used here in a generic sense to refer to any confrontation with an evil spirit aimed at overcoming his influence. Deliverance, then, can encompass the whole range of encounters with evil spirits, from repulsing satanic temptation to exorcising

---

[99] Gombis, *Drama of Ephesians*, 160–179.
[100] Gombis, *Drama of Ephesians*, 183.
[101] Gombis, *Drama of Ephesians*, 183.
[102] Michael Scanlan and Randall Cirner, *Deliverance from Evil Spirits: A Weapon for Spiritual Warfare* (Cincinnati, OH: Franciscan Media, 1980), 1. Though this book is more than thirty years old it is in constant demand, as can be seen in its Amazon sales. At the time of its writing, Scanlan was the chancellor of Franciscan University in Steubenville, Ohio. He held that position for twenty-six years.
[103] Scanlan and Cirner, *Deliverance from Evil Spirits*, 5–11.
[104] Scanlan and Cirner, *Deliverance from Evil Spirits*, 15–19. A strength of this work is the numerous quotations from the early church fathers.

a possessed person."[105] For Scanlan and Cirner the devil works in three major ways: temptation, opposition, and bondage. The devil tempts humankind in order "to lead men away from God," as can be seen in the example of Adam and Eve. In addition, the devil opposes the word of God. He seeks to prevent the preaching of the gospel. The magician Elymas's attempt to dissuade the proconsul from listening to Paul and Barnabas is their example (Acts 13:6–11). Lastly, the devil puts some into bondage through possession, as he did with the demoniac of Mark 5.[106]

How, then, according to Scanlan and Cirner, is the satanic to be defeated? They suggest two weapons. The first is the word of command: "You evil spirit, I command you in the name of the Lord Jesus to leave."[107] This is the weapon of offense. The second is living a dynamic Christian life that embraces the means of grace (e.g., daily prayer, daily Bible reading, fellowship, hearing sound teaching, sacraments, and serving others). This is the weapon of defense that protects such a Christian from giving a place to the devil.[108]

Our two authors are writing for a wider audience than a Catholic readership.[109] However, their Catholic commitments surface strongly when they distinguish "a simple exorcism, from solemn exorcism."[110] They contend that simple exorcism is a practice that laity can do. Its purpose is "curbing the devil's power."[111] Solemn exorcism requires the priest and the permission of the local ordinary (bishop). This kind of exorcism requires the "driving out of the devil from a possessed person."[112] Since they are writing to laity, they leave solemn exorcism out of their discussion and concentrate on deliverance ministry that curbs the devil's power. Here, categories multiply: personal or self-deliverance, fraternal deliverance, pastoral deliverance, and specialist deliverance.[113] The procedure for deliverance is outlined in seven steps: preparation, introduction, listening and discerning, repentance, deliverance, healing and blessing, and finally pastoral guidance by way of follow-up.[114]

Another area where Catholic theology and practice come to the fore is

---

[105] Scanlan and Cirner, *Deliverance from Evil Spirits*, 1.

[106] Scanlan and Cirner, *Deliverance from Evil Spirits*, 27–35. In the next chapter (chapter 4), Scanlan and Cirner use the three categories to analyze their experiences with various people who they claim were victims of satanic temptation or opponents of the gospel, or were in satanic bondage.

[107] Scanlan and Cirner, *Deliverance from Evil Spirits*, 60–61.

[108] Scanlan and Cirner, *Deliverance from Evil Spirits*, 61.

[109] See Scanlan and Cirner, *Deliverance from Evil Spirits*, 59, which has a section on "Participation in a Christian Group," with no reference to the Catholic Church.

[110] Scanlan and Cirner, *Deliverance from Evil Spirits*, 65.

[111] Scanlan and Cirner, *Deliverance from Evil Spirits*, 66.

[112] Scanlan and Cirner, *Deliverance from Evil Spirits*, 66.

[113] Scanlan and Cirner, *Deliverance from Evil Spirits*, 63–65. Apparently one can, according to Scanlan and Cirner, cast out a demon from oneself by commanding the evil spirit to leave one's life. The evil spirit will be named in doing so (e.g., anger, lust, etc.). Where is the scriptural basis for such a practice? Fraternal deliverance involves others. Pastoral deliverance requires a designated person with such a responsibility, and the specialist has a special gift to effect deliverance.

[114] Scanlan and Cirner, *Deliverance from Evil Spirits*, 80–91.

in their discussion of sacraments and "sacramentals." They claim, "Sacraments and sacramentals have a definite role in helping us become free of evil spirits."[115] Sacraments (e.g., baptism, Eucharist), they contend, put the receiver into direct contact with the action of Christ: "This direct contact with the Lord and his holiness is powerful enough to free us from evil spirits."[116] Sacramentals are objects set aside by the Church as means of grace (e.g., holy water and holy oil). These, they say, "have a special place in spiritual warfare."[117] What needs to be done in preparing water for baptism provides an instructive example. The minister prays, "God's creature, water, I cast out the demon from you in the name of Jesus Christ His Son and Lord and in the power of the Holy Spirit."[118] For all its sincerity, this is tradition uncontrolled by God's self-revelation.[119]

There is much to commend the approach of Scanlan and Cirner. It is thoroughly supernaturalistic. Their use of a kingdom framework provides a robustly biblical basis for their reading of the biblical evidence. They make illuminating use of the early church fathers. Their Roman Catholic commitments are in evidence but their intent is broader than that. They recognize that not all human maladies are satanic in origin. Discernment is needed to distinguish, for example, disease from the demonic.

What is of concern in Scanlan and Cirner's treatment of spiritual warfare, however, is that when addressing today's context there is so much presented that would not be anticipated from a careful reading of Scripture. Tradition and present-day experiences appear to displace the biblical testimony in key places. When they turn their attention to the practical, so much on view is textless as far as Scripture is concerned, or tenuously connected with Scripture. Extrabiblical categories multiply. Such multiplication of categories appears to characterize charismatic theology and practice, whether Protestant or Catholic. However, their patent pastoral concern for the afflicted cannot be faulted, only admired.

A Protestant Pastoral Model: Peter Bolt and Donald West

Peter G. Bolt and Donald S. West argue that the essentials of Christian ministry are independent of culture but are dependent upon the gospel of the NT: "The essentials of ministry, in relation to both principle and practice, arise from the gospel of Jesus Christ."[120] They adopt an inaugurated, now-but-not-yet eschatology, which leads them to see struggle, pain, and suffering as

---

[115] Scanlan and Cirner, *Deliverance from Evil Spirits*, 107.
[116] Scanlan and Cirner, *Deliverance from Evil Spirits*, 108.
[117] Scanlan and Cirner, *Deliverance from Evil Spirits*, 108.
[118] Scanlan and Cirner, *Deliverance from Evil Spirits*, 108.
[119] It is hard to square the emphasis some traditions place on sacraments given 1 Corinthians 1:13–17, where Paul clearly prizes preaching the gospel above the practice of baptism.
[120] Peter G. Bolt and Donald S. West, "Christ's Victory over the Powers and Pastoral Practice," in *Christ's Victory over Evil*, 211.

the common lot of the believer this side of the return of Christ. However, the Christian has the great hope of the resurrection and ultimate deliverance.[121] Indeed, they maintain that "any 'victorious Christian life' will be experienced only on the resurrection day."[122] Christians should not be swayed by facile promises of deliverance in this life, especially when the demonic influence card is played.

On their view, the ministry of the word of God and prayer are the staples of congregational life in the midst of the powers of evil.[123] Spiritual warfare is nothing less and nothing more than the Christian life, a life lived in the light of Christ's definitive victory on the cross.[124] The question may be asked as to how, then, might the Christian deal with the devil? They write,

> When the NT is surveyed, there are surprisingly few direct instructions in regard to dealing with the devil—seven only in fact: (1) married couples are warned against abstaining from sex, lest the devil takes opportunity of their lack of connection to tempt them (1 Cor. 7:5); (2) the Ephesians are instructed not to sin in their anger, and so (presumably) not to give a place for the devil in the midst of their congregation (Eph. 4:27, "opportunity"); (3) they are instructed to put on the whole armor of God, so that they might stand against the methods of the devil (Eph. 6:11); (4) they are instructed to take up "the shield of faith," which will enable the extinguishing of the evil one's darts (Eph. 6:16; cf. Ps. 91:5); James calls upon his readers to submit to God, and to resist the devil, with the promise that he will flee (Jas. 4:7) (6) Peter urges watchfulness, because of the devil's penchant to wander around like a lion seeking some prey (1 Pet. 5:8); and (7) John warns his readers to love and not to be like Cain, who belonged to the evil one (1 John 3:12).[125]

They also persuasively contend that the Christian should not address the devil but should pray to their heavenly Father: "This means that there is no biblical justification at all for the practice in some deliverance ministries of directly conversing with evil spirits."[126] (I was once asked at a seminar whether I would speak directly to the devil. I replied that we were not on speaking terms.)

Provocatively, Bolt and West argue that Christians are to deal with the evil powers indirectly and not directly: "The 'battle' that Christians find themselves caught up in . . . is therefore, just like Christ's victorious battle beforehand, *indirect*."[127]

There is much profit to be found in the Bolt and West argument, with which I am largely sympathetic. However, in places it reads as reductionist. It

---

[121] Bolt and West, "Christ's Victory," 213.
[122] Bolt and West, "Christ's Victory," 215.
[123] Bolt and West, "Christ's Victory," 217.
[124] Bolt and West, "Christ's Victory," 219–221.
[125] Bolt and West, "Christ's Victory," 225.
[126] Bolt and West, "Christ's Victory," 226.
[127] Bolt and West, "Christ's Victory," 219, emphasis original.

is worth noting also that Ephesians 6:10–20 is given no sustained exegetical treatment, and there are Pauline instructions in that passage that are left unaddressed (e.g., those that concern the breastplate, the shoes, the helmet, and the sword, let alone prayer).[128] Moreover, it is hard to square the idea of indirectly battling the devil with 1 Peter 5:9: "Resist him [the devil], firm in your faith." This, prima facie, seems direct rather than indirect. That being said, Peter gives little hint as to the practicalities of such resisting.

Toward a Biblically Defensible Model of Spiritual Warfare

Thus far in this chapter, seven models of spiritual warfare have been surveyed and their varied strengths and weaknesses have been discussed. But it is hardly satisfactory to leave it at that. What then is the way forward, since a full treatment of the topic of spiritual warfare is beyond the scope of this present work? Even so, some indication of my own approach is in order. Recall my working description of spiritual warfare as that aspect of our common struggle as Christians against the machinations of malevolent spiritual creatures who are intent on thwarting God's redemptive plan for his human creatures. We begin with Christology.

The Victory of Christ

Death could not hold Jesus. The devil and his minions could not defeat Jesus. Jesus is indeed *Christus Victor*.[129] (This is a strength of Boyd's model.) Jesus's purposeful incarnation (Heb. 2:14–15), his atoning death on the cross (Col. 2:13–15), his triumphant resurrection from the dead (1 Pet. 3:21–22), his ascension to the place of executive authority at the right hand of the Father (Eph. 1:18–22), his pouring out of the promised Holy Spirit on the Day of Pentecost (Acts 2:32–36), his ever living to intercede for his people as our great high priest (Heb. 7:23–25), and the prospect of his kingly return (1 Cor. 15:20–28) reveal the depth of his triumph and the definitive nature of his victory over sin, death, and the devil.

Any approach to the topic of spiritual warfare must factor in a robust, biblically informed Christology.

Our Eschatological Setting

The fact is that in this life we do not yet see Jesus the Lord on the throne with our own eyes (1 Pet. 1:8). We live in the present by faith, not sight (2 Cor. 5:6–7). We experience what scholars call the now-but-not-yet. We have so many of

---

[128] This lacuna is true of the book as a whole.
[129] For a fuller discussion of how Christ is victor through his sacrifice on the cross and subsequent vindication by the Father, see my *God the Peacemaker: How Atonement Brings Shalom* (Downers Grove, IL: InterVarsity Press, 2009), chapter 6, esp. 124–130.

the blessings held out in the gospel now: forgiveness of sins (Col. 1:13–14), the indwelling Holy Spirit (1 John 4:4), eternal life (1 John 5:13), and so forth. But so much more is yet to come: the *visio dei* (the vision of God; 1 John 3:1–2), the definitive overthrow of evil (Rev. 20:7–10), no more death or tears or pain (Rev. 21:4), the new heavens and the new earth (Revelation 21–22), inter alia. In this light, we must avoid an overly realized eschatology.[130] An overly realized eschatology expects all the blessings of the gospel to be available now. On this view, enough faith banishes sickness and can even raise the dead. A now-but-not-yet eschatology is aware that the devil is still working his mischief, even though the cross has signaled his ultimate overthrow (cf. John 16:7–11 and Rev. 20:7–10).

A biblically defensible model of spiritual warfare needs to get eschatology right. I argue that the now-but-not-yet eschatology (technically, inaugurated eschatology) is such a model.

Three Key Assurances

Warfare involves struggle. As we struggle against the world, the flesh, and the devil, three key assurances are especially relevant to facing the devilish with confidence.

The first is the assurance that to be in Christ means that there is no divine condemnation. Paul's words are striking (Rom. 8:1): "There is therefore now no condemnation [*katakrima*; "condemnation," "judgment"] for those who are in Christ Jesus." Paul elaborates (vv. 33–34): "Who shall bring any charge against God's elect? It is God who justifies. Who is to condemn [*katakrinōn*, "condemning"]? Christ Jesus is the one who died—more than that, who was raised—who is at the right hand of God, who indeed is interceding for us." The devil has no claim on us. We belong to another. The death, resurrection, and intercession of Christ are the foundation for this first assurance.

Second, Paul makes it clear that nothing can separate believers from the love of Christ. This claim is the second key assurance, and Romans 8:35–39 is the relevant text:

> Who shall separate us from the love of Christ? Shall tribulation, or distress, or persecution, or famine, or nakedness, or danger, or sword? As it is written,
>
>> "For your sake we are being killed all the day long;
>> we are regarded as sheep to be slaughtered."
>
> No, in all these things we are more than conquerors through him who loved us. For I am sure that neither death nor life, nor angels nor rulers, nor things

---

[130] We must also avoid a futuristic eschatology, the view that all the blessings of the gospel are future. I know of no evangelical theologians or scholars who hold this view.

present nor things to come, nor powers, nor height nor depth, nor anything else in all creation, will be able to separate us from the love of God in Christ Jesus our Lord.

The reference to "angels," "rulers," and "powers" in this context provides further evidence that there are malevolent spirit beings. Otherwise why would Paul have included such in a list of what or who may separate us from the love of Christ? As with the first assurance, with regard to this second assurance the death and resurrection of Christ are the foundation.

The third assurance has to do with pneumatology rather than Christology. In 1 John 4:4 we read, "Little children, you are from God and have overcome them, for he who is in you is greater than he who is in the world." The context is significant. John is warning about the presence of antagonistic spirits (antichrists) at work through false prophets. The comparative claim is vital: the Holy Spirit is greater than the evil one. That it is the Holy Spirit who is the indwelling one in this context is evidenced by the earlier reference to the Spirit in verse 2 and the later reference to the Spirit in verse 13. As for Jesus, according to 1 John 2:1, he is our advocate with the Father. So Jesus is not on view in 4:4.

A biblically defensible model of spiritual warfare needs to make the Christian aware of the position of strength that these three assurances provide, if the believer is to be strong in the Lord (Eph. 6:10). Such assurances provide no rationale for passivity on the believer's part, as Paul's admonitions concerning the armor of God will show us next.

The Significance of the Armor of God

Any model of spiritual warfare must take into its purview the context of the warfare, as does Paul's description of the armor of God in Ephesians 6:10–20. (This is a strength of Powlison's model.) This is not the place to exegete the passage at any great length. However, some exposition is in order.

The context for admonition to wear the armor of God is our setting, in which malevolent spirits are at work (vv. 11–12):

> Put on the whole armor of God, that you may be able to stand against the schemes of the devil. For we do not wrestle against flesh and blood, but against the rulers, against the authorities, against the cosmic powers over this present darkness, against the spiritual forces of evil in the heavenly places.

Paul thus makes his readers very much aware of the context of conflict in which we live. That context includes more than the devil, as his minions are also mentioned, albeit obliquely (e.g., "cosmic powers," "spiritual forces of evil"). There is no room for demythologization in a biblically defensible model of spiritual warfare, although there is something in Walter Wink's thesis that human institutions can be vehicles for the devilish.[131]

The whole armor of God is extensive in its coverage. All of it is needed if the Christian is to stand (*stēnai* in v. 11, and *stēte* in v. 14) and withstand attack (*antistēnai* in v. 13). The language of "stand" and "withstand" suggests to me that a defensive rather than an offensive posture is on view. Put another way, I do not see the passage calling for Christians to seek out the devil and his entourage for combat. However, if we are engaged in gospel ministry, devilish attacks are to be expected. In verse 14 Paul refers to the belt of truth, in verse 14 the breastplate of righteousness, in verse 15 shoes for the feet, in verse 16 the shield of faith, in verse 17 the helmet of salvation, and in verse 17 the "sword of the Spirit, which is the word of God." I contend that all of these items are gospel-related. The truth on view in verse 14 is gospel truth. The righteousness mentioned also in verse 14 is the righteousness that comes to us through the gospel. In verse 15, Paul mentions the "gospel" explicitly. With our feet shod, we can actually stand firmly for the gospel. In verse 16, I take the shield of faith to be the gospel because Paul writes of "the faith" (*tēs pisteōs*). The faith protects from the onslaughts of the devil. The helmet mentioned in verse 17 consists of salvation, which is the term used in the most general way in the NT to speak of the benefits of the gospel. Lastly, also in verse 17, we read of "the sword of the Spirit, which is the word of God," which for Paul is the gospel message (see 1 Thess. 2:13). (Emphasizing the gospel is a strength of Bolt's model.) Moreover, Paul, having described the armor of God, calls for prayer on his behalf that he might proclaim the gospel boldly (Eph. 6:19). (The accent on prayer is another strength of Bolt's model.) Paul's call for such prayer reinforces in my mind the idea that he has the gospel in view in the passage. We also need to note that Paul is addressing a congregation and not just the individual Christian. This spiritual warfare is not conducted alone. (This is the strength of the Gombis model.) A biblically defensible model of spiritual warfare must seek to ground believers on the gospel of peace.

Importantly, Ephesians 6:10–20 begins and ends with God. In verse 10, the admonition is to be strong in the Lord, and in verses 18–20 Paul calls for prayer for his gospel ministry. Again, it is worth observing that Paul does not call upon his readers to pray that he might launch a "seek and destroy" mission against the demonic.

A biblically defensible model of spiritual warfare is both theocentric and gospel informed.

---

[131] To recall an example given earlier in the chapter, Nebuchadnezzar made idolatry the law of the land (Dan. 3:1–7). A law can be the vehicle for sin. Institutionalized evil is a real phenomenon. What needs to be avoided is Wink's reductionism.

Two General Principles to Observe

In broad terms, two principles are vital to engaging in spiritual warfare in a biblically sound way. The first is the principle of embracing the biblically warranted. The evangelical has a high doctrine of Scripture as God's word written. Any beliefs about spiritual warfare that are text-less are suspect, unless they can be shown to be consistent with divine special revelation. With regard to consistency, then, a judgment call is necessary as to the propriety of a belief or practice (e.g., the belief that the believer can be demon-possessed, and the practice of claiming territory from evil spirits). The second principle is that of avoiding the fanciful. The fanciful goes well beyond what is written in Scripture (e.g., providing buckets of water for exorcised demons to enter).

Informed by these two principles, we next turn our attention to the implications of our discussion for belief and practice.

IMPLICATIONS FOR BELIEF AND PRACTICE

My own approach to spiritual warfare is to observe the need to be biblical in belief, attitude, and action on the one hand, and the need to avoid the fanciful, on the other. What then is biblically warranted when it comes to spiritual warfare, and what needs to be eschewed?

Embracing the Biblically Warranted

First, the Christian needs to believe that, as Scripture makes plain, spiritual warfare is real and the struggle is cosmic in scope (Eph. 6:12). The demonic is not simply the dark side of the "Powers" (contra Wink's reductionism). There are malevolent intelligences destructively at work. Chief among these is Satan, the prince of darkness. His demonic entourage is real too. Ignorance of this reality is dangerous.

Second, there is the need for alertness (1 Pet. 5:8). We are in a combat zone, spiritually speaking. Life individually, congregationally, and in wider society can take a destructive turn. The devil works his mischief, even in churches. The aware Christian should always be disappointed by this but never surprised, if he or she is alert. In particular, we need to be alert to the devil's two guises in this world. He can be the angel of light using false teachers and their teachings to do harm (2 Cor. 11:12–15), and he can use the persecution of God's people to wreak havoc (1 Pet. 5:8). With regard to the first guise, the believer needs to stand firmly on the apostolic gospel, and not be tempted to embrace "a different gospel" (2 Cor. 11:4). The roaring lion's guise is to be met with resistance, firm faith, and the hope of "eternal glory in Christ" (1 Pet. 5:8–10). Regarding the roaring lion, we are not alone in facing his onslaughts, as 1 Peter 5:9 shows: "Resist him, firm in your faith, knowing that the same kinds of suffering are

being experienced by your brotherhood throughout the world." This knowledge should serve to encourage believers. It is that much harder for us to stand
in the face of evil if we think that we are alone in experiencing it.[132]

Third, the aware and alert Christian needs to be intentional about wearing
the armor of God described in Ephesians 6, and about adopting the life stance
that goes with wearing it: namely, to stand and withstand the devil. Even so,
Christians are nowhere commanded to seek out the devil or the demons for
combat. Instead, we engage in gospel ministry, knowing that devilish attacks
may come. On this point we need to note in evidence that Paul's call for prayer
in Ephesians 6:18–20 is that he might proclaim the gospel with boldness (*en
parrēsia*, "in boldness"). His call presupposes that there will be opposition.
Hence the need for boldness. Interestingly, in Acts 4:23–31 the first Christians
also called upon God that they might speak the word (the gospel, in the context
of Acts) with boldness (v. 29; *meta parrēsias pasēs*, "with all boldness") in a
climate of opposition. Indeed, Peter and John had earlier been arrested on account of the word (Acts 4:1–3).

When it comes to devilish attacks, the word of God, the sword of the
Spirit, is especially important. Jesus used the word of God in the wilderness
in countering the devil (Matt. 4:1–11). It is the word of God that the psalmist encourages the believer to store in his or her heart that we might not sin
against our God (Ps. 119:11). There is no substitute for an intimate knowledge
of Scripture. Memorized Scripture is an asset when temptations come (e.g.,
1 Cor. 10:13; Rom. 8:1, 38–39; 1 John 4:4 and Rev. 12:11).

Moreover, on this matter of knowing the Bible, the believer needs to be
aware that the devil is the great opponent of the word of God. In Jesus's famous parable of the sower, the devil snatches the seed of the word that fell
along the path (Mark 4:15): ". . . Satan immediately comes and takes away the
word [the gospel of God, in the Markan context] that is sown in them." If this
is so with the spoken word of God, we can safely assume the devil is the opponent of the written word of God. The evil one recognizes the value of the word
of God. Jonathan Edwards rightly argued, "The devil has ever shown a mortal
spite and hatred towards that holy book the Bible: he has done all in his power
to extinguish that light. . . . He is engaged against the Bible, and hates every
word of it."[133] The word of God is an essential weapon in this spiritual war.

Fourth, whether the Christian is both aware and alert will also show itself

---

[132] Elijah comes to mind (1 Kings 19:10): He said, "I have been very jealous for the LORD, the God of hosts. For the
people of Israel have forsaken your covenant, thrown down your altars, and killed your prophets with the sword,
and I, even I only, am left, and they seek my life, to take it away." The Lord reassures him (v. 18): "Yet I will leave
seven thousand in Israel, all the knees that have not bowed to Baal, and every mouth that has not kissed him."
Elijah was not alone.

[133] Quoted by J. I. Packer in the foreword to R. C. Sproul, *Knowing Scripture*, 3rd ed. (Downers Grove, IL: Inter-
Varsity Press, 2016), 5.

in the life of prayer. As the ancient rule says, "*lex orandi lex credenda*" ("the law of praying is the law of believing"). Our prayers reveal our true theology. If the demonic is never mentioned in our prayers, then how aware and alert are we? I for one, whenever I preach, teach, or lecture, pray not only that Christ is honored and God's people edified but also that the strong man is discomforted yet again. In liturgical churches, congregants pray the Lord's Prayer every week and in doing so are hopefully reminded of the need to be delivered from the evil one. In non-liturgical churches, the pastor's prayer provides the opportunity to show an awareness of the spiritual warfare in which congregants are engaged. Prayer, too, is an essential weapon. Indeed, if I suspected that satanic disruption was at work in a situation, my first recourse would be to raise that possibility in prayer to God, and ask for his protection and his wisdom to know what to say and do.

Fifth, there is a virtue or strength of character that is vital to spiritual warfare, and that is humility (1 Pet. 5:6–7). Pride, on the other hand, can undo us (1 Tim. 3:6). As Scripture warns (1 Cor. 10:12), "Therefore let anyone who thinks that he stands take heed lest he fall."

Sixth, the Christian is to give the devil no place. This is Paul's counsel in Ephesians 4:26–27: "Be angry and do not sin; do not let the sun go down on your anger, and [*mēde*, "neither"] give no opportunity [*topos*, "place"] to the devil." How is the devil given a place in the Christian's life? In this Ephesians text, anger that is not dealt with seems to provide the devil opportunity to work mischief. There are contexts in which a Christian is right to be angry. Jesus, after all, was rightly angry on occasion (Mark 3:5). However, there is a devilish danger, when it comes to anger and its expression. John R. W. Stott comments,

> Paul's third qualification is *give no opportunity to the devil* (verse 27), for he knows how fine is the line between righteous and unrighteous anger, and how hard human beings find it to handle their anger responsibly. So he [Satan] loves to lurk round angry people, hoping to be able to exploit the situation to his own advantage by provoking them into hatred or violence or a breach of fellowship.[134]

Is the danger that anger can lead to a loss of self-control, and is that when the devil can work? The issue of self-control is certainly on Paul's mind in 1 Corinthians 7:5. In discussing husband-and-wife sexual relations he writes (v. 5), "Do not deprive one another, except perhaps by agreement for a limited time, that you may devote yourselves to prayer; but then come together again, so that Satan may not tempt you because of your lack of self-control [*akrasia*]."

Seventh, affliction arising from persecution may provide an opportunity

---

[134] John R. W. Stott, *God's New Society: The Message of Ephesians* (Downers Grove, IL: InterVarsity Press, 1980), 187, emphasis original.

for the devil, as Paul makes clear to the Thessalonians in 1 Thessalonians 3:5: "For this reason [because of afflictions], when I could bear it no longer, I sent [Timothy] to learn about your faith, for fear that somehow the tempter [clearly Satan] had tempted you and our labor would be in vain." Leon Morris suggests, "It is likely that, while the Gentiles were persecuting them, the Jews were urging them to abandon the Christian way and accept Judaism, which would, of course, immediately free them from their plight."[135] Affliction is difficult to bear, and because of it, one is tempted to lose heart or to blame God. The devil knows our weaknesses and how to exploit them. Happily, Timothy brought back good news to Paul that the Thessalonians were faithful despite the suffering (1 Thess. 3:6).[136]

Eighth, another avenue for Satan's malevolence to express itself is when forgiveness is withheld. Such a withholding appears to provide a devilish opportunity to work harm. This seems to be Paul's concern in 2 Corinthians 2:5–11, where he encourages the Corinthians to be forgiving toward a repentant congregational member (vv. 10–11): "Anyone whom you forgive, I also forgive. Indeed, what I have forgiven, if I have forgiven anything, has been for your sake in the presence of Christ, so that we would not be outwitted by Satan; for we are not ignorant of his designs." Paul Barnett comments, "Satan, who is ever ready to destroy churches, will, in the absence of love and forgiveness, quickly bring bitterness and division. Now that the man has turned from his evil ways it is important that he, and the group who support him, be reconciled through forgiveness with the main body of the congregation."[137]

Avoiding the Fanciful

The key to avoiding the fanciful is positively to embrace the biblical; that is to say, to embrace what is in the text or consistent with it. In practical terms, have the expectations that the NT fosters. Methodologically speaking, it is useful to ask the question whether reading the NT, and especially letters addressed to churches and individuals, would lead me to expect X or Y or Z? For example, I remember being told of a practice of exorcism which involved having a bucket of water placed in the room so that the demons had somewhere to go, as per Mark 5:13.[138] A description of what happened on one recorded occasion became a contemporary practice for some; bad interpretative method leads to bad practical theology. What is so striking about the letters of the NT is the

---

[135] Leon Morris, *1 and 2 Thessalonians*, TNTC (Downers Grove, IL: InterVarsity Press, 1984), 70.

[136] Scripture is also positive in places about affliction. In the providence of God, affliction may lead to growth in Christian character and joy, as James 1:2–4 shows. The key is steadfastness under such pressure.

[137] Paul Barnett, *The Message of 2 Corinthians*, TBST (Leicester, UK, and Downers Grove, IL: InterVarsity Press, 1988), 46. Jonathan King, in private conversation, has suggested to me that the accent in the Lord's Prayer on forgiving others and deliverance from the evil one may be linked (e.g., cf. Matt. 6:12–13 and 14–15).

[138] Chapter 5 of the present work addresses the question of whether there are exorcisms today.

absence of any hint of what passes for spiritual warfare in some circles today.
Why doesn't Paul list exorcism as a gift of the Spirit in 1 Corinthians 12, or
exorcist as an "office" of the church in Ephesians 4 alongside apostle, prophet,
evangelist, and pastor-teacher? The 1 Corinthians passage is particularly intriguing because it does list distinguishing spirits as a gift (12:10).[139]

As a general rule it is sound to argue that the absence of evidence is not
evidence of absence, yet in some cases silence is pregnant with meaning, as in
the detective mystery short story "Silver Blaze," by Arthur Conan Doyle. The
story involves both theft and murder. Silver Blaze was a racehorse that had been
stolen from its stall. Sherlock Holmes notes that there was a curious absence of
barking by the dog on the night in question. Holmes concludes it was because
the dog knew the culprit and that it was none other than Silver Blaze's trainer,
John Straker. Holmes was right. The silence was meaningful.[140]

The claim that there are territorial spirits that need to be combated
provides a case in point. Nigel G. Wright relates how in 1977, at the annual
Dales Bible Week at the Harrogate Showground, the assembly was called
upon "to bind a powerful, national evil spirit which he [Ern Baxter, from
Fort Lauderdale, Florida] called the 'prince of Great Britain.'"[141] This putative evil prince was "that dark winged spirit that hovers over the Parliament
building."[142] The idea that Christians are to engage putative territorial spirits is described by Peter R. Schemm Jr. as "specious angelology."[143] He asks,
"Is there a biblical basis, either by instruction or by positive example, for
engaging territorial spirits in order to bind demons in preparation for the
proclamation of the gospel in a particular city?"[144] He thinks decidedly not.
He states, "In the New Testament no explicit teaching exhorts believers to
engage territorial spirits in spiritual warfare."[145] I take his point. Why, for

---

[139] Interestingly, the gift of discerning spirits precedes the gift of tongues in the list, and the gift of tongues is
followed by the gift of the interpretation of tongues (1 Cor. 12:10). I suggest that these three gifts form a cluster.
Distinguishing spirits enables a congregation to know the origin of the tongue—whether it is heavenly or devilish.
The interpretation of tongues adds a further check because the content of the tongue is thereby made known to all
present. These three gifts safeguard the congregation from devilish deception.

[140] Sharon Beekmann and Peter G. Bolt (*Silencing Satan: Handbook of Biblical Demonology* [Eugene, OR: Wipf &
Stock, 2012], xiv), suggest, "The challenge, then, is to say only what the Bible has to say and to honor the Bible's
silences." As general counsel this is most wise, but as argued, some silences may indeed be meaningful.

[141] Nigel Wright, "Charismatic Interpretations," in *The Unseen World: Christian Reflections on Angels, Demons,
and the Heavenly Realm*, ed. Anthony N. S. Lane (Grand Rapids, MI: Paternoster/Baker, 1996), 159.

[142] Wright, "Charismatic Interpretations," 159. Wright is highly critical of the entire charismatic approach to territorial spirits and argues that it "has no place in a healthy theology." This is one of his milder comments. His own
approach is too demythologizing in my view, too indebted to Walter Wink. However, a number of his criticisms have
purchase, especially the difficulty of distinguishing fantasy and reality. Even so, the charismatic movement—the
Pentecostal movement as well—laudably bears witness to the fact of cosmic conflict in ways that other churches
in the West muted or forgot.

[143] Schemm, "Agents of God: Angels," 275.

[144] Schemm, "Agents of God: Angels," 276.

[145] Schemm, "Agents of God: Angels," 276. I think that Schemm's use of "specious angelology" is a little too strong.
"Mistaken angelology" would be a less polemical phrase. Commendably, those Christians who seek to engage
putative territorial spirits do take seriously the machinations of the devil and his entourage, albeit in a mistaken
way in my view.

example, didn't Peter counsel his readers in his first letter who were experiencing hostility in Asia Minor to reclaim the cities of that region from territorial spirits? Positively, as Schemm rightly points out, the apostolic strategy on entering a city was to proclaim the gospel. He quotes Wayne Grudem to good effect: "Christians just preach the gospel, and it comes with power to change lives."[146]

CONCLUSION

There is a legend, dating from late in the sixteenth century, that Martin Luther (1483–1546), during his stay at Wartburg, threw an inkwell at the devil.[147] As a technique of spiritual warfare, of course, this is pious nonsense. However, spiritual warfare takes the dark kingdom and its machinations with utmost seriousness, just as Luther did.[148] The world, the flesh, and the devil work their mischief. However, there is the whole armor of God to wear, and there is much in the NT that counsels resistance informed by reliance upon God, and with humility as a virtue to embrace and cultivate. There is controversy at present in certain Christian circles surrounding the nature and the number of practices that make up spiritual warfare. The charismatic movement has largely been responsible for the rise of the awareness of the spirit world in the church.[149] Gratitude is rightly due for this. However, there is much criticism in the literature concerning some of the charismatic interpretations of the unseen world and its influence on this one. This criticism is well founded wherever there are no clear biblical warrants that justify a given practice. Nigel Wright offers wisdom here: "Binding the devil, rebuking the devil, engaging in spiritual warfare will not avail if the supply lines of sin which enable the power of darkness to replenish itself parasitically from the human race are not also dealt with."[150] The Christian engaged in spiritual warfare, whatever the form it takes, is a person who needs to be ever ready to practice 1 John 1:9: "If we confess our sins, he is faithful and just to forgive us our sins and to cleanse us from all unrighteousness." Above all, the Christian needs to embrace a biblically defensible model of spiritual warfare, and to avoid the fanciful.

---

[146] Schemm, "Agents of God: Angels," 277. He also offers a vigorous critique of prayer walking as a spiritual warfare strategy. C. Peter Wagner and Rebecca Greenwood define "prayer walking" as follows in "Strategic-Level Deliverance Model," 190: "Prayerwalking is just what it sounds like: walking while praying. . . . These prayers are filled with fervor and expectancy that God will release dramatic breakthroughs of love, that souls will find the truth of salvation, and that righteousness will penetrate a segment of society."

[147] Scott A. Hendrix rightly comments, "Although definitely a fabrication, this legend points to an important truth about Luther. He was a deeply devout man of his age who believed strongly in the existence of the Devil." See his "Legends about Luther," http://www.christianitytoday.com/history/issues/issue-34/legends-about-luther.html, accessed 3/24/2016.

[148] As Luther's *Catechism* shows, according to Hendrix (Hendrix, "Legends about Luther").

[149] As Nigel Wright rightly points out ("Charismatic Interpretations," 149).

[150] Nigel Wright, *The Satan Syndrome: Putting the Power of Darkness in Its Place* (Grand Rapids, MI: Zondervan, 1990), 48.

Excursus: How to Test the Spirits

I recall reading somewhere that when you listen to a sermon or read a book or an article, be prepared to have "YBH" ready. YBH stands for "Yes, but how?" It is one thing to be informed as to what needs to be done. It is quite another to be helped in knowing how to do it. If Satan and demons are at work, how is their activity to be discerned? Some examples are needed. Is there a difference between reading a horoscope in a magazine for fun or to pass the time on a long flight, and using a Ouija board for guidance? (More anon.) Are both harmless? Are both harmful? Is one harmless and one harmful? If so, which one? And above all, how do we tell?

The NT writers would not have us be ignorant. Gullibility is not next to godliness. Discernment is an important biblical practice. Two NT witnesses make that clear: Paul and John. Take Paul. He writes to the Thessalonians (1 Thess. 5:19–22), "Do not quench the Spirit. Do not despise prophecies, but test [*dokimazein*; "to put to the test," "to prove by testing"] everything; hold fast what is good. Abstain from every form of evil." The idea of testing here means exercising quality control on alleged prophecies, but not in such a way as to block the Spirit's ministry. Importantly, there is a clear moral dimension to the testing, as the contrast is drawn between good and evil.

Interestingly, the discernment challenge was soon in evidence in the sub-apostolic period. In the second century, there were so-called prophets who preyed on the faithful. The *Didache* or the *Teaching of the Twelve* addresses the issue in a very practical way. The visitors were to be welcomed but also observed. The tests were simple. First, "If any prophet, speaking in a trance, says, 'Give money (or anything else),' do not listen to him. On the other hand, if he bids you to give it to someone else who is in need, nobody should criticize him."[151] Another test seeks to determine whether the prophet's espoused theology and operational theology were in contradiction. That is to say, if he speaks one way and lives another, he is a fraud. One more, if the prophet stays more than two days, he is not genuine but is freeloading on other people's faith and goodwill.

However, it is one of the Johannine letters that is especially pertinent to our subject. John writes to his beloved children and calls upon them to test the spirits (1 John 4:1): "Beloved, do not believe every spirit, but test [*dokimazein*, same word that Paul uses in 1 Thess. 5:21] the spirits to see whether they are from God, for many false prophets [*pseudoprophētai*] have gone out into the world." The epistemological question is, how are such spirits operating through false prophets to be discerned? The answer is Christological (vv. 2–3): "*By this*

---

[151] Maxwell Staniforth, trans. and ed., *Early Christian Writings* (Harmondsworth, UK: Penguin, 1968), 233. Staniforth translated "prophet" as "charismatist." I have reverted to "prophet"; see his footnote 7 on page 236.

you know the Spirit of God: every spirit that confesses that Jesus Christ has come in the flesh is from God, and every spirit that does not confess Jesus is not from God." The false prophets deny the reality of the incarnation. In so doing they show that they are not of God but of the world (v. 5). The "world" [*cosmos*] is humanity in its opposition to God. Another epistemological test is offered (v. 6): "We are from God. Whoever knows God listens to us; whoever is not from God does not listen to us. *By this we know* the Spirit of truth and the spirit of error." The spirit of truth affirms the incarnation. The spirit of error denies it. Moreover, to whom John's readers listen reveals whether they are of God or not. We could call this second test the apostolic one. In this test, the teachings of the apostles are applied to the claim on view.

John's first letter offers another epistemological test alongside the Christological one and the listening-to-the-apostle one. One's morality is revelatory of one's relation to the light (1 John 3:7–8): "Little children, let no one deceive you. Whoever practices righteousness is righteous, as he is righteous. Whoever makes a practice of sinning [*ho poiōn*, "the one continually doing the sin"] is of the devil, for the devil has been sinning from the beginning." But how can one tell the devil's progeny from those who belong to God? First John 3:10 offers this consideration: "By this it is evident [*phaneros*; "visible," "plain"] who are the children of God, and who are the children of the devil: whoever does not practice righteousness is not of God, nor is the one who does not love his brother." The idea of those who do not love their Christian brothers occurs a number of times in the epistle (e.g., 3:14, implied; 4:20, explicit). It seems that a feature of the schismatic community was its detestation [*misein*, "to hate"] of the faithful ones—namely, John's readers (e.g., 2:9, 11; 3:13, 15; 4:20). John points out the great disconnect between affirming love for God and hatred of his children (4:20).

The Christological and the apostolic tests can be done quickly with some well chosen questions. What view of Christ is being commended or assumed? Does what is being affirmed undermine the apostolic witness? The moral test helps discern good from evil over time. The person's lifestyle and practices need to be observed.

Paul's letters also are of relevance to our question. In 1 Corinthians 12, Paul lists gifts of the Holy Spirit given for the common good of the congregation (v. 7): "To each is given the manifestation of the Spirit for the common good." Their use in this context presupposes a Christian gathering. The practice of tongues seems to be safeguarded by listing discernment of spirits before it and the interpretation of tongues after it (v. 10): ". . . to another the ability to distinguish between spirits [*diakriseis pneumatōn*, "discernings of spirits"], to another various kinds of tongues, to another the interpretation of tongues." The former gift discerns the origins of the tongue, while the latter one expounds its content. If both of these gifts are operating, then a "pseudo-tongue" would be exposed as such and rejected. Is this the discernment on view in the book of Acts? Nigel Wright sums up the evidence well with reference to Arnold Bittlinger's work:

> Arnold Bittlinger understands this as the "ability to distinguish between divine, human and demonic powers" and sees this gift manifested in the encounter of Peter with Simon Magus (Acts 8:20–24) and his exposure of Ananias and Sapphira (Acts 5:3). Paul exhibits the gift in his recognition that Bar-Jesus is a son of the devil (Acts 13:10) and in perceiving that the slave girl in Philippi was controlled by a spirit of divination (Acts 17f).[152]

Unfortunately, the NT text leaves so much unexplained. Did discernment in these instances involve discursive thought, or was it an intuition, or a mixture of both? This question for me remains an open one.

According to P. T. Forsyth, writing in the early decades of the twentieth century (1848–1921), "Logic is rooted in ethics, the truth we see depends upon the men [generic] we are."[153] Importantly, the truth does not depend on character or the lack of it. For Forsyth, truth is objective. The observation he makes is epistemological. He links the *discernment* of truth to character. In arguing this, Forsyth is on solid NT ground. We read in Hebrews 5:14,

> But solid food is for the mature, for those who have their powers [*aisthētēria*; "senses," "faculties"] of discernment trained by constant practice [*gegymnasmena*, prefect passive participle] to distinguish [*pros diakrisis*; "with a view to judgment," "with a view to discernment"] good from evil.

Once more the distinguishing of good from evil is on view. Significantly, the mature believer is trained by experience to do so. The formation of godly character or virtues over time develops a disposition to discern good from evil. What would that look like *in situ*? It would mean recognizing very quickly that some claim does not seem to comport with what else is known or valued, even though it may be hard to put into words then and there just what the problem is.

A case in point is the use of a Ouija board to find direction for life. The mature Christian, whose maturity lies in a developed godly character made up of Christian virtues, would recoil at such an attempt to seek guidance on such a matter from something other than God. Scripture has much to say on where true guidance is to be found. Here there may be a mature Christian's

---

[152] Nigel Wright, *Satan Syndrome*, 100.
[153] P. T. Forsyth, *The Principle of Authority in Relation to Certainty, Sanctity, and Society* (Eugene, OR: Wipf & Stock, 1996), 10.

equivalent to the "Yuk!" factor in moral philosophy. In moral philosophy, the "Yuk!" response betrays a deep moral intuition (e.g., repugnance at hearing a story of pedophilia). Philosopher Julian Savulescu describes the "Yuk!" response as "intuitive feelings of revulsion or disgust."[154] Such a Christian would know Scripture well enough to have immediate questions about such a practice, I would hope. The relevant term may not be "Yuk!" but "Really!" The "Really!" response should lead us to search the Scriptures, where it would be found that such a practice has no precedent and prima facie is inconsistent with the overall biblical testimony. Here we can learn from the Berean Jews, who upon hearing Paul's message about Jesus searched [*anakrinō*; "examined," questioned"] the Scriptures to see if they backed Paul up. The narrative makes plain that the Bereans were to be admired for this practice as they are described as "more noble" [*eugenēs*, "noble minded"] than the Thessalonians (Acts 17:11).

For some this will be an unsatisfactory conclusion, as it would be so much more convenient if there were, say, six steps to provide an algorithmic way of discerning the demonic evil from the good.[155] The issue of discernment is not new. John Wesley in the eighteenth century wrestled with the discernment question, of how one recognizes the genuine witness of the spirit as opposed to a manifestation of human nature or devilish deception.[156] He candidly confessed,

> To require a more minute and philosophical account of the manner whereby we distinguish these, and of the *criteria*, or intrinsic marks, whereby we know the voice of God, is to make a demand which can never be answered; no, not by one who has the deepest knowledge of God. Suppose when Paul answered before Agrippa, the wise Roman [*sic*] had said, "Thou talkest of hearing the voice of the Son of God. How dost thou know it was his voice? By what *criteria*, what intrinsic marks, dost thou know the voice of God. Explain to me the *manner* of distinguishing this from a human or angelic voice." Can you believe, the apostle himself would have once attempted to answer so idle a demand? And yet, doubtless, the moment he heard that voice, he knew it was the voice of God. But *how* he knew this, who is able to explain? Perhaps neither man nor angel.[157]

---

[154] Julian Savulescu, "Julian Savulescu on 'Yuk!'," in *Philosophy Bites*, ed. David Edmonds and Nigel Warburton (Oxford: Oxford University Press, 2010), 2. As a secular thinker, Savulescu is doubtful of the value of the response as changing times lead to changes in what is considered "Yuk!" He sees homosexual practice as an example of such a change from general disapproval to more general acceptance. He argues that the response needs sound ethical principles to inform it; it cannot stand alone, seems to be his gist. Even so, he acknowledges that he experiences the "Yuk!" factor when he reflects on sex with animals, or on cannibalism (4–5, 8–9). A virtue ethicist might say that contemporary changes in the "Yuk!" response may be a matter of character and its loss.

[155] An "algorithmic" method would provide the right answer every time, as in mathematics.

[156] For a famous treatment of discernment and the criteria it requires, see Jonathan Edwards, *Jonathan Edwards: On Revival*, new ed. (Edinburgh: Banner of Truth, 1984).

[157] John Wesley, "The Sermons of John Wesley—Sermon 10," http://wesley.nnu.edu/john-wesley/the-sermons-of-john-wesley-1872-edition/sermon-10-the-witness-of-the-spirit-discourse-one/, accessed 4/9/2015. Although I myself am more in line with George Whitefield theologically, there is much to learn from this other great eighteenth-century evangelist. The lack of punctuation in places is in the original.

The way of wisdom is to pay attention to the voices of the Christian past such as Wesley's. Such intuitions, deeply rooted in Christian character, formed over years of Christian service and the practice of a Christian piety, are to be taken with utmost seriousness.[158] There are places in the world where the need for godly discernment is pressing.[159]

---

[158] There are voices in the present that also need to be heeded. Beekmann and Bolt, *Silencing Satan*, 198, offer five wise tests to apply to assess whether angelic visitations and "divine" dreams are counterfeit: (1) assume that you can be fooled; (2) use Scripture to evaluate experience; (3) speak directly to Jesus as mediator about the experience; (4) trust God to guide; and (5) step out in faith. I have truncated these steps.

[159] James Nkansah-Obrempong ("Angels, Demons and Powers," *ABC*, 2nd ed., ed. Tokunboh Adeyemo [Grand Rapids, MI: Zondervan, 2006], 1480) offers an interesting African perspective on demonic deception: "[I]t would be more accurate to say that demons can impersonate deceased people by appearing in a form that resembles them. Many people in Africa claim to have received messages from deceased family members, delivered either physically or in a dream. Many such incidents actually involve impersonation by demons." Addressing such claims with pastoral sensitivity requires a high order of theological and practical wisdom. Such wisdom is to be found in Yusufu Turaki, "The Role of Ancestors," *ABC*, 480, and also in Matthew Michael, *Christian Theology and African Traditions* (Eugene, OR: Wipf & Stock, 2013), 98–99.

CHAPTER

EIGHT

THE DESTINY OF THE DARKNESS
AND THE VICTORY OF THE LIGHT

INTRODUCTION

In broad strokes, we have been following the biblical plotline in this study. The biblical plotline, as we have previously argued, following Leland Ryken, takes the U-shape of comedy. That is to say, harmony gives way to disharmony before harmony is finally regained. A more common way that the biblical plotline has been characterized is as a movement from creation through fall and redemption to consummation.[1] We have now reached that part of the plotline which speaks of the consummation of all things. As we shall see, the angels are integrally involved in the eschatological resolution of the history of salvation. Jean Danielou is correct to claim, "The angels . . . appear associated with various moments of the eschatological drama; they are the ministers of the resurrection of the dead, the gathering together of the elect, and the separation of the just from the wicked."[2] The disharmonies of the groaning creation of Romans 8:18–22 will give way to the conflict resolution of the world to come. The disunities of the present evil age will give way to the unity of a restored creation. Paul Copan rightly argues that "the ultimate resolution to evil is (a) rooted in the *past*—in the cross-work of Christ, who stripped 'rulers and authorities' of their power, triumphing over them (Col. 2:15); but (b) its hope will be fully manifested in the *future* in the new heavens and the new earth (Rev. 21–22)."[3] In that light we turn our attention to the coming judgment, the witness of the book of Revelation, the ultimate winning ways of God, and the promise that evil will be finally defeated. As for

---

[1] For example, John Stott, *Issues Facing Christians Today*, 4th ed. (Grand Rapids, MI: Zondervan, 2006), 62–64. Stott describes these four motifs as "The Fourfold Framework" (62). This fourfold framework, like the comedy idea, is to be viewed in heuristic terms. As a heuristic device, it is most useful as a Bible reading strategy.
[2] Jean Danielou, *The Angels and Their Mission according to the Church Fathers*, trans. David Heimann (Notre Dame, IN: Ave Maria, 1957), 107.
[3] Paul Copan, *Loving Wisdom: Christian Philosophy of Religion* (St. Louis: Chalice, 2007), 133.

the demonic, with its leader, Satan, we will ask if there is hope for them in general, and hope for him, in particular.

The King Is Coming Again

The firm expectation of the NT and the early church is that the Jesus who walked the streets and dusty roads of Palestine, who in his resurrection and ascension was declared to be Lord and Christ by Peter on the Day of Pentecost in Acts 2, shall return in glory (1 Pet. 4:13).[4] NT writers use a variety of terms to describe the event.[5] The King's coming is his *parousia*, a royal visit (1 Thess. 4:15). It was a term used in the first century of a dignitary's visit to a city or town. The King's coming is his *epiphaneia* ("appearance"). The return will be visible (1 Tim. 6:14). It will also be an *apocalypsis* ("unveiling"). In a very real sense, revelation has not quite finished (again, 1 Pet. 4:13). There is a great revelatory disclosure to come. The return of the King will prove to be nothing less than the day of the Lord (*hē hēmera tou kuriou*), as 1 Corinthians 1:8 shows. For some he will come as Savior, for others as Judge, and it is to the matter of judgment we now turn.

The Coming Judgment

We live in a morally serious universe. There is an accounting. The God of biblical revelation is not only love but also light. God is holy, righteous love. His love is seen in salvation history. Jesus "will save his people from their sins" (Matt. 1:21). The light is seen in the judgments of God, stretching from the expulsion of the primal pair from the garden (Genesis 3) to the great white throne judgment at the end of the story (Revelation 20).

The need for an accounting is graphically captured in these words from Miroslav Volf. He has in mind those in the comfortable West, especially theologians, who find the idea of God's judgment too violent to entertain:

> To the person inclined to dismiss it [divine judgment], I suggest imagining that you are delivering a lecture in a war zone (which is where a paper that underlies this chapter was originally delivered). Among your listeners are people whose cities and villages have been first plundered, then burned and leveled to the ground, whose daughters and sisters have been raped, whose fathers and brothers have had their throats slit. The topic of the lecture:

---

[4] Second-century writer Justin Martyr, in his dialogue with the Jew Trypho, sums it up well: "Of these and such like words written by the prophets [he has a passage from Isaiah specifically in mind], O Trypho, . . . some have reference to the first advent of Christ, in which He is preached as inglorious, obscure, and of mortal appearance: but others had reference to His second advent, when He shall appear in glory and above the clouds; and your nation shall see and know Him whom they have pierced, as Hosea, one of the twelve prophets, and Daniel, foretold" (*Dialogue with Trypho*, chapter 14). Justin's reference to Hosea is mistaken. Zechariah 12:10 is the relevant text. I am grateful to John Feinberg for pointing out Justin's mistake.
[5] For this paragraph I am particularly indebted to Michael F. Bird's stimulating discussion in *Evangelical Theology: A Biblical and Systematic Introduction* (Grand Rapids, MI: Zondervan, 2013), 259–260.

a Christian attitude toward violence. The thesis: we should not retaliate since God is perfect noncoercive love. Soon you would discover that it takes the quiet of a suburban home for the birth of the thesis that human non-violence corresponds to God's refusal to judge. In a scorched land, soaked in the blood of the innocent, it will invariably die. And as one watches it die, one will do well to reflect about many other pleasant captivities of the liberal mind.[6]

Volf's words remind us that all theology is contextual, located in a particular time and a particular space.[7] Volf, a Croat, wrote these words out of his own experience of war in the former Yugoslavia. His is no armchair comment.

The Old Testament and Judgment Day

The God of OT revelation knows both how to save, as he did with Israel, and how to judge, as he did with Pharaoh. The song of Moses thematizes both (Ex. 15:1–2):

> I will sing to the LORD, for he has triumphed gloriously;
>> the horse and his rider he has thrown into the sea.
> The LORD is my strength and my song,
>> and he has become my salvation;
> this is my God, and I will praise him,
>> my father's God, and I will exalt him.

The judgment motif is found not only in the Torah. The OT prophets knew of a day in which God would hold the world accountable. The key phrase is "the day of the Lord." Isaiah's words have lost none of their rhetorical power (Isa. 2:6–22). He prophesied in the context of the southern kingdom, caught up in occult practices, the accumulation of treasure, and idol worship. This people needed humbling. Pride has no future in God's creation. Humbled they will be (v. 11): "The haughty looks of man [adam, "humankind"] shall be brought low, and the lofty pride of men shall be humbled, and the LORD alone will be exalted in that day." And what is that day? Isaiah describes it in these terms (vv. 12–16):

> For the LORD of hosts has a day
>> against all that is proud and lofty,
>> against all that is lifted up—and it shall be brought low;
> against all the cedars of Lebanon,

---

[6] Miroslav Volf, *Exclusion and Embrace: A Theological Exploration of Identity, Otherness, and Reconciliation* (Nashville: Abingdon, 1996), 304.

[7] As I have written elsewhere, "Recognizing that theology is situated does not lead necessarily to postmodern conclusions. Quite the reverse! The fact that we recognize our situatedness (the insight of postmodernity) shows that there is something in our anthropology that transcends situatedness. Whether it is an aspect of reason or imagination (my guess), human beings have the ability to establish a critical distance between themselves and their own beliefs and values that on occasion enables their reform." See my *God the Peacemaker: How Atonement Brings Shalom* (Downers Grove, IL: InterVarsity Press, 2009), 76n36.

> lofty and lifted up;
> > and against all the oaks of Bashan;
> against all the lofty mountains,
> > and against all the uplifted hills;
> against every high tower,
> > and against every fortified wall;
> against all the ships of Tarshish,
> > and against all the beautiful craft.

Judgment is coming, and with it (v. 17), "the haughtiness of man shall be humbled, and the lofty pride of men shall be brought low, and the LORD alone will be exalted in that day." That day will bring an end to not only Judah's idolatry but that of all humankind (vv. 20–21):

> In that day mankind [adam, "humankind"] will cast away
> > their idols of silver and their idols of gold,
> which they made for themselves to worship,
> > to the moles and to the bats,
> to enter the caverns of the rocks
> > and the clefts of the cliffs,
> from before the terror of the LORD,
> > and from the splendor of his majesty,
> > when he rises to terrify the earth.

The living God is not to be trifled with. He has a day in store. Those who desire that day may be in for a surprise (Amos 5:18–19): "Woe to you who desire the day of the LORD! Why would you have the day of the LORD? It is darkness, and not light, as if a man fled from a lion, and a bear met him, or went into the house and leaned his hand against the wall, and a serpent bit him."

NT writers know of the day too. In this they stand in continuity with the OT prophets. Paul wrote to the Romans in these terms (Rom. 2:1–3). The language is generic, as "O man" of verse 1 makes clear:

> Therefore you have no excuse, O man [anthrōpos, "human"], every one of you who judges. For in passing judgment on another you condemn yourself, because you, the judge, practice the very same things. We know that the judgment of God rightly falls on those who practice such things. Do you suppose, O man—you who judge those who practice such things and yet do them yourself—that you will escape the judgment of God?

Whether the Jew or the pagan moralist is on view in this text, judgment is coming. Wrath is coming. And divine wrath is not to be made banal and dismissed as the depiction of a celestial temper tantrum unworthy of a modern person's belief. Rather it is the holy opposition of a good God to that which spoils creation.

Jesus and Judgment Day

It would surprise many a modern person to find that the Jesus of the Gospels spoke so often of judgment. Rather than being a first-century version of to-day's humanitarian, Jesus stood in line with the prophets of Israel as far as the coming day of the Lord was concerned. John's witness provides a case in point. For example, in John 5, Jesus presents a dichotomy to his hearers. He speaks of himself as having authority from the Father to judge humankind (v. 27). He will be the Judge in terms of the Son of Man role depicted in Daniel 7. For some this will mean life at the resurrection of the dead, and for others judgment. The determinant of destiny will be whether one has done good or has done evil (John 5:29). This is not a statement to be trifled with, because in the Johannine idiom it is prefaced by "Truly, truly, I say to you" (v. 25). The statement is a sober warning to the Jews about judgment. These Jews were criticizing Jesus for healing on the Sabbath (v. 16).[8] In contrast, for those who embraced Jesus there is no condemnation, but they have "passed from death to life" (v. 24).

The Synoptic Gospels also make the connection between the Son of Man of Daniel, Jesus, and the Day of Judgment. Maxwell J. Davidson sums it up well:

> Jesus taught that he would come to earth again as the Son of man "in clouds with great power and glory" (Mk 13:26; cf. 14:62) and accompanied by angels, to execute judgment (Mt 16:27; Mk 8:38; cf. Lk 9:26). Such allusions derive from Daniel 7, with its figure "like a son of man" who is presented before God and given an everlasting kingdom (Dan 7:13–14). God is depicted as sitting in judgment, attended by innumerable angels (Dan 7:9–10).[9]

Jesus's worldview was apocalyptic, with himself as the central player in carry-ing out the Father's will (John 6:38).

Paul and Judgment Day

Like Jesus, Paul stood in line with the OT prophets concerning the day of the Lord. This comes out clearly in his famed address to the Athenian intelligentsia gathered on Mars Hill in Acts 17. The apostle to the Gentiles gives his hearers a lesson in "OT 101." There is only one Creator God. Idolatry is foolish. With great rhetorical power he declares (vv. 29–31),

> Being then God's offspring, we ought not to think that the divine being is like gold or silver or stone, an image formed by the art and imagination of man.

---

[8] "Jews" in John's Gospel has a variety of meanings. Some are positive, as in John 4:22, "salvation is from the Jews." Others are negative, especially when the Jewish authorities are in view, as in John 5:15–16.
[9] Maxwell J. Davidson, "Angels," in *DJG*, ed. Joel B. Green, Jeannine K. Brown, and Nicholas Perrin, 2nd ed. (Downers Grove, IL: InterVarsity Press, 2013), 8.

> The times of ignorance God overlooked, but now he commands all people everywhere to repent, because he has fixed a day on which he will judge the world in righteousness by a man whom he has appointed; and of this he has given assurance to all by raising him from the dead.

The man Paul referred to is obviously Jesus, and the "day" is the day of the Lord. The only appropriate response to what is coming is repentance, which for the Athenians would show itself in the abandonment of their idolatry. And on that occasion some of Paul's Athenian listeners did indeed repent (Acts 17:34).

Second Peter and Judgment Day

Skepticism about the return of Christ is no new phenomenon. It was in evidence long before the Enlightenment of the eighteenth century. In fact, it began very early. Peter's second letter, in chapter 3, speaks of those who scoff and who say (v. 4), "Where is the promise of his coming? For ever since the fathers fell asleep, all things are continuing as they were from the beginning of creation." In reply, Peter draws attention to the divine patience (vv. 8–9):

> But do not overlook this one fact, beloved, that with the Lord one day is as a thousand years, and a thousand years as one day. The Lord is not slow to fulfill his promise as some count slowness, but is patient toward you, not wishing that any should perish, but that all should reach repentance.

Similar ideas are found in Paul's letter to the Romans (Rom. 2:4–5):

> Or do you presume on the riches of his kindness and forbearance and patience, not knowing that God's kindness is meant to lead you to repentance? But because of your hard and impenitent heart you are storing up wrath for yourself on the day of wrath when God's righteous judgment will be revealed.

Christ will return, and the Day of Judgment is coming. But before those events occur, our present time frame provides the opportunity to repent, and it is the divine kindness, forbearance, and patience that make this possible.

The Role of Angels and Judgment Day

During the period between the Old and New Testaments, angels played a significant role in the coming judgment in Jewish apocalyptic thought. Davidson sums it up well: "They function as a kind of heavenly police force, arresting offenders, presenting evidence and executing punishment." Similar ideas are found in the teaching of Jesus too. As Davidson goes on to argue,

> Angels will be dispatched to gather God's people from all over the earth (Mt 24:31; Mk 13:27; cf. 1 Enoch 100:4), and they will be with the Son of man

when he sits in judgment (Mt 25:31). They will also assist in inflicting punishment on evildoers (Mt 13:41–42, 49–50; cf. *1 Enoch* 90:20–26; CD 2:5–7). When Jesus taught that those who acknowledged him and his teaching would ultimately be acknowledged before God's angels at his coming, the angels were being cast in the role of hearing evidence in the heavenly courtroom (cf. *1 Enoch* 99:3). Those ashamed of him will be denied before the heavenly court (Mk 8:38; Lk 9:26; 12:8–9).[10]

In Paul there is an intriguing reference where there appears to be a role reversal. The saints judge angels. The context is his criticism of Corinthian Christians taking a brother or sister to court. Surely such disputes should be handled within the body of Christ. Why? Paul provides an answer in 1 Corinthians 6:3: "Do you not know that we are to judge angels? How much more, then, matters pertaining to this life!" The a fortiori argument is typically rabbinic in style, as in the scheme of things the relatively light matters of judgment in this world are compared to the heavy matter of judgment in the next. Who are the angels on view? Are they fallen or unfallen, or both? W. Harold Mare comments,

> To make his argument even stronger for the validity and competence of Christians to settle cases at Corinth, Paul teaches that Christians will even judge angels, but he does not specify any details (v. 3). By using *angelous* without the article, Paul is not necessarily including all the angels. He must mean that Christians, when ruling in the future with Christ, will have a part in judging the devil and the fallen angels at the Second Coming (cf. Rev 19:19; 20:10).[11]

Not all agree. Charles Hodge took a more expansive view. He maintained that the Christian judges angels fallen and unfallen.[12] This seems a stretch.

Judgment Day and Works

If there is a judgment day coming, on what relevant principle will it be based? The testimony of both Old and New Testaments is consistent. Judgment is according to works. Proverbs 24:12 is representative of the older covenant: "If you say, 'Behold, we did not know this,' does not he who weighs the heart perceive it? Does not he who keeps watch over your soul know it, and will he not repay man according to his work?" In the new covenant era, Paul writes similarly (Rom. 2:6–8): "He [God] will render to each one according to his works: to those who by patience in well-doing seek for glory and honor and immortality, he will give eternal life; but for those who are self-seeking and do not obey the

---

[10] Davidson, "Angels," 8.

[11] W. Harold Mare, "1 Corinthians," in *EBC*, comment on 1 Corinthians 6:3.

[12] Mare, "1 Corinthians." Mare explains Hodge's view as follows: "Or, the statement could mean, as Hodge suggests, that Christians will judge angels, even the good ones, in the sense of presiding with Christ over the angelic host (in loc.). Compare the statement of Matthew 19:28 about sitting 'on twelve thrones, judging the twelve tribes,' i.e., presiding over them."

truth, but obey unrighteousness, there will be wrath and fury." Paul goes on to argue, however, that the class of those who are awarded eternal life because of their works is a null set (Rom. 3:23): "for all [whether Jew or Greek] have sinned and fall short of the glory of God."

The book of Revelation shows the same understanding of the last judgment. I quote *in extenso* (Rev. 20:11–15):

> Then I saw a great white throne and him who was seated on it. From his presence earth and sky fled away, and no place was found for them. And I saw the dead, great and small, standing before the throne, and books were opened. Then another book was opened, which is the book of life. And the dead were judged by what was written in the books, according to what they had done. And the sea gave up the dead who were in it, Death and Hades gave up the dead who were in them, and they were judged, each one of them, according to what they had done. Then Death and Hades were thrown into the lake of fire. This is the second death, the lake of fire. And if anyone's name was not found written in the book of life, he was thrown into the lake of fire.

The scene is graphic. Twice the accent falls on retributive justice: "And the dead were judged by what was written in the books, according to what they had done" (v. 12), and, "they were judged, each one of them, according to what they had done" (v. 13).

The Christian is saved by works. God is just. However, the good news is that the works of Christ, in both his active and passive obedience, are the Christian's. How can this be? The Christian is in union with Christ, a member of his body, animated by the same Holy Spirit who animates the humanity of Christ.[13] This is beautifully captured by Calvin in his *Institutes*:

> We must examine this question. How do we receive these benefits which the Father bestowed on his only-begotten Son—not for Christ's own private use but that he might enrich poor and needy men? First, we must understand that as long as Christ remains outside of us, and we are separated from him, all that he has suffered and done for the salvation of the human race remains useless and of no value for us. . . . all that he possesses is nothing to us until we grow into one body with him. . . . To sum up, the Holy Spirit is the bond by which Christ effectually unites us to himself.[14]

The Christian is in Christ (*en tō christō*, to use the ubiquitous Pauline phrase), and that will make all the difference when the "books" of Revelation 20 are opened.

---

[13] I argue this in *God the Peacemaker*, 158–160.

[14] John Calvin, *Institutes of the Christian Religion*, 3.1.1 (*CJCC*). Calvin's heading for chapter 1 is, "The Things Spoken concerning Christ Profit Us by the Secret Working of the Spirit," and that of the first section is, "The Holy Spirit as the Bond That Unites Us to Christ."

So much for the believer, but what of Satan's future? What does the divine future have in store for the devil? To answer that question, we turn to the controversial matter of the millennium.[15] To anticipate a later section, the devil too will receive retributive justice.

The Binding of Satan and the Millennium

In relation to the millennium, Grant R. Osborne correctly states, "few issues have divided the church for as long a time as this."[16] The idea of the millennium (a thousand years) is found explicitly only in Revelation 20.[17] For John it is a visionary experience involving an angel, the dragon, and a pit. The language is symbol-laden. What else could binding a spirit with a chain be! We read in Revelation 20:1–3,

> Then I saw an angel coming down from heaven, holding in his hand the key to the bottomless pit and a great chain. And he seized the dragon, that ancient serpent, who is the devil and Satan, and bound him for a thousand years, and threw him into the pit [abbyson; "pit," "abyss"], and shut it and sealed it over him, so that he might not deceive the nations any longer, until the thousand years were ended. After that he must be released for a little while.[18]

We must ask what will happen in the millennial period while Satan is so bound.[19] John's visionary experience continues (vv. 4–6):

> Then I saw thrones, and seated on them were those to whom the authority to judge was committed. Also I saw the souls of those who had been beheaded for the testimony of Jesus and for the word of God, and those who had not worshiped the beast or its image and had not received its mark on their foreheads or their hands. They came to life and reigned with Christ for a thousand years. The rest of the dead did not come to life until the thousand years were ended. This is the first resurrection. Blessed and holy is the one who shares in the first resurrection! Over such the second death has no power, but they will

---

[15] In this work, various eschatological positions will be treated only briefly. This series, when complete, will include a work on eschatology, to which the reader may turn.

[16] Quoted with approval by Eckhard Schnabel, *Forty Questions about the End Times* (Grand Rapids, MI: Kregel, 2011), 267.

[17] That the millennium appears only in Revelation 20 in an explicit way should not suggest that it is doctrinally unimportant. Some significant events and passages in the biblical witness appear only once in any explicit way and their importance is not to be denied (e.g., Babel in Genesis 11 and Pentecost in Acts 2). Hans Schwarz, *Eschatology* (Grand Rapids, MI, and Cambridge: Eerdmans, 2000), 336, seems somewhat dismissive of the significance of Revelation 20:1–6 when he describes it as being in a book which "does not occupy the center stage of the New Testament message but is on the periphery." How one determines the center of the stage he leaves unexplained.

[18] This pit is also mentioned in Revelation 9:2. Walter C. Kaiser Jr., *Hard Sayings of the Bible* (Downers Grove, IL: InterVarsity Press, 1997), 763, comments, "The Abyss is apparently the prison of demons and fallen angelic beings (some Jews believed demons were fallen angels, while others distinguished them as being their offspring). This explains the fear of the demons in Luke 8:31. They wanted to remain free, not be placed in prison. Jesus apparently allows them freedom because the time of judgment has not yet arrived. Likewise it explains why Satan is imprisoned in the Abyss, for it is the standard place to imprison such beings."

[19] Schnabel, *Forty Questions*, 268–269, points out there are some who take the millennium to be a literal 1,000-year period, while others see it as symbolic of a long epoch, which is Schnabel's own view. Schnabel also points out that in Jewish expectations the period ranges from 40 to 365,000 years (267).

be priests of God and of Christ, and they will reign with him for a thousand years.

There are four major lines of interpretation of the millennium, which we shall examine in turn. I will follow the history of the discussion and when a particular eschatological scenario first became prominent. Each of these scenarios represents a synthesis of a number of biblical texts. Our focus, however, will be mainly on Revelation 20.[20]

The Historic Premillennialist Reading

Historic premillennialism affirms that, at a future time in human history, Christ shall return and set up his kingdom on earth and will reign there for a thousand years. We call it "historic" because it was held by a number of early church fathers. Justin Martyr (c. 100–c. 165 AD) is but one example. Irenaeus (c. 130–c. 200) is another. (Interestingly, even as early as the second century there was a diversity of opinion on the millennium.[21]) According to historic premillennialism, Christ's return will be visible and public. There will be no secret rapture. Judgment day will follow the millennium. Before the dawn of the millennium, Christians will experience a time of increasing tribulation because of persecution. Michael F. Bird describes this period as "the rage of Satan against the church."[22] It is in a sense a pessimistic view: The millennium begins with the binding of Satan (Rev. 20:2). Then ensues a period of enormous blessings. Satan is removed from the scene until the end of the period. This is the period in which the faithful departed and/or the martyrs find their vindication and reward. They reign with Christ (v. 4). In this scenario, the binding of Satan is a future event.

The Amillennialist Reading

Amillennialism is something of a misnomer. Amillennialists believe in a millennium but interpret it in spiritual terms as the period of time in which Christ reigns from heaven as King before his public return and the ushering in of the last judgment. (There is no secret rapture of the church.) Perhaps

---

[20] Exploring the eschatology and angelology of Revelation is a fascinating task, but beyond this work. Regarding angelology, Herbert Lockyer, *All the Angels in the Bible: A Complete Exploration of the Nature and Ministry of Angels* (Peabody, MA: Hendriksen, 2012), 117, rightly describes the book of Revelation as "the angel book" of the NT, with seventy-seven references to them, which far exceeds any other book in the canon. Stephen F. Noll offers an excellent brief treatment of the angels in the book of Revelation in *Angels of Light, Powers of Darkness: Thinking Biblically about Angels, Satan, and Principalities* (Eugene, OR: Wipf & Stock, 1998), 190–197. However, his claim that there are well over a hundred references to angels in the book (191) seems incorrect.

[21] Justin Martyr, in his *Dialogue with Trypho*, said, "I and many others share this opinion, and I believe that such will take place . . . but, on the other hand, many who belong to the pure and pious faith, and are true Christians, think otherwise." Quoted in Dana Netherton, "Historic Premillennialism: Taking the Long View," *Christian History* 18/1 (Issue 61, 1999): 11.

[22] Bird, *Evangelical Theology*, 291. Bird prefers the phrase "messianic interregnum" to the term "millennium" (282).

"symbolic millennialism" would be a better name for this view, or as Michael Horton suggests, "*semi*realized millennialism." For Horton the latter phrase captures the idea that "Not until Christ returns in glory at the end of the age will the kingdoms of this age become the kingdom of Christ."[23] This view arose early in church history. It was, for example, Augustine's eschatological position.

On the amillennial view, we are in the millennium now. Horton sums up this view well: "According to an amillennial interpretation, then, we are presently living in the 'thousand years' of Revelation 20, longing not for a literal millennium with yet another fall into sin but for the everlasting kingdom of righteousness and peace that will dawn with Christ's return in judgment and restoration."[24] Christ rules from heaven now.[25] This is a matter of faith, not sight, especially since the argument runs that before Christ's second coming life will get increasingly worse for believers because of persecution. Like historic premillennialism, it is a pessimistic view. As for the binding of Satan that took place on the cross (see Matt. 12:26–29, esp. v. 29), this is how Augustine understood its applicability to Revelation 20:2: "The devil is bound throughout the whole period, from the first coming of Christ to the end of the world, which will be Christ's second coming."[26] As for those who come to life to reign with Christ (Rev. 20:6), they are those who are born again. This is the first resurrection, and it is a spiritual one—so Augustine argued.[27] One may ask, since there is so much evil in the world, in what sense is Satan bound? He is bound in such a way that he cannot deceive nations. But he is not so bound that he cannot deceive individuals.[28] On this amillennial scenario, Satan's binding is a past event.

---

[23] Michael Horton, *The Christian Faith: A Systematic Theology for Pilgrims On the Way* (Grand Rapids, MI: Zondervan, 2011), 935.

[24] Horton, *Christian Faith*, 945.

[25] Horton, *Christian Faith*, 935, finds fault with dispensationalism for not doing justice to the "already" and "not yet now" dialectic he sees in the NT witness. This criticism may apply to classic dispensationalism but not so obviously to progressive dispensationalism.

[26] Augustine, *The City of God*, quoted in David Wright, "Amillennialism: Millennium Today," *Christian History* 18/1 (Issue 61, 1999), 14.

[27] Wright, "Amillennialism: Millennium Today," 15.

[28] In one class I taught on eschatology, students asked how individuals could be deceived but not nations. Wasn't the German nation deceived during the Nazi years? An amillennial answer might be that the leadership of the nation (e.g., Hitler) was indeed deceived by Satan but not the nation per se in any direct satanic way. I find the idea of satanic inability to deceive nations during the present era exegetically and existentially unconvincing, as does Bird, *Evangelical Theology*, 280–281. On this question Craig Blaising, "The Kingdom that Comes with Jesus: Premillennialism and the Harmony of Scripture," *SBJT* 14/1 (2010): 12n11, writes, convincingly I would say,

> Considering the whole of the New Testament's teaching on the activity of the devil, one needs to note that the deception prior to the second advent is presented as an increase or escalation in activity, not as a contrast between activity then and inactivity at the present time. Both John and Paul underscore this by stressing the link between present and future activity: while the antichrist is coming in the future, many antichrists have already come (1 John 2:18–23). While the man of lawlessness is coming, the mystery of lawlessness is already at work (2 Thess 2:7–8). While there is a present restraint on that future full manifestation (2 Thess 2:6–7), it does not constitute the complete cessation of activity described in Rev 20:1–3. The latter is fittingly descriptive only of a post-advent situation.

Blaising writes from a progressive dispensationalist perspective.

The Postmillennialist Reading

The Postmillennial view, in contrast to the previous two readings of Revelation 20, is optimistic.[29] The millennium is a period of enormous blessing that takes place before Christ's second coming. Princeton theologian A. A. Hodge (1823–1886) wrote,

> Christ has in reserve for his church a period of universal expansion and of preeminent spiritual prosperity, where the spirit and character of the "noble army of martyrs" shall be reproduced again in the great body of God's people in an unprecedented measure, and when these martyrs shall, in the general triumph of their cause, and in the overthrow of that of their enemies, receive judgment over their foes and reign in the earth; while the party of Satan, "the rest of the dead," shall not flourish again until the thousand years be ended, when it shall prevail again for a little season.[30]

As with amillennialism and historic premillennialism, there is in postmillennialism no secret rapture of the church. Puritans in the seventeenth century held this view, and so did many others in the nineteenth and early twentieth centuries. It is very much a minority position today. The bloody tragedy of World War I made it difficult to entertain the same optimism about human progress that the nineteenth century allowed. World War II reinforced the picture. On this view, the millennium may have already started in a sense with the spread of Christianity in places like China and the fact that more Muslims are coming to Christ than at any other time in history—or it is yet to come. Moreover, there is a concern for human rights that was not the case in the ancient or medieval worlds. And technological advances increasingly make human life so much more enjoyable and healthy. Although not his eschatological preference, Bird captures the putative evidence for the postmillennial idea well: "[P]ostmillennialists point to the success of Christianity in the world with the frequency of conversions, the multiplication of theological colleges, the number of missionaries sent out, and the proliferation of Christian media on radio, television, and the internet."[31]

Regarding the binding of Satan, Kenneth L. Gentry Jr., a prominent contemporary postmillennialist, argues,

> Satan's binding begins in the first century. Christ initiates it during his earthly ministry: "if I cast out demons by the Spirit of God, then the kingdom of God

---

[29] Loren T. Stuckenbruck, "Revelation," *ECB*, ed. James D. G. Dunn and John W. Rogerson (Grand Rapids, MI, and Cambridge: Eerdmans, 2003), 1567, appears quite confused in arguing, "So formulated, this question has produced traditions of interpretation which, respectively, are labeled 'premillennial' and 'postmillennial.' Whereas the former regards the millennium as the culmination of a gradual improvement brought about by the church in the world, the latter expects that the world will only be changed decisively when God's activity intervenes in a world in a downward spiral of evil." The reverse is actually the case.
[30] Quoted in Bird, *Evangelical Theology*, 277.
[31] Bird, *Evangelical Theology*, 277.

has come upon you. Or how can anyone enter the strong man's house and carry off his property, unless he first binds the strong man? And then he will plunder his house" (Mt 12:28–29).[32]

Like amillennialists, postmillennialists hold that the binding of Satan does not nullify his activities; rather, the key point is that he deceives the nations no more. Gentry writes,

> Satan's binding continues throughout the Christian era (i.e., the "thousand years"), except for a brief period just prior to the second advent (Rev 20:2–3, 7–9). It does *not* result in the *total inactivity* of Satan; rather it enforces Christ's complete control of his power. . . . John carefully qualifies the purpose of Satan's binding: it is "in order that" (Gk., *hina*) Satan not "deceive the nations."[33]

Like the amillennialist, the postmillennialist understands the language of Revelation 20 to be metaphor-laden and needing a spiritualized reading.

The Dispensationalist Reading

Classic dispensationalism is a species of premillennialism.[34] One of its features is the advocacy of a literal hermeneutic. That is to say, unless the result is nonsense, biblical texts are to be taken at their literal face value. (A nonsense result would be to hear that Jesus claimed to be the "door," and then to ask, "Mahogany or cedar?") For the dispensationalist, a literal hermeneutic means taking OT prophecies about a future state of bliss as literal predictions of the divine intent (e.g., Isa. 35:1–2, 7). What is striking about this eschatology is the positing of a secret rapture of the church (e.g., Matt. 24:34–41 and 1 Thess. 4:16–17).[35] This doctrine is not a feature of the other three eschatological schemas. Another key defining characteristic that makes the dispensationalist eschatological schema distinctive is that it envisages a future for ethnic Israel.[36]

---

[32] Kenneth L. Gentry Jr., "The Binding of Satan," http://postmillennialismtoday.com/2014/02/03/the-binding-of-satan/, accessed 4/24/2015. See also his essay, "Preterist," in C. Marvin Pate, ed., *Four Views on the Book of Revelation* (Grand Rapids, MI: Zondervan, 1998), esp. 82–84.

[33] Gentry, "Binding of Satan."

[34] Classic dispensationalism, according to some (e.g., Charles C. Ryrie), is to be clearly distinguished from progressive dispensationalism (e.g., Darrell L. Bock), which is a newer theological position and which is seen by the classic dispensationalists as a deviation. For our purpose there is no need to delve deeply into this debate, as this is not a monograph on eschatology. Suffice it to say that the progressive dispensationalist believes that the ascended Christ is on the throne of David now and reigns. However, the reign of the ascended Christ on the earth awaits the millennium. For the classic dispensationalist, Christ's reign as King in heaven and on earth awaits the millennium per se. In the interim, he ministers as the great high priest depicted in Hebrews (passim).

[35] Christopher J. H. Wright, *The God I Don't Understand: Reflections on Tough Questions of Faith* (Grand Rapids, MI: Zondervan, 2008), 171n2, wrongly dates the origins of the contemporary form of dispensationalism to 1930. The year when Margaret MacDonald shared her prophetic visions with Edward Irving was 1830. This is a minor blemish in an otherwise very helpful work. See Thomas D. Ice, "MacDonald, Margaret," in *Dictionary of Premillennial Theology*, ed. Mal Couch (Grand Rapids, MI: Kregel, 1996), 244.

[36] John S. Feinberg, "Systems of Discontinuity," in *Continuity and Discontinuity: Perspectives on the Relationship between the Old and New Testaments—Essays in Honor of S. Lewis Johnson, Jr.*, ed. John S. Feinberg (Westchester, IL: Crossway, 1988), 81.

Of all the eschatological schemas, dispensationalism gives the most detailed attention to the role of Satan in the end times.

For the classic dispensationalist, then, the millennium lies in the future. Before Christ ushers it in he will snatch away or "rapture" the church (e.g., 1 Thess. 4:13–18).[37] Before that event, however, Christians will face increasing persecution in this the church age. Merrill F. Unger argues, "Although demonic activity in human history has always been undeniably great since the sin of our first parents exposed mankind to its baneful attacks, yet the full realization and augmentation of its destructive power are reserved for the consummation of the age."[38] So, like historic premillennialism and amillennialism, but unlike postmillennialism, this is a pessimistic view which posits "the last-day upsurge of evil supernaturalism."[39]

After the secret rapture of the church, according to classic dispensationalism, God's program for Israel will kick back into action. Seven literal years of tribulation will follow. Midway through that period, the Antichrist will reveal himself and claim to be the Messiah. The catalyst of this upsurge in demonic activity is the war in heaven of which Revelation 12:7–9 speaks. John F. Walvoord claims in his discussion of the rapture, which he finds in 1 Thessalonians 4:13–18, "Michael [the archangel] is also mentioned in Revelation 12:7–9 as fighting with the devil and the demon world (Satan's angels); in the middle of the seven-year period preceding the Second Coming he will cast them out of heaven."[40] On this view, Jesus may even have had this event in mind when he spoke proleptically in Luke 10:17–18: "The seventy-two returned with joy, saying, 'Lord, even the demons are subject to us in your name!' And he said to them, 'I saw Satan fall like lightning from heaven.'"[41] According to Unger, "It will be pre-eminently the period of Satan's sway."[42] During the tribulation period, faithful Jews and some Gentiles will convert to a form of messianic Judaism, and will be persecuted for failing to worship the Antichrist. These believers are the "Tribulation saints."[43] During this second half of the tribulation period (three and a half years), Satan will work through his agents, the

---

[37] Pretribulationists hold that the rapture occurs before the seven years of tribulation or Daniel's seventieth week. Daniel 9:27 is the putative proof-text cited by Schwarz. That pretribulationists appeal to this text is a mistake on Schwarz's part. Midtribulationists hold that the rapture occurs three and a half years into the tribulation or three and a half weeks into Daniel's seventieth week. Christians face the tribulation. For these distinctions see Schwarz, *Eschatology*, 335.

[38] Merrill F. Unger, *Biblical Demonology: A Study of Spiritual Forces Today* (Grand Rapids, MI: Kregel, 1994), 201. See also C. Fred Dickason, *Angels: Elect and Evil* (Chicago: Moody, 1995), 229–234.

[39] Unger, *Biblical Demonology*, 201.

[40] John F. Walvoord, "End Times: Understanding Today's World Events in Biblical Prophecy," in *Understanding Christian Theology*, ed. Charles R. Swindoll and Roy B. Zuck (Nashville: Thomas Nelson, 2003), 1263.

[41] Walvoord, "End Times," 1353. Walvoord allows that it may simply be a reference to Christ's future victory at the cross. The present writer is not persuaded by this reading of Revelation 12 which views Luke 10 as a "prophetic anticipation" of the Revelation 12 text, but it needs to be noted that the view is held by a number of serious scholars of the Bible.

[42] Unger, *Biblical Demonology*, 207.

[43] J. Randall Price, "Tribulation, Various Views of the," in *Dictionary of Premillennial Theology*, 417.

beast and the Antichrist.[44] At the end of the seven years of tribulation, Christ returns in triumph with myriads of angels. Satan is bound and Christ begins his thousand-year reign from the reestablished throne of David in a restored Jerusalem. Satan is released from his bondage and returns to action only after the thousand years are over. Progressive dispensationalist Darrell L. Bock puts it like this: "At the end of this stage of the kingdom, evil itself will be destroyed in a display of Christ's judgment against satanic and human rebellion, and death along with sin will be eliminated."[45]

Each of the positions hitherto discussed affirms the binding of Satan. The key difference lies in the when. Only historic premillennialism and dispensationalism make the binding of Satan a future event and therefore are relevant to a discussion of the future of the devil.[46] Hans Schwarz makes an excellent point concerning these eschatological schemes:

> All of the eschatological timetables that we could devise miss the intention of this vision [Revelation 20:1–15] that shows, in the face of seeming defeat, the victory of Christ and those who are faithful to him. Therefore the millennium is not to be understood in a triumphalistic manner, but as a pastoral comfort. It shows the conviction that God will ultimately make his kingdom triumph. Those who belong to God will not be abandoned, and their reward will be sure.[47]

It is to that triumph we next turn our attention.

---

[44] Charles C. Ryrie, *Basic Theology: A Popular Systematic Guide to Understanding Biblical Truth* (Colorado Springs: ChariotVictor, 1997), 471.

[45] Darrell L. Bock, *Progressive Dispensationalism* (Grand Rapids, MI: Baker, 2000), 283.

[46] I hold a variant of historic premillennialism, which some call end-historical premillennialism (e.g., Boyd Hunt). On this view, the end of history and the beginning of the world to come overlap in a period symbolized by the millennium. An observation among others by Schnabel, *Forty Questions*, 277, comports with this view: "When we follow John's description of his vision of the millennium in Revelation 20:1–6, we are led to believe that we should not make a hard and fast distinction between life during the millennium and life on the new earth." Schnabel points to the idea that the saints who reign during this period are resurrected and therefore have the bodies of the new earth. In this period Christ rules on earth, the martyrs are vindicated, and Satan is bound. Although this view reflects a covenant theology rather than a dispensationalist one, it has a family resemblance to progressive dispensationalism at some points (e.g., the progressive dispensationalist idea of the millennium and eschatological kingdom making up the Zionic dispensation). It must be said, however, that careful Bible believers are both covenantal and dispensationalist in theology. Even the most ardent amillennial theologian holds to at least two dispensations (the old one and the new). The chief issue is what idea is in the foreground as opposed to the background. Is covenant the chief organizing principle as a reading strategy for the whole Bible, or is it the notion of dispensations? A difficulty I have with the amillennial and postmillennial positions is that I do not find the fact that Satan won't deceive the nations during this time frame satisfactorily treated by these schools of eschatological thought. C. E. Arnold, "Satan," in *DPL*, ed. Gerald F. Hawthorne and Ralph P. Martin (Downers Grove, IL: InterVarsity Press, 1993), s.v., captures my concern well: "The language and imagery of the text is too strong to allow for this particular binding to have occurred in the work of Christ on the cross. The writer of the apocalypse uses a series of five aorist indicative verbs to express this total suppression of Satanic opposition: (1) the angel seizes Satan, presumably with the chain he carries, (2) binds him for a thousand years, (3) throws him into the Abyss . . . (4) locks the Abyss with the key he possesses, and (5) seals it over him. The seizing, binding, casting, locking, and sealing imagery leaves little room for seeing Satan as active on earth, even in a partial sense." Moreover, I find it difficult to reduce the first resurrection to regeneration—despite my considerable respect for Augustine. Resurrection in the NT appears to mean a bodily phenomenon. For a careful treatment of possible understandings of the resurrection motif in the NT, see N. T. Wright, *The Resurrection of the Son of God* (Minneapolis: Fortress, 2003), 472–476. I do not find Wright's own suggestion concerning Revelation 20 that convincing.

[47] Schwarz, *Eschatology*, 337. There is no reason that the Revelation 20:1–15 cannot be both triumphant and pastoral. I am grateful to John Feinberg for pointing out the false dichotomy in Schwarz's remarks.

God Wins: The Victory of the Light

The last book of the Bible, Revelation, ends the canon on the note of victory and expectation. Christ is returning. God wins. Evil is defeated. Barbara R. Rossing captures the thrust of Revelation vividly: "Like other apocalypses, the book has a narrative framework. It tells a story . . . the story of the Lamb Jesus who defeats evil and leads the community on a great exodus out of the unjust empire [i.e., Rome], personified as a dragon. The narrative journey ends in a utopic new city, the bridal new Jerusalem, with a river of life and a healing tree in a renewed creation."[48]

Satan's Doom

The last eschatological battle involves Satan being released from the pit (Rev. 20:7).[49] He deceives the nations and musters his forces of Gog and Magog (v. 8). Leon Morris argues, "The expression *Gog and Magog* seems to mean all people."[50] Jerusalem is the object of their attack, but a fiery response from heaven ends the campaign (v. 9). As for Satan, he is thrown into the lake of fire to face never-ending torment (v. 10). Retributive justice is served. The devil has company. Those anti-God personages of the beast and the false prophet provide him company (v. 10). Of the beast and the false prophet, Walter Kaiser writes,

> What, then, can we say about the beast? John saw in his vision a personage coming at the end of time who would be the devil incarnate and demand worship. This personage would be accompanied by a second who would seem to be harmless enough ("two horns like a lamb," perhaps suggesting a likeness to Christ, the Lamb), but would speak for the devil ("he spoke like a dragon," Rev 13:11). The second personage will direct worship toward the first.[51]

This is somewhat puzzling, as Kaiser gives the distinct impression that only two personages are on view in the passage, with the beast as "the devil incarnate." The more natural reading is to see three figures at work: the beast, the false prophet, and the dragon (Satan) acting through them.

---

[48] Barbara R. Rossing, "Revelation," *The New Testament Fortress Commentary on the Bible* (Minneapolis: Fortress, 2014), 716. Rossing sees the Roman Empire and the dragon as synonymous. In her view, the seer sees only a little beyond the fall of the Roman Empire. I would argue, in contradistinction, that the Babylon of Revelation is the agent of a very real devil and that the Rome ("Babylon") that John lived in was also a pointer to what is to come. Even so, there is much insight in her commentary, and her point about the narrative framework of Revelation is a fine one.

[49] Charles H. H. Scobie, *The Ways of Our God: An Approach to Biblical Theology* (Grand Rapids, MI, and Cambridge: Eerdmans, 2003), 226, states, ". . . after the thousand years are over, Satan *escapes* from prison and rallies the forces opposed to God for one last battle" (emphasis mine). The biblical text actually states that Satan is released (*luthēnai*, v. 3; and *luthēsetai*, v. 7) from his bondage. The divine sovereignty in this is implied.

[50] Leon Morris, *Revelation*, TNTC (Downers Grove, IL: IVP Academic, 1987), 232.

[51] Kaiser, *Hard Sayings*, 772. It may also be questioned whether incarnation language should be used of the devil at all.

As with so much in this apocalyptic text, interpretations are varied. For example, can the beast from the sea and the false prophet be reducible to first-century figures such as the Roman Empire and rulers like Nero or Domitian?[52] Patent, however, is that Satan, the beast, and the false prophet all lose the contest.[53] Their fate is "the eternal fire prepared for the devil and his angels," of which Jesus spoke (Matt. 25:41).[54]

Evil Defeated

Evil, like its agents Satan, the beast, and the false prophet, has no future in God's new creation.[55] The description in the book of Revelation is stunning (Rev. 21:1–4). It begins with language drawn for the prophetic end-time vision of Isaiah 65–66:

> Then I saw a new heaven and a new earth, for the first heaven and the first earth had passed away, and the sea was no more. And I saw the holy city, new Jerusalem, coming down out of heaven from God, prepared as a bride adorned for her husband. And I heard a loud voice from the throne saying, "Behold, the dwelling place of God is with man. He will dwell with them, and they will be his people, and God himself will be with them as their God. He will wipe away every tear from their eyes, and death shall be no more, neither shall there be mourning, nor crying, nor pain anymore, for the former things have passed away.

The sea, which symbolizes the forces of destructive chaos, has gone (Rev. 21:1). The indicators of evil's presence are gone too: tears wiped away; death removed; mourning, crying, and pain are no more (v. 4). This indeed is a new world.

WILL SATAN BE SAVED?

The answer to the question of Satan's salvation appears to be a firm no. Revelation 20:10 seems definitive: "and the devil who had deceived them was thrown into the lake of fire and sulfur where the beast and the false prophet were, and they will be tormented day and night forever and ever [*eis tous aiōnas tōn aiōnōn*, "into the ages of the ages"]."[56] However, some in the early church

---

[52] Kaiser (*Hard Sayings*, 772) appears to open the door to this contention: "That means that John could be shifting from a vision of literal Rome and its emperors to one of a succession of empires."

[53] The presentation of the beast and false prophet in the book of Revelation shows that Satan is aping God. The Creator works through his agents (angels and humans) to achieve his purposes. Likewise the devil, in his counter kingdom, works though his agents (demons, the beast, and the false prophet).

[54] There is a fascinating asymmetry in Matthew 25:31–46. Consider the fate of the cursed of humanity (v. 41): "Then he will say to those on his left, 'Depart from me, you cursed, into the eternal fire prepared for the devil and his angels." The cursed find their end in a place not intended for them but for fallen celestial beings. In contradistinction, the righteous find their end in a place divinely intended for them (v. 34): "Then the King will say to those on his right, 'Come, you who are blessed by my Father, inherit the kingdom prepared for you from the foundation of the world.'"

[55] For a brief but fine discussion of the beast and the false prophet see Eckhard Schnabel, *Forty Questions*, chapters 19 and 22 respectively.

[56] E. A. Litton, *Introduction to Dogmatic Theology* (Bellingham, WA: Lexham, 2018), 128, argues that angels—and presumably this applies to fallen angels as well—are aeviternal. That is to say, such beings have a beginning as creatures, but no ending. Revelation 20:10 comports with this view. The classic discussion of this concept in contradis-

period took an optimistic view. Clement of Alexandria, for example, thought that, given God's limitless mercy, there may even be hope for the devil. His pupil Origen took it further. He argued for *apocatastasis*, which is the idea that all things made by God will return to him. Origen found a scriptural basis for this view in Acts 3:21; 1 Corinthians 15:26–28; Romans 5:17; 11:36; Philippians 2:10; and 1 John 4:8.[57] So how does the salvation of the devil work? The Platonic notion of evil as the absence of good is vital to Origen's theory. In other words, the devil will cease to be the devil per se and will have his angelic nature restored. Latin-speaking fathers such as Jerome and Augustine would have none of this, nor did Constantinople II, which in AD 553 roundly anathematized the idea of the *apocatastasis* and the idea that the demonic could revert back to the angelic in nature.[58]

The condemnation of the *apocatastasis* doctrine has firm NT basis. It is true that the Greek word *apokatastasis* ("restoration") does appear in Acts 3:21, where Peter speaks of a "time for restoring" as promised in the holy prophets. In Acts 3:19–21 Peter declared,

> Repent therefore, and turn back, that your sins may be blotted out, that times of refreshing may come from the presence of the Lord, and that he may send the Christ appointed for you, Jesus, whom heaven must receive until the time for restoring all the things about which God spoke by the mouth of his holy prophets long ago.[59]

However, this same Peter is found preaching in the very next chapter an exclusivist rather than a universalist gospel (Acts 4:11–12): "This Jesus is the stone that was rejected by you, the builders, which has become the cornerstone. And there is salvation in no one else, for there is no other name under heaven given among men by which we must be saved." Kaiser rightly comments, "In other words, the teaching throughout Acts (and the rest of the New Testament, for that matter) is that there is only one way to escape God's judgment and receive his favor, and that is through Jesus. This exclusivity is a consistent claim of the early church."[60]

Implications for Belief and Practice

For the Christian, the eschatological horizon does not shrink to the next vacation or public holiday. After all, Jesus taught us to pray for the kingdom to

---

tinction to eternity and time is found in Thomas Aquinas's *Summa Theologica*, I, Q 10.5: "Aeviternity differs from time, and from eternity, as the mean between them both. This difference is explained by some to consist in the fact that eternity has neither beginning nor end, aeviternity, a beginning but no end, and time both beginning and end."

[57] None of the biblical texts that Origen appealed to provide exegetical footing for the claims he made.

[58] For the substance of this paragraph I am indebted to Jeffrey Burton Russell, *Satan: The Early Christian Tradition* (Ithaca, NY, and London: Cornell University Press, 1987), 122–123, 144–148.

[59] The NRSV begs the question, though, when it paraphrases the Greek in the following way: "the time of *universal* restoration" (emphasis mine). This rendering appears to favor a soteriologically universalist reading.

[60] Kaiser, *Hard Sayings*, 516.

come and for God's will to be done on earth as it is in heaven. In practical terms, this eschatological mind-set shows itself in two attitudes: confidence and expectation.

Confidence

We live in a society that appears to be moving from tolerant indifference toward Christianity on the part of the secular elites to increasingly open hostility at the verbal and judicial level. As Russell D. Moore correctly argues, Christians in the United States have to learn how to move from being the moral majority to a prophetic minority.[61] More and more, the pre-Constantinian church in general seems relevant, and in particular the Pauline confidence that the future belongs to God and his people. Paul states his own confidence in writing to the Romans (Rom. 8:38–39):

> For I am sure [*pepeismai*, perfect aspect; "I have been persuaded and still am"] that neither death nor life, nor angels nor rulers, nor things present nor things to come, nor powers, nor height nor depth, nor anything else in all creation, will be able to separate us from the love of God in Christ Jesus our Lord.

In the list Paul notably includes angels, rulers, and powers, understood as opponents of God's purposes and people.

Hope

The initial readers of 1 Peter knew growing hostility toward their faith. Indeed, as we saw in an earlier chapter, Peter describes the devil as a roaring lion seeking prey to devour (1 Pet. 5:8). Be that as it may, the letter right from its opening makes it clear that the Christian's future is secure. Such is the great Christian hope. Peter writes (1:3–5),

> Blessed be the God and Father of our Lord Jesus Christ! According to his great mercy, he has caused us to be born again to a living hope through the resurrection of Jesus Christ from the dead, to an inheritance that is imperishable, undefiled, and unfading, kept in heaven for you, who by God's power are being guarded through faith for a salvation ready to be revealed in the last time.

The inheritance is safe because God is its guardian and Christ's own resurrection is its guarantee.

According to Jesus, humanity's state in the world to come is to be like the angels. Jesus made this claim in his debate with the Sadducees, who denied the resurrection of the body (Matt. 22:23–33). He pointed out that their

---

[61] Russell D. Moore, interviewed by Naomi Schaefer Riley, "Russell Moore: From Moral Majority to 'Prophetic Minority,'" in http://www.wsj.com/articles/SB10001424127887324769704579010743654111328, accessed 4/27/2015.

argument exhibited two errors. The first error was their ignorance of their Scripture. They had a more limited OT canon than their rivals the Pharisees. However, they did believe the Torah, and in the Torah, Exodus 3:6 makes it plain that God continues to be the God of Abraham, Isaac, and Jacob. Cleverly, Jesus appeals to a Scripture which was authoritative for the Sadducees and uses it against them by showing its implication. Their second error was in their not believing the Scriptures' witness to the power of the living God. It is instructive, in a society where relativism is so prevalent at the level of ideas and morals, that Jesus taught that a person *can* be mistaken. Those same two errors of which he spoke can be made today, even in theological colleges and divinity schools.

In the course of the argument Jesus teaches that, in the future state, humans are like the angels, "For in the resurrection they neither marry nor are given in marriage, but are like angels in heaven" (Matt. 22:30). R. T. France comments,

> In this new deathless life there will be no place for procreation, and the exclusive relationship within which this takes place on earth will therefore not apply. . . . The Sadducees' question may have been cynical, but the issue it raises is a real one for those who have married more than once; Jesus' reply points them to a possibility of fulfilment of these relationships in the risen life which the exclusiveness of the marriage bond in earthly life would have rendered unthinkable.[62]

In the world to come Christ has a bride, the church. Marriage in this life is a pointer to what is to come (cf. Eph. 5:31–32 and Rev. 21:1–2). Members of Christ will find their fulfillment as the bride of Christ, whether they are male or female.

With reference to the future state and the expression of our sexuality I have written elsewhere,

> The question is whether human sexuality and expression continues in the new heavens and new earth. Jesus cryptically said that in the new world disciples would not marry. They would be like the angels (Matt. 22:30). The seer writes that in the world to come, there will be marriage, but a marriage between the Lamb and his bride, the church (Rev. 19:1–10 and 21–22). It seems that human sexual expression in one flesh union is now transposed to another plane. Human eros now has a Christological focus. Grace has both redeemed eros and transposed it.[63]

"Like the angels" is a hard word to hear in our over-sexualized culture, which seems to make the expression of our sexuality the defining charac-

---

[62] R. T. France, *Matthew*, TNTC (Downers Grove, IL: IVP Academic, 2008), 320.
[63] Graham A. Cole, "Sexuality and Its Expression: With Reference to Homosexuality," *Interchange* 51 (1994).

teristic of our humanity. As Michel Foucault argued, for moderns, sex has replaced the soul.[64]

CONCLUSION

The darkness won't extinguish the light. The destiny of the darkness is its destruction. Fallen angels will experience the eternal fire. The devil may be the prince of this world. Be that as it may, in the next he has no kingdom, according to the biblical witness. The Christian, according to Paul, can have confidence that not even angels can separate him or her from the love of Christ (Rom. 8:31–39). Gregory of Nyssa (c. 330–c. 395) captures the joy of this prospect:

> Up until now creation groans and travails in pain, subject because of us to vanity, seeing in our fall a loss to itself, until the revelation of the sons of God, for which the angels never cease to wait in eager expectation for us—until the sheep which has been saved is reunited to the holy hundred fold. For we are the sheep, we whom the Good Shepherd, in becoming man, has saved. But then in a heart-felt sentiment of gratitude they will present their thanksgiving to Him who by His First-Born has called back the straying sheep to the Father's hearth.[65]

The final picture in Scripture is of a redeemed humanity serving the Lord as priests and kings in a new heaven and a new earth (Revelation 21–22). However, we are not left thinking that this is the total picture. For earlier in Revelation, there is the seer's vision of the heavenly throne room (Revelation 4–5). God has other servants. These servants have never creased in their praise and adoration of God. It is these angelic servants we join to worship the living God. True worship throughout creation will be restored.

EXCURSUS: THE ARCHANGEL MICHAEL
AND THE MAN OF LAWLESSNESS

The King is coming again. Judgment Day is coming. However, before then a mysterious eschatological figure, the man of lawlessness, will appear working mischief. Satan will be the architect of this rebellion. The one NT passage that describes this personage is 2 Thessalonians 2:1–12. In this passage Paul, out of pastoral concern, counsels the Thessalonians (vv. 1–2), "Now concerning the coming of our Lord Jesus Christ and our being gathered together to him, we ask you, brothers, not to be quickly shaken in mind or alarmed, either by a spirit or a spoken word, or a letter seeming to be from us, to the effect that the day of the Lord has come." There are clearly those in the background with

---

[64] Stuart Sovatsky, *Words from the Soul: Time, East/West Spirituality, and Psychotherapeutic Narrative* (Albany, NY: SUNY Press, 1998), 157.
[65] Quoted in Danielou, *Angels and Their Mission*, 113–114.

an overly realized eschatology, who deceptively mask their own machinations with an illegitimate use of Paul's name (v. 3): "Let no one deceive you in any way." So Paul corrects the troublers' eschatology (vv. 3–5):

> For that day will not come, unless the rebellion comes first, and the man of lawlessness is revealed, the son of destruction, who opposes and exalts himself against every so-called god or object of worship, so that he takes his seat in the temple of God, proclaiming himself to be God. Do you not remember that when I was still with you I told you these things?

Thus Paul introduces the mysterious figure of "the man of lawlessness, . . . the son of destruction." Who is this personage? Eckhard Schnabel comments, "Paul's description of the Lawless One combines the two types of anti-messiah figures of Second Temple Judaism: the figure of the false prophet, and the figure of the tyrant who opposes God. Paul appears to be thinking of a future pagan ruler who will recapitulate the blasphemy of Antiochus IV Epiphanes . . . and who will be the supreme embodiment of evil which will appear at the end."[66] Michael Bird adds to the picture when he argues, "This 'man of lawlessness' can be correlated with the 'antichrist' (1 John 4:3; 2 John 7) and 'the beast' (Rev 13–17). This figure, resembling a mixture of Antiochus IV Epiphanes and Nero, opposes God, persecutes God's people, and leads nations astray."[67]

More mystery follows in 2 Thessalonians 2:6–8:

> And you know what is restraining him now so that he may be revealed in his time. For the mystery of lawlessness is already at work. Only he who now restrains it will do so until he is out of the way. And then the lawless one will be revealed, whom the Lord Jesus will kill with the breath of his mouth and bring to nothing by the appearance of his coming.

Who or what, then, is this restraining force? Significantly, the appearance on the stage of history of the man of lawlessness is no accident. Paul explains the dark personage behind this figure's rebellious activities (vv. 9–10): "The coming of the lawless one is by the activity of Satan with all power and false signs and wonders, and with all wicked deception for those who are perishing, because they refused to love the truth and so be saved."

For our purposes the key question which arises from this fascinating passage is, Who or what is the restrainer? Colin Nicholl makes this interesting comment:

> One of the most enduring exegetical enigmas of the Pauline corpus is the iden-tification of *ho katechōn*/*to katechon* ["the one holding back"] in 2 Thess.

---

[66] Schnabel, *Forty Questions about the End Times*, 160.
[67] Bird, *Evangelical Theology*, 299.

2:6–7. Discussion of the issue has reached something of an impasse, with some recent contributions expressing pessimism regarding the whole enterprise and a few even postulating that the author himself had no particular referent in mind.[68]

Nicholl weighs into the question with a proposal of great interest for this study. He argues that the restrainer is no lesser figure than Michael the archangel. To this proposal we turn our attention.

Nicholl considers the number of contenders for the restrainer which have been proffered. These include: the Roman Empire per se, a particular ruler or principle of law and order, Paul or the proclamation of the gospel, Satan or rebellion, God's will or plan, and the Holy Spirit. Each of these he finds wanting.[69] Following earlier suggestions, Nicholl offers the archangel Michael as this mysterious figure. This earlier suggestion is found in works which range from H. Gunkel in 1895 to D. Hannah in 1999.[70] According to Nicholl, what is missing from these earlier suggestions is any explanation of the most important point of 2 Thessalonians 2:6–7, which is the removal of restrainer.[71] He offers his own remedy for this lacuna, but not without first establishing the plausibility of Michael as the restrainer.

In establishing the plausibility of Michael as the restrainer, Nicholl shows the stature of Michael in extrabiblical literature. Canvassing a wide range of such sources, he shows how they present Michael as a major figure (e.g., *1 Enoch* 24:6), who is charged with defending Israel (e.g., *Pirque Rabbi Eliezer* 26, 33, 36, 38, 42, 50), interceding for it (*Testament of Abraham A* 14:5–6), and as the opponent of Satan/Belial (*1QM* 17:5–6).[72] Nicholl contends that "The pre-eminence of Michael in contemporary Jewish thought, especially as *archistrategos*, opponent of Satan and protector of God's people, renders him an especially plausible candidate for the role of restrainer."[73] As for the role of restrainer, Nicholl argues that the writer of 2 Thessalonians—whom I believe to be Paul—in chapter 2 alludes to Daniel 11:36–37 and other Danielic texts. In fact he contends that Daniel 10:1–12:3, which casts Michael as a restrainer, provides the background to the Thessalonians passage. He provides evidence that this conception of Michael's role as "a restrainer of eschatological evil" is found in Second Temple Judaism. After detailed and lengthy argument he offers this proposal: "We suggest that Michael could plausibly have been viewed

[68] Colin Nicholl, "Michael, the Restrainer Removed (2 Thess. 2:6–7)," *Journal of Theological Studies*, n.s. 51/1 (2000); 27.

[69] Nicholl, "Michael, the Restrainer," 30–32. Schnabel, *Forty Questions*, 161, lists another candidate whom some champion, although he leaves the question open: "In this case, the restraining power is the Jewish state, while the restrainer is perhaps James, the leader of the Jerusalem church."

[70] Nicholl, "Michael, the Restrainer," 33n21.

[71] Nicholl, "Michael, the Restrainer," 35n31.

[72] Nicholl, "Michael, the Restrainer," 33–35.

[73] Nicholl, "Michael, the Restrainer," 35.

as a restrainer-figure, based on Daniel 10–12 and that there is evidence that he was viewed in precisely this way in subsequent Jewish thought."[74] The question begged by Nicholl's impressive study is that, if all this was well known in Second Temple Judaism, why doesn't the apostle name Michael per se? The exegetical fact is that Michael is not mentioned in the text. If Nicholl is right, I am at a loss to understand why the apostle does not name names, especially since, given 1 Thessalonians 4:16, Paul clearly knows of the existence of archangels and the eschatological role of at least one of them.[75]

In a work on pneumatology, I suggested that either the Roman Empire or the Holy Spirit is the main contender for the restrainer. In that work, I "leaned" toward the Holy Spirit as the restrainer.[76] I am not yet persuaded that Nicholl is right, but in the light of his plausible argument I would now have to say that there are three main contenders for that figure: the Roman Empire, the Holy Spirit, and Michael the archangel. An important question that Nicholl's argument raises is the dogmatic status of his proposal. As suggested above, in my view it is to be entertained as one of the possibilities, but doctrine is not to be built on it.

---

[74] Nicholl, "Michael, the Restrainer," 50.

[75] I am not endorsing Nicholl's proposal, but if I were to offer an explanation as to why Paul does not mention Michael by name, I would draw attention to Colossians 2:18–19: "Let no one disqualify you, insisting on asceticism *and worship of angels*, going on in detail about visions, puffed up without reason by his sensuous mind, and not holding fast to the Head, from whom the whole body, nourished and knit together through its joints and ligaments, grows with a growth that is from God." Clearly, for this NT congregation, the worship of angels was a temptation to be eschewed. Perhaps, *ex hypothesi*, Paul feared that, if Michael were mentioned, too much weight might be placed on it. This is conjecture on my part.

[76] Graham A. Cole, *He Who Gives Life: The Doctrine of the Holy Spirit* (Wheaton, IL: Crossway, 2007), 236–237.

NINE

CONCLUSION

Roman Catholic theologian Jean Danielou opens his book on angels in modest terms: "To devote an entire book to the subject of angels might seem at first glance unwarranted."[1] Protestant theologian Hendrikus Berkhof is of a much stronger and contrary opinion. In Shakespearean terms, Berkhof believes that angelology, if not much to do about nothing, is very much a matter of much to do about very little. He writes, "For no matter how often the Bible may speak of incidental appearances of angels, there is hardly any reflection on it, and one finds no basic outlines of an angelology. . . . From the Bible no angelology can be constructed."[2] Berkhof would find this concluding chapter quite a disappointment.

It is true that Scripture is addressed to us and not to angels. (A point that needs to be remembered.) So, unsurprisingly, there is so much that we simply don't know about these spiritual creatures. They are minor players in the divine comedy.[3] But players they are, and they appear, as we have seen, at key junctures in the history of redemption (e.g., the nativity of the incarnate Son of God). And, enough is revealed to provide the substance for a monograph like this one on angelology. Indeed there is hardly a major doctrine in which angels play no role. So then how does this doctrinal suitcase—to use the N. T. Wright analogy once more—relate to the rest of the luggage?

Angels as creatures are part of the story of creation. The biblical account reveals a creation multiplex. Creatures are of different kinds and of differing capacities. Some creatures are persons who are self-aware and morally accountable for their actions. Both humankind and angel-kind are members of the realm of the personal and the morally accountable. Both angels and

---

[1] Jean Danielou, *The Angels and Their Mission according to the Church Fathers*, trans. David Heimann (Notre Dame, IN: Ave Maria, 1957), vii.

[2] Hendrikus Berkhof, *Christian Faith: An Introduction to the Study of the Faith*, trans. Sierd Woudstra (Grand Rapids, MI: Eerdmans, 1979), 176. Berkhof distinguishes four levels of material in Scripture: direct witness, insights, representations that figuratively express insights but without a definite connection to them, and representations that originate from other traditions. Angels and the devil belong to the third category (90). This is far too dismissive.

[3] A point well made by Kevin J. Vanhoozer, *Remythologizing Theology: Divine Action, Passion, and Authorship* (Cambridge: Cambridge University Press, 2010), 229.

humans can self-consciously say "I." Both humankind and angel-kind are judged. Scripture gives no hint that other creatures are part of this realm of the personal. The nature of angels as spirits was considered in our study and their roles both in heaven and on earth discussed. In nature, they are spirits without bodies. In this they are like God, who is spirit. In terms of function they are servants. Angelic service is directed not only toward individuals, but also toward nations. Angels appear to be in some kind of hierarchy. They are many, a host. Angels have made their appearances on the stage of human history.

Angels raise important questions about theological anthropology and especially about the image-of-God idea. The substantive view sees the *imago dei* residing in certain properties such as rationality and volition. However, as we saw, these too are qualities of angels. So one can reasonably ask how adequate the substantive view is as it stands. What we saw is that humankind was given a dominion task and a stewardship role over creation which angels do not appear to have been given. So at the very least, a theological understanding of the *imago dei* needs the functional understanding in its definition.

Angels are also part of the story of hamartiology. Satan is the great spoiler, the great disuniter and death-bringer. He is a fallen angel and leads other fallen angels. Indeed, there is ongoing rebellion in the angelic order. How this rebellion came about seems to be hinted at in the OT. Pride is a common explanation in the history of theological discussion. As a consequence, the created order in which we now live is a dramatic one. That is to say, there is a great conflict underway between good and evil. We examined Satan's role in the great rupture, and the exact nature of his condemnation. We explored his nature as a fallen spirit and his activities as the enemy of the divine purpose. Importantly, as Otto Weber rightly argues, "To be sure, as Christians we do not believe 'in' the devil. The devil is not mentioned in the creed. But we do believe 'against' the devil."[4]

Hamartiology deals not only with sin and Satan but also with the demonic disorder. Satan is not alone in his rebellion. There are other principalities and powers involved. We examined their nature and how they relate to Satan. Their activities have also come into view. It is a debated question as to whether demons possess human beings or inhabit them or demonize them to varying degrees which may include possession or inhabitation. The debate applies to the question of whether Christians can be possessed or demonized. This study rejects the idea that the Christian who is the temple of the Holy Spirit can also be the residence of demons. The controversial question of the interpreta-

---

[4] Otto Weber, quoted in Nigel Wright, *The Satan Syndrome: Putting the Power of Darkness in Its Place* (Grand Rapids, MI: Zondervan, 1990), 25.

tion of "the sons of God" in Genesis 6 was addressed. We concluded that the Genesis 6 passage was not relevant to angelology but deals with godly human beings marrying ungodly ones—although not all would be satisfied with my approach.

Angels also play their part in the Christological story. Key events in the Christological story have an angelic presence or a fallen angelic presence: the news of the conception, the nativity, the temptations, the demonized confronting Jesus, the agony in the garden, the resurrection and ascension. We examined Jesus's ministry as an exorcist, as well as the role of the Holy Spirit in Jesus's binding the strongman and spoiling his goods. We gave particular attention to the story of Good Friday's cross and how Jesus defeated Satan there. Robert W. Jenson captures the significance of both Jesus's death and vindicating resurrection admirably when he writes, "Then, too, if you read the story as the Bible does, then this worst thing that ever happened—the crucifixion of the Messiah, the Christ—and the triumph over that worst thing—the resurrection of Christ—can be construed as the final or at least the decisive victory in the warfare between God and evil."[5] Jesus proved indeed *Christus Victor*. The motif *Christus Victor* featured prominently in this part of the study, and how exactly Jesus overcomes the evil one was explored in some depth.

Angels play their part in the soteriological story, especially in the area of progressive sanctification as the Christian struggles with the world, the flesh, and the devil. We considered spiritual warfare as seen in Jesus's ministry, and as found articulated in the writings of Luke–Acts, Paul, Peter, and John. Seven contemporary views of spiritual warfare as related to the demonic were critically examined. Popular ideas of spiritual warfare were discussed, such as reclaiming territory from territorial spirits. At the popular level, much of the discussion of spiritual warfare appears to make claims with limited biblical backing. Even ecclesiology is touched by angelology. Through the church, the body of Christ, Christ is making a point to the principalities and powers, and in Christian assembly decorum needs to take into account angelic observers. An excursus examined the question of how to discern whether a spirit is from God.

Angels also figure in the story of eschatology. We reflected on the end of history, the destiny of the darkness and the ultimate victory of the light. The witness of the book of Revelation was especially important here. "God wins" is its message. Satan and his minions are doomed. The world to come reveals order restored and evil defeated, with God's people at home with God, living in shalom. In the end, the light prevails. Various understandings

---

[5] Robert W. Jenson, *A Theology in Outline: Can These Bones Live?* (Oxford: Oxford University Press, 2016), 83.

of the millennium were also canvassed and the role of Satan and his agents examined. Importantly all these views posit the defeat of the evil one. The Christian can be confident and expectant. The biblical language that we are more than conquerors is no mere rhetorical flourish, although in this life it is mostly a matter of faith, not sight.

THE CREATION MANIFOLD

Angels are creatures and so are we. Unlike us, they are pure spirits. Like us, they are persons. In this appendix, I aim to locate them in relation to us and to other kinds of creatures. To do so, some metaphysical thinking is in order. That is to say, we need to think about the very nature of what is real.

The fundamental metaphysical distinction is not that between being and becoming, or the infinite and the finite, but between the Creator and the creature. Creatures are internally related to the Creator. That is to say that, without the will of the Creator, they are not. An internal relation is a relation without which X is not X. For example, maleness is internally related to kingship. Without maleness, a king is not a king, but something else. An external relation is one without which X remains X. I can lose all my hair and still be me. Put another way, the relation between the Creator and the creature is asymmetrical. In terms of the logic of relation, $X(R)Y \neq Y(R)X$. An example of $X(R)Y \neq Y(R)X$ is the relation of a father to his son. However, two brothers would be represented by $X(R)Y = Y(R)X$. Y is the brother of X and X is the brother of Y.[1]

The Creator relates to creatures in three possible ways for some, and in two ways for others. God can relate to angels and us in three possible ways. For self-conscious beings such as angels and humankind, God relates as a singer to a song. If he stops singing, we stop being. He also can relate to us as primary cause to secondary cause. And so Cyrus acts as the anointed one who delivers God's people from Babylonian bondage albeit unconscious that he is Yahweh's agent (Isa. 45:1): "Thus says the LORD to his anointed, to Cyrus, whose right hand I have grasped, to subdue nations before him and to loose the belts of kings, to open doors before him that gates may not be closed." Saul of Tarsus is arrested by the risen Christ on the road to Damascus. He is personally addressed by Christ as person to person or, in Martin Buber terms, as a Thou to an I (Acts 9:4–5): "And falling to the ground, he heard a voice saying to him,

---

[1] Philosopher and theologian E. L. Mascall draws upon the logic of relations—pioneered by Bertrand Russell—in a useful way to articulate the doctrine of the essential Trinity in his *The Triune God: An Ecumenical Study* (Eugene, OR: Wipf & Stock, 1986), chapter 6, "Light from the Logicians."

'Saul, Saul, why are you persecuting me?' And he said, 'Who are you, Lord?' And he said, 'I am Jesus, whom you are persecuting.'" However, God related to the strong east wind, an impersonal force, in Martin Buber terms, as a Thou to an It, which drove the waters back at the exodus. He related to the wind as primary cause to secondary cause and used it to save his people from Pharaoh (Ex. 14:21): "Then Moses stretched out his hand over the sea, and the LORD drove the sea back by a strong east wind all night and made the sea dry land, and the waters were divided."

Creatures exist at different levels.[2] Angels are personal: namely, they can use "I" language and are morally self-aware. They are conscious: namely, they are aware of the other. They are living, but are not material beings. Human beings are personal, conscious, living, and material. We are the microcosm. Since angels and human beings are personal in the foregoing sense, they are held morally accountable and are therefore judged. Dogs are conscious, living, and material beings, but not personal. Trees are neither personal nor conscious, but they are living and material. Gold is material, but not personal, nor conscious, nor living, nor organic. There is no scriptural reason for thinking that dogs, trees, or gold are to be judged. The point is not a trivial one. Creatures need to be differentiated, whereas often Christians appear to have only one category, which is creature, and one language for causation: namely, primary to secondary cause.

---

[2] The view that I am advocating here is not to be confused with the notion of a great chain of being. Great chain of being language too easily lends itself to an emanationist understanding of reality. On an emanationist view, lesser reality flows out of the supreme reality of the One, or God, as in Neoplatonism. I am, however, comfortable with a "great chain of creatures" notion, where there is a hierarchy of creaturely complexity and value. Jesus appears to have had such a hierarchy in mind when he described human beings as of more value than sparrows or sheep (cf. Matt. 6:26; 10:31; and 12:12). On this view, the Creator-creature divide is not compromised.

ANGELS, IBLIS, AND JINN IN ISLAM

Islam, like Christianity, takes the supernatural with utmost seriousness and does not fall into the blind spot that Paul Hiebert identified in chapter 1.[1] Some years ago I was in small group listening to Sheik Fehmi at the Preston mosque in Melbourne, Australia. Sheik Fehmi went on to become the chief mufti of Australia. (A mufti is a scholar who is a legal expert in Islamic law.) He explained that the Muslim goes through life with an angel on one shoulder and a jinn (evil spirit) on the other. Both are recording deeds. The angel records good deeds and the jinn records evil ones. But Sheik Fehmi claimed that a good deed far outweighs the bad, and so on the day of judgment most Muslims would be safe. Islam has its angelology, and its debts to Christianity are patent because, along with angels and jinn there is Iblis, the devil. In this appendix we will consider all three.[2]

ANGELS

One of the most influential Muslim thinkers of the last century was S. Abul A'La Maududi (1903–1979). His book *Towards Understanding Islam* has been described as "timeless wisdom" and the "most famous exposition of what Islam is about."[3] For this scholar, the doctrine of angels is the second most important doctrine in Islam after the doctrine of God. It is that important. He contends that, in nature, angels are neither male nor female, but "are made of light energy."[4]

---

[1] On Hiebert, recall our discussion introduced in chapter 1. On Islam, one might ask, why treat it at all in a work of evangelical systematic theology? I do so because Islamic angelology and demonology show what the doctrine of angels, Satan, and demons can look like when the Christian Scriptures are not the norm of norms for theological proposals, and when extrabiblical putative special revelation (the *Qur'an* in particular) is appealed to as the norm of norms.

[2] As suggested in the previous note, some readers may be surprised to find an appendix on Islam and angelology in a work of Christian systematic theology. The writer has found it helpful in teaching to employ the principle of comparison and contrast to throw Christian theology into sharper relief, and so for many years the principal conversation partners in my lectures have been modernity, postmodernity, and Islam.

[3] Ashrafuz Zaman Khan, "Foreword" to Abul A'la Maududi, *Towards Understanding Islam* (New York: Islamic Circle of North America, 2005), revised by Yahiya Emerick and based on the translation of Khurram Murad, n.p. This work and that of Sayyid Qutb, *Milestones*, 2nd rev. ed. (Damascus, Syria: Dar al-ilm, n.d.), are essential reading for anyone who wants to understand the rise of militant Islam.

[4] Maududi, *Towards Understanding Islam*, 130. Maududi provides no Quranic textual evidence for his assertions. Interestingly, the Qur'an gives angels wings: "messengers flying on wings, two, three, and four" (Surah 35:1). See

He wrote of angels, "Muhammad revealed to us that there is a class of unseen spiritual beings, whom people misidentified as deities or gods or God's children that are called angels. . . . God merely employs them to administer His Kingdom, and they carry out His orders exactly and accurately."[5] They are not to be worshiped. Only God is to be worshiped. Moreover, for a human being to worship angels is degrading. To justify this latter claim Maududi argues, "For on the very first day of humanity's creation, God made them [angels] bow themselves before Adam, granted to him greater knowledge than they possessed, and bestowed upon Adam the stewardship of this earth in preference to them. What debasement can, therefore, be greater for a human being than bowing himself before those who had bowed themselves to him."[6] Surah 2:30–34 provides the Quranic backing for Maududi's claims. It reads in part, "And when the Lord said to the angels, I am going to place a ruler on the earth. . . . And when We said to the angels, Be submissive to Adam, they submitted."[7] Scripture knows nothing of this divine command. From a Christian perspective this is a text-less doctrine, which is to say a doctrine without biblical warrant, and thus question-begging in the extreme.

According to Maulana Muhammad Ali, angels in this life surround humans, attracting them to the good.[8] However, it is on the Day of Judgment that they play a much more critical role. Maududi maintains,

> They [angels] observe and note all our actions, good and bad. They preserve a complete record of every person's life. After death, when we will all be brought before God, they will present a full report of our life's work on earth, wherein we will find everything correctly recorded. Not a single action will be left out, however insignificant or carefully concealed it may be.[9]

Surah 82:10–12 is warrant for his assertion: "And surely there are keepers over you. Honorable recorders. They know what you do." Likewise, Surah 17:13 provides support for this proposition: "And we have made every man's actions to cling to his neck, and We shall bring forth to him on the day of Resurrection a book which he will find wide open." Noticeably absent is the notion of divine grace.

Gabriel is especially important in Islamic thought. According to some scholars of Islam, Gabriel is the angel through whom the Qur'an came to Muhammad. For example, Michael Cook maintains, "According to Muslim tradition, the Koran was revealed to Muhammad by God through the agency

Maulana Muhammad Ali, *The Holy Qur'an: Arabic Text with English Translation and Commentary by Maulana Muhammad Ali*, new ed. (Lahore, Pakistan: Ahmadiyyah Anjuman Isha'at Islam, 2002), 857.
[5] Maududi, *Towards Understanding Islam*, 105.
[6] Maududi, *Towards Understanding Islam*, 105.
[7] Maulana Muhammad Ali, *Holy Qur'an: Arabic Text with English Translation and Commentary*, 18–20.
[8] Maulana Muhammad Ali, *Holy Qur'an: Arabic Text with English Translation and Commentary*, 76n177b.
[9] Maududi, *Towards Understanding Islam*, 19–20.

of the angel Gabriel; this took place partly in Mecca, his hometown, and partly in Medina, where he succeeded in creating a state in an otherwise stateless tribal society."[10] The Quranic verse which informs the tradition at this point is Surah 53:5: "One Mighty in Power has taught him [Muhammad]."[11] However, other scholars, for example Maulana Muhammad Ali, argue that this verse is referring not to Gabriel but to Allah himself.[12] Gabriel is also thought by some to be referenced obliquely in Surah 17:1: "Glory to Him who carried His servant by night from the Sacred Mosque to the Remote Mosque, whose precincts We blessed, that We might show him Our signs."[13] This is known as the Night Journey, or the Ascent. According to one explanation, Gabriel takes Muhammad from Mecca to Jerusalem. From thence Muhammad ascended to the very presence of Allah. The details need not detain us, and there is debate in Islam as to whether this surah refers to an actual journey involving Gabriel (e.g., Cyril Glassé) or to a vision with no reference to Gabriel (e.g., Maulana Muhammad Ali).[14]

In Islam, as in Christianity, there is the dark side of angels, and it is to that dark side we now turn.

IBLIS

In Islamic thought, the devil (*Iblîs*, in Arabic) is the great adversary. He is the one angel who refused the divine command to bow down to Adam.[15] In the Qur'an, in Surah 18:50, the sin of Iblis is described: "And when we said to the angels: Make submission to Adam, they submitted except Iblis. He was one of the jinn, so he transgressed the commandment of the Lord."[16] According to Surah 7:12, the devil argued with Allah, "I [Iblis] am better than he [Adam]; Thou hast created me of fire, while him Thou didst create of dust."[17] For this prideful refusal to obey, Iblis was cast out of heaven to earth, where

---

[10] Michael Cook, *The Koran: A Very Short Introduction* (Oxford: Oxford University Press, 2000), 5.

[11] Maulana Muhammad Ali, *Holy Qur'an: Arabic Text with English Translation and Commentary*, 1029.

[12] Maulana Muhammad Ali, *Holy Qur'an: Arabic Text with English Translation and Commentary*, 1029n5a. One religion where there is no ambiguity about an alleged angelic agent conveying divine revelation is Mormonism and its teaching about the visits of the angel Moroni to Joseph Smith. For a scholarly account see Terryl L. Givens, *Wrestling the Angel: The Foundations of Mormon Thought: Cosmos, God, Humanity* (Oxford: Oxford University Press, 2015), 139–141. From a Christian perspective, this is another doctrine without biblical grounding and thus question-begging in the extreme. It also has the same epistemological problem to be seen in Islam: namely, extra-biblical sources are used for the construction of doctrine. In the case of Islam it is the *Qur'an* (and allied materials such as the hadith) and with Mormonism it is the Book of Mormon.

[13] Maulana Muhammad Ali, *Holy Qur'an: Arabic Text with English Translation and Commentary*, 563.

[14] See Cyril Glassé, *The New Encyclopedia of Islam*, 3rd ed. (Lanham, MD: Rowman & Littlefield, 2008), 395–396; and Maulana Muhammad Ali, *Holy Qur'an: Arabic Text with English Translation and Commentary*, 563n1a.

[15] The idea of Satan's refusal was not new. It appears in a first-century pseudepigraphical work *The Life of Adam and Eve*. In this Jewish work, Satan's refusal to worship Adam becomes the explanation for his fall and that of the angels he leads. See the discussion in George H. Guthrie, "Hebrews," in *CNTUOT*, ed. G. K. Beale and D. A. Carson (Grand Rapids, MI: Baker Academic, 2007), 932.

[16] Maulana Muhammad Ali appeals to this verse to argue that Iblis was never an angel (*Holy Qur'an: Arabic Text with English Translation and Commentary*, 599n50a). For a contrary view, see Glassé, *New Encyclopedia of Islam*, 214–215, who argues that Iblis was an angel at one stage.

[17] Maulana Muhammad Ali, *Holy Qur'an: Arabic Text with English Translation and Commentary*, 330.

he subsequently tempted Adam and Eve.[18] Interestingly in Islamic thought, Iblis sins after Adam's creation by Allah. There is no pre-mundane fall. There is a Sufi tale that evidences this tradition. Sufi Abu al-Qasim al-Junayd (c. 825–c. 910) longed to see in a vision what Satan looked like. One day he met an old man in the mosque and knew the terrifying face was that of Satan. The Sufi asked why Satan had refused to bow to Adam. Satan replied that he would only bow down to God. To which Sufi al-Junayd retorted that Satan was lying, for if he had been God's servant he would have obeyed the divine command.[19] According to Islam, Iblis continues his nefarious activities in this world. In his comment on the so-called "Satanic verses," Maulana Muhammad Ali sums up that activity in these terms: "Now, what every prophet desires is the establishing of the Truth that is revealed to him, and it is with this desire of every prophet that the devil interferes, instigating men, making suggestions to them, as stated here, to oppose the Truth."[20] Again, the Bible knows nothing of this divine command to bow down before Adam and this act of disobedience. In Islamic thought, Satan on account of his disobedience became a jinn ("a dark spirit") and thus forfeited his angelic nature.[21]

JINN

Unlike angels, who are created of light, and humankind, who are made out of clay, jinn are made of fire.[22] Surah 15:26–27 contrasts the making of humanity and jinn: "And surely We created man of sounding clay, of black mud fashioned into shape. And jinn, We created before of intensely hot fire."[23] According to Cyril Glassé, "Some *jinn* are friendly to humans, others are hostile; some are beautiful, and others, the '*ifrīt* and *ghūl* (from which the word "ghoul" derives), are hideous."[24] There are signs by which these latter dark spirits may be recognized. Glassé provides an excellent summary:

---

[18] Glassé, *New Encyclopedia of Islam*, 215. The Qur'an appears to have been influenced by the *Life of Adam and Eve* in this contention. See Philip C. Almond, *The Devil: A New Biography* (Ithaca, NY: Cornell University Press, 2014), 39. This fascinating text has none of the brevity of the biblical text when it comes to Adam and Eve. It is rife with religious imagination. For example we learn that Adam allegedly was given charge of the North and East parts of Eden while Eve had responsibility for the South and West parts. For the text, see http://www2.iath.virginia .edu/anderson/vita/english/vita.lat.html, accessed 1/30/2018.

[19] See the account in Glassé, *New Encyclopedia of Islam*, 215.

[20] Maulana Muhammad Ali, *Holy Qur'an: Arabic Text with English Translation and Commentary*, 678 and footnote 52a. The key passage is found in Surah 53:19–21 which a few have taken as showing that Muhammad lapsed into idolatry in endorsing three female pagan gods. Maulana Muhammad Ali will have none of this, 1031n21a. For a brief but illuminating discussion of the "Satanic verses" (Surah 22:52), see Cook, *Koran: A Very Short Introduction*, 126–127. For more detail see Malise Ruthven, *Islam: A Very Short Introduction* (Oxford: Oxford University Press, 2000), 33.

[21] Glassé, *New Encyclopedia of Islam*, 273. Seyyed Hossein Nasr, ed., *The Study Quran: A New Translation and Commentary* (New York: HarperOne, 2015), 21n30, relates that at least one Muslim commentator claimed that jinn were a particular tribe of angels, who unlike the other angels were not created out of light but out of smokeless fire.

[22] It is important to note that, in some contexts, "jinn" refers to human beings from foreign tribes, as in Surah 38:37–38. See Maulana Muhammad Ali, *Holy Qur'an: Arabic Text with English Translation and Commentary*, 899 and footnote 38a. Also worth noting: many Muslim commentators argue that jinn "inhabited the earth before human beings." See Nasr, ed., *Study Quran*, 21n30.

[23] Maulana Muhammad Ali, *Holy Qur'an: Arabic Text with English Translation and Commentary*, 527.

[24] Glassé, *New Encyclopedia of Islam*, 273.

Among the traditional signs of "dark spirits" are the following: first, that they say the opposite of the truth; second, that they deny their own faults and attribute them to others, preferably to someone who is completely innocent; third, that they continually change their position in an argument, the purpose of argument being only to subvert, to turn aside from truth and goodness; fourth, that they exaggerate the evil of what is good, and the good of what is evil, that is, they define good as evil because of a shadow of imperfection, and evil as good because of a reflection of perfection; they glorify a secondary quality in order to deny an essential one, or to disguise a fundamental flaw; in short, they completely falsify true proportions and invert normal relations.[25]

As noted above, angels attract humankind toward the good. In contrast, the jinn attract humanity toward doing evil.[26]

Exorcism of jinn is practiced in Islam. This is unsurprising given that beyond the Qur'an, there are stories of Muhammad exorcizing jinn. David Albert Jones writes of a story in which Muhammad allegedly opens an afflicted boy's mouth. He then blows into it three times and commands, "In the name of Allah, I am the slave of Allah, get out, enemy of Allah."[27]

GABRIEL AND THE HOLY SPIRIT

The angel Gabriel plays an important role in Islam. Michael Cook sums it up well:

> The heavenly archetype of the Koran is a book. The Koran we have here on earth is likewise a book. It might therefore seem natural to expect that God would have revealed His speech as a complete text—sending it down "all at once," as the carping unbelievers thought that He should have done (Q25:32). Instead, the Muslim sources describe a process of revelation which is at once oral and piecemeal. The revelation is transmitted orally by Gabriel to Muhammad, who recites it, and has scribes write it down.[28]

Some of the putative revelation took place in Mecca and some in Medina.[29] What the role of Gabriel shows is that such an angel could play a mediatorial role in an epistemological sense.

Interestingly, some Muslims believe that the Holy Spirit (Arabic, *Ruh Al-Qudus*) is none other than the angel Gabriel, as in Surah 19:17–19: "Then we sent to her [Mary] Our spirit and it appeared to her as a well made man. . . . He [the spirit] said: I am only bearer of a message of thy Lord: That I will give

[25] Glassé, *New Encyclopedia of Islam*, 215.
[26] Maulana Muhammad Ali, *Holy Qur'an: Arabic Text with English Translation and Commentary*, 76n177b.
[27] David Albert Jones, *Angels: A Very Short Introduction* (Oxford: Oxford University Press, 2011), 114. See also http://www.islam-universe.com/Exorcism.html, accessed 3/2/2016. This Muslim website has footage of an exorcism and interestingly cites Surah 2:275 as the relevant Qur'anic verse, as does http://www.islamicexorcism.com/, accessed 3/2/2016. Both websites distinguish disease and possession.
[28] Cook, *Koran: A Very Short Introduction*, 127.
[29] Cook, *Koran: A Very Short Introduction*, 5.

them a pure boy."[30] The alert Christian reader asks, but what of Jesus's teaching about the Paraclete in the Upper Room in John's Gospel (John 14–16)? In fact, there is no suggestion in this, the most extensive teaching of Jesus on the subject of the Holy Spirit, that the Holy Spirit is an angel. Surprisingly, in Islamic thought, Jesus was predicting not the coming of the Holy Spirit but Muhammad as the prophet greater than himself.[31] This is a stretch, to put it mildly.

CONCLUSION

Islam takes the supernatural seriously, and so should any professing Christian. There are scriptural echoes in the Qur'an. The Muslim believer lives in a dramatic universe in which good is at war against evil. So does the Christian. Even so, there is so much in the Qur'an that speaks where Scripture is silent on the matter of angels, Satan, and demons. Moreover, there is so little awareness of the depths of human sinfulness in human nature and its actions, and of the grace of God, which addresses the need of humankind adrift from its Creator. This should not surprise. In Islam there is no doctrine of original sin. Human beings are born with good natures. Both Scripture and experience show the folly of such a belief.[32]

---

[30] Maulana Muhammad Ali, *Holy Qur'an: Arabic Text with English Translation and Commentary*, 616. According to Nasr, ed., *Study Quran*, 768n17, most Muslim commentators believe in this identification. See also the discussion of the Holy Spirit as Gabriel, the angel, in, "Ask about Islam," http://www.islamonline.net/askabout islam/display.asp?hquestionID=4987, accessed 2/2/2005. The online article is a response to the question: "What is the Holy Spirit?" The identification of Gabriel with the Holy Spirit is attempted by linking Matthew 1:18, Luke 1:26–27, and Surah 19:17–19.
[31] See my *He Who Gives Life: The Doctrine of the Holy Spirit* (Wheaton, IL: Crossway, 2007), 88.
[32] For example, I had to teach each of my three children when they were very young to speak the truth. They needed no lessons in how to lie.

CREEDS, ARTICLES OF FAITH, CATECHISMS, AND CONFESSIONS

Creeds, articles of faith, catechisms, and confessions show what a religious community finds of fundamental importance to say as worthy of Christian belief
and adherence. In that light it is interesting to observe how little angelology
features in the historic creeds, articles, and confessions of the church right up to
and including the Reformation period. In the Patristic era, the Apostles' Creed,
for example, which dates from the third to fourth century, but in present form
from the eighth century, makes no mention of angels, Satan, or demons. The
Nicene Creed of AD 381—strictly speaking, the Niceno-Constantinopolitan
Creed, which incorporated the Nicene Creed of AD 325—begins with confessing
belief in "God the Father Almighty; Maker of heaven and earth, and of all things
visible and invisible." Traditionally "invisible" has been regarded as including the
angelic realm.[1] In contrast, other early church practices were different as far as
angelic emphasis is concerned. In Patristic baptismal liturgies, for example, there
was a formal repudiation of the devil and his works. In the St. Cyril's *Catecheti-
cal Lectures* of the fourth century, we find that the one to be baptized turns west
and renounces "Satan, his works, his pomp and his worship."[2] The Athanasian
Creed (dating from at least the sixth century) is silent on the subject.

In the Middle Ages and in the West, the Fourth Lateran Council of 1215
does refer somewhat obliquely to angels and more explicitly to the devil and
devils. Angels are referred to in the first of the constitutions. We read, ". . . creator of all things invisible and visible, spiritual and corporeal; who by his
almighty power at the beginning of time created from nothing both spiritual
and corporeal creatures, that is to say angelic and earthly, and then created

---

[1] As can be seen in the title of Anthony N. S. Lane, ed., *The Unseen World: Christian Reflections on Angels, Demons, and the Heavenly Realm* (Grand Rapids, MI: Paternoster/Baker, 1996). See also page 192, which explicitly
refers to the Nicene Creed.
[2] See J. N. D. Kelly, *Early Christian Creeds*, 3rd ed. (London and New York: Continuum, 1972), 33.

human beings composed as it were of both spirit and body in common."³ The devil and demons also feature in this constitution with reference to the fall of humankind: "The devil and other demons were created by God naturally good, but they became evil by their own doing. Man, however, sinned at the prompting of the devil."⁴ The fate of the devil is also clearly stated:

> He will come at the end of time to judge the living and the dead, to render to every person according to his works, both to the reprobate and to the elect. All of them will rise with their own bodies, which they now wear, so as to receive according to their deserts, whether these be good or bad; for the latter perpetual punishment with the devil, for the former eternal glory with Christ.⁵

In the Reformation period, the sixteenth-century Church of England's Thirty-Nine Articles of Religion (first drafted in 1563) is also silent on angelology. However the Second Helvetic Confession (1562 and revised 1564) has a chapter (VII) on creation in general and on angels, the devil, and man in particular. Regarding angels and the devil it confesses,

> OF ANGELS AND THE DEVIL. Among all creatures, angels and men are most excellent. Concerning angels, Holy Scripture declares: "who makest the winds thy messengers, fire and flame thy ministers" (Ps 104:4). Also it says: "Are they not all ministering spirits sent forth to serve, for the sake of those who are to obtain salvation?" (Heb. 1:14). Concerning the Devil, the Lord Jesus Himself testifies: "He was a murderer from the beginning, and has nothing to do with the truth, because there is no truth in him. When he lies, he speaks according to his own nature, for he is a liar and the father of lies" (John 8:44). Consequently we teach that some angels persisted in obedience and were appointed for faithful service to God and men, but others fell of their own free will and were cast into destruction, becoming enemies of all good and of the faithful, etc.⁶

This is a fulsome statement, pointing out the servant function of angels and the nefarious ways of Satan.

Creeds, articles of religion, and confessions are not the only ways that churches show what is important in their theological understanding. Catechisms are significant too. Catechisms are educational tools that articulate the faith, often but not always in question-and-answer form.

As a Reformer, Martin Luther (1483–1546) saw the need for catechizing both children and less-informed adults. The result was *The Large Catechism*. Luther's last revision of this catechism was published in 1538. In it Luther hoped to provide "the minimum knowledge required of a Christian." *The Large Catechism*

³ "Fourth Lateran Council (1215)," https://www.ewtn.com/library/COUNCILS/LATERAN4.HTM, accessed 8/30/2016.
⁴ "Fourth Lateran Council (1215)."
⁵ "Fourth Lateran Council (1215)."
⁶ See http://www.reformed.org/documents/, accessed 2/19/2016.

expounds the Ten Commandments, the Apostles Creed, and the Lord's Prayer, in that order. Thus Luther provided his supporters with an ethic, a faith, and a spirituality. There are only three references to the good angels in the catechism. The devil is another matter entirely. In Luther's brief preface alone there are nine references to the devil and one to the devils. In the preface, Luther exhorts the reader to meditate on the word of God, as the word "is the true holy water, the sign which routs the devil and puts him to flight." He writes of the "incessant attacks and ambushes of the devil." Of particular interest is the accent Luther places on prayer in spiritual warfare: "This I say because I would like to see the people brought again to pray rightly and not act so crudely and coldly that they become daily more inept at praying. This is just what the devil wants and works for with all his might, for he is well aware what damage and harm he suffers when prayer is in proper use." Luther is aware of the weakness of the believer in the face of such a mighty foe: "This we must know, that all our safety and protection consist in prayer alone. We are far too weak to cope with the devil and all his might and his forces arrayed against us, trying to trample us under foot. Therefore we must carefully select the weapons with which Christians ought to arm themselves in order to stand against the devil." The chief weapon is prayer: "But by prayer alone we shall be a match both for them [human plotters against him and the Reformation] and for the devil, if we only persevere diligently and do not become slack."[7] Anyone socialized through *The Large Catechism* would have a deep sense of the battle between good and evil, and of the supernatural realm.

Another important product of the Reformation is the Heidelberg Catechism of 1563, beloved of the Reformed church tradition. In this catechism, Question 14 describes angels as exemplars of willingness and faithfulness whom Christians are to emulate in carrying out their duties. This is the only reference, though, to angels in the catechism. As for demons, there is not one reference. However, with regard to the devil the picture changes. Right from the start in Question 1 the devil is described as an enemy whose power is broken.[8] Question 9 makes it clear that man fell at the instigation of the devil. According to Question 32 the Christian life is a kingly fight against sin and the devil. Question 34 claims that Jesus as Lord frees us from the devil's power. Lying and deceit are described in Question 112 as the devil's works. Question 123 states that, in praying that God's kingdom come, we are praying for the destruction

[7] For the substance of this paragraph and the quotations I have drawn on *The Large Catechism*, https://www.lutheransonline.com/lo/903/FSLO-1330564903-111903.pdf, accessed 3/26/2016.
[8] In expounding Question 1, Karl Barth, *Learning Jesus Christ through the Heidelberg Catechism*, trans. Shirley C. Guthrie Jr. (Grand Rapids, MI: Eerdmans, 1964), 31–32, describes Satan as a "foreign power" whose sphere is "the anti-divine and therefore anti-human."

of the devil's works. Question 127 locates the devil as one of our three sworn enemies. The other two are the world and the flesh.[9]

From the seventeenth century, the *Westminster Confession of Faith* (1643) refers to Satan in several places but is not explicit about angels per se. Chapter 1 speaks of "the malice of Satan" against the church. Chapter 3 refers to "the subtlety and temptation of Satan" in seducing "our first parents." Chapter 8 describes the ascended Christ as returning "to judge men and angels, at the end of the world."[10] Unlike the Second Helvetic Confession, these references are slim in content.

The recent massive *Catechism of the Catholic Church* has much to say about angelology. We find in the 1994 document that angels are non-corporeal beings.[11] They are spirit in nature, and both servants and messengers in function.[12] Our knowledge of them is "a truth of faith" found in Scripture and testified to in the tradition.[13] Angels belong to Christ and were created for him.[14] They are intimately involved with us: "From infancy to death human life is surrounded by their watchful care and intercession."[15] As for the devil, he is a fallen angel, a good angel gone wrong. In this he is joined by the demons.[16] Their fall was the result of "free choice."[17] No repentance is possible for them.[18] Satan's power is limited: "He cannot prevent the building of God's reign."[19] Even so, he has "by our first parents' sin . . . acquired a certain domination over man."[20] Mysteriously, divine providence allows "diabolical activity."[21] However, the devil will not prevail over Christ. The *Catechism* sounds the *Christus Victor* note loudly.[22]

Returning to the Protestant world, as a member of the faculty of Trinity Evangelical Divinity School I am bound by the Evangelical Free Church of America's Statement of Faith of 2008. This contemporary statement does not leave Satan out, as can be seen in paragraph 3, which concerns the human condition: "We believe that God created Adam and Eve in His image, but they sinned when tempted by Satan. In union with Adam, human beings are sinners by nature and by choice, alienated from God, and under His wrath.

[9] For the substance of this paragraph I have drawn on http://www.wts.edu/resources/creeds/heidelberg.html, accessed 3/22/2016.
[10] See http://www.reformed.org/documents/, accessed 2/19/2016.
[11] CCC (Liguori, MO: Liguori, 1994), 328. The numbers in this and the following references refer to the paragraphs in the CCC.
[12] CCC, 329. The *Catechism* explicitly follows Augustine on this point.
[13] CCC, 328.
[14] CCC, 331.
[15] CCC, 336.
[16] CCC, 391.
[17] CCC, 392.
[18] CCC, 393.
[19] CCC, 394.
[20] CCC, 407.
[21] CCC, 395.
[22] CCC, cf. 395, 538, 539, and 550.

Only through God's saving work in Jesus Christ can we be rescued, reconciled and renewed."[23] However, apart from this reference to Satan, the statement is silent on angelology.

In the creeds, articles of faith, catechisms, and confessions of the church, both past and present, angels, Satan, and demons feature sparingly compared to passages referring to the Father, Son, and Holy Spirit as well as to soteriological matters. This should not surprise, given the emphases in Scripture itself.

---

[23] See http://go.efca.org/resources/document/efca-statement-faith, accessed 2/19/2016.

The theological topic of angelology, with its subsets of devil, demons, and spiritual warfare, continues to attract attention. A fine general treatment of angelology is to be found in David Albert Jones, *Angels: A Very Short Introduction* (Oxford: Oxford University Press, 2011), and the same applies to Darren Oldridge, *The Devil: A Very Short Introduction* (Oxford: Oxford University Press, 2012). For the early church period and views of Satan, see Jeffrey Burton Russell, *Satan: The Early Christian Tradition* (Ithaca, NY, and London: Cornell University Press, 1987). A very valuable discussion by a variety of authors on the unseen world is to be found in Anthony N. S. Lane, ed., *The Unseen World: Christian Reflections on Angels, Demons and the Heavenly Realm* (Grand Rapids, MI: Paternoster/Baker, 1996). Karl Barth's provocative but not always convincing treatment of the subject in his *Church Dogmatics*, III/part 3/chapter 11/section 51, remains a landmark discussion. From an evangelical perspective, C. Fred Dickason, *Angels: Elect and Evil* (Chicago: Moody, 1995) is a clearly written and very useful work. The same is true of Stephen F. Noll, *Angels of Light, Powers of Darkness: Thinking Biblically about Angels, Satan, and Principalities* (Eugene, OR: Wipf & Stock, 1998). Michael S. Heiser has written two thought-provoking volumes: *Supernatural: What the Bible Teaches about the Unseen World—and Why It Matters* (Bellingham, WA: Lexham, 2015), and the more academic, *The Unseen Realm: Recovering the Supernatural Worldview of the Bible* (Bellingham, WA: Lexham, 2015). I am not persuaded, though, about the degree to which he draws on ancient Near Eastern sources and how he uses them. For a most stimulating monograph on Satan, see Gregory A. Boyd's provocative *Satan and the Problem of Evil: Constructing Trinitarian Warfare Theodicy* (Downers Grove, IL: IVP Academic, 2001). On the matter of spiritual warfare, the volume edited by James K. Beilby and Paul Rhodes Eddy, *Understanding Spiritual Warfare: Four Views* (Grand Rapids, MI: Baker Academic, 2012), is well worth reading. So too is the book by Clinton E., Arnold, *Three Crucial Questions about Spiritual Warfare* (Grand Rapids, MI: Baker, 1998). A major monograph on spiritual conflict is Gregory A. Boyd's provocative *God At War: The Bible and Spiritual Conflict* (Downers Grove, IL: IVP Academic, 1997). From a charismatic perspective, Michael Green lucidly discusses Satan in his *I Believe in Satan's Downfall* (London: Hodder & Stoughton, 1999). The subject of demonology is classically addressed by Merrill F. Unger in his *Biblical Demonology: A Study of Spiritual Forces at Work Today*

(Grand Rapids, MI: Kregel, 1994). For a recent and most helpful treatment of demonology with practical, biblically informed strategies for engaging the demonic, see Sharon Beekmann and Peter G. Bolt, *Silencing Satan: Handbook of Biblical Demonology* (Eugene, OR: Wipf & Stock, 2012). This work also has an extensive bibliography. See also Peter G. Bolt, ed., *Christ's Victory over Evil: Biblical Theology and Pastoral Ministry* (Nottingham, UK: Inter-Varsity Press, 2009). For a stimulating philosophical defense of the existence of angels see Peter S. Williams, *The Case for Angels* (Carlisle, UK/Waynesboro, GA: Paternoster, 2000). Peter Kreeft, *Angels and Demons: What Do We Really Know about Them?* (San Francisco: Ignatius, 1995) provides a Roman Catholic perspective on the questions surrounding angels, Satan, and demons. For Islam, see the respective articles on angels, Satan, and jinn in Cyril Glassé, *The New Encyclopedia of Islam*, 3rd ed. (Lanham, MD: Rowman & Littlefield, 2008). Finally, Paul G. Hiebert's seminal article, "The Flaw of the Excluded Middle," may be found in a volume containing a collection of some of his collected essays, *Anthropological Reflections on Missiological Issues* (Grand Rapids, MI: Baker, 1994). This work also contains his very useful "Biblical Perspectives on Spiritual Warfare."

accommodatio: Latin, "accommodation." The idea that God, in communicating his will and ways to humanity, stoops to our level, like a great rhetorician, in order to connect.

angel: Broadly defined, angels are created spirits who are messengers and servants of God (seraphim, cherubim, archangels, angels, etc.). Narrowly defined, angels fall into two classes (archangels and angels). In Islam, angels are spirits made of light that attract human beings toward the good.

angel Christology: The view that Jesus fulfilled an angel role. That is to say, he was a messenger, so "angel" is an appropriate title for him. However, others in the early church period really did think that Jesus was an angel—that he was a spirit and only appeared to be human.

angel of the Lord: Many identify this OT figure with Christ in a preincarnate manifestation. Others believe that the angel of the Lord was simply an angel, albeit of singular importance.

angelism: The view that humans are like angels in their sinlessness, and that embodiment has no value.

angelology: The study of angels, their origins, nature, and activities.

angelophany: The appearing of an angel.

anthropomorphic angelophany: The appearing of an angel in human form.

antichrist/the Antichrist: That which is opposed to Christ; a minion of Satan who will emerge as an eschatological opponent of the people of God.

apokatastasis: The idea that, in the end, all will be restored to right relation to God, including Satan and his demonic servants.

archangel: An angel such as Michael, with leadership over lesser angels.

binding of Satan: According to Revelation 20, Satan is bound by an angel and put in a pit for a thousand years.

canonical hermeneutics: Any given text of Scripture is to be interpreted in its context in its literary unit in its book in the canon of Scripture, in the light of its location in the unfolding redemptive history.

cherubim: An order of celestial creatures that guard God, the divine presence, and sacred spaces.

Christology: The doctrine of Christ's person and work.

Christological moments (sometimes, **Christological mysteries**): A theological device for understanding Christology as presented in the Gospels by reference to the key points in Christ's life and work. Traditionally there are seven such moments: birth, baptism, temptations, transfiguration, death, resurrection, and ascension.

Christophany: An appearing of Christ, whether pre-incarnation or post-ascension.

Christus Victor: A theory of the atonement that accents the victory of Christ through his atoning death over the devil. This view was made famous by Swedish theologian Gustaf Aulén.

composite angelophany: The appearing of an angel that combines human and animal characteristics.

demon: A fallen angel in the service of Satan and therefore an enemy of God and his people.

demonization: The oppression of human beings by a demon or demons. Some scholars prefer this broad term to demon-possession.

demonology: The study of demons and the demonic realm.

demon-possession: The occupation or "ownership" of a human being by a demon or demons. This traditional phrase has been challenged in recent scholarship. Some prefer the term "demonization," which allows for different degrees of demonic control or influence. Still others prefer the phrase "demon inhabitation."

devil, the: An angelic leader, Satan, who fell away from God's service, traditionally through pride, and is now the archenemy of God and his people and his creation. Some argue that Satan was originally a cherub.

economy: The administration of a plan, e.g., of salvation.

eschatology: Greek, *eschaton*, "last." Traditionally narrowly defined as the Four Last Things: Death, Resurrection, Heaven, and Hell. But increasingly a broader definition is in play, whereby eschatology is the story of the unfolding of the divine purpose in time and space, from creation through redemption to new creation.

evidence: Information that counts toward establishing the truth or falsity of a proposition.

evidence-based approach: The use of evidence to support truth claims.

exorcism: The expulsion of a demon or demons from a state of indwelling a human being.

Heilsgeschichte: German for "salvation history." See redemptive history, below.

historia salutis: Latin, "history of salvation." Refers to those unique events that are integral to the provision of salvation, from the calling of Abraham on (e.g., election of Israel, incarnation).

Iblis: The Islamic name for the devil, meaning adversary. Some scholars argue that Iblis was originally an angel. Others argue that Iblis was always a jinn.

jinn: In Islam, a spirit made of fire that can work evil by attracting human beings toward evil.

living creatures: An order of celestial beings also associated with the heavenly throne and who may be either cherubim or seraphim.

Lucifer: A traditional name for Satan found in the Latin Vulgate translation of the OT, meaning "morning star" or "bearer of light."

method of comparative difficulties: This method applies when truth claims are in dispute and asks where the difficulties lie in a position in terms of number and weightiness. The position to be embraced—if a position is to be embraced at all—is the one that has the fewer and/or the least weighty difficulties.

norma normans: Latin, "norming norm" or "standardizing standard." With regard to various possible authorities (Scripture, reason, tradition, experience), the *norma normans* as the supreme authority is the final court of appeal. For the evangelical, with regard to truth claims, it is Scripture.

norma normata: Latin, "ruled norm' or "ruled standard." For example, for the evangelical, reason is a norm but may be overruled by Scripture when there is a dispute between them.

ordo salutis: Latin, "order of salvation." Refers to the order of the elements in the application of salvation to the individual, beginning with calling and culminating in glorification.

redemptive history: The plotline of the canonical revelation from old creation to new, from Genesis to Revelation, with its accent on redemption.

revelation: What God has made known about his reality, character, will, and ways.

salvation history: See redemptive history.

Satan: The personal name for the fallen angel opposed to God and his people, who leads other fallen angels in their infernal rebellion. "Satan" as a personal name is to be distinguished from "the satan," who can be either Satan or a human in the role of an adversary.

seraphim: An order of celestial being associated with God's heavenly throne, God's glorious presence, and his purifying fire.

special revelation: What God has made known about his reality, character, will, and ways to certain people at certain times (e.g., Ps. 19:7–14; Heb. 1:1–2).

spiritual warfare: Those practices used by believers to thwart the evil purposes of Satan and his demons. It assumes a dramatic universe in which good is in conflict with evil.

theophany: An appearing of God.

visionary composite angelophany: The appearing of an angel in a vision experienced by a human subject, where the appearing has both human and animal characteristics.

visionary angelophany: The appearing of an angel in a vision experienced by a human subject.

on, 118–120; and false worship, 120–122; final defeat of, 162, 211n18; hindrance of believers by, 127–128; in Islam, 233n1; mental illness and, 135–137; modern lack of interest in, 21–25, 102n99, 178, 193, 239–243; nature of, 112; possession by, 122–124, 129–131; superstition and, 134–135; teaching of Jesus about, 145–146; warring of against other angels, 125. See also demonic disorder, the; exorcism; "testing the spirits"

Descartes, 18, 43n60

descriptive vs. prescriptive nature of accounts in Acts, 73, 166

Destroyer and the Lamb, The (Hoffmann), 64n43

"Destroying Angel, The" (Bar), 59n24

"Deuteronomy" (Rogerson), 62nn32–33

Devil, The (Oldridge), 104n109

devil, the. See Satan (the devil)

Devil: A New Biography, The (Almond), 80, 80n4, 87n37, 98n83, 99n88, 101n93, 115n18, 116n25, 118n37, 141, 149n31, 236n18

Dickason, C. Fred, 32n16, 68n66, 91–92, 91nn51–52, 95, 120n47, 129, 151n38

Dictionary of Biblical Imagery, 39n49, 40n51

Dictionary of Latin and Greek Theological Terms (Muller), 137n122

Didache (Teaching of the Twelve), 197

Dionysius the Areopagite, 51, 65–68, 66n54, 66nn58–59

Disappearance of God, The (Friedman), 59n24

discernment, 76, 134–138, 185, 195n139, 197–201. See also "testing the spirits"

docetism, 64

Doctor Faustus (Marlowe), 89n47

doctrine as a suitcase, 31, 88n42, 227

Dodd, C. H., 163n1

Dome of Eden, The (Webb), 42n56, 83n20, 94n65, 144n10

domination system model of spiritual warfare, 173–175

dragon, great red, the, 144n10

Drama of Doctrine, The (Vanhoozer), 22–23, 23n31, 55n14

Drama of Ephesians, The (Gombis), 182n96

dualism, 80n5, 81n10, 98, 99n88, 104, 107, 107n120, 136n120. See also substance dualism

Dumbrell, William J., 145n15

Duriez, Colin, 41n54

Dutch couple's encounter with demons, 111

Ebert, Daniel J. IV, 44n66

Eddy, Paul R., 172, 172n31, 173n33

Edwards, Jonathan, 192, 200n156

ekklēsia, lack of mention in 1 Peter, 44n67

Elijah, 58, 192n132

Elisha, 74

Ellul, Jacques, 84

Elymas, 101, 184. See also Bar-Jesus

"embodying the divine warrior" model of spiritual warfare, 182–183

"End Times" (Walvoord), 216n41

Engaging the Powers (Wink), 125n67, 126

epistemic humility, 105–106

Erickson, Millard J., 23, 24–25, 31, 42, 42n58, 63, 68, 82, 114, 120n46, 140

eschatology, 96, 203, 211n15, 212n20, 220–223; eschatological setting of the church, 187–188; futuristic, 188n130; inaugurated eschatology, 163n1, 185, 188; realized eschatology, 163n1. See also man of lawlessness; millennium, the

Eschatology (Schwarz), 211n17, 216n37, 217n47

espoused vs. operational theology, 146, 158–159, 197

Eusebius, 121n49

Evangelical Free Church of America's Statement of Faith, 242

"Evangelical Religion" (Ryle), 28, 28n45

Evangelical Theology (Bird), 204n5, 212n22

evangelical theology, 19–21, 19n14, 28, 29n2, 48, 49n96, 68, 96n75, 118–119, 140, 188n130, 233n1

evangelicalism, 19, 75, 89, 173, 175, 191

Evans, Craig A., 123, 133n106

evil: problem of, 103–108, 103n104, 104n110, 104n112, 105n113; reality of, 103–104

Evil and Christian Ethics (Graham), 104n109

"evil one, the," 100–101, 103, 106, 111, 130, 142, 144–148, 154, 161, 162, 166, 168, 171, 172, 189, 192, 193, 194n137, 229, 230. See also Satan (the devil)

evil triad, the, 164n6

exegesis vs. eisegesis, 20

exorcism, 122–124, 127, 142, 147, 162, 164, 165–166, 176–177, 183–184, 191, 194, 195; baptism as form of, 132n99, 184–185, 185n119; contemporary accounts of, 131–135, 132n104, 137; in Islam, 237

"Exorcism" (Howard), 122n54

Exorcist, The (movie), 80

extrabiblical/extracanonical sources, 32n15, 96n75, 118–120, 120n43, 185, 225, 233n1, 235n12

Ezekiel 20–48 (Allen), 92n56

faith seeking understanding, 139

Faith Seeking Understanding (Vanhoozer), 23n31

faith: expressed most clearly in prayer, 166, 166n12; faith vs. reason and faith vs. fear,

Guinan, M. D., 84
Gunkel, H., 225
Guthrie, George H., 43n62, 235n15

Hades, 149–150, 210
Hagar, 63
Hagner, Donald A., 72, 73nn85–86, 155
Hall, Douglas John, 23
Hamilton, James, 142, 142n6
Hamlet (Shakespeare), 29, 29n1
Hammond, T. C., 68, 68n67
"handed over to Satan," 131
Hannah, D., 225
Hard Sayings of the Bible (Kaiser), 40n51, 59n24,
    73n86, 99n86, 138n125, 211n18, 219n52
"harmful spirit from the Lord," 122
harmony to disharmony to harmony (plotline of
    Scripture), 83–84, 97n80, 144, 203
Harris, Dana, 147n24
Harris, Murray J., 107, 107n120
harrowing of hell, the, 149
Hartley, John E., 121
Hawthorne, Gerald F., 144
Hays, Richard B., 89n45
He Who Gives Life (Cole), 73n87, 132n105,
    238n31
Hebrew Bible, 171
"Hebrews" (Guthrie), 43n62, 235n15
"Hebrews" (Peterson), 148n25
Heidelberg Catechism, The, 241–242
Heiser, Michael S., 40n51, 61–62, 131, 152n46
Hendrix, Scott A., 196n147
Henze, Matthias, 62, 62n35
Herod Agrippa, 57, 59
Hiebert, Paul, 46, 48, 143, 233, 233n1
Hippolytus, 149
"Historic Premillennialism: Taking the Long
    View" (Netherton), 212n21
History of Christian Thought, A (González),
    143n8
Hodge, A. A., 34, 34n22, 49, 49n96, 214
Hodge, Charles, 209, 209n12
Hoffmann, Matthias Reinhard, 64n43, 161
Holmes, Michael W., 128
Holy Qur'an (Maulana Muhammad Ali),
    235n12, 235n16, 236n20, 236n22
Holy Spirit, the, 27, 39, 58, 88, 96, 124, 137, 147,
    150, 185, 237–238; believers indwelt by,
    129–130, 188–189, 210; gifts of, 198; more
    prominent in NT, 100; at Pentecost, 187; as
    prosecutor for a world on trial, 105; as the
    "restrainer" of 2 Thessalonians, 225–229
Hooker, Morna D., 153n50
Horton, Michael, 213
How to Hear Your Angel (Virtue), 74n91

*How to Understand and Apply the New Testa-
    ment* (Naselli), 118n36
Howard, J. Keir, 122, 122n56
Hum of Angels, The (McKnight), 61n30
Hymenaeus and Alexander, 131

I Believe in Satan's Downfall (Green), 95n69,
    104n107
Iblis (the devil, in Islam), 235–236
imago Dei, 42, 228
immigrant African churches in Britain, 135
In Understanding Be Men (Hammond), 68n67
incarnation, 27, 52, 55, 60, 64, 64n43, 77n98,
    94n65, 130, 143, 143nn8–9, 148, 151,
    160–161, 187, 198
Institutes of the Christian Religion (Calvin),
    66n55, 210, 210n14
Introduction to Dogmatic Theology (Litton),
    219n56
Introduction to the New Testament, An (Car-
    son), 43n65
Irenaeus, 94, 152, 183, 212
Issues Facing Christians Today (Stott), 203n1
IVP Bible Background Commentary, The, 33n18,
    168n18

Jacob, 53, 76
Jacob's Ladder (Bulgakov), 30n5, 41n55, 42n59,
    45n74, 75n94, 77n98
James (author of letter), 169, 225n69
James (brother of John), 57, 59, 165, 170, 186
jealousy, as root of all evil, 94n65
Jekyll or Hyde, 126
Jenkins, Philip, 96n75, 120n44, 132n99, 135,
    135n112, 136n117
Jenson, Robert W., 229
Jerome, 30n5, 71, 71n75, 93, 220
Jeshurun, 121
"Jesus and the Psychiatrists" (Brewer), 136n117,
    136n119
Jesus and the Victory of God (Wright), 144n14
Jesus Christ: active and passive obedience of, 210;
    ascended, 122, 242; assurances because of,
    188–189; as atonement, 148; confidence in,
    161–162; conquest of the devil, 143–148;
    contrasted with Adam, 86; creator, 34; cross
    of. See cross, the; "descended into hell,"
    149–151; his equality with God, 40n51; as
    the faithful Adam and faithful Israel, 162;
    fullness of God dwells in, 41; future return
    of, 95, 208, 211–217; greater than the devil,
    130; humiliation and exaltation of, 37;
    humility and obedience of, 86; our hope,
    221–223; incarnation of. See incarnation;
    love of, 162, 221, 223; justification through
    faith in, 188; Lamb of God, 40, 41n55, 111,

the

FOUNDATIONS OF EVANGELICAL THEOLOGY

series

EDITED BY JOHN S. FEINBERG

The Foundations of Evangelical Theology series incorporates the best exegetical research, historical theology, and philosophy to produce an up-to-date systematic theology with contemporary application—ideal for both students and teachers of theology.

For more information, visit **crossway.org**.